Power, Culture, and Economic Change in Russia

Utilizing cutting-edge theory and unique data, this book examines the role of power, culture, and practice in Russia's story of post-socialist economic change, and provides a framework for addressing general economic change.

No other book places power and culture as centrally as this, and in doing so it provides new insights not only into how Russia came to its present state under Putin, but also how economies operate and change generally. In particular, the importance of remaking authority and culture—creating and contesting new categories and narratives of meaning—is shown as central to Russia's story, and to the story of economies overall.

Power, Culture, and Economic Change in Russia is an excellent research tool for advanced undergraduate and postgraduate students of sociology, political science, economics, area studies, and other related disciplines.

Jeffrey Hass is Associate Professor in the Department of Sociology, University of Richmond, USA. He has published extensively on post-socialism and economic sociology, including *Economic Sociology: An Introduction* (Routledge, 2007) and numerous journal articles.

Power, Culture, and Economic Change in Russia

To the Undiscovered Country of post-socialism, 1988–2008

Jeffrey Hass

Routledge
Taylor & Francis Group

LONDON AND NEW YORK

First published 2011
by Routledge
2 Park Square, Milton Park, Abingdon, Oxon, OX14 4RN

Simultaneously published in the USA and Canada
by Routledge
711 Third Avenue, New York, NY 10017

Routledge is an imprint of the Taylor & Francis Group, an informa business

British Library Cataloguing in Publication Data
A catalogue record for this book is available from the British Library

Library of Congress Cataloging in Publication Data
Hass, Jeffrey Kenneth, 1967-
    Power, Culture, and Economic Change in Russia : to the
    Undiscovered Country of post-socialism, 1988-2008 / Jeffrey K Hass.
        p. cm.
    1. Russia (Federation)–Economic policy–1991- 2. Russia (Federation)–
    Economic conditions–1991- 3. Power (Social sciences)–Russia
    (Federation) 4. Social change–Russia (Federation) 5. Post-communism–
    Russia (Federation) I. Title.
    HC340.12.H37 2011   2010049057
    306.30947–dc22

ISBN: 978-0-415-66691-6 (hbk)
ISBN: 978-0-203-81729-2 (ebk)

Typeset in Baskerville by
HWA Text and Data Management, London

Printed and bound in Great Britain by the MPG Books Group

In memory of Mitchell Kenneth Hass
August 15, 2000–February 11, 2002

"For all sad words of tongue or pen,
The saddest are these: 'It might have been.'"
(John Greenleaf Whittier)

And for Daniel and Peter, for teaching me how to laugh,
and to live, again.

Contents

Tables and figures

Tables

Figures

Acknowledgements

Writing on Russia's market revolution is akin to duck hunting from the back of a moving haywagon in a fog. This made the challenge immense, maddening, at times enjoyable. One does not do this alone, and I have amassed a debt of gratitude that words cannot convey. Miguel Centeno, Paul DiMaggio, and Stephen Kotkin provided key ideas when they supervised my dissertation, and afterward they and Viviana Zelizer continued to give advice and support. This is a continuation of and challenge to what they taught. At the University of Pittsburgh, Bob Donnorummo, Jon Harris, and John Markoff were always willing to provide feedback and friendship. In what was once a series of weekly meetings, Ric Colignon not only helped me work out ideas, but also helped raise my own analytic skills. My thanks go to Roberto Franzosi, Jorge Rodriguez, Tanya Cassidy, and Andy Buck for sage advice and help on this and other issues during my time in the UK. Colleagues at the University of Richmond provided the support for setting up a new life while continuing this work from the old. Jan French has read various chapters too many times. David Brandenberger, John Treadway, and Joe Troncale have provided support and springboards for ideas about Russia. In providing intellectual banter and demonstrating their own growing passion to scholarship, Alison Heslin and Brian Brower helped me adapt to and accept that new home; teaching them made it all worthwhile. I also owe thanks to those in Russia who provided tactical help, intellectual stimulation, and friendship in a second home: Nikita and Nastya Lomagin, Maksim Storchevoi, Sergei Podbolotov, and Sergei Afanas'ev, among so many others. Colleagues at the St. Petersburg Institute of Sociology of the Academy of Sciences provided a sociological home, replete with myriad discussions and tea. I learned much in the intellectual company of the late Valerii Golofast, from conversations we can never have again. The staff of the Academy of Sciences in St. Petersburg, in particular Dmitrii Donskoi and Svetlana Sergeeva, provided logistical and visa support. The Council on Regional Studies and the Center for International Studies at Princeton University and the American Council for Teachers of Russian (Title VIII funding) supported the fieldwork that became the dissertation and this book. The International Research and Exchanges Board (IREX) provided a summer grant to return to St. Petersburg in 1999 to mine yet more veins of raw material. I owe a debt of gratitude to Gerhard Boomgaarden, my editor at Routledge, for his faith in this book and for moving it smoothly through the entire publication process (much as he did for my first book on economic sociology). Thanks as well to Alexa Richardson for patiently working with the manuscript and helping bring it to its finished form. A last word of thanks goes to friends and family for support in these turbulent years: Jan Davies, James Garvey, Irene Petten, John Schmalzbauer, Gary Susman, Bob Toner, and Gray Wheeler. My parents provided shelter from myriad storms. My father not only put up patiently with me but also with the fact that I remained unemployed and in need of support. My wife Irina has stood on the front lines of this entire process—putting up with moodiness, frustration, and sociology.

The following publishers have kindly given permission to reprint excerpts from these works: Robert Pirsig, *Zen and the Art of Motorcycle Maintenance* (New York: HarperCollins, 2008), p. 88; Umberto Eco, *Name of the Rose* (New York: Houghton Mifflin Harcourt, 1983), p. 502.

Yet whatever illumination it may provide, this book lives under a dark shadow. On February 11, 2002, hours before he would have been 18 months old, my son Mitchell Kenneth died from an undiagnosed metabolic disorder. Besides grief over how Mitya was deprived of what would have been a happy, loving life, I am left with the hollow feeling that this book is a banal nothingness compared to this loss—a little boy who was incredibly smart, loving and good-natured, caring and compassionate, who gave and taught so much. I tried to make this something he would have been proud of, a testimony to his wonder. But no book, no matter how brilliant or profound, will make up for his absence, and for the hours that were rightfully his that instead I spent on this.

In the years that followed, Daniel and Peter came into this world and my life. I have tried to find that balance between this book and their lives; I have not found that golden mean, but I hope I have come closer. Mitchell taught me the meaning of life from one perspective; as they have grown, Daniel and Peter have taught me its meaning and value from another. To you all, Mitchell, Daniel, and Peter—my sons—for what it is worth, I dedicate this work.

JKH

St. Petersburg, Russia, and Richmond, Virginia

Transliteration note

For transliteration from Russian into English I have generally followed the Library of Congress system, except for formal names that are better-known in a different form (thus Yeltsin not El'tsin).

Introduction

To the Undiscovered Country: a journey through post-socialism

> There are more things in heaven and earth, Horatio,
> Than are dreamt of in your philosophy.
>
> > (*Hamlet*)

> Russia is lacking some fundamental economic logic.
>
> > (Russian graduate student in economics)

Russia's post-Soviet story is one of conflict, confusion, and innovation. In 1988, with a narrative of viable socialism, Mikhail Gorbachev introduced reforms to stimulate the moribund Soviet economy; early hopes were dampened as the Soviet economy unraveled. Ten years later, in early 1998, as inflation declined, the economy improved, and privatization had rewarded a few over the many, a myth of a liberal market and polity was starting to take root. By August 1998, this narrative was a shambles. Ten years later, in 2008, it seemed Vladimir Putin had rebuilt state power with a new narrative of a strong and economically active technocratic elite, as he dispensed with democratic procedure and played to the myth of the state as guarantor of stability and growth. Yet Russia's health, based on high hydrocarbon profits for state-owned companies, was again exaggerated and the narrative oversimplified reality. Elites and a small middle class benefited, but poverty and social inequality persisted.[1] Oil wealth reduced state debt and made Russia an investor's darling (despite lessons of *Soviet* oil wealth), but the trap of oil rents exacerbated corruption and Kremlin *hubris*, retarded structural reforms, spurred enormous corporate debt in foreign loans, and hid economic problems all too clear by 2009.[2] Traditional economic weaknesses persist twenty years after socialism's end: low-quality output, weak business reliability and marketing, low competitiveness, weak research and development (e.g. patentable output), low transparency, rising state predation and corruption, underdeveloped financial structures, and an unbalanced economy aimed at resource extraction.[3] Recent policies of national champions and innovation by fiat (e.g. in nanotechnology) or reducing inflation by prosecuting food producers for "speculation" betray quasi-Soviet logics.[4] Russian leaders are anxious that WTO entry will betray suboptimal productivity and practices.[5] Russia's economic revolution is not over.

Russia's journey to its post-socialist Undiscovered Country is a laboratory of social change and an opportunity for theory and data to interact, to enrich analyses while concurrently improving theory and leaping beyond present confines. The death of Soviet socialism and birth of Russian post-socialism as project and journey involved remaking and imposing narratives while reconstructing fundamentals of power and authority, culture and meaning, and everyday practices.[6] In fact, this has been two journeys: that of Russians, and all those who experience social change; and that of theory. The usual analysis of post-socialist economic change involves identifying elite alliances and conflicts, laws and institutions, state capacity, and financial structures.[7] The Soviet/post-Soviet crisis was primarily financial and legal, to be solved with liquidity, financial controls, and smarter laws. Weakened control of rubles and resources in the late 1980s unraveled the Soviet economy; inflation, taxes, and capital hunger forced firms to use barter, avoid formality, stay small, follow short-term planning, and avoid major changes in production and output. I do not deny these are important pieces of the puzzle as to why and how post-socialist change—or any change—occurs; but such accounts are at best incomplete, at worst misleading on sources and mechanisms of action. Concretely, such explanations of post-socialist change and economic change generally 1) too readily assume the primacy of instrumental action and rationality, to the neglect of meaning-laden action or multiple rationalities, 2) fixate on how contexts (e.g. laws or finances) shape actors and actions without sufficiently examining how actors negotiate these in the first place, and 3) take "institutions" for granted rather than problematize them. To make sense of our stories, we must look beyond macro-level indicators or "institutions" and explore dimensions of power, culture, and practices, and how these are intertwined.

Diving into the wreck: from institutions to power, culture, and practice

Post-socialism's story, like the rise of the West, is often told in terms of institutions. Economics, political economy, much sociology, and post-socialist research elide what "institutions" are or take this intellectual elephant in the seminar room for granted as formal rules.[8] In instrumental approaches, institutions are rules that shape costs; research in this vein addresses legal details. This risks tautologies: institutions construct interests, begging where institutions come from; or interests construct institutions, begging the reverse. "Institutions" in state-centered theory are close to formal organizations and elide mechanisms of reproduction and change. These approaches have produced insights: analyses of East Asia and Latin America note how historical constellations of actors and rules begat policies and structures. If this partly answers "how," "why" still beckons that we examine what lies underneath. As David Woodruff notes, "institutions" involve meanings and justifications that give sense to structures.[9] We need a dynamic model, not a simple input–output model with little concern for process,[10] that unpacks what "institutions" are and how they operate and change. This will help us tackle thorny issues of change and continuity. For example, contingency is important in historical change: power structures weaken and normality of existing narratives comes into question, especially if alternatives emerge as challenges. One key aspect of contingency is what components of the dominant narrative are questioned: this helps shape the nature of change and continuity.[11] We must pay attention to interpretations, categories, and practices as they are worked out, challenged, and enforced.

I conceptualize institutions as manifestations and collective instantiations of power-culture brought to life via practices. In sum: culture, power, practices, and logics. *Culture*: institutions are categories and meanings people use and reproduce, "experienced as existing over and beyond the individuals who 'happen to' embody them at the moment," that we use to navigate uncertainty. This includes knowledge and considerations of legitimacy and normality for the context. Institutions as cultural phenomena are collectively but imperfectly shared, ritualized meanings of normality, reified and externalized as objective, natural procedures and categories, embodied in and enforced by everyday practices and logics that involve "symbolic signposts" such as laws.[12] *Power*: institutions enforce meanings by sanction against deviations that threaten interests or certainty, or by smothering actors with meanings, as institutions "by the fact of their existence, shape action through defined patterns of conduct, which channel it in one direction as against the many other directions that would theoretically be possible."[13] *Practices and logics*: institutions exist as actors perform and justify sets and sequences of meanings and authority in particular contexts. Change involves creating new meanings and knowledge and enforcing them in relations of power, practices, and logics of justification.

Power and culture, practices and logics are the heart of our story. Reforms and shocks broke power relations and made existing meanings and practices appear abnormal, undermining institutional reproduction. Creating new culture, power, and practice depended on how actors—managers, entrepreneurs, financiers, employees, and state officials—used existing culture, power, and practices. *Legislating change* involved reacting to shocks (articulating blame) and proposing new procedures and practices. *Learning change* entailed adapting to changes by coming to grips with new strategies and logics of action and categories for perceiving the social world. *Enforcing change* involved creating capacity to implement new strategies and practices by imposing them on others or defending autonomy. Further, these processes occurred on several fronts simultaneously: remaking firms and work, reorienting sales and exchange, redefining and enacting property and governance. All the while, managers, employees, owners, and state officials were embedded in a patchwork discourse of global logics and local knowledge. With no strong, central power to impose uniformity, processes and trajectories varied. Alongside this was institutional design—i.e. social *reconstruction* of reality. Economists expect information asymmetries or distributional conflicts; I expect confusion over articulating and grasping new knowledge to make policies operative as practices. We should see contention over *competing normalities*, stemming from differing interests and differing views of normality. We should see conflict over new authority, as remaking institutions reshapes participation in discourse and deliberation and breeds contention. Preexisting knowledge and assumptions color design: Soviet-era knowledge and logics not delegitimated in shocks or deliberations could survive. Small wonder institutional design faced hurdles in Russia; small wonder the crisis of 2008 frightens us as it does.

All this occurred against the backdrop of sometimes dramatic politics: shock therapy and protest in Moscow, privatization and industrial collapse, surprising electoral outcomes, and changes in the state's structure and role. I do not ignore big politics, but one goal is to move beyond a restricted focus on Moscow elites, to average Russians whose everyday practices made big politics important. To assume the Big Event occurs and the remainder of the populace automatically follows in step, like soldier ants, is problematic. Ethnographic studies easily show that in everyday life non-elites may follow commands from above; but they also maneuver within and around them, negotiate them, warp or misuse them, even resist them (perhaps in a hidden, passive manner). Further, *empirical* discussions of post-Soviet Russia reveal the problems inherent in implementing new practices, codes, categories, and the like of the post-Soviet economy. Let me note here briefly that studies of enterprise change paid little attention to conflict and authority relations, let alone variation in change; and while many scholars raised the issue of fit between Soviet-era managerial skills and intended post-Soviet reforms and normality, they did not sufficiently explore or problematize this issue as one of culture (knowledge and skills, but also categories), practices, and authority to define and enforce (or resist) "normal" skills.

Beyond instrumental rationality and institutions assumed

A market economy does not arise magically.[14] As Max Weber, Emile Durkheim, Karl Marx, and others noted, the social world is enacted through meanings and practices that, as socially constructed collective rules and rituals, govern social life.[15] Part of post-socialist reconstruction was rewriting a "narrative of normality" of a post-Soviet landscape and how to create it.[16] Michael Kennedy called this "transition culture," a shift in meanings for interpreting and framing events and claims; Elaine Weiner dubbed this a metanarrative of post-socialism.[17] Yet too often scholarship misses or does not adequately address how change operates because it assumes institutions and relies on instrumental rationality.[18] My goal is not to discard existing scholarship *in toto*, nor to subject competing approaches to empirical tests, as has been done;[19] but we must be aware of weaknesses to be addressed. Take economic theory. Armies of economists have produced observations and insights, especially in game theory, but these gains have come with costs: e.g. assumptions of instrumental rational action and the supremacy of efficiency persist despite numerous critiques from research on cognition, social psychology and small-group interaction, and broader economic organization.[20] Neoclassical economic theory works best in certain contexts of collective meanings and stable power relations that economists take for granted. Yet economists' discourse is trapped in its own assumptions and categories. Mainstream theory assumes change through market clearing and adaptation of efficient practices, backed by threats of market exit and consumer power. Strategies, structures, and change follow costs; efficient strategies and structures survive competition to become the norm. In Russia, the Soviet state corrupted possible market signals,[21] and shock therapy thus prescribed reduced the state's role via rapid liberalization, privatization, and austerity policies to unleash rational market forces.[22]

Yet seeming irrationalities confounded economic theory. Why did Russian managers have difficulty altering sales and production strategies—especially when they confronted serious collapses in income and sales? Why adopt "marketing" departments that provided few material returns and only drained resources? How did enterprise restructuring lead to conflict in some cases but not others? At the micro-level, the atomized rational actor at the heart of economic theory is problematic: people are not as instrumentally and objectively rational as economists assume,[23] and the classic view of cognition assumed, where the brain merely sorts objective data, is problematic.[24] Information costs and asymmetries are important, as game theory suggests, but as used these concepts cannot capture the complexity of heuristic devices and *interpretation* of information. Put differently, economic theory cannot handle *framing*, and why individual interests and actions do not fit with predictions.[25] Thus, economic life is inadequately problematized: what are "prices" or "costs," how are they interpreted, how do people act on them? Just because managers consider "costs" (but which?) does not make them objective rational actors; they are embedded in meanings and power and need to interpret contexts and formulate and justify actions to colleagues, competitors, and themselves. Meanings are elided, especially for the very concept at the center of economic theory, "market," which remains vague and undefined.[26] Yet humans are not amoebae reacting automatically to supply–demand stimuli; they are creative, confused, and confusing. To make sense of economic behavior and change, we cannot leave culture, power, and institutions exogenous. They must be scrutinized, not cast off as epiphenomenal.

James Millar noted, "Standard [economic] theory assumes…the existence of the necessary legal, social, financial and regulatory institutions essential for a market economy to function."[27] New Institutional Economics (NIE) and political science correct this by taking institutions as their point of departure.[28] Economies reflect constellations of "institutions:" instrumental rules of procedure and structure (akin to the definition of "organization"). By structuring access to and use of resources (including people) and sanctioning transgressions, institutions shape costs and benefits of action. Post-socialism becomes a process of institutional design, creating rules and governance structures that shape costs, hopefully to society's advantage. In particular, the state plays a crucial role as the ultimate enforcer of these rules.[29] To NIE's analysis of how institutions shape economies, political economy adds politics of institutional design and implementation, and conflict over allocation of rewards and pain.[30] Economic institutions arise from conflicts and compromises between the state, elites, foreign powers, and other organizations, with interests and power bases whose operation is sometimes unquestioned.[31] Identify interests, institutionally shaped costs, and loci and balances of power, and you explain or predict change. Extrapolating, we could say that post-socialist change is a struggle of identifiable groups such as *nomenklatura* and Red Directors, financial elites, and state officials to shape rules to maximize resource returns. The engine of change is a mesh of transactional efficiency and accumulation of property, social capital, or legal power.[32] Political economists and *dependentistas* should be ecstatic over how Russia's recent history supports their overall framework.

This brief overview of NIE and political economy does not do justice to their insights that guide my way. My concern is that core ideas are underdeveloped due to fixating on instrumental actions, e.g. elite tactics, governance rules, distributional politics. While I do not deny costs and benefits, analyses cannot end with this oversimplistic approach. One key problem is that these approaches are caught in a *one-dimensional analysis*: constrained within instrumental rationality, where ends are assumed and the focus is on calculating optimal means to obtain those ends.[33] This blinds analysts to meanings and socially constructed knowledge.[34] As well, most of these analyses are trapped in a single dimension of power, material resource control. How policy leads to multiple outcomes depends on heuristics and assumptions of interpreting and implementing them (culture, power). This will be a recurring theme: reforms invoked different reactions because of different material interests *and* because of different logics of normality and of interpretation. Further, reliance on instrumental rationality misses everyday practices and claims that make up laws and institutions; knowing rules and actors' institutional contexts does not warrant assuming we know their interests and thinking. Ethnographic work suggests that rules provoke myriad reactions; whether laws and institutions "work" depends on how actors' meanings and practices (re)constitute them.[35] NIE in particular faces unpleasant historical evidence that inefficient economies persist over time and that institutional configurations might not emerge because they improve efficiency gains.[36] Our data will suggest that in Russia's post-Soviet journey, efficiency, productivity, and profit were not absent from considerations of strategy and structure; but they were not alone, and *aiming for* efficiency is not devising means *to obtain it*.

Organized power enters as class or group struggle over resource allocation, but power itself is undertheorized (e.g. mere superior access to material resources), and meaning is left out.[37] Classes, states, authority do not emerge full-blown like an economic Athena; they are socially constructed and reconstructed.[38] This is a problem in state-centered approaches, where the state is a universal magic wand of explanation, even in works that investigate state capacity. The state is important as a ganglion of power in the body politic, but we must not assume or reify power—we must explore its creation and operation. "Authority" is absent: legitimation and cultural sources of obedience are foreign to political economy, and we cannot explain how new rules appear as everyday practices are disseminated or enforced.[39] To fixate on classes and states or to assume institutions blinds us to deeper mechanisms of how agents construct meaning and authority. The picture of elite wars over Russia's soul is oversimplistic: where does all that authority come from, anyway? This will help us avoid an all-too-common tautology: to invoke bad institutions to explain failure is saying that laws are weak because laws are weak.

That is, NIE and political economy elide *what* institutions are, *how* they operate, and how they *change*.

In short, despite insights they have generated, economic theory, NIE, and political economy *do not adequately explore social forces that make costs, finances, property, institutions, organizations, states, and the like operational in real social life*. They are stuck in the worldview of lawyers and accountants: institutions, strategies, and structures are formal or informal rules and relations in which agents calculate costs and constraints (of capital, information, mobilizing allies and assets, contract). Such is one point of economic sociology, which leaves the lawyer's office and moves beyond the one-dimensional analysis, taking a *constitutive* approach to institutions and institutional design: institutions constitute not only costs but also identities, knowledge, and consciousness. Much good economic sociology fits in political economy, especially state-centered analyses of social change, policy, and the like,[40] and analyses of networks and culture have added micro-level mechanisms and forces.[41] Yet despite rich insights on social construction, power, and culture, economic sociologists focus too much on refuting economists' oversimplifications and devote too little time to elucidating mechanisms of power, culture, practice, and change. Also, few economic sociologists have ventured into post-socialism. David Stark and László Bruszt have addressed East European post-socialism: post-socialist managers and states were embedded in networks that constrained or facilitated deliberation and institutional reconfiguration; yet conflict and power are missing from their analyses.[42] Other economic sociologists have extolled post-socialist innovation amid uncertainty,[43] but some innovation was superficial adaptation decoupled from practice, and with innovation came conflict.[44]

One approach has emerged to help us face the eternal challenge of developing structure and culture, change and reproduction, and investigating institutions: sociological neoinstitutionalism. Seminal work by John Meyer, Brian Rowan, Paul DiMaggio, and Walter Powell outlined this framework to address such troubling issues as why organizations in different niches resemble each other or follow seemingly irrational practices.[45] Neoinstitutionalists posit that organizations and economies are "myth and ceremony," with an important cultural, non-rational dimension. Organizational actors seek to minimize uncertainty and pursue legitimacy. Organizational fields—communities of organizations with perceived affinity—create pressures via isomorphic mechanisms to conform to set practices and structures.[46] Thus, neoinstitutionalism introduces power and culture in a more sophisticated view of culture than elsewhere.[47] This allows neoinstitutionalists to explore efficiency as contextualized social constructions and make variation across space and time more intelligible; convergence to a norm works through isomorphism and fields. Adding political sociology, Neil Fligstein created an embryonic theory of institutional change. Field leaders defend "normal" strategies and structures in fields, maintaining status hierarchies and certainty. When such shocks as depressions or state policies weaken field structures, field leaders or "raiders" from outside the field use these opportunities to enforce new field logics.[48]

Paradoxically, power and culture still remain underdeveloped, including power dynamics and actual cultural meanings. While Meyer and Rowan noted "decoupling" between form and practice, the possibility of contradictory meanings within and between fields and organizations is missing. Neoinstitutionalists often elide actual practices that produce meanings and institutions.[49] Fields and isomorphism are inherently about power, but *how* power operates requires more study; resistance is also marginal.[50] Neoinstitutionalism also does not adequately engage change *and* continuity, not as opposites but as simultaneous occurrences, in different spheres, practices, and levels of organization. Action and agency are often elided as well.[51] Finally, neoinstitutionalism dances around "institutions." Many oversights stem from a research focus on stable economies or gradual change, which restricts exploration of how power-culture and practice produce meanings underpinning institutions, structures, organizations, and economies. Engaging neoinstitutionalism with Russian post-socialism will address this because Russia approaches *revolutionary* change: depths of institutions, structures, and practices are unveiled.[52]

Finally, neoinstitutionalists use Bourdieu incompletely, as Mustafa Emirbayer and Victoria Johnson claim.[53] As Bourdieu himself noted, fields are sites of struggle and status competition. Also, Bourdieu used fields *fractally*, as social dynamics and patterns recurring at different levels; this is related to his principle of homology.[54] As well, neoinstitutionalists must better integrate capital (cultural, economic, social, human, institutional, etc.) and *habitus*. Fortunately, some studies have started addressing these weaknesses, and I draw on their rich insights. In his study of Arthur Andersen & Co., Tim Hallett showed how *habitus* was critical to change and continuity: newcomers to the firm brought new meanings and practices, yet existing routines were a counterweight inculcating existing practices into *habitus*.[55] In an innovative study of Russian post-socialism, Yoshiko Herrera uses Bourdieu to explain variation across regions that, from a structural perspective, should have had *similar* interests and identities. Her explanation invokes *habitus* and *doxa*, social rules taken-for-granted as natural and beyond human intentionality. System shocks weaken *doxa*; elites reassemble orthodoxy to maintain social order, but this allows heterodoxy (alternative claims about normality) to emerge. However, questions still remain, e.g. *how* shocks and challenges weaken *doxa* and orthodoxy, or how heterodoxies develop.

Before examining how post-socialist change in Russia occurred *on the ground*, in social reality, in Chapter 1 we dive into the dimensions of culture and power and how they change, and the logics and nature of those practices through which power and culture come alive as institutions at the heart and soul of analyses, policies, and everyday life—the wreck of Russia's post-socialism *and* of that very modernity we share. If we are to enhance our understanding of how change really operates, as real practices of real people—and if we are to make sense of the massive and confounding changes that have beset Russia over the last twenty years (helping bring about Putin and company, with consequences for geopolitics)— we can no longer elide or assume micro-level power, culture, and practice that are everyday life. This is hunting big game; given globalized crises, peak oil, and ecological threats, it may be big game is hunting us. This heart of modernity beats in us as well, and Russia's trials could one day be ours. To these fundamental building blocks of the social world we now turn.

1 Power-culture, practice, and economic change

Outlines of a framework

But to tear down a factory or to revolt against a government...because it is a system is to attack effects rather than causes...[I]f a factory is torn down but the rationality which produced it is left standing, then that rationality will simply produce another factory. If a revolution destroys a systematic government, but the systematic patterns of thought that produced that government are left intact, then those patterns will repeat themselves in the succeeding government.

(Robert Pirsig, *Zen and the Art of Motorcycle Maintenance*)

Post-Soviet change was a Kuhnian-style paradigm shift and search for new narratives and practices of normality in enterprises, exchange, and property.[1] What are fundamental processes and variables of economic change and variation in trajectories and outcomes? How do contingent power-culture processes create innovation and stasis? How and why do past practices persist or combine with new practices? For answers, I propose an outline to a framework on economic change drawing on different dimensions of culture and power and their interaction. To note a parallel to chemistry: organic chemistry works on the principle that electrons move from spaces of high to low density. Yet something deeper creates electron movement: electrostatic attraction, weak and strong forces, strings. Political economy, economics, and economic sociology follow surface rules. Let us dive beneath to look for strings that make these rules operative—there is order in the seeming chaos of post-Soviet change, and now we set out to find it.

My premises arise from three observations. First, political action involves culture. Logically, if culture shapes politics, why should economies be immune?[2] Western capitalist institutions and practices did not emerge automatically from natural pursuit of rational self-interest and "correct" policies, but from specific historical configurations difficult to reproduce. Macro-level structures are reproduced via micro-level practices embedded in cultural assumptions; assuming a universal market *mentalité* is misguided. Second, reality reveals various factors at work in economies. People are rational in contexts of meaning, knowledge, and practice. They calculate costs and follow routines, assume perceptions of opportunity are objective, and seek legitimacy. Costs affect decision-making, but action also stems from wellsprings of meaning and rituals. Not all action is a mechanistic, instrumental response to "institutions" with questionable ontological status. Third, economic change has two stages: legislation and implementation, in which blame and normality are assigned and groups compete over new rules. These observations lead to a fundamental point: market-building is like polity-building, where multidimensional power and culture figure prominently. As power and culture fragmented in Russia, multiple logics of action and authority emerged, of which actors' knowledge was not complete, breeding confusion and conflict over remaking the economic order. This resulted in variation: negotiated evolution or confusion (e.g. sales), conflict (property), paternalism, low trust, and reliance on networks.

My framework departs from straightforward interests and decision-making of stable economies, where practices and logics are taken for granted as truths. Policies are not hard rules but are totems for discourse and authority mediated through practices. To develop this framework of fundamental change in power-culture and practice, we need a radical case where everyday "webs of signification," in Max Weber's phrase, unravel and differences between previous and intended systems are vast. Russia fits the bill. As pillars of post-Soviet reform were discipline and productivity, privatization and governance, and exchange liberalization, I examine enterprise restructuring, remaking property and governance (fields and state–society relations), and practices of sales and production. I use interviews, ethnographic data, enterprise newspapers, and other primary and secondary data, covering mostly 1987–96 but sometimes to 2008. To analyze change mechanisms, we must follow how this experiment unfolded: *what* historical baggage was, *how* it was bequeathed, *how* it changed as it did. Thus, I start at the end of the Soviet era, close enough to the event to experience it, far enough for cooler analysis. We who were there for the revolution are in a unique position to assess this history and its impact.

Culture and power, logics and practice

To begin, I invoke a wealth of scholarship to suggest three ground rules of economic life.[3] First, *economies are socially constructed and embedded*. They involve structured control of material and symbolic resources and collective enactment of ritualized meaning. Change involves altering mechanisms and content reproduced. Second, *knowledge and meaning support authority and practices that then support knowledge and meaning systems*. Shifts in power create opportunity for new organization, practice, and authority. Third, *contingencies in strategies, power, and outcomes shape meanings and practices then reified into institutions*. Outcomes include little change, conflict, confusion, or true innovation.

I take these rules from four sets of works. From Weber, I make *verstehen* and power central. Action stems from meaning *and* material forces, and economies are forms of power and culture that emerge from historical accidents and constellations of power-culture. Alas, Weber left culture and *verstehen* underdeveloped. Our second foundation, Berger and Luckmann's social constructionism, makes meaning and knowledge crucial to social life. Knowledge is produced in historically contingent situations and reproduced via plausibility structures, collective structures of power and meaning. Russia's transition becomes competing paradigms (forms and content of knowledge) and attempts to reify those paradigms as social normality through "legitimations"—authoritative knowledge in set domains, and symbolic universes integrating meaning and action. Yet Berger and Luckmann did not develop *structured* power, learning, and practices. Pierre Bourdieu offers *habitus*, *doxa*, capital, and fields to address practices and non-material roots of conflict and construction.[4] Application of power through socialization in institutions and structures shapes knowledge, dispositions, and logics of action in the *habitus*, which in turn shapes capacity to act. Change involves learning and situating new knowledge in *habitus*. Also, *habitus*, capital, and strategies are embedded in *fields*: sites of game-like struggle and imitation structured by rules and rituals. *Doxa* ("field logics") are rules that organize the use of practices and capital in fields. As sites of reproduction and contestation, fields work fractally: from an encompassing "master field" or "field of power" as canopy of rules and meanings, to localized fields (regions, sectors). Economic change creates conflict over *doxa*, field boundaries, hierarchies, and authority—at multiple levels and over foundations of economic organization. Bourdieu's insights are powerful but incomplete, however; he said less about mechanisms by which actors compete over power, meaning, and knowledge. For this I bring in political sociology.[5] Economies inherently are politics and power. Take the firm. To economists it is a profit maximizer in a market. To institutional economists it is a governance structure to reduce opportunism. In political economy and sociological neoinstitutionalism, it is a function of classes, states, or fields.[6] Yet this gives little attention to internal dynamics. I follow Jeffrey Pfeffer's claim that organizations are polities;[7] we can then apply political sociology to follow change and resistance in firms and fields. Employees and managers use available material and symbolic resources—money, discourse, institutional position, legitimacy—to engage in blaming and legitimating new structures and practices. Attention should go to structures of power, alliances and negotiations, and access to resources and discourse; how actors frame claims and actions; and contingencies of conflict.[8]

These are our foundations. Instead of rational choice's simplistic short-cut for micro-foundations of action, we have an approach that can get to roots of dynamics and problems of changing fundamental practices. Unlike neoclassical economics, we expand our understanding of "economy" with knowledge and authority. Unlike institutional economics and political economy, we see institutions as meaning and authority and can examine the guts of institutions and institutional change. This foundation in fact takes economic sociology and neoinstitutionalism to their logical conclusion. Yet this foundation requires more development. For example, why did Russian managers propose changes in business practice (marketing, decentralization) without coherently implanting their substance in real practices? Turning claims into practices assumes actors understand what they want to create and that there are no contradictions between practices. This also assumes one group has power and legitimacy; otherwise, enforcement becomes problematic. Only by exploring meaning and knowledge (culture) and implementation (power) can we make better sense of these issues. Thus, we need to open up the dimensions of power and culture, address how these dimensions interact and how power and culture interact, and examine how fundamentals of power-culture for one set of practices interact with those for others (e.g. sales and production knowledge and practices changing in different firms in different ways at the same time). We have made our story more complicated than corrupt state officials, capital hunger or oil wealth, or problematic laws; we must ask *why* officials are "corrupt," *how* capital and value are embodied and used, and why laws and implementation are problematic in the first place.

For methods, I follow an informal rule of qualitative studies: embed method and theory in the narrative, especially when the goal is not testing hypotheses but to engage theory and data to draw out insights from an important case and develop a framework. This follows Bourdieu's plea for "theories which are nourished less by purely theoretical confrontation with other theories than by confrontation with fresh empirical objects."[9] To this end I use a mix of qualitative methods: ethnography, interviews, and written primary and secondary sources that add to discourse. I draw on Michael Burawoy's extended case method,[10] which relates well to Bourdieu's call, to discover how organizations, fields, power, and meanings operate by looking at practices and meanings in wider contexts. Like grounded theory, this method uses cases and comparisons; but it also uses data to expand theory and generate genetic (context-bound) claims. Attention to micro-level detail elucidates practices, constellations of actors and forces, and mechanisms that make up structures, organizations, and institutions.[11] As one goal is to trace claims, categories, and logics of practices, I looked through several sources for issues, claims and categories, and practices in contexts of disputes, counterfactuals, and problematic outcomes. The problem of creating new practices is best seen when actors complain about each other or themselves: relating problems (to me as interviewer or to journalists) in devising and using new concepts, e.g. marketing or decentralization. I sought variation across claims and practices, not only comparing and correlating variables, but asking *how* variables operated. I followed how claims and practices related to experiences of interactions (one's own or others') and contexts.[12] What other practices are discussed, and how are they evaluated (by whom)? What does this say about normality and status? When system shocks perturb existing logics and interpretations, do actors offer or carry out a new template of action, or does their template closely resemble past practices (perhaps masked by new buzzwords)? Equally important is what actors do *not* say or do—which past practices were not blamed or changed, which actions were not taken during a perturbation. Actors might resist criticisms or proposed changes; this suggests a boundary of illegitimacy and abnormality has been crossed, and we can use this to map out logics of normality.

Practices and logics

Changing an economy is changing practices and logics making up its components: property, production, sales, organizational structure and authority, and so on.

Yet by framing economic change in terms of institutions, scholars elide what institutions are: shadows of practices that enact and reify collective meanings. Focusing on practices helps us see mechanisms of change and continuity and sources of conflict and confusion in operation. It also forces us not to assume organizational structures or public policies work merely through costs or operate in the same way for all. By addressing practices we move beyond a superficial view that change is a function of legislating new rules. I conceptualize practices as sets of routines and acts with structured improvisation, repeated in specific material, symbolic, and temporal contexts.[13] Practices include specifics of routines and imply a logic or rationale linking them. Also, practices are neither entirely routine and taken-for-granted nor entirely rationally calculated or *ad hoc*. They are general sets of acts in contexts where we believe they naturally fit, but that we can finesse tactically. Practices thus have a preconscious level anchored in habit, and a conscious level of manipulation and transposition. We can alter superficial aspects of practices, but changing the general action of practices takes more conscious effort and thus is more difficult. In a stable context, institutions and practices are assumed to be, reinforcing reproduction. Fundamental change requires more than marginal shifts in laws; it needs forceful application of power to change collective foundations of practices. It is convoluted because practices are partially taken-for-granted and contextualized as social reflexes. Older practices tend to persist, perhaps with a new façade, and deflect reforms. Change in practices also involves enforcing new meanings and routines for *many* individuals. Because states are creatures of power, institutional change often comes from above, but such reforms might be absorbed "below" in the sea of everyday practices. Studies of change that focus on state and elites miss this complexity that makes radical change messy.

A logic is assumptions, knowledge of how to do something, and rationales that assemble and bind routine acts into practices.[14] Using language as metaphor, practices are vocabulary and logic is grammar. Logics emerge as people perform practices and apply tacit knowledge of what to do—producing a good, making a sale, writing a contract. A crucial facet of economic change is reshaping logics *and* practices—transforming multiple meanings for many people. Remaking the post-Soviet enterprise meant inculcating new logics and practices of production and authority: shopfloor autonomy, economizing, scientific study of demand, profit-based production for consumers. These changes affect knowledge, meanings, and assumptions of normal practices and boundaries for different people and organizational routines. These practices and logics are also part of wider practices and logics: "enterprise" and "economy," one level higher. Market logics of profit via accumulation, rights to residuals, and assessment by value consumed and a financial "bottom line" ran counter to Soviet primacy of production for a plan, property for social use not sale, and assessment via quantity. Not all Soviet practices and logics were delegitimated:[15] paternalist logics and practices persisted as normal, adding to confusion and contention of change.

The link between logics and practices runs as shown in Figure 1.1. A practice is the collection of repeated acts 1, 2, and 3, as an entirety in a context. Linkages binding these individual routines or acts together—rationales, knowledge,

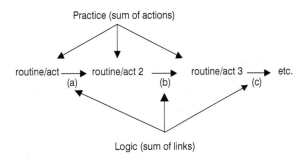

Figure 1.1 Logics and practices

assumptions in (a), (b), (c)—are the logic of the practice. Two notes are in order. First, logics and practices are *fractal*, i.e. they can recur at different levels. Making a car is practice; the operation of an auto firm is a set of practices; the economy in which the factory is embedded is a set of practices. We must note how changes in different levels interact. Second, contradictions in a practice or between practices might create confusion or conflict. These may persist unresolved if other actors enforce quiescence or actors are ambivalent to the contradiction. With power lifted, these contradictions might spawn disorganization and contention. These practices and logics are best observed through qualitative methods such as participant observation or open-ended interviews that trace routine acts, contexts, and justifications (including the inability to explain what seems natural). Perturbations leave practices in disjunction with new contexts, and so I pay attention to what happens to practices and logics when contexts change: if actors continue previous practices or change them, and what they need to do for change. As participant observation is not always feasible, we must use other sources: actors' descriptions and rationales of what they do, especially everyday behavior and reactions to shocks and perturbations (what they did and why). One important detail is *criticism*: what people accentuate as dysfunctional, and what problems they see as persistent and why. Alternatively, we seek solutions people champion as "correct" and why, and how to enforce them—descriptions and justifications of new routines and their fit with new contexts.

The utility of analyzing change via practices and logics is that we avoid reifying institutions or assuming laws shape behavior through costs alone. Institutional mechanisms and change become visible as concrete acts. Private property is realized through practices and justifications of decision-making authority. But there is more. Practices involve meanings attached to actions routine for particular contexts. When we act, practices remind us of meanings, assumptions, and categories, and they reproduce power and authority. We must now unpack culture and power.

Multidimensional culture

Culture is a diverse and multifaceted complex of meanings, knowledge, and assumptions by which we interpret and react to the world.[16] It is not monolithic, perfectly consistent, or overdetermining; differential change across culture's dimensions might create confusion and conflict.[17] More concretely, I see culture as "elements" organized imperfectly on two levels (superficial and fundamental) and in individuals and collective contexts (tool kits and logics). In individuals, elements make up a "tool kit"; those elements are inserted, altered, and discarded in interactions, making culture game-like and interactive,[18] and *habitus* organizes elements. Elements as basic units include categories (ways in which we interpret the world), norms (conceptions of normal action), knowledge, identities, and assumptions of normality and cause–effect relations. I refer to these when relevant: "meanings" in one context, "knowledge" in another. Some elements such as categories or symbols are relatively discrete; others (assumptions) are broader and less conscious. One crucial element is knowledge: manifested as human capital (skills), symbolic capital (status), and cause–effect interpretations, knowledge shapes how we interpret and respond to events. Actors can adopt new strategies, but whether this breeds new practices depends on whether they have sufficient knowledge. Reformers and scholars focusing on macroeconomic concerns downplayed "the lack of training and experience of Russian managers in management skills and techniques to a market economy," such as "sales promotion, marketing, cost and capital accounting [and] management systems such as lateral integration."[19]

Categories, norms, knowledge, and assumptions are not isolated from each other or contexts. To examine change and continuity, we examine how categories and meanings change according to actors' discussions; how assemblages of categories change; and how this happens in conjunction with events and other categories and meanings. This can help us follow and make sense of confusion, conflict, stasis, and real change, especially when new categories correspond to new actions and practices. Further, the empirical narratives will show the importance of culture's multidimensionality, and how culture is linked to power through legitimacy and normality.

Levels

One useful schema suggests two basic levels of culture, a superficial/tactical dimension and a deeper fundamental/tacit dimension.[20] The superficial level includes categories, symbols, values, and skills. These elements are relatively close to consciousness, are easier to manipulate, and are more readily formalized, codified, and structured; with some effort, they can be counted and coded quantitatively. One can consider what skills one has or what categories and words to use for discussing the world. Learning this superficial level of culture is classroom learning, e.g. via supervised practice and repetition. The tacit level runs deeper into consciousness, as assumptions of normality and unexpressed, nearly instinctive knowledge of meaning, cause–effect, and what one does in contexts: "highly subjective insights, intuitions and hunches…and accumulated skills and experience."[21] Culture at this level is preconscious, assumed, and taken-for-granted; we rarely question it even if we change categories.[22] Learning tacit knowledge or meanings requires internalization via experience or trial-and-error, which in turn needs investment of time and resources—a luxury in a rapidly and radically changing context. Also, learning can be complicated when competing knowledge and claims abound; what tacit knowledge is normal and that one is supposed to learn? Finally, if enforcement and support of new tacit knowledge are weak or inconsistent, learning is hindered. For example, a manager can learn new strategies and their tacit knowledge (e.g. via foreign training and apprenticeship programs) but face older knowledge on return to the context of "work as usual" back home. For these reasons, it is crucial that we consider levels of culture and change, for this multidimensionality of culture makes fundamental shifts in practice more difficult.

Legitimacy and normality

Most people do not like to offend God or nature: legitimacy and normality are central to reproduction, learning, and implementing new culture and practices. We have seen legitimacy and normality hiding in institutions as collective meanings linked to conceptions of a normal social order. Legitimacy is acceptance that actions or claims follow humanly constructed principles of proper procedure or moral order. Normality is assumed reality of cause–effect relations beyond human control, by which the social world operates. Legitimacy is humanly constructed ethics, normality is natural laws. The illegitimate violates human strictures of behavior and risks sanction; the abnormal violates nature's rules and risks negative outcomes. If people minimize uncertainty and are risk-averse,[23] the immoral, unknown, or odd create anxiety people try to resolve. Finally, legitimacy and normality are not static but are constantly reproduced: we should talk of "legitimation" and "normalization" as processes of reproducing the normal social order. This links legitimacy and normality to culture, power, and reproduction.[24]

An important aspect to (de)legitimation and normality is "framing." Frames are "schemata of interpretation," assemblages of symbols, rhetoric, and claims accepted as legitimate and normal that actors use as reference to make sense of social life.[25] Further, frames have levels: a "master frame" encompassing a polity, and subframes for subfields. Through framing, people use existing meanings and rhetoric to imbue claims with normality. By providing legitimate grounds for claims and mobilization, they act as signposts or totems for challenges or as a defense of the status quo. That is, when framing actors try to show their claims fit generally understood and accepted rules of human conduct and nature; opposing them is immoral and risky. As actors draw on frame content, they may devise new combinations. If these have sufficient logical consistency, clarity, and halos of success (perhaps averting direct falsification), they can alter broader frames.[26] Frames can also constrain claim-making to existing contents; straying beyond these bounds poses a risk until challengers shift them. In radical change, initial shocks and delegitimation may weaken frames; fundamental and radical change inherently involves altering master frames and the nature of legitimacy. When constructing normality, participating actors can raise chances of success by using claims that tap into broader normality and legitimacy. Such claims have less likelihood of facing resistance or confusion, as they more likely resonate with the audience's experiences and knowledge of the normal social order.[27] Alternatively, proposed changes can gain legitimacy and normality from a halo effect: being linked to other legitimate or normal phenomena, e.g. groups or policies with perceived status and success. One implication is that reformers may need to frame opponents and their policies as abnormal, illegitimate, and to blame for social ills. We will see that some aspects of the Soviet system were widely perceived as abnormal and were easy targets for attack; others, such as paternalism, retained normality and were difficult to alter. Finally, multiple claims of (ab)normality and (il)legitimacy can emerge, breeding confusion and conflict over competing models of behavior.

Culture and change

A common view is that change is a gradual accretion and follows a combination of socialization, copying, and imposition, although fundamental change may be punctuated.[28] Actors might adopt new strategies and practices that appear normal or useful and are imposed, e.g. gatekeepers promote one version of normality and punish "deviance." Yet the universe of available categories, logics, and practices is sufficiently broad that actors can mix and match elements to maneuver and innovate, given power and opportunity. Contradictions and gaps in knowledge and practice prevent total hegemony and allow innovation. Yet uniform change is not so easy. The number of people involved might raise costs of change and increase the chances of resistance, confusion, and competing claims. Culture's multileveled nature also significantly affects this process. Rules and incentives shift but do not filter quickly into tacit knowledge; tactics appear to change (e.g. new organizational forms) when real practice and understanding follows older knowledge. Superficial adaptation of formal rules is faster than change in knowledge or practice, creating a lag between form and substance of change.[29] The conscious, tactical/surface level is straightforward human capital and formal knowledge (e.g. technical skills); change means acquiring new skills, credentials, or vocabulary. Adopting new practices (fundamental change) means learning new tacit knowledge, habitual responses, and assumptions that we do not question but simply do.[30] Actors may deduce tactics from costs and benefits of change versus continuity, but this assumes the capacity to deduce costs and that costs are not ambiguous. Actors may copy solutions to common problems, but this is complicated by learning and inculcating new logics (the how and why of practices). Education may instill buzzwords or formulae, but changing tacit knowledge and practices requires time and resources. This is one source of stasis and reproduction: through *habitus* we reproduce old tacit meanings and knowledge because this is natural; in so doing we pass on culture to others. This can occur even with change around us: we might accept new claims or categories to survive, but unless we change our tacit level, we reproduce past practices in new form. Embeddedness also complicates change: an individual may try to change, but his/her context (e.g. networks of older employees) might reinforce older elements. Knowledge needs expertise and conceptual capital to be transferred beyond its original generating context;[31] yet when training is over, agents return to older contexts and reproduce older practices, meanings, and logics. Finally, while some older categories might be delegitimated, others might persist. Global capitalism provided new practices, frames, and justifications, but Soviet claims and conceptions persisted, such as paternalism and nationalism.

Combining elements (knowledge, categories), levels, and organizing principles (frames, logics), we have a richer picture of change. The tacit dimension means logics and practices change more slowly than laws or discourse. From 1985 on Russia/USSR and East Europe were enveloped in transition culture, an extension of Cold War dichotomies, global neoliberalism, and capitalism. Transition culture, discourses on post-socialism carried through market actors, framed global capitalism and socialism in contrasting normal–abnormal dichotomies: progress–regress, freedom–constraint, development–stasis, dynamic–stagnant.[32] As Soviet elites acknowledged problems and reform movements took root, transition culture gained a foothold as less tainted by failure and linked to powerful actors with legitimacy and resources (e.g. dynamic American consumerism, economists) and local actors such as "reform" journalists and politicians. Yet transition culture's dichotomies and support did not mean frictionless change. New market categories might be transposed onto Soviet logics and practices. Let me illustrate with post-Soviet marketing (Chapter 4). The conscious level includes such elements and categories as consumers, taste, price, and quality. Ideally, marketing/sales personnel collect and analyze data on consumer tastes and wants; managers prioritize goals (profit, market share, survival) and set production strategies accordingly, to optimize the fit between these goals, the firm's capacities, and consumer tastes and demand. Russian managers tried to implement marketing; yet the superficial level changed while the fundamental level did not. Rather than adopt marketing elements *and* logic, Russian managers transposed marketing elements onto Soviet production logics. They created marketing departments that did little more than study others' prices. Comprehensive change required managers to have tacit knowledge of marketing, which they did not.

This is only half the story. Members of organizational fields may share particular categories, logics, and practices; and they may do so because such knowledge and culture benefit them all. Yet given the human capacity for innovation, and given that there is as yet no single, clear economic path that is first among equals, persistence of shared meanings likely does not come from agreement alone. Fields and social groupings survive, and share meanings and practices, in part because these are imposed. Further, there is much to gain from defining legitimacy and normality, or being its prime recipient.

Multidimensional power

Power supports change (breaking resistance or inertia) and underpins reproduction (defending against challenges). Power is also dynamic, operating via rituals, interactions, and exchange. As legitimated authority, power is part of everyday practices that involve positions and status *vis-à-vis* others. Yet power is not sufficiently explored despite its centrality to economies (extracting surplus, enforcing obligations, etc.). Economic theory marginalizes or assumes it. State-centered scholars narrow it to state structure and assume the economy reflects state capacity or that failure reflects state *in*capacity.[33] Class-centered analyses have a similar logic. Yet power is not limited to states or classes; it has many forms and bases and plays out in many ways. Scholars who focus on regions expand *nodes* of power,[34] but power's roots, operation, and justifications remain underexplored. In a masterpiece on power, John Gaventa applied Steven Lukes's three-dimensional model to understand Appalachian miners' quiescence, which was inexplicable from other theoretical perspectives. William Roy showed how the corporate form was not adopted for efficiency but was *enforced* by investors who viewed it as normal organization. Douglass North noted that only power could explain the persistence of inefficient institutional arrangements as beneficial to those with power. Yet to say "power is important" is a truism; *how* does power operate?

Dimensions of power

Like culture, power operates at different levels and locales. I follow Steven Lukes's and John Gaventa's innovative model of power:[35] I refer to the three dimensions as *resource power*, *discursive power*, and *narrative power*. Resource power is control of material and symbolic resources that can shape actors' options. This is dependency, and it involves manipulating social provision and even violence.[36] Discursive power involves controlling discursive sites and agendas to articulate claims for mobilization or legitimacy and to invoke the use of resource power to enforce rules (e.g. using the police). Closed access to voice means no claims and less chance for mobilization or legitimation. Discourse can also be a signaling device facilitating mobilization: in an open press, the dispossessed can complain openly and learn that others share their views. Material factors can affect this dimension, e.g. money for newspapers or politicians, coercion to silence challenging voices. Narrative power is capacity to shape categories, arguments, and logics into narratives that plausibly explain and justify existing events, inequalities, and organization. By framing narratives that provide plausible meanings to events, actors can shape expectations, meanings, and interests, and from here obedience or resistance.[37] Explanation becomes power when target populations cannot conceive alternatives, feel others will not accept their non-hegemonic narrative, or cannot provide a counter-narrative with clarity and coherence. Elites cloak power in legitimating meanings (e.g. progress) or lose it when their competence and right to rule is disproved. Successful challenge involves devising and articulating a counter-narrative with sufficient explanatory power and resonance with a target audience; correlating the new narrative with "success" provides legitimacy and empowerment; failure or repression of alternatives deprives challengers of a rallying cause. Narrative power is initially built on other dimensions, although it can sustain structures if other dimensions weaken. Dependency and silence make groups think powerlessness is natural; material autonomy and discursive freedom invite the powerless to articulate and act. Also, hegemony is never perfect as it creates its opposite.[38] Market outlines could come from reversing Soviet socialism.

Forms of power relations

I collapse power relations into three types: vertical authority, horizontal autonomy, and unresolved.[39] The essence of *vertical authority* is rights and capacity to control another. Relations and dimensions of power are structured hierarchically around control, command, and obedience, even domination. The Soviet command economy, property, and bureaucracy involved vertical authority. The essence of *horizontal autonomy* is rights and capacity of autonomous action; actors are relative equals. Power and authority are embedded in enforcement of autonomy and obligations. Parties shape each other by using discourse or resources to enforce obligations.[40] Horizontal autonomy may involve leverage, but this is not control or institutional power. When both sets of rules and logics persist, we have *unresolved authority*. Vertical authority partially fractures, and horizontal autonomy is not consolidated, leaving confusion and contention as different groups try to articulate and enact a resolution and create stable authority and autonomy that defends interests and identities.

Power relations are also organized through property and fields. Property, as William Roy notes, normalizes power relations into legitimate authority. Property operates both through resource power (control over residuals and decision-making) and through the other dimensions. How property is defined and defended in public narratives can legitimate or demonize new classes (e.g. property owners as engines of growth or as parasites), and owners will likely try to influence that discourse. If property becomes a natural part of the narrative of normality, it can be seen as unavoidable: e.g. the narrative of American history gives private property a sacred role as necessary guarantor of economic growth *and* as bulwark against state tyranny.[41] Here the state plays a key role in defining and defending "property" by defining its own role and power *vis-à-vis* society. Yet if not hegemonic, ambiguities in "property" can generate contention and confusion over its limits (e.g. owners versus managers or employees, majority versus minority shareholders). A second structured form of power relations is the field. Fields as communities of organizations are not simple associations of the like-minded; field leaders set general logics of normal organizational strategy and structure and punish challengers. As Neil Fligstein showed, fields allow us to understand waves of corporate change and continuity in American history.[42] Further, the relation of fields and the state is crucial: is the state an enforcer of field limits and autonomy or at the center of the field of power, dictating to other fields? If field creation is about remaking power, we expect fields to be central to contention in Russia: contention over remaking field boundaries and leaders, over status and rules within fields, and over competing logics between fields. Finally, the principle of fractals—social processes operate at different levels (although different specific meanings might be involved)—suggests we apply field insights to organizations themselves. As we will see in Chapters 2 and 3, only by analyzing organizations as political sites and fields can we understand processes of change, contention, and variation.

Power and change

Severe shocks and change disrupt resource control, discourse, and conceptualizations of normality, creating opportunity for action. Alternative resources (jobs, goods, protection) weaken dependency, lowering costs of resistance or exit. Liberalization and democratization expand second-dimensional opportunity to set agendas and to articulate alternative identities and forms of economic organization. Experiences of systemic problems and mounting criticisms of failure open the third dimension to new concepts of normal relations and practices. Further, change need not be uniform across all three dimensions: dependency may weaken while discourse is controlled. Finally, changes in each dimension and their impacts are contingent. Non-elites might not be able or willing to take advantage of opportunities for mobilization, articulation of alternative relations, and empowerment. Contingent confrontations can create polarization, with all sides articulating differing versions of normal social order, or lead to negotiations, depending on actors' perceptions and relations. For our concrete case, *glasnost'* and *perestroika* (liberalization), destatization, and corruption reduced state capacity to enforce laws and hegemony. State withdrawal from the economy and a growing private sector fractured state power over society and managerial power over employees. (Compare this to China, where state power remained intact, or Poland and Hungary, where post-socialism involved transfer of power, not its decomposition.[43]) Perceived weaknesses in Soviet socialism and encroaching transition culture empowered alternative normalities, although social democracy persisted. Paradoxically, propaganda hindered narrative power: citizens appreciated welfare and superpower status, but most knew reality did not coincide with over-the-top propaganda.[44] People's performances of front-stage conformity, a surreal "living the lie," empowered: playing to the lie was a denial of the regime's truth-claims and an expression of hidden autonomy.[45]

Remaking power is no easy task and likely will elicit resistance. Rebuilding resource power requires changing resource control and dependency. Rebuilding discursive power requires leverage anew over discourse and agendas. Rebuilding narrative power means creating a hegemonic narrative and expectations that alternatives will be ignored, punished, or fail. This means elites must do more than secure control of property or capital—they must rebuild dependency and normality, e.g. sanctify private property or managerial prerogative. They must also inculcate the expectation that resistance to new normality will be crushed. However, elites cannot simply legislate new rules and relations of power. They must enact them through negotiations with non-elites, impose them during confrontations, and create alliances (e.g. between owners or managers and politicians) for the perception of broad support.

Processes of economic change

It is time to embed power-culture, logics, and practices in contingent shocks, legislating, and implementing. Culture underpins power via categories that legitimate and normalize power as natural authority. Power underpins culture by enabling and blocking alternative meanings. Change involves altering power-culture and normality: relations and practices weaken when elites cannot support them, non-elites blame them, and alternative claims challenge them. This suggests multiple permutations to remaking power-culture; change is not straightforward. If plausibility structures behind meanings and practices are stable—actors have adequate knowledge of desired practices and can manipulate power relations—opportunities for resistance are low, and the powerful can reward those who adapt and punish those who do not. (Economists assume markets do this.) If power fragments, groups articulate and act on meanings. Actors must negotiate meanings and practices or turn to direct conflict. There is also the issue of "fit" between new rules and old knowledge that may hinder legitimation. Finally, power and culture contingently interact in complex manner: in multiple contexts (finance, production), groups (owners, state, demographic cohorts), levels (national, regional, sectoral), and content of meaning and knowledge.

Power relations, culture, and change

In the USSR, the Party, state, and informal networks were plausibility structures reinforcing command economy logics. As they weakened, new meanings and logics could emerge, but they too required plausibility structures, making change in power important. If change is *marginal*, authority relations shift trivially. For *fundamental* change, authority is redefined and plausibility structures collapse. With radical delegitimation and change, the combination of learning new logics while remaking authority (and trying to impose new logics) created conflict and confusion. Vertical authority can facilitate change from above, although success is not inevitable—sufficient resistance may emerge, or incomplete knowledge may complicate enforcement. Where vertical authority gives way to stable horizontal autonomy but weak fields, isomorphic spread of new strategies and structures becomes knotty. No commanding power is there to enforce new practices or to weed out those who do not adapt; change depends on individual leaning or facilitated sharing of knowledge. For example, organizing the *act* of exchange expedited shared meaning and practices in a way that independent sales *strategies* did not.[46] For organizing production and property, actors perceived chaos as a central problem solved by rebuilding hierarchical authority. Whose idea of legitimate authority would dominate became the focus of conflict.

From our power relations (vertical, horizontal, unresolved) and cultural levels (superficial, fundamental), we can conceive of power shifting in three paths:

vertical → *vertical, vertical* → *horizontal,* and *vertical* → *unresolved.*[47] (These might include multi-step paths or oscillation.)

Vertical → *vertical*

This sees no change in power or its quick consolidation vertically. Superficial/tactical change is possible, legislated and implemented from above. This might be merely changing exchange partners. Fundamental change depends on whether actors with power have sufficient knowledge of new practices and of the requisite organizational politics and tactics to enforce new knowledge and practices among subordinates. Change also depends on distance and fit between legacies and target practices—the greater the distance, the more power is necessary. Part of cultural change will involve justification of new verticality.

Vertical → *horizontal*

These are relations of relative autonomy in which coordinated change in logics and practices is difficult, with possible conflict over competing interests or authority claims (turf wars). Cultural change will be linked to how actors interact and learn logics and practices. Fundamental change is harder without a central actor evaluating practices and enforcing change. Contagion is easier for repertoires that can be negotiated or copied; a deeper logic involves intense learning absent from formal interactions. Further, a plurality of logics can coexist. While actors devise common tactics of exchange (networks, prepayments), fundamental strategies might diverge (waiting for clients versus seeking them). For fundamental change I expect plurality of practices and decoupling between proposed changes and real deeds.

Vertical → *unresolved*

Practices and power relations exhibit horizontal *and* vertical traits, leading to contradictory authority. This occurs if vertical authority changes partially, or rules collapse without negotiated replacements. Material dependency could end while formal rules maintained vertical decision-making authority. Unresolved power allows multiple logics and practices to survive; culture is linked to conflict over competing practices. In enterprises, subdivisions received some autonomy, yet managers claimed ultimate authority (Chapter 3). A related form is vertical → unstable horizontal → vertical (Chapter 5, property and fields). Unstable horizontal relations emerge from a confused collapse of vertical authority. With property reform, the state nominally owned firms, but officials rarely engaged decision-making, giving firms *de facto* autonomy. Privatization encouraged vertical authority via shareholding. Amid cash hunger, ownership promising investment could create first-dimensional dependency. Oligarchs gave privatization a bad name, but Soviet state-run property fared worse in discourse.

Combinations of power-culture and contingent processes of legislating (framing, blaming) and implementing (enforcing, learning) lead to four possible processes of change.

Innovation

New practices take root or old and new combine to create hybrids. As fundamental change faces obstacles, this is most likely in *consolidated vertical authority*: innovative owners or managers have sufficient knowledge of target reforms in practice—they know how the target system works—and have power and tactics to inculcate them. This occurred in some cases of enterprise change and of business logics (Chapters 3 and 4); the Atlas tour firm in Chapter 2 is our epitome of innovation and fundamental change. I do not discount that successful learning and fundamental change is possible in horizontal autonomy,[48] although this might be vertical authority at another level, e.g. within firms. (One case would be autonomous firms learning and negotiating common tactics, e.g. defending exchange and contract.)

Decoupling

In this second process and outcome, new procedures are legislated and adopted superficially or with confusion; real practices follow previous logics. This can occur in *consolidated vertical authority* when levels of culture do not shift in tandem, or there is a gap of knowledge and power. An owner/manager with stable authority might lack knowledge to enforce new practices and logics (through training, surveillance, reward); this was the case for Economics Inc. (Chapter 2) and many Red Directors who imperfectly implemented marketing. Alternatively, *unresolved authority* can breed decoupling: actors who grasp target logics and practices may lack sufficient power to impel others to follow their lead or to overcome resistance.

Contradiction

In this scenario, only some components in a set of logics and practices change. The result is an incomplete shift that brings practices into conflict. Alternatively, different groups' interests, identities, and conceptions of normal practice differ fundamentally. Contradictions in cases of *consolidated vertical authority* more likely result in confusion and inefficiencies, as actors with power restrict conflict (marketing in Chapter 4, restructuring in Chapter 3). Managers who tried to reform labor practices could not discard paternalism, leading to conflict between employees and managers over normality and retaining more workers and welfare than needed.[49] Contradictions in *unresolved authority* can breed confusion or conflict, especially if related to power. This occurred in some cases of enterprise restructuring and remaking governance and fields, where conflict emerged between competing groups and their logics.

Continuity

This scenario results from stable power relations (usually vertical), where commanding figures' logics and practices do not shift. This might result if switching costs are high or returns low: change is difficult, current knowledge is cheap, and power-holders support old practices. This might also result if previous logics and practices are not noticed and blamed.

These processes led to outcomes varying by subject (altering structure, production and sales, etc.). In Chapter 3 we will see consolidated vertical authority *and* unresolved authority as consequences of restructuring—the latter leading to conflict and confusion over normal enterprise practice and operation. In the Conclusion I also propose four contemporary business logics: market engagement, *dirigisme*, muddling, and retreat. Each was related to the processes noted above: contradiction led to weak firms and market retreat; continuity led to *dirigisme* in firms still state-owned and to muddling or retreat in others; successful change and innovation led to market engagement; and decoupling bred muddling through due to superficial change.

Legislating and implementing change: framing, knowing, enforcing

Change in culture and power follow processes of *legislation* and *implementation*: articulating the subject and process of change, and structuring its enforcement. I begin with legislation. Iurii Lotman noted that Russian change involves rejecting the past; Yeltsin's framing of the USSR and Putin's framing of the 1990s follow this.[50] Legislating change is articulating what of the social order is rejected and why, and maneuvering power relations to frame solutions. This begins with system shocks that destabilize a system and signal dilemmas that call into question existing structures and practices. Actors blame: they seek roots of dilemmas that delegitimate by deeming practices abnormal and a source of problems.[51]

Table 1.1: Trajectories of change

Vertical → *vertical* Cases: limited enterprise change (Chapters 2, 3)	Power located in minority of wielders. 1. Stasis of practices (continuity). 2. Possible fundamental change if power-wielders have knowledge (innovation), otherwise potential decoupling (superficial change)
Vertical → *horizontal* Cases: Exchange, radical enterprise change (Chapters 3, 5)	Power dispersed; outcome dependent on contingent relations: 1. Negotiated innovation between actors (if shared interaction) 2. If independent decision-making, independent learning; variation 3. Inter-group conflict over normality and interests (contradiction)
Vertical → *unresolved* Cases: Enterprise restructuring (Chapter 3) and property/field relations (Chapter 4)	Elements of authority and autonomy. Culture/logics/practices as focus for conflict: setting new rules of structure and legitimacy/normality. 1. Conflict over new practices and authority/autonomy (contradiction) 2. Negotiated innovation or decoupling if power perceived as marginal (outcomes depends on learning and levels of culture)

Content of blame and solutions emerges through filters of categories, perceived interests, identities, and knowledge that informs what is possible and desirable or not. Solutions are the proposed new normality. However, shocks can unleash myriad actors with their own frames and trigger defenses of existing various meanings and relations. Further, group identities, interests, and articulations can shift with broader changes in power-culture. Legislation can involve change *and* stasis. One example of paradoxical change and continuity is paternalism: it was not delegitimated immediately, but only when able managers shifted paternalist provision from providing goods and services to providing stable wages. Further, just as important as was blame for abnormalities was what was *not* targeted for blame. A practice not blamed might persist to contradict reforms because actors will assume it and reproduce it. Employees criticized enterprise structure as relevant and immediate but were less concerned about distant "marketing." While economists criticized paternalism, state elites, managers, and employees did not blame but remade it.[52]

Legislating change is muddied by contingencies and power, including actors' political skills *vis-à-vis* framing and structuring alliances. What issues come up in discourse (or not) is partly shaped by contingent politics of framing: attacking centralized distribution was easy because it could be solved easily and because it was less controversial than private property, which confronted a key tenet of Soviet socialism and threatened a redistribution of wealth and disempowerment of employees and managers. We will see this for enterprise restructuring: outside ownership became an important tool managers used to augment their legitimacy. Power as well muddies our waters. Participation in blaming and framing depend on opportunity. Shocks alter groups' access to resources, discourse, and position to rebuild authority and normality. Yet not all groups may be empowered or willing to act. Early on, managers and employees were positioned to act. Managers gained autonomy from ministries, and employees gained voice to vote for managers and reforms. Yet employees' opportunity depended on how far managers took restructuring. Financial elites gained resources to participate, e.g. networks with Yeltsin's Kremlin. State officials lost institutional power through liberalization, destatization, and delegitimation of the Soviet command economy. Yet as reforms created disorder, state elites under Putin gained opportunity and legitimacy to frame and legislate.

Implementation turns legislation into practice through enforcing real practices to make them operational. The first aspect of this stage concerns knowledge and learning. Learning marginal change (e.g. a few new laws) might be annoying, but learning fundamentally new practices is a challenge involving cognitive and structural issues and tacit knowledge of numerous logics. The cognitive side involves complexity and levels. Complexity involves the number of practices and logics to be learned; the more to learn, the more difficult the process. Enterprise restructuring was complex; simultaneous privatization and marketing further complicated learning. Complexity also involves levels of knowledge and practice. Learning new logics and tacit knowledge (the fundamental level) requires active, conscious attempts to learn and embed new practices in routines. If actors do not understand deeper logics, they may adapt only superficially. This is related to "fit," distance or affinity between legacies and targets of change. If solutions appear normal and are understood—they fit or resonate with knowledge and normality— actors are more likely accept and implement them. If target practices and logics do not resonate with experiences, requiring learning new tacit knowledge and logics, confusion or resistance and further blame might result. For example, capitalist enterprise structure and marketing entail knowledge and logics actors might not understand, requiring altering existing relations of work and authority. If multiple models are available, actors might not know which is optimal, although they may mimic others with needed resources or who discovered optimal solutions.[53] Structurally, if change is individuals learning on their own, as in horizontal autonomy, adaptation might not spread effectively. Marketing and restructuring were firm-specific; managers could copy each other but did not negotiate common practices. If groups are cooperative or ambivalent to each other, chances for negotiated learning improve. If identities are oppositional, negotiated change and sharing practices are hindered: accepting another's practice is tantamount to denying one's legitimacy and status. Radical enterprise restructuring unfolded in this way. Finally, decoupling—adopting a new form without its real practice— might occur if actors with power do not have sufficient knowledge of those practices. Such actors may still reproduce older logics and practices despite new organizational structure. Managers socialized in the Soviet era tried to implement new marketing divisions and strategies, but they inadvertently reproduced the Soviet production logic. Alternatively, actors might resist change by adopting it superficially. Managerial accounting has been awkward, as managers resisted transparency.[54] Persistence of contradictory practices can also occur when reforms are incomplete: older practices and knowledge remain legitimate and opera- tive to contradict newer strategies. Managerial paternalism remained operative, contradicting "downsizing" and using unemployment to increase efficiency.

Implementation also depends on capacity to enforce change: if not blamed or blocked, older practices persist out of inertia or resistance.[55] Actors might resist change if costs appear high, if change threatens interests and identities, or if change is sufficiently different to evoke trepidation.[56] Implementation thus involves enforcing practices and knowledge through criteria of evaluation and procedures of selection. Firms and entrepreneurs whose skills and practices do not fit criteria of normality are punished through exit or marginalization, leaving the "normal." However, this assumes selection mechanisms and authority to reward or punish. One natural enforcer is the state, yet post-socialist state capacity was compromised when reforms (e.g. privatization) deprived the state of levers of power. *Glasnost'*, reduced coercion, and democratization hindered state capacity to control agendas and legislation. Corruption and weak knowledge deprived state officials of capacity to understand or enforce new norms, a legacy of *prikhvatizatsiia* and absence of practices sanctifying the rule of law.[57] Bolsheviks derided "bourgeois" law and stressed the primacy of politics and the will of the Party. Under Brezhnev, state and Party cadres made themselves the law rather than its agents. Gorbachev's reforms intensified *prikhvatizatsiia* by reducing Party and state monitoring: authority in the state became personalized, and ritualistic appeals to the state became appeals to individuals.[58] Private actors played along, accepting bribes as akin to fees or using networks with state agents for gain or advantages.

Post-Soviet state power varied across time and context. For privatization, the state was a variable actor: sometimes supporting managers, other times owners but then turning on them. In exchange/sales, the state did not defend contract well; actors innovated defenses. In enterprise restructuring, the state set bounds of reform and left the process to managers and employees. State power was also confounded by a gap between new rules and officials' practices and knowledge. To enforce reforms, state agents had to understand new policy logics—difficult when the logic of the state shifted from running the economy to refereeing it. Yet we focus solely on the state and laws at our peril. Non-state gatekeepers such as investors can apply criteria—debt repayment, P/E ratios, models of share value—to determine which actors are following accepted logics and deserve reward (further investment, recommendations) or punishment (criticism, lawsuits, investigations). Unsurprisingly, post-Soviet Russia had no coherent private gatekeepers: the stock market was primarily a site of speculation in a handful of natural resource firms, and banks did not provide sufficient capital for leverage over firms.[59] In response to problematic gatekeepers, weak rule of law, and a predatory state, private actors constructed means to enforce of practices. To guard contracts, actors used prepayments, reputation within networks, and even *mafiia*.[60] Within enterprises, managers augmented authority through law (privatization and share ownership), material means (paternalist provision), and framing (opposing outside shareholders as speculators). In short, part of market-building was not just learning new logics and practices but also creating means independent of the state and elite to enforce or guard practices.

Historical legacies: that which weighs on or abets the living

Narratives, *habitus*, resources, and rules do not come from thin air; they come from history. A central theme to Russian history has been a dream of modernity. Framing Russia *vis-à-vis* the West and relying on state bureaucracy, Peter the Great and his heirs built an incomplete foundation for capitalism with one fundamental contradiction: state sovereignty versus market autonomy. The state was a jealous god defending sovereignty, demanding economic initiative yet fearing autonomy. Weak private property, finance, contract, civic association, and rule of law (power outside the tsar) retarded emergence of entrepreneurial groups and market institutions.[61] Private property was tenuous, mitigated by patrimonialism in which rights stemmed not from assumed natural franchise but from the sovereign. Merchants and entrepreneurs helped reproduce this logic. Fearing expropriation, coerced into such duties as collecting taxes and maintaining infrastructure, and facing underdeveloped capitalist structures, merchants and emerging entrepreneurs developed coping strategies: petty trading, short-term deals, and personal networks; opportunistic behavior to strangers but not to friends; selling below cost to poor customers and demanding high prices from the wealthy; using cut-throat competition and personal credit. Merchants distrusted innovation, credit, and competition, and investment and accumulation were weak driving forces. While laws did not encourage property and capital accumulation, merchants seldom lobbied for new freedoms and focused primarily on making money to retain status and improve consumption. Merchants, intellectuals, small producers, and workers maintained a distance hindering civic association and coevolution of social practices.[62]

Despite contradictions between tsarism and capitalism, by the 1870s Russia experienced growth of industry, social classes, state-led financial institutions, and a nascent legal structure. Yet Russian society, bereft of sufficient social capital, exploded in 1917 under strains of World War I. In the Civil War the Bolsheviks launched War Communism: nationalizing production and distribution, abolishing money, instituting planning, and expropriating peasant produce. Its failure led to quasi-market experiments of the New Economic Policy (NEP). Heavy industry was state-run, but small production and agriculture were private. Industrial organization combined market and socialist logics in trustification (*trestifikatsiia*): the state used market mechanisms to arrange state-owned enterprises in trusts (*tresty*) and syndicates (*sindikaty*) for efficiency of production and economies of scale.[63] Managers were to obtain capital, use it efficiently, and make profit; profitable firms could "buy" the worse-off. The Bolsheviks believed this would reveal efficient enterprises and managers. Some syndicates and trusts failed; others were little more than Civil War administrative units (*glavki*) with the same personnel and practices, relying on state largesse—drawing criticism of bureaucratic "glavkism" and "glavokratiia." Managers demanded prices they felt they deserved despite demand and held to state paternalism.[64]

NEP's contradictions (market inequality, private wealth), ideological battles for power, and the threat of a European war led Stalin to champion Party-state control over planning, production, and distribution. This would fulfill promises of 1917, defend the homeland, and demonstrate Soviet superiority to the West. Bureaucrats, planners, and ministries now controlled economic decisions from pay to production to prices. Despite legitimation from victory in World War II, insiders considered economic reforms. Nikita Khrushchev's reforms, politically motivated decentralization, led to resistance. Leonid Brezhnev and Aleksei Kosygin forged ahead with competing policies. Kosygin—head of state and reformers' champion—initiated changes in 1965 in accounting and performance evaluation. Economists A. Birman and E. Liberman suggested profit (difference of costs of inputs and output returns) be the primary indicator of enterprise success. Two items central to this agenda were *realizatsiia* and *rentabel'nost'*: output counted towards plan fulfillment when buyers paid for it, and fulfillment meant the relation of income to production costs, gross output plus profitability. Both were linked to an incentive fund and bonuses the state could use as economic levers.[65] Yet legal contradictions and soft budgets undercut full implementation of reforms. Revised plan indicators confused bureaucrats and managers, and bureaucratic politics and rule-skirting hindered reforms. Many managers were unable or unwilling to reorient to new indicators; one claimed, "for many enterprise-management people, it was incomprehensible to operate" via different indicators, and managers and ministers continued to follow the "same old thinking."[66]

In Brezhnev's conservatism, a key linchpin of authority was the "little deal." Formal authority was centralized in rules and procedures, but real authority slipped to individuals and informal patronage.[67] Officials had stable careers in bailiwicks in return for quiescence; citizens had jobs and welfare in return for political obedience. This embedded institutional schizophrenia in the Soviet political economy. Formal structure and accountability masked real informal use of state authority and created the dual nature of the Soviet economy: formal rules and procedures versus an informal world of the shadow economy, whose logic of personal networks of reciprocity and patronage (*blat*), driven by survival and opportunism, spread to the entire state.[68] Formal and informal revolved around collective totems of Party-state, enterprise, and plan. The economy was imbued with paternalism—formal state welfare provision and informal patronage— that reproduced patron–client authority relations. Criminal interests emerged, although their links to the economy were less blatant until Gorbachev's reforms (e.g. co-operatives) provided opportunity and incentives for money laundering.[69] The ubiquity of shadow practices harmed performance and legitimacy. Formal claims were more fiction than reality, giving credence to the perception of the Soviet system as "the lie." Brezhnev's tolerance of informality made informality easier, legitimating shadow practices as the reality in the illusory formal economy.

Brezhnev's vision of welfare for support meant glacial change. Supply bottlenecks and troubled technological development were endemic. Paternalism meant workers had jobs; intensive development (increasing output through labor) prevailed over extensive (technological) development. By the 1980s, long-term trends and short-term shocks endangered the economy, and younger political elites began to support reform. As well, in East Europe the USSR was occupying power *and* colony, supplying cheap resources and buying overpriced manufactured goods.[70] Cold War competition and military production warped the economy: military production made up 30 percent of GDP, and declining petrodollars in the 1980s reduced hard currency reserves for imports.[71] Intensive production had fewer returns, and bureaucracy and theocracy hindered innovation by stifling discussion of problems and solutions. Finally, a post-war generation came of age. Lacking direct experience of World War II—of great significance to Soviet legitimacy—they did not share strong identification with the system. Their elders built communism; they wanted its rewards, were more ambivalent to communism, and engaged in underground counter-culture.[72] The values shift did not mean inevitable change, but it made liberalization more likely. Malaise set in as the regime aged gracelessly, captured in witty political anecdotes.

Gorbachev, Yeltsin, and Putin faced Soviet legacies that we too must address to make sense of change and everyday post-Soviet economic life. Mikhail Gorbachev began by increasing discipline, but when this failed he turned to limited liberalization and enterprise restructuring. Ultimately, contradictions in the socialist economy expanded, economic performance dropped, and the shadow economy (*tenevaia ekonomika*) grew through new opportunities for speculation. With the economy near collapse, Yeltsin took the double leap of destroying the USSR and vaulting into capitalism, resulting in contradictions and deformities, problems of creating new practices, and unraveling of authority.[73] In hindsight it is clear how unprepared Russia was for these leaps. There was a dearth of cadres in the state and economy trained in market logics such as marketing, accounting, or contract law. Those with an inkling of such logics, whether by training, experience, or intuition, did not have power to enforce their practices. The state could not change from dictator to neutral referee overnight, when officials were used to power and privilege and private actors to hiding in the shadow economy. Managers persisted in seeing the firm as a *productive* unit rather than as a *revenue-generating* unit (the reigning understanding of the firm in Anglo-American capitalism) and as their own bailiwicks rather than as property under ultimate control of whoever owned that property. Laws and procedures were weak or in flux, making it difficult for competent and honest officials to turn firms or the state around.

Legacies of economies past

Legacies as initial conditions are social endowments that emerged from socialization in institutions and discourses—arrangements of rules and relations, categories and knowledge, *habitus*, authority and practices—that are tools *and* sunk costs too great to abandon.[74] What follows is a reduction of rich analyses of the tsarist and Soviet eras. Legacies were a production-centered logic, with the plan as central totem (bureaucratic over consumer needs); vertical authority, studied distrust, and the economy as game of power and resistance; reliance on informal networks; paternalism as a normal organizing principle; and social rather than private property. Structural legacies included physical dispersion of factories across the USSR, investment in military production, monopolies, and lack of autonomous information networks.[75]

Production-centered logic of economic activity

Enterprises were units of production, not sales and profit,[76] with a *raison d'être* to produce goods and welfare. This logic had strong historical roots: from Peter the Great's military-oriented industrialization, to 1920s *trestifikatsiia* to discover enterprises and managers that were the most efficient, to Stalinism. A combination of Bolshevik logics were at work: Cold War competition (outproducing the West) and militarization, Marxist anti-capitalism that exalted work and output rather than demand as the fount of value, and a spin on modernity privileging technocratic rationality over market irrationality. The Brezhnev era reinforced this logic, especially policies concentrating decision-making in "production associations" (*obedinenie*) to improve interaction between producers of similar goods or of inputs and outputs, akin to vertical integration to reduce the number of entities the state had to administer and supply. By the 1990s this logic and enterprise mission privileged production-centered managerial skills and practices, especially

Table 1.2 Logics of legacies

Practices/Logics	Culture (categories, assumptions)	Power
Primacy of production	Work centered on producing goods and obtaining inputs. Value measured in physical output. Production (not profit) as raison d'être.	Dependency on suppliers and state. Production structures through centralized supply and plan.
Enterprise power from managers to shopfloors.		
Centralized vertical control	Overall vertical hierarchy and lower-level hierarchies, justified by distrust, claims to knowledge and ideological wisdom. Legitimated through collectivism and class rhetoric.	Centralized control of resources and distribution; authority via elitism, practical need for production knowledge; informal networks within the bureaucracy and Party
Informality and resistance	Resistance as norm. Informal relations and practices of real action. Distrust unknown and state.	Informal access to needed resources. Informal authority personalized.
Paternalism	Elite prerogative and duty to provide; expectations for provision (not only in return for loyalty).	Resource dependency, legitimation of pseudo-feudal relations of fealty.
Socialized property	Property run by those with technical knowledge, owned collectively (not accountable). Private ownership of means of production a threat, linked to paternalist duty (ownership and provision).	Soviet control by proletariat via Party-state blurs control boundaries. Private property does not automatically confer right of use (boundaries vague). Formal collectivist rationale of authority.
Conceptualizing markets	Response to bureaucratic failure, shadow practices, shortage economy. Market as expanded assortment of goods, freedom (awaiting rather than seeking buyers/suppliers or serving officials)	Response to vertical authority: autonomy from the state, bordering on anarchy (rather than autonomy constrained by system of laws and practices); informality as default for authority and recourse

Table 1.3 Logics of change

Legacy Logics	Target Logics (global capitalism)
• Paternalist provision of goods/services (welfare) legitimate;	• Paternalism illegitimate or provision of wage
• Manager (or state) supreme	• Owners and consumers supreme
• Production knowledge, labor as primary capital	• Finance, share ownership as primary capital
• Industrial organization = mutual aid, sector-oriented (Soviet ministries as template)	• Industrial organization = finance, profit, diversity (Western firms as template)
• Risk = lose supply, production; profit = money for supply	• Risk = lose investment; profit = return for more investment
• Acquisition skills (obtaining supplies) as key survival skill	• Salesmanship (obtaining sales, income) as key survival skill

orienting strategies and contingent tactics towards manufacture. Relations of authority were fundamentally different from those of capitalism.[77] Authority was located in planning ministries and suppliers who kept production going, rather than in consumers whose purchases paid wages and supplies. Production for its own sake guided strategies, from risk-aversion to hoarding materials and labor to "storming." Working their way up the ranks, managers, shopfloor bosses, and engineers identified themselves with this technological *raison d'être*. Managers were judged on their ability to produce output rather than profit, and their practices and logics followed accordingly. The instinct was to produce first; health and success meant producing goods, and shipping them out demonstrated use.

Vertical authority and studied distrust

Party-state supremacy was central to political and economic practice. Historically, Russian moral, intellectual, and political authority was collective (collective priority over the less rational individual), manifested in the elite and especially its apex (tsar or Communist Party) and exercised by subordinates.[78] While in rhetoric workers were the source of moral authority, in practice they were bound to the Party-state. Via homology, managers as *nomenklatura* were agents of the theocratic Party-state. Further, this elite was historically insecure and jealous in its authority. Tsarist authority became increasingly suspicious of autonomous social groups, but Bolshevism's ideology and conspiratorial history produced even stronger tendencies to centralized power and institutionalized, studied distrust of autonomous social action.[79] Unlike dialectical systems, where "truth" is attained through competition (as in democratic elections or market competition), theocracies pin legitimacy on having keys to truth through revelation of the rules to the social universe. They cannot admit error that questions their knowledge of truth and right to rule. Marx's teachings, interpreted and augmented by the Party's "priests," were such keys. Hence, autonomy was a particular danger.

As markets involve autonomous social forces, there could be no real market, which by definition would be to a degree outside elite control (regulation being too weak a form of control). Economic structures and procedures were predicated on resource control (funds, material inputs, cadres) and assessment of their use through complex reports and audits.[80] The obsession with and confidence in the supremacy of scientific rationality over the chaotic market encouraged state-run social engineering and economic micromanagement.[81] This was manifested in economic totems and practices, such as the Five-Year Plan and paternalist provision. This also undercut the rule of law and made the bureaucratic economy subject to arbitrariness and informality. This logic was first a context, especially of state behavior, in which post-Soviet reforms and actions were embedded. It became an "anti-totem" of abnormality against which to articulate blame and define illegitimacy. Studied distrust became a taken-for-granted logic of state–society relations in the post-Soviet era, and it also seeped into broader social relations: distrust of the unfamiliar generally. Building markets and generalized trust faced this daunting obstacle.

Informality and resistance

Studied distrust and vertical, centralized authority bred logics and practices of resistance and informality, manifested as plan manipulation and the shadow economy (*tenevaia ekonomika*). Resistance is not unique to Russia,[82] but institutionalized distrust of autonomy made the informal an oppositional logic of state–society relations. The Party-state's ubiquitous presence and paranoia also made autonomy akin to treason, fusing it to resistance and ingraining it as second nature. Facing hyperbureaucracy and distrust, managers and citizens developed networks and informal practices—*znakomstvo i sviazi* (acquaintances and ties) and *blat* (nepotism)—to navigate the system, obtain deficit goods, act opportunistically, and survive.[83] Formal relations were distrusted because the unknown (*chuzhoi*) person could be a threat (KGB informant, cheat) in a context where forgiveness was rare. Like pre-revolutionary peasants who used foot-dragging or the tsar's name against landlords,[84] Soviet workers used labor shortages to employ absenteeism, labor turnover, foot-dragging, and a "cult of non-work."[85]

Informality was normal because, paradoxically, the state treated it as normal. Brezhnev's "little deal" and demands for ideological loyalty led officialdom to wink at marginal violations of rules. Officials grabbed state authority for personal use: this is "*prikhvatizatsiia.*"[86] Rules were obstacles to avoid or (mis)use—a logic antithetical to the rule of law.[87] Using networks, falsifying documents, and working outside the law were "reality" versus "the lie" of formality. The rule of law was not second nature and offered only weak recourse; patronage promised security. Managers colluded in informal supply and falsifying reports to show plan fulfillment and avoid ratcheting, i.e. raising norms based on past performance.[88] Employees worked *nalevo* (on the side) or stole for informal trade—marginal, everyday privatization (or *prikhvatizatsiia*) of work in the formal economy.[89] Post-Soviet state tactics of control and predation reinforced informality's normality.[90] Laws demanded firms deposit hard cash in bank accounts and hold only enough to pay wages, insurance, and immediate needs. Money transactions had to use traceable, *beznalichnye* money (money not in physical form). In one 1994 survey, two-thirds of managers admitted that they concealed at least a quarter of their transactions by using hard cash.[91]

Practices and logics of informality and shadows did not mean a market economy would emerge full-blown once state control ended. The shadow economy may have been driven by needs or utility, but its ultimate logic was speculation and parasitical use of property rather than creating use value.[92] Exchange was based on personal relations; value was set in kind as often as in money. Investment was not important because interactions were short-term. Independent contracts had no formal enforcement. Ethics embodied a moral economy of resistance: one could steal from the state or strangers because the concept of "property" was corrupted. *Nalevo* was normal but speculation immoral. Logics of informality, personalized authority, and resistance to or corruption of formal rules contradicted the rule of law that is essential to capitalism.[93]

Paternalism

William Blackwell noted, "By the 1850s, some of the owners of the larger factories were pointing out that, in contrast to European capitalists, they were maintaining churches, hospitals, pharmacies, children's schools, orphanages, pensions, and other services, in some cases amounting to 30 percent of the total overhead expenses of an enterprise."[94] Change the year and this was a Soviet firm. One logic central to Russian economic history is paternalist authority—state, enterprise, and manager as creator, provider, father. The enterprise produced not only goods: it produced welfare and dependency. Paternalism was grounds for authority via material dependency and symbolic status (role of provider), and a component to organizational normality and community. State provision through the enterprise, of employment, wages, and social goods (apartments, vacations, medical care) demonstrated Soviet ideology at work. It also linked citizens to the Party-state: in a state-run economy of shortage, people received many of their goods through enterprises. Instead of being grounded in contractual relations between free individuals, authority was grounded in a construction of master and subject, with the former assumed to understand better the needs of the collective.[95] This construction justified elite rule, yet it had a reciprocal side: those few owed welfare support to the many they ruled.

Managers and elites, under state tutelage, reenacted paternalism as source of authority (employee dependency, moral claims) and as values and obligations. While paternalism is not foreign in the West, Western capitalists could more easily extract themselves from welfare, claiming primacy of profit, private property, and shareholder value—arguments used since the 1980s to roll back corporate and state support for employees and the broader population, in healthier economies! In Russia, paternalism had a longer, more deeply embedded history that wound through structures and conceptions of normality that market reforms would confront head on.

Social property

In his study of the corporation, William Roy discussed "socialization" of capital and property—a change in power extending ownership via mass shareholding shares. Property in pre-revolutionary Russia was on difficult ground, given tsarist supremacy over law; personal belongings aside, Soviet property (land, capital) did not belong to physical or legal individuals. Rather, it was "social property," belonging to the collective and administered by the Party through the state in the collective's name of the people. Like low prices, social provision and property were a contract over authority between state and society.[96] A Soviet firm without social property and provision was not "Soviet" and violated Bolshevik anti-capitalist logic. Also, power, institutionalized through property, belonged to and flowed from the proletarian Party-state and collective. This gave workers a potential claim to authority through ultimately sovereignty over property as well as through labor value. Yet Soviet property was directly administered by managers, a pseudo-technocratic elite claiming knowledge as its grounds for authority. This set up potential conflicts over privatization and governance. One unexpected outcome was general disrespect for property: property was collectively owned, making its unapproved use and *prikhvatizatsiia* morally inoffensive.[97] Creating private property meant not only changing rules and relations of social power and sovereignty; it also meant inculcating new sanctity.

Logics and practices of actors

Legacies could survive in collective knowledge and practices of actors' perceived identities and practices, and I suggest ideal types of important collective actors in our story. Initial positions shaped and restricted initial interests and identities of post-Soviet directors, entrepreneurs, employees, owners, and state officials (e.g. *siloviki*, security officials),[98] but as fundamental changes unwound structure, groups could reexamine meanings and interests.[99] I propose ideal types for analysis; they are from a collage of claims in the Soviet and early post-Soviet eras. Employees had labor skills and claimed labor's primacy in producing value. Soviet-era managers, "Red Directors," were likely to carry Soviet knowledge and practices as natural default, even if they understood the problematic nature of their knowledge. They claimed their skills brought material support for survival, their organizational position provided a complete view of production (institutional capital), and their paternalism benefited laborers. Younger entrepreneurs and new owners developed conceptions of normal economic behavior from experiences and interaction with or opposition to new discourses and other actors such as Red Directors or foreign investors. This group used capitalist normality, financial knowledge and economic capital, and authority of property. State officials claimed responsibility for social order to justify actions and authority and relied on political capital (legitimate use of force and *kompromat*, i.e. material for legal prosecution).[100] They began with different tool kits of knowledge, assumptions, and ideologies: from "red governors" and local officials for whom the state was prime mover, to reformers who wanted the state to be a neutral referee supporting the rule of law. I summarize these aspects of actors' positions, capital, *habitus*, and logics of action and legitimacy in Table 1.4.

One useful way to sum up different groups' logics and practices is as "economies." Employees articulated a social-democratic *moral economy of labor* that claimed sovereignty stemmed from those who produced. Given how socialization and skills from the command economy inculcated conservatism, enterprise sovereignty, local knowledge of production, and a sense of paternalist propriety over their firms,[101] Red Directors developed a *managerialist moral economy* in which enterprise community and production were sacred. Financial entrepreneurs, especially those who became "oligarchs," developed a post-Soviet *profit economy*. With backgrounds in Party politics (e.g. Komsomol), they learned to maneuver around rules and laws, not to maintain production and output but to advance careers.[102] Less socialized in Soviet economic logics, they had an easier time with market logics: money and accumulation were normal, and money was means *and* end. This does not mean Red Directors ignored personal gain, but they did not perceive accumulating capital to further expand profit as a key normality. Finally, state officials' logic was *political economy*: economic action subservient to political directives and national glory that officials could play for status or personal gain.[103] State and nation were sacred; Brezhnev's "little deal" favored state power and facilitated rent-seeking inside the state (corruption).

These interests and identities shaped what actors framed as sources of and solutions to problems. Managers found state interference a hindrance to efficient production; why should external shareholders be different? Employees saw

Table 1.4 Groups, capital, and logics

Group	Primary capital	Source/logic of sovereignty
Employees	Human capital (skills) and labor power	Source/logic: Social-democratic ethic of labor primacy. Labor, technical knowledge of production. Defensive of status quo versus uncertain change. Moral economy of labor
Managers	Technical skills, networks to local elites	Source/logic: Bureaucratic/technical (position). Knowledge of production, politics; paternalism. Defensive of status quo versus uncertain change. Moral economy of managerialism.
Owners, financiers and oligarchs	Economic and social capital (money, networks)	Source/logic: Financial knowledge and resources; property ownership (shareholding). Capitalist logic. Profit economy.
State officials	Political capital (laws), kompromat, networks	Source/logic: Custody of the social order; physical coercion. Political economy of *dirigisme*.

threats from outsiders and focused on jobs, provision, and justice. Entrepreneurs and financiers blamed state-owned property for economic woes and proposed privatization and liberalized exchange. State officials blamed legal incoherence and private corruption (rent-seeking Red Directors and speculating oligarchs) and championed the state as defender of national well-being. Note I do not claim stasis. Innovation was in the Soviet tool kit: dealing with worn-out machinery and maneuvering to obtain deficit goods clearly demonstrated creative thought. Yet particular innovations could make change in the fundamental level of culture and practice more difficult, especially in the presence of competing logics. Whether an "old" or "new" logic was implemented depended on contingent framing and mobilization: whether actors could frame one logic as normal and the other as abnormal or enforce changes against challengers. Sometimes old logics survived in original or altered form, while in others some actors learned new practices imperfectly (e.g. marketing and sales).

Change dynamics could unleash contentious identities if reforms created cleavages, distrust, and counter-claims—e.g. labor power versus managerial knowledge, managerial authority versus shareholder governance.[104] One key aspect of identities and change was whether groups perceived cooperation or contradiction as the natural state of relations, and how rituals and discourse produced such relations—whether "studied trust" or "studied distrust" was the operative logic. (The central idea of "studied" trust or distrust is that these are produced in ritualized interactions; they are not essential traits of actors, nor are they static qualities in space and time.[105]) While global institutions pushed the neoliberal model as the sole legitimate economy, local knowledge and ideologies supporting some form of social democracy persisted, easily seen in votes for communists and nationalists. If Soviet logics were illegitimate because they failed, reforms could lose sanctity if they did not "succeed."

The remaining chapters use various cases and themes to bring this framework to life and to show how these factors and processes—dimensions of power and culture, vertical and horizontal authority, learning and contradicting, legislating and implementing, conflict and negotiation—contingently interacted to produce complex post-Soviet change. This is not a story of hypothesis testing—it is too early in the game for that. The next chapters merely suggest value added by this framework. Rather than assume interests, we will see interests in action, interacting with power-culture of identities, contexts, and practices. This is also a story of contingencies. But such is the landscape in a revolution: never pretty, never straightforward, but always intriguing.

2 Remaking strategy and structure in post-Soviet entrepreneurship

> One more innate defect of Soviet-style business—a deep-seated habit after decades of an economy of the absurd, to count not so much on one's own efforts, initiative, and professionalism, as on networks.
>
> (Entrepreneur Igor Sagirian[1])

In 1995 I had a long conversation with Denise, an American hired in July 1994 as co-director of St. Petersburg tour firm Atlas. Charged to change the firm, Denise wanted to inject order into work routines to make Atlas "professional." Too much energy was lost in disorganized, inefficient work lacking forethought. Atlas's main problem was that employees saw it as a seasonal source of wages and were nonchalant about work—this would change when they understood and accepted her grand scheme and fulfilled tasks. Her plans included office organization (systematizing data); a schema of tasks for each person; and "professional behavior," with discipline the norm when "each person knew what his job was and what he was supposed to do." In autumn 1995 Economics Inc., a non-profit organization, was sinking into financial despair: short of funds to pay wages or taxes and a bank debt threatening but held at bay thanks to ties to bank directors. Employees were unmotivated to work efficiently, money was wasted with little accountability, and projects fell short. "The Captain," a former submarine captain hired as assistant director, claimed there was profit to be made if organization was improved. Two months later, he was gone. Economics Inc. muddled through with a new cohort of employees devoted less to the firm than its resources—and even then, in 2007 founder and manager Misha closed it down. In sum: in a financial crisis, Economics Inc. had greater incentives to reform, yet it changed little and managed to muddle through for twelve more years. Atlas had a small niche yet exhibited fundamental change. Denise created and enforced new myths and narratives of a normal firm, and along with this introduced and supported new logics and practices of everyday work. Misha did not, despite greater incentives. This paradox is the heart of this chapter, and of Russia's story.

These firms were not unique: other entrepreneurs and managers related similar stories, and economists and business journalists bemoaned problematic inculcation of market norms. Capitalism is rooted in rationalized practices of structured discipline, calculated production and sales oriented to consumers.[2] Yet such everyday logics did not appear magically. "Soviet entrepreneurship" emerged from Soviet institutions. Post-Soviet entrepreneurs and managers had to forge "post-Soviet capitalism"—no small task for a varied group inexperienced with capitalism (even if mythic) in practice. Unlike in developed market economies, Russian entrepreneurs and managers had no concrete, pervasive model of strategies and practices to imitate, nor were there requirements such as business plans (e.g. to receive loans) enforcing market terms. Their context included non-market rules, practices, and experiences. The deficit and shadow economy experiences bequeathed normality of using networks to facilitate speculation with state resources.[3] A perceived need to discover "market" organization is central to their stories. To make sense of change, we need to examine organizational dynamics of reconstructing power, culture, and normality. Laws and costs might explain cosmetic change, but given weaknesses of mechanisms to enforce market norms, how managers and entrepreneurs handled change was paramount. This was not easy: Soviet legacies of resistance, production, paternalism, and informality interacted with new conceptions of discipline, accumulation, and profit. We see this at its starkest in stories of small private firms. One expects obstacles in large bureaucratic organizations, with legacies embedded in complex structures and procedures not altered overnight. Yet at small firms, where entrepreneurs use personal authority and direct enforcement,[4] managers and employees faced such baggage. These mythic engines of capitalism provide a glimpse of basic confrontations of Soviet socialism and post-Soviet capitalism,[5] and a contrast of two small firms as microcosms of post-Soviet business lays bare raw, fundamental politics of post-Soviet change and continuity in strategy and structure.

Soviet entrepreneurship, small firms, and market-building

Russian and Western studies of transitions rarely explore deeper forces of change in normality of everyday work and authority. Most empirical studies of small post-Soviet firms, dwarfed by studies of banks or large firms, focused on employment, laws, macroeconomic environment, and contracts.[6] This is not surprising: such analytic categories are typical in studies of stable markets. Yet they elide social forces underpinning "economy" and are less helpful for extracting insights on radical change, when deeper forces are torn asunder. Shock therapy implicitly assumed quick liberalization and privatization would force Russians to become market animals. Gradualism, shock therapy's competitor, highlighted small firms and entrepreneurship. The state would keep "dinosaurs" alive until small firms could grow and absorb labor, so that dinosaurs could go under.[7] But shock therapy and gradualism assumed fairly frictionless adaptation driven by instrumentally rational managers and entrepreneurs primarily after profit. More institutionally informed economists and political scientists focused on how state policies (taxes, registration laws), inflation, and capital availability set costs and opportunities that shaped entrepreneurial practices and small firm structures.[8] Some studies claim competition, property rules, laws, and regional effects shape restructuring, yet their broad data do not follow processes of change and continuity.[9] Environmental factors are not unimportant; but *how* they work requires study. Further, this says little of change dynamics when institutions develop alongside firms, and the environment provides fairly clear and consistent signals and tools for change. What if the environment is inoperative or ambiguous, with vague or contradictory laws and officials unable to use them?[10] A law alone cannot breed one narrow set of practices and actions.[11] Laws are totems for practices; people react creatively, not mechanically, with tools from *habitus*, networks, and discourse. Facing capital hunger, red tape, and taxes, entrepreneurs could go underground, work in the system, or recruit allies in the state to navigate laws. More crucial is how they devised and understood practices, as informed by logics of normal practice and authority, and how these shaped the creation of organizational routines and meanings that make up firms large and small.

While small firms are less important than fields and larger businesses in neoinstitutionalism and much economic sociology, insights from these frameworks are not irrelevant. In entrepreneurial firms we see forces from Chapter 1 in their starkest form; post-Soviet entrepreneurship can flesh out mechanisms of change and continuity, claim-making and constructing power-culture, and contingency and contention. Following the principle of fractals, change of practices in small, entrepreneurial firms should follow political and cultural processes Pfeffer and Fligstein observe in corporations and fields.[12] Organizational change is about skills and human capital, and tactics and technologies to actualize power and practices (including framing and legitimating). Power and its legitimation as authority involve material tools (wages, fines) and meanings, what James Q. Wilson called organizational mission: what the organization is about, and meanings of normality underpinning authority and legitimate practices.[13] Entrepreneurs and small firm managers mobilize material and symbolic resources *vis-à-vis* agendas, goals, and procedures to interpret the context and (re)define organizational authority and normality; employees might articulate counter-claims drawn from networks, work in another firm, or previous work in that firm. A reforming manager frames authority and reforms as normal and natural by interpreting sources of ills plaguing a firm (work habits, environmental instability, corruption) and proposing solutions to fix a new normality. If that manager can demonstrate causal links between proposed reforms and success and can plausibly assign blame for failures to others, he/she can establish superiority of managerial knowledge and deflect alternative authority and normality claims. In contrast, managerial confusion or incompetence, or a competitor's appropriation of success symbols, might leave managerial authority resting on formal rules alone, increasing resistance or opportunism. A complementary strategy is to bring employees' identities into line with those of the firm as a moral project worthy of investment and discipline, rather than an instrument (source of wages) or imposition—giving the manager authority as head of a sacred group.

What skills and tactics facilitate the politics of transforming meanings and practices? A manager or entrepreneur must be convinced of the need for change:

an important cause is an event that shocks that person's understandings of economic normality. The potential reformer must also notice and understand an alternative model of business—and this raises decoupling and levels of knowledge and culture. If a reforming manager adopts a new model and grasps how it works in practice, then he or she must articulate, promulgate, and defend the new mission, its organizational logics, and its narrative of normal work and authority. This can set the foundation for implementing new practices, knowledge, and authority, although it is no guarantee of success. This also raises explaining and justifying new logics, akin to framing and maneuvering in the second, discursive dimension of power. Thus, this first task involves control of organizational discourse and confronting legacies of normal mission and practice—the reformer must devise a new "public transcript" and counter potential path dependency in "hidden transcripts."[14] The second process involves creating and applying authority: legitimating and normalizing not only new power relations but also the reformer's right to rule, by initially enforcing changes, embedding them in myriad banal practices, and demonstrating their normality by defining "success" and framing how reforms led to it, e.g. better profit and sales or improved wages. But there is a danger. Transition culture normality posited Soviet culture and carriers as abnormal, providing a template for change (older practices as abnormal), but transition culture could breed a conservative antithesis, including claims to local knowledge in contrast to claims to more general abstract knowledge about fundamental, invariant laws of business (e.g. buy low and sell high, the customer is always right, etc.).[15] As we will see, at Atlas Ivan framed his identity against transition, and change came to Economics Inc. less because of the environment and more because of opportunism. Overall, we have cases of relatively vertical authority (but variation in its use), and contrasts in having tacit knowledge of the target system.

Post-Soviet entrepreneurship and small business

The general model of entrepreneurship across space and time has some constants: risk-taking, impulses for creativity or expressing autonomy, livelihood or profit.[16] There are also differences in conceptions of normal practice and structure.[17] When entrepreneurs tire of jumping between quick deals and settle down to routine activity, they build structures and rules learned in socialization, experience, and environmental contingencies. Unfortunately, much discourse presumes entrepreneurs are ready-made market actors and growth engines, yet risk-taking, initiative, and optimizing gains do not make a "market" or "market actor" *per se*.[18] Rushing into a deficit market or realizing the need to compete do not equal stable market practices. To differentiate entrepreneurship from administration of state-owned firms by citing risk-taking only suggests correlations in psychological states, not logics of practice.[19] Alexei Yurchak claims Soviet and Western "entrepreneurial governmentality" are similar, especially the capacity to navigate rules that was inculcated in formal and informal organizational experience of the late Soviet era (e.g. in the Komsomol).[20] Yet post-Soviet entrepreneurs were tempered by non-market strategies, categories, and logics I suggest below. The explosion of small firms plying deficit goods for speculative profit makes them seem market-like, but this means only that entrepreneurs found niches with immediate demand, not that strategies, practices, and logics were "market." A capitalist entrepreneur maneuvers in the market, innovating and adapting to produce and sell.[21] The Soviet entrepreneur could maneuver in the command economy, innovating with rules for survival or gain.

Entrepreneurs were supposed to emerge from the shadows, pay taxes, employ labor, and fuel growth.[22] Despite crime, corruption, and bureaucracy, non-agricultural small firms (less than 50 people) grew in waves: 14,000 co-operatives in 1987, 270,000 registered firms in 1991, and 900,000 by 2000. The first wave arose with *perestroika*.[23] Entrepreneurs felt alienated in the Soviet system, could not realize their potential, or wanted money. Some created new businesses, others legalized informal work, e.g. in construction. Many early co-operatives grew from desires to realize dreams as well as profit, and many entrepreneurs re-registered co-operatives as small firms to avoid the stigma of speculation or money laundering.[24] Liberalization in 1992 bred a second wave: entrepreneurs emerged as intermediaries trading domestic and imported goods.[25] Opening a firm remained bureaucratic, especially in regions where officials did not follow law appropriately. Finding office and facilities space was troublesome, as was defending contracts. In the third wave (1993–4) entrepreneurs faced draconian and confusing tax laws, increased competition and decreased consumer spending, and hurdles to obtaining loans and capital, and the state did little to incubate entrepreneurship.[26] After 1995 entry costs and competition increased, and market entrants were offset by exits through self-liquidation, debt, and occasional bankruptcy.[27] As numbers reached a plateau, entrepreneurial activities expanded from simple trade to production and services. In 1995, 877,000 private small firms accounted for 14 percent of employment, 12 percent of GDP, and one-third of profit, and they paid average wages.[28] Despite quandaries of high taxes, red tape, *mafiia*, and the 1998 crisis, entrepreneurship persisted, and small firms became part of the post-Soviet landscape.

Russian entrepreneurs soon learned they had to exercise initiative and self-reliance and learn on the job—and there was much to learn. Constructing and enforcing new normality should be easy in small firms. With less capital and internal procedures as shields from environmental pressures, managers of small private firms should be more likely to adopt market norms, strategies, and structures. Unlike larger firms—with myriad operation rules and informal practices—newer small, private firms were closer to *tabula rasa* (supposedly free of path dependency): they had fewer employees, simpler structure, and fewer Soviet-era rules and relations. Yet Soviet baggage there was, making change far from easy. Many entrepreneurs felt the impact of coming of age in a non-market economy. Moving into a niche or buying and selling was one thing; market planning and strategizing, using routines such as marketing or formal hiring, were different. Many admitted the need to accept lower returns or that certain skills and attitudes were paramount but hard to find: individual initiative, creative and adaptive thinking, specific skills such as technical or financial analysis, disciplined and coordinated work, and replacing or complementing networks with formalized rules and relations of sales and hiring.[29] Even smart directors and entrepreneurs were disoriented by rapid post-Soviet changes—this was a work in progress.[30]

In light of this theme, consider two generations of entrepreneurs from one study. The first generation was socialized in the late Soviet period—they had higher education, were likely to be in the Komsomol, and worked in Soviet-era firms. A member of this first wave, who worked in a Soviet import–export enterprise, noted, "The socialist system raised the majority of people, who do something: they enumerate, talk, travel, hold negotiations, but there are no results from these activities. For them results are not important."[31] The next generation was in their late teens when they entered "business" and was less likely to have a higher education or have worked in Soviet enterprises. As the command economy crumbled, they jumped ship, often into finance, using mathematical or other scientific skills. As one from this wave noted, "At the start of *perestroika* we did not manage to become Party functionaries or shadow actors (*teneviki*)." Or: "For me... there was no psychological tension at the moment of the break with state service. Maybe because of [young] age or because we did not manage to settle our roots in old structures."[32] Entrepreneurs in both generations targeted deficit goods and services that promised quick, large returns. The former generation was attracted to distributing deficit goods, the latter to capital accumulation.

From old to new: legacies and power-culture in small firms

Ideally, competition, financial procedures for loans and repayment, bankruptcy, and market expertise make survival dependent on engaging market demand. In Russia, these were weak or faced contradictory practices. The influence of competition and prices is mediated by knowledge, networks, and power—embodied in legacies and processes of reorienting the post-Soviet firm. Legacies noted in Chapter 1 suggest templates for entrepreneurial practices. Russian founders and employees of post-socialist firms were socialized until recently in Soviet institutions and discourses, or by older colleagues carrying those Soviet logics from the old regime.[33] Legacies entrepreneurs most directly confronted were these. *Informality* of structures, procedures, and authority—non-codified rules outside public view—were conditioned by a bureaucratic, parasitic state.[34] Most entrepreneurs could not avoid exposure to shadow economy practices, especially reliance on informal relations. Small private firms could not always avoid the second legacy, *identifying organizations with a moral economy of provision*. This took two forms: formal paternalism, and informal provision or *prikhvatizatsiia*. Expectations of social provision could appear in small firms, even if shallower than in larger firms. A widespread form of informal provision was a logic of personal ties and friendship, a small-scale moral economy or "micro-paternalism" with the right to make claims, including employment, and expect fulfillment and reciprocity. (Because of this I obtained most of my interviews.) The second form of provision was a "parasitic" view of the firm. To employees or managers with this view, a small firm's status was like that of state-run organizations: host rather than generator of value, with sovereign significance.[35] Rituals and rules embodying the Soviet logic of studied distrust created a third legacy, *ingrained resistance* to formal authority and discipline (the Soviet command economy and exploitation). Weak law, accountability, and recourse made open challenges to the regime dangerous. Citizens learned passive resistance as a universal tool. A fourth legacy resulted from post-1991 economic instability that made long-term planning difficult: identifying business with *quick gratification and returns* rather than investment and growth. Institutional incentives and state-led education created the fifth legacy, investment in *non-market skills*, e.g. non-market accounting or market planning skills, weak skills in management and organization that involve flexibility and negotiation rather than command and control. Finally, experience in maneuvering *vis-à-vis* the state and leaping between deals created the ability to *innovate* with rules, even if superficially.

Given legacies, creating a market firm meant redefining normality and integrating it into employees' worldviews and identities. Knowledge of new practices and politics of change were vital to authority and capacity to act. Managers might create rules but lack knowledge or competence to make them operational. One tool was material incentives (wages), *if* there was something to be lost. Small firms might pay better and timelier wages than factories, but not all avoided arrears or hardship.[36] Also, in personalized settings of small firms, power was embedded in personal relations. Authority might come from status as founder, paternalism, charisma, or strategic use of networks. The successful reformer had to create alliances, draw on existing authority, and fashion a power base. The reformer might frame success as a sign of knowing the secrets of business and deserving to rule, just as priests and scientists gain authority from wielding arcane knowledge. To augment power and consolidate change, reformers had to embed authority in new procedures, positions, and demonstrations of success and get these to take root in everyday routines and new assumptions and myths about normal everyday work.

Restructuring in a nutshell: Atlas versus Economics Inc.

I flesh out these processes in narratives of Atlas and Economics Inc., where I directly observed everyday work and change.[37] The processes in these stories are paradigmatic for this book and capture much of the post-Soviet story. Less complicated structures and histories give us a stark view of power-culture and change. Atlas and Economics Inc. were born with market-building, Atlas in communism's last years and Economics Inc. after its death. Soviet logics were not so well congealed in formal rules or intergenerational socialization of "how things are done"; but individuals still carried legacies into the firms from elsewhere, embedding them in individual and collectively informal, assumed logics and practices. Both firms initially relied heavily on networks and informal practices. Work was not rigorously organized or disciplined. Employees and managers looked on the firms parasitically; there was little medium- or long-term vision. Managers and employees at neither firm followed practices of rationalized study of the market, linking marketing logics to production. Production, pricing, and sales were formulaic at best, haphazard at worst. Both faced similar economic environments, vague tax and other laws, and uncertainty. While employees brought traditions from elsewhere, both firms were new and initially did not have intrinsic, firm-specific rituals of authority, work, and resistance. While Atlas was in better financial health, Economics Inc. had potential. Both faced emerging competition but had niches. Economics Inc.'s non-profit status did not seem to affect its strategies or condition. Both faced problems of productivity, work quality, and discipline. Here similarities end. Economics Inc. was worse off than Atlas in 1994 and 1995, and one would expect incentives for change were greater there than at Atlas. In fact, Atlas changed more. Shocks created perceptions of the need to change strategies and structures, and both firms engaged in restructuring—with different outcomes. Soviet legacies confronted new contexts, and the issue was whether actors had and used sufficient power and knowledge to inculcate new practices of organization and business.

This is not a story only of managerial competence; it is an exploration of any metric of normality against which to measure competence (e.g. "efficiency"). This is a story of what "competence" is in the context of fundamental change. The empirical narrative will show that Denise's competence was a combination of tactics (not always consciously devised) and luck. Simply citing "competent leadership" or "the market" to explain or expect change is unwise when selection mechanisms— logics, institutions, and practices enforcing a particular normality—are inoperative. The outcome of changes was the opposite of that expected in a simple market model. Finances and shocks at Economics Inc. were worse than at Atlas, and it faced increasing competition. Atlas had a relatively stable niche, providing enough income for a reasonable existence. Both firms' managers relied on networks for resources, clients, and sales; by 1996 these were secondary at Atlas but vital for Economics Inc. Atlas changed fundamentally, despite being better-off and less in need of change.

In this comparison, we will see shocks and changes in perceived organizational needs, as well as the capacity to devise a new organizational model and put it into action. We will see the importance of organizing authority—creating alliances, framing change and legitimacy, creating procedures that set and routinize lines of authority—through its successful creation at Atlas and continuing difficulties at Economics Inc. We will also see multilevel culture: both Denise and Misha realized the need for change, but only Denise could articulate *and* implement a new, operational system, along with a narrative of normality and abnormality. We will see normality in Denise's and Misha's proposed changes, and counter-claims (some openly, others more covert or articulated "in action" rather than words), but Denise will play organizational politics to defeat opposition and create her new firm; Misha, unable and unwilling to play such games, will be far less successful. Change was a function less of market or institutional environments than *internal* process of power, culture, and practice, and how actors used power to create and impose new identities, normalities, logics, strategies, and work practices. The narratives of these two firms not only address small Russian business in transition; they illuminate essences of generic organizational change. Table 2.1 summarizes change dynamics.

Table 2.1 Change dynamics at Atlas and Economics Inc.

Atlas	Economics Inc.
Legacies (culture/practice) Undeveloped work procedures. Weak discipline, high informality of structure, work. Parasitic-provisional, short-term view of firm.	Legacies (culture/practice) Weak discipline, undeveloped structure. Moral view of firm. Resistance to discipline.
Power (legacy and change) Authority from individuals, not position; used and translated into formal authority, aided by legitimacy and symbolic capital.	Power (legacy and change) Formal, moral authority with founder/positions, real authority weak, untapped, inoperative—symbolic resources marginal.
Change process (basics) and outcome Personal shocks start change. Denise expands authority, legitimacy to change practices, identity and create new normality.	Change process (basics) and outcome Shocks to firm; reforms superficial. Older interpretations of firm and practices persist. Networks, new cohort enable survival.

Creating the market machine: the transformation of Atlas

Atlas's transformation centers on the inculcation of procedures, identities, and discipline. Once a firm living hand-to-mouth and viewed as a source of rents for lifestyle or speculation, Atlas became a "professional" organization, with staff dedicated to tasks and firm, and income plowed back into the firm. This took place not amidst operative market mechanisms demanding certain behavior but in a context of economic normality in flux. This transformation did not occur automatically or overnight. Denise needed eighteen months to lay the foundations and two more years for the new schema to gel. She succeeded because she tapped into informal authority and created her own status. Through imposition and training, she inculcated new practices and logics that became embedded in everyday procedures and conceptions of the normal firm. In short, power and knowledge made this transformation possible: power structured to facilitate transformation, plus knowledge of the new firm's operations and the will to impose her vision.

Soviet logics at work

This small tourist firm was born in 1990 as Aleksei's dream. Aleksei and friend Sasha were dissatisfied working as chemists. Aleksei dreamed of status and freedom. Sasha, now a father, needed better wages for his family. Athletics were important in Soviet culture, and Soviet and East European amateur sportsmen traveled to Leningrad for competitions. Aleksei was inspired to form a small tourist firm to cater to these sportsmen or to occasional groups of foreign tourists. This limited liability partnership (*tovarishchestvo s ogranichenoi otvetstvennost'iu*) organized summer housing and services (meals, transportation) for partial payment in foreign currency. Originally only side work to augment income, Atlas became a long-term project in 1991. Nikolai, a university lecturer who once taught Aleksei and Sasha, ran a program for American graduate students studying Russian. He arranged for Atlas to care for his first group, whose group leader was a young woman named Ellen. Atlas arranged dormitory housing, ensured the students had three meals a day, organized cultural excursions (ballet, opera, trips), provided daily transport to the university, and made sure the Americans were safe and happy. The seven-week program went well and provided Atlas with its first significant hard currency profit. This and the August 1991 putsch convinced Aleksei to stay in the business. The next summer they catered to more of Nikolai's American students, plus additional groups Ellen brought in.

Personal networks guaranteed one or two student groups each summer, and by 1993 in the fall and spring groups from various universities and inter-university programs. Aleksei's networks were crucial: contacts at Party and city-run hotels and elsewhere facilitated work, and he used networks to hire employees, such as Ivan (who worked at the railroad and gained connections there). Nikolai introduced Aleksei and Sasha to three acquaintances who worked at Atlas until 1994. They helped students and ran side projects, such as buying and selling guns, Ukrainian sugar, and boots. (They left in 1993 to open a brokerage house and speculate on currency.) It was not unusual in 1993 to see cigarette cartons (raided for personal use) stacked in the office or to hear Aleksei setting up a deal. Not all deals were successful: an arrangement to import guns faced trouble from a customs officer's shady interpretation of law. (Aleksei wrote off the guns in 1994.) Profits were not colossal, but they covered wages, investments (e.g. repairs or bribes), and expenditures. Aleksei speculated or invested in auxiliary business deals, not all of which were successful, e.g. refurbishing the edifice of an office complex nobody would rent.

The typical working day was not chaotic or lethargic, but rhythm, structure, and sense of mission were weak.[38] Ivan, Shura, or Sasha and Aleksei might show up at 9:00 a.m. early in a group's tenure to accompany students to the cafeteria; they would stop as students learned a routine. At 10:00 other staff would arrive. Aleksei or Sasha might run around town on errands—changing rubles for dollars or vice versa, negotiating a side deal, or meeting with appropriate officials of banks or the state (e.g. for visas). Sometimes Ivan would handle documentation. These tasks might be carried out on that particular day, depending on matters arising. There was no rigorous schedule—contingency drove tactics and decisions. In the afternoon Aleksei or Shura might negotiate with university administrators or sit idly in the office, with Sasha and Ivan playing computer games or reading newspapers. As Denise complained of her first days at Atlas,

> Work was more of a social thing than it actually was work…If you look at how many cups of tea they drink…four hours a day they'll drink tea, maybe four hours a day they'll do something…Come in when I want, leave when I want, go get my hair cut while I'm at work, go get my teeth fixed while I'm at work.

Logics and practices were of sketchy organization of labor and the lack of rhythm or structured time and practice. Things got done when they needed to be done, not following measured pace or planning. When projects would come due or contingencies would arise, employees would go into "storming" mode, and energy and spontaneous structure would arise. The rule of thumb was that the division of labor followed skills and networks, i.e. who was best at an issue (e.g. negotiating with administrators or bankers). However, this was not so precise; Sasha might have to handle visas and passports, or Ivan rather than Aleksei might have to meet an important client or negotiate with university lecturers. Secretaries filled out mundane documentation, fielded phone calls, greeted visitors, and made coffee—although Sasha might do this as well. On a hectic day, Aleksei would return from one part of town, make quick phone calls, and rush off. Ivan might be in transit, setting up excursions or negotiating with hotel or dormitory administrators about new students. Sasha would watch the office and handle important messages or issues.

A core organizing principle of work relations, procedures, and authority was informality, of which Aleksei was the central authority; he was the charismatic leader in business and social life. The office was in a dormitory and near student clients' rooms, which facilitated after-hours parties. This created rapport with college students, for whom socializing was as important as instruction. Aleksei ran the show. He suggested when and how the party would work and might send Ivan across town to fetch his guitar and play for them; never shrinking from the limelight, Ivan would oblige. Several times Aleksei *et al* invited this author for all-night merriment beginning at pubs and continuing at the office perhaps until 4:00 a.m. Sasha was divorced and Ivan single. At formal or informal gatherings (e.g. farewell banquets for students), Aleksei was the master of ceremonies. In disagreements Aleksei would look astounded at contradictory suggestions or would answer with a quick and authoritative stream of objections. Sasha, Ivan, Shura, and others did not protest: he set up Atlas, he watched out for their welfare, and he did not have a large ego. He was a benevolent leader, and financial wizardry and relations to those with money augmented his authority. Finally, Aleksei was energetic, stepping in with ideas or decisions when needed—even if they lacked an organizing logic— and not giving others the chance to take charge.

If survival was success, Atlas was successful. When dollar payments were legal, Aleksei and Sasha invested some hard currency profit into their work, but other investments were less wise. They lent money to acquaintances with myriad proposals—developing real estate near a hotel, a small lumber firm, and the like—without requesting specifics of these plans or the capacity to recoup the investment. All they asked was the return they would make. Yet by 1994 dollar income was drying up—formal payment had to be in rubles, and money wasted on bad investments drained reserves. Aleksei realized room for improvement if one expanded the definition of "success." Employees could work hard when necessary, but pace and tasks were not well structured or disciplined. Needed services such as dormitory or hotel space were obtained via networks, information on which was privileged to individuals with those contacts. To employees, profit meant wages. Occasionally drunkenness led to troubles; lax discipline and informal division of labor made for sporadic confusion and inefficiency. Firm and work were necessary evils, not worthy of effort or creativity. Employees were friendly, and so students' evaluations were positive. Why have discipline or vision if the firm provided consistent rents?

The environment supported *and* contradicted Atlas practices. Transition culture was spreading in discourse; journalists and average Russians beat their chests about Russian deficiencies *vis-à-vis* the West. Business actors were relatively receptive to vague ideas of change, although some at Atlas, such as Ivan, found the state of affairs normal. Outside forces also encouraged existing practices and logics. Uncertainty put a premium on survival; changes might not pay off and result in wasted effort or even crises. State officials demanded bribes, paperwork, and post-Soviet fealty, encouraging resistance. Other business actors were a mix of rugged entrepreneurs (with whom Aleksei started to mingle) following intuition, and others focused on survival or tried-and-true past scripts. There seemed little reason to change when few around them were changing and, at the same time, the economy was undergoing rapid, incomprehensible change. *De facto* ignoring new rules and demands was a Soviet tactic that made sense. It would take a shock to Aleksei and a new player with a different version of business and organizational normality for serious change in Atlas's logics and practices to begin.

The transformation begins

Atlas's primordial logics and practices became clear as the firm changed—like a perturbation of an entity's "ground state,"[39] contingent shocks that trigger change in logics and practices. At issue is what knowledge, logics, and power actors have to interpret shocks, formulate responses, and enforce responses as new normality and everyday practice. Change at Atlas came from Aleksei, who in 1994 experienced three shocks that triggered a rethinking of what normal "business" was. The first shock was a near-miss with personal bankruptcy in late 1993. Aleksei loaned money to various groups but did not worry about getting his money back—given his talent for finances, it was ironic he thought little of risk. Many loans were not paid back, and in the winter of 1993 he had debts but declining income. At the time he was depressed, turning down my request for an interview by claiming I "would not want to talk to someone who was bankrupt." He had not yet decided to reform Atlas, but he was becoming receptive to the idea. A second incentive to change was a scandal in June 1994. Ellen, an occasional student group leader who was personally close to Aleksei, complained about Atlas's recent service. She had worked constantly with Atlas since 1991, even spending time living independently in Russia and helping with their work. Heading a student group in June–July 1994, Ellen raised concerns about problems such as changing light bulbs and repairing locks. Underlying these problems was vodka: Ivan, Sasha, and Shura were often too drunk or hungover to fulfill tasks on time. Denise, a group leader in 1993 and 1994 and who interacted personally and professionally with Atlas, also had conversations with Aleksei. She used Ellen's complaints as ammunition to back up her claim that Atlas had to change work procedures and organization to improve its finances and to grow into a more serious tourist firm. Denise saw untapped potential, but work had to be structured and based on market sense. Aleksei defended Atlas but began to think about Denise's point.

The third stimulus for change was exposure to different ways of work that he interpreted as disciplined and "professional"—an interpretation stemming in part from Denise's framing of his experiences. Aleksei went to the United States with Denise in summer 1994 to observe American business first-hand. Reeling from his impressions as he returned to Russia, he received a job offer from a former classmate who ran the daughter firm of his father's chemical company, importing Western chemical goods for Russian firms. The firm needed someone with a head for numbers and contacts with financial gatekeepers. Aleksei was just the person, and he accepted the job in late summer 1994. At this point his manner began to change to the "professional" character of his colleagues at the new firm—dressing in newer, fashionable suits, carrying a new briefcase, riding in his own car with a chauffeur, and sitting in a new office in a reconstructed building with young professionals. Aleksei's manners changed (he became a Russian yuppie) as did his attitude (serious all-day work and a constant rhythm). The two proximal experiences—seeing American business up close, and entering a new job at a slick firm with more capital and that worked with American businessmen—were the final shocks to Aleksei's business thinking.

These events and shocks set change in motion: not only the shocks, but also being in constant dialog with Denise, who was itching to work on Atlas and explained to him *what* he had experienced and why. That is, she framed his experiences and helped reconstruct his new version of normality. Aleksei now began to formulate and articulate this need for new normality, which included inculcating the American penchant for constant, disciplined work. He claimed Atlas's strength *and* weakness was that it was typically Russian. In Soviet fashion, work methods were undisciplined "storming." Employees could drink and sleep 28 days of the month and then in 48 hours of superhuman effort fulfill tasks. Aleksei highlighted this in a discussion on November 1, 1994. Employees had a long Halloween party the day before; the next day nobody came in until 2:00, and Aleksei was annoyed because he had important business to discuss with Sasha. This "typically Russian" approach to work would not do: if Americans could not accomplish a heroic 48-hour effort, they did not need to because work was rhythmic. Storming was useful—he noted approvingly how Soviet workers quickly built Magnitogorsk from scratch. Not to throw out the baby with the bathwater, he wanted to combine strengths of the two systems: heroic efforts from the Soviet culture, constant disciplined tempo from the American side as the basis of normality.

Aleksei asserted personal authority by framing blame, i.e. abnormal practices creating problems. Atlas earned most of its income in spring and summer; side trade provided marginal returns. Work attitudes needed improvement. All was okay while Atlas served undergraduates and had moderate expectations, but Aleksei saw this as a hindrance. He began change symbolically by re-registering the firm in early August 1994, closing "Atlas" and opening "Atlas Inc."; Denise claimed "Inc." signaled professionalism. Aleksei moved to his new job and needed someone to run Atlas day-to-day. Sasha, his friend and right-hand man, wanted to run a timber firm he and Aleksei acquired (then later sold) and did not bring new thinking. Denise did, and she had Aleksei's confidence from earlier work together. In 1993 and 1994, as student group leader, she spent evenings smoking, conversing, and drinking with them. This made Denise "one of the boys," trusted in the inner circle and as much a friend as client—and now a legitimate actor in the politics of Atlas's rebirth. She impressed Aleksei and others with a straightforward, no-nonsense attitude, self-confidence, and knowledge of how to coordinate activities (which she did as group leader)—in other words, she exhibited authority. After Aleksei's shocks in 1993, Denise provided useful advice. To her, it was common sense that a firm should grow based on hard work, dedication to firm and clients, and "professional" behavior. This was key to her logic: Russia's problem was low professionalism. On good terms with Aleksei, she could use his informal authority. Her self-confidence and willingness to assert herself—crucial in a patriarchal society—served her well in Atlas. As an American she gained legitimacy from knowledge.

In 1994 Aleksei brought in Denise as associate manager alongside Ivan. She could draw on his support and authority, even if he was not around and formally she and Ivan were equals. Aleksei understood Ivan was "Soviet," less than disciplined, unconcerned with developing Atlas's potential; but to make him subordinate to Denise would be a slap in the face to an old friend.[40] Denise would balance this, and hopefully her energy would counter Ivan's penchant for passivity. Denise lobbied for her position, constantly discussing with Aleksei and Sasha how the firm needed a professional image and business practices. She saw this as a challenge, "an opportunity to start a company from scratch, in Russia," and make something good. In August 1994, initially accepted by employees as a known commodity, she set out to transform Atlas.

Denise goes to work: formalization and professionalism

Reflecting years later on her first days and initial reforms at Atlas, Denise said:

> Whoever was available did whatever. What I did was basically to come in and say, [Ivan], for example, his first responsibility in the company is to conclude contracts with the Russian rail station. He set up a system for them for bank transfers, contracts, and also for the bookkeeping. His second responsibility, for example, would be transportation, auto transportation. To make sure that all is in order. [I would make] them each do folders, for example, on their information, so there was no reason why a client would call our office and somebody [would say], "The person who does that is not here, call back later." Everybody knew where the folders were and [I] made them do mini-presentations [on what they were for]: "Here you'll find the train folder. You will find in here the prices back and forth from Moscow to St. Petersburg, you'll find how reservations are taken, how we pay, [and so on], what we need from the client, information, and so on. Here's an example of our reservation request forms, we need it filled out…"

Denise's attempt to instill Weberian rationality—formal procedure and structure, dependency on the organization, observation and evaluation of work and results—and create a disciplinary structure embodying and enforcing new logics was a daunting task. This required changing organization and work (e.g. documentation, procedures), sales and supply (e.g. pricing, clientele, hotels), hiring, overall view of the firm, and business principles. She began with "office management," creating a structured organizational schema. Information on clients and suppliers was crucial for arranging services and deciding on cost and quality, to optimize profit and product. Russian tourism and tax laws required a client's *written* request for service, with specifics on services, payment, and passports. Such data were kept chaotically: taken by whoever answered the phone, written on scraps of paper or in private diaries. This caused the poor bookkeeper grief: tax documents required receipts and detailed information on payment to suppliers or to Atlas, but these were scattered among various employees. Denise felt following the law was part of a normal firm, and she cleaned up the bookkeeping chaos: "to make everyday activities that we did correctly so that the bookkeeper would not have to go back and do extra paperwork." She also felt a key to success was having information readily available for dealing with clients and optimizing work. She created a filing system: documents and data on prices, services, bills, tour groups, and past and potential partners were organized in ring-bound folders, labeled "hotels," "dormitories," "transportation," "guides," "theater," and so on. Denise developed reservation forms including required information, and procedures for linking them to the client: e.g. faxing requests to clients for a signature. Auditors hired to help with taxes complimented her on the system, which they had not seen before. After initial confusion and resistance, Atlas staff went along.

Denise also created a formal division of labor. Earlier, tasks went to whoever was available at the moment; without specific tasks, employees could shirk responsibility. Denise addressed this with double bureaucratization: she posted an organizational hierarchy and formal division of tasks for each person so that "everyone would know his place." She was responsible for general strategy, negotiations with clients and suppliers (e.g. hotel managers), and quality. Ivan was responsible for arranging transportation or other work involving travel around the city. He might obtain train tickets in the morning, and in the afternoon meet guides or museum officials to arrange excursions. Sasha's tasks were less strenuous because of his commitments to the timber firm. He became Denise's right-hand man for negotiating with clients and handling finances (balancing books, obtaining loans or depositing money, etc.). Shura was an intermediate between clients and Atlas, constantly available to address problems, guide clients around the city, and communicate concerns to Denise. For each client group, Denise posted schedules of where each employee should be at specific times: Ivan and Shura at the airport or train station at X o'clock to meet clients, and afterward Denise and Shura to meet them for dinner while Ivan confirmed hotel accommodations. With information and procedures generalized and available to all, if somebody was sick, another person could fill in. Denise said this would end the problem of Atlas being "paralyzed because that person was not there. And that was a big problem earlier."

Changing logics of business

While I examine change in logics of business and sales in Chapter 4, I touch on this issue here briefly to show how fundamental logics of business could change—concepts of strategic markets and consumers, costs to calculate and how, formal versus informal relations, and the like. Until 1994 Atlas muddled through, surviving and profiting from a niche (visiting students) and rudimentary side activities. Payments were often undocumented, including bribes or favors for access to dormitory or hotel rooms or transportation (e.g. railroad tickets). Customers and services came through networks (e.g. Nikolai). In the off season Atlas employees used networks to buy and sell goods and make enough money to survive, and at times even to invest. The circle of primary clients and markets was limited to input from these networks. This did not mean there were no attempts to expand. In 1992 Aleksei tried to widen the circle of potential tourist clients by entering more traditional markets. The thrust of the new strategy was a brochure—one sheet folded twice and not laminated—with text and some pictures of St. Petersburg as "Venice of the North." Promised services were vague mentions of excursions or clients staying in nice hotels. The English was not perfect; grammar was incorrect and several words were misspelled. In 1992, Ivan and Sasha mailed out hundreds of these brochures to American tour firms and some universities but did not receive a single reply. As a result they abandoned the expansion tactic and focused on core clientele and usual business practices.

In normal business practice, networks were sacred, formalized relations profane. One's networks were a personal resource; this reproduced informal authority and autonomy. Connections held business together—partners whose birthdays and telephone numbers were in little black books and memories. Networks gave their owner dependency power within Atlas and shaped status and tasks. While work at Atlas was not well structured, an employee's tasks sometimes correlated to their networks. Ivan's connections made him one general trouble-shooter, especially regarding obtaining tickets. If train transportation was needed, Ivan obtained tickets through his connections. He also spent time at the hotel bar, chatting up staff and creating social capital for possible use. Aleksei's networks made him a natural for some pressing needs as well, especially as per money or protection via *mafiia*. Aleksei negotiated loans from banks or well-off private financiers. Aleksei, Sasha, and Ivan had overlapping connections that allowed Atlas to gain clients and space for them. Atlas housed their sportsmen and student clients in a former Party dormitory where, in theory, they had no right to live. However, Aleksei cultivated personal connections with the head of the dormitory and its associated hotel, and until 1995 used the dormitory for student groups and the state hotel for other clients. In theory, only students of a nearby institute could live in the dormitory, and only guests of the Mayor's office on official business could stay in the hotel.[41] However, by cultivating relations with the hotel director, Atlas obtained passes for students to stay at the dormitory. These ties to the director were cultivated on the last Friday of every month, when Aleksei, Sasha, and Ivan would go to the hotel director's office with champagne and candy to celebrate her "birthday." A Yeltsin decree transferred the dormitory to local government; Russian students had to leave, but Atlas could remain.

An initial symbolic change came in late 1993 when Aleksei moved Atlas down the street to a building with cheaper office space and bank offices. The symbolism was not subtle: from the dormitory of Atlas's past, to a context of suits, security, credentials (e.g. passes to enter the building), and the glitter of money. In winter 1993 Sasha looked at other dormitories for students—the city complex now wanted $10 per room per day—but Sasha did little more, still preoccupied with the timber firm. To move beyond symbolic changes and slow searches for better accommodations, Denise set out to attack informality and rough calculations of strategies and prices. Discourse privileged formalized exchange between positions, not people, as normal. At Atlas, surviving as it did through informality, such change would not have occurred had Denise not framed problems in terms of reliance on networks. One of her earlier attempts to change practice and logics of sales and business came when she questioned price-setting tactics.

> A lot of times when I came into that [Atlas], they had an attitude of sitting and waiting for that foreigner to come along. The first question was, "How much do we charge him," and the second question was, "What is his title in business," "Did he have money or did he not have money." Then they charged accordingly...I basically thought that was insane.

Denise suggested that Atlas would add 15 percent to overall costs for services as profit, as 15 percent was the going mark-up for tourist services in the city. Shura felt prices should vary because of fairness: from each according to his ability to pay. Denise noted that students had worse accommodation and would pay less anyhow; but Shura stuck to principles. For three days they debated pricing until Shura threw up his hands and gave in. Here Denise revealed inexperience. This "cost + profit" formula, as I suggest later, is a crude market logic; she could have factored in competitors' prices and supply-and-demand or season. However, she was attempting a general switch in logics from justice to Atlas's needs, and she applied a formula simple enough to help the firm develop. On the surface, Shura's flexible approach may seem market-like, but it was guided by a sense of justice, not profits. Denise also included flexibility, such as special pricing for repeat clients or negotiating prices for potentially important or repeat clients. Alongside this was a debate over presenting the breakdown of charges to clients. Denise was in a fit: Ivan and Shura presented a simple sum from costs and profit for clients. To address this, she did an exercise with them, pretending to be a client. How would they explain where this sum came from? Shura scratched his head in bewilderment. Ivan raised his eyebrows, walked to a desk and sat silently, lighting up his nth cigarette. Clients were supposed to pay bills, not ask questions. Denise's point was counter-intuitive: a bill was not a mystical number but had to be justified so the client knew what (s)he was charged for and so that Atlas would have a rationalized breakdown of expenses.

Despite Denise's rising star, her reforms did not automatically take root. Ivan remained an obstacle. He relied on personal ties for business; his little black book of telephone numbers and birthdays was so important ("gold") that he refused to relinquish it or show it to anyone. Denise believed in formal contractual relations, stemming from stereotypes of business absorbed in her American upbringing; the importance of the form of relations stemmed from the value they brought, and formal relations were more "professional" and, if done with the proper clients or hotels, would bring in more income. After the incident with the Important Client (below), the tug-of-war with Ivan, rising prices at the city hotel and dormitory, and the need to upgrade Atlas's image to attract business travelers, Denise decided that it was time for Atlas to move on to "professional" business relations with reputable hotels and dormitories. For Denise "professional" was a key word: it meant organization, formal relations, courtesy, competitiveness, strict rules of operation and hierarchy—legalistic, quasi-bureaucratic practice. Costs and events did play a role in the decision to switch hotels: rising costs of city buildings, potential problems from relying on networks and needing to keep them fresh, in contrast to contractual relations. But ultimately what mattered was Denise's *interpretation* of why problems occurred and how to solve them and develop Atlas. She gained authority, and her interpretations and solutions mattered most.

In autumn 1994, this clash of normalities led to tension, although Ivan claimed there was no clash and that he was helping Denise survive Russian business. One key step was to end exclusive dealings and informal relations with the city dormitory complex and deal formally with hotels through contracts or long-term agreements for reduced rates. Denise could not make this change at once; she needed to delegitimate older practices (and hope there were enough hotels, especially foreign-owned, where hotel staff would share her thinking). In November 1994 she got her chance with the case of the Important Client. In late 1994, with Denise out of town, Ivan arranged for the Important Client's stay at the city hotel. When he arrived, hotel staff announced he did not have a place and had no right to stay there. (He was not a formal guest of the Mayor's office.) Ivan pleaded but could only provide the Important Client with a sub-par room. On her return, Denise was outraged and could only apologize, but she did use this to reframe reliance on personal relations as abnormal. Denise got help pushing this logic of relations via position to position (e.g. manager to manager, not friend to friend) as contractual relations became more accepted. By 1995 it was easier to defend contract in courts, although far from straightforward. In 1995 federal law forced contracts to leave a paper trail for the Tax Inspectorate—contributing to contract nonetheless. More private hotels and tourist services dealt with dollar-wielding foreigners and were amenable to formal relations and practices as business practice. Elite hotels (e.g. Nevskii Palace and Grand Hotel Europe) were already foreign-owned, and new staff, trained in Western practices, negotiated professionally—especially with people like Denise, who went to "professional" rather than to unreformed hotels. This also helped her legitimacy: not only did her strategies succeed; they demonstrated that there was change in other Russian organizations, legitimating the entire project of change at Atlas. Atlas employees learned a new logic which, if not ideal-typical market behavior, was closer to Western practice. They learned the market because Denise taught it to them— made possible by her knowledge, authority, and will to impose it, and sufficient changes in environment to suggest Denise was not off the mark.

Employee, firm, and identity

Part of Denise's logic was inverting relations of dependence between employees and the firm, not only to increase discipline and control over employees, but also to create a broader, embracing sense of collective identity in which the firm's mission came first.[42] By formalizing documentation and work, she broke reliance on networks—moving information from little black books to formal structure deprived employees of leverage *vis-à-vis* Atlas. Having disarmed some employees, she reinforced her own power-knowledge position through the spectacle of training. Turning formal structure and procedure into normal, taken-for-granted practice required interacting with them to inculcate the new logic and make it natural practice. As Michel Foucault noted, power is located in relations of bodies and wielders of power with a "gaze"—the claim of those with power and knowledge to observe, pass judgment, and punish/reward. Denise worked carefully with employees early on, inculcating respect for professional work—respect of other employees, for working as a team and following rules, punctuality and timely, rhythmic work, and so on. With Ivan and Sasha, whom she "inherited," the job was a little more difficult. Sasha constantly procrastinated and was not energetic or proactive. He would call a hotel to inquire about available rooms and not argue when told there was nothing available; Denise would immediately call back, complain that Atlas was an important customer, and "suddenly" get a booking. Sasha learned his lesson, however. A group of clients was coming in three months, but Sasha did not reserve hotel rooms ahead of time. Denise told him he should do so to avoid last-minute complications, but he waved aside such worry. At the last minute Sasha had incredible trouble finding accommodations. Needless to say, after this he was more careful with planning ahead to avoid uncertainty and last-minute trouble. It was interesting how Denise framed this episode. Russian business, i.e. the hotel—something Sasha could not control—was not at fault; Sasha was to blame for waiting until the last minute.

To change business logics, Denise took employees under her wing to train them. She showed them price-setting, evaluating hotel quality and price, negotiating, and forming contracts and other documents. Here the arrangement of space was crucial to her "gaze": the ability to watch, interact, and judge. While Atlas changed office locations four times from 1994 to 1997, rooms in each place were connected for easy access and visibility. Denise would look or wander into rooms and talk with employees about work, argue with them, discuss certain problems or possibilities with them. She would call Shura in to discuss recent pricing policy; she would ask Ivan how a project was coming along as a way of encouraging him to work rhythmically. She would warn Sasha and others that if they did not work consistently, tasks would pile up and lead to potential catastrophes. She would ask advice as one way of engaging others. In addition to this physical component of interaction and training, another part of Denise's "gaze" was specific instructions for procedures. Contracts and financial documents were to be completed in a certain way; the last line on these instructions was, "Make sure you show the document to Denise," reminding workers that she would double-check their work, in part so they would understand they could not hide, but in part to make sure that no serious mistakes were made—a central part of the "training." While Denise could not watch over every employee (e.g. when they were around town on errands), she could examine their handiwork or documents and ask about work and results.

For future employees, Denise used the hiring process to instill new logics of formality, discipline, structure, and professionalism. At the initial interview with a candidate, she would give a small booklet with the rules of work and ask the person to read it—he or she "would understand that there was a different type of mindset, that it was very structured, that you have a lunch break thirty minutes every day…They knew they had their set of rules, and that cleared a lot of problems instantly…" If that person wanted to work at Atlas and follow the rules, he or she could call back for a follow-up interview. When occasional problems of conflict or breaking professional norms broke out, Denise calmly called the employees into her office to let them know that continued violation of norms of work and civility would have grave consequences. In one notable case, Denise confronted two female employees at war:

> Let's talk about professionalism. While you're here, you are not [Lena], you are not [Inna]. You are personnel…If you want to bitch at each other, go down to the street corner and say whatever you want to each other, beat each other up, I don't care. But when you're in this office, there will be no yelling, no raising your voice…no name calling, there will be no judgmental reactions. If you're going to do that, you're going to have a direct conflict with me, and if you have a direct conflict with me, you'll lose your job.

Denise did not reshape everyone: Ivan was a constant competitor. His conception of normal business was stereotypically Soviet: a parasitical view of the firm, leisurely work, reliance on networks. He resisted Denise's reforms through foot-dragging. Denise insisted Atlas needed a new computer and laser printer to give materials a polished look and improved image. Before they sent materials to a printing firm; a laser printer would do the job and pay for itself. Aleksei supported Denise, but Ivan time and again responded, "Why? We don't need it." As Denise studied computer and printer information, Ivan walked slowly around the office or sat and smoked, subtly showing displeasure. Asked if he had read these materials, he casually answered yes and said no more. Other disagreements between Denise and Ivan emerged. Denise wanted a constant stream of business clients and to change pricing policy. Ivan thought Atlas could live off summer income and trading activities; new pricing policy was unnecessary. Rather than engage Denise or suggest alternatives, Ivan disagreed but did not contribute. He claimed his job was acclimatizing Denise to Russian business, showing her the ropes and helping out. Essentially, Ivan was claiming local knowledge that he assumed Denise lacked— knowledge of Russians and Russian business, which he described through an endless stream of witty anecdotes and sayings, personal connections he thought Atlas needed, wisdom about how to hire or anticipate and react to contingencies. Denise found him an obstacle, more annoying or sad than dangerous, given that he did not actively foment rebellion or intrigues.

Consolidating authority, practice, and change

But reform required more than new strategies—it required new power. Initially Denise relied on Aleksei's authority, but she needed to consolidate her own. Early on, personal relations and authority lay underneath ownership arrangements. If in August 1994 Atlas was officially registered in *Ivan's* name, Aleksei was still the real boss and Atlas required his contacts and financing. As the chemical job and side investments began to bear fruit, Aleksei kept around $10,000 at any time in the firm's safe for its use, even though on paper the firm had less money than this and Aleksei was not linked to Atlas. In theory, Ivan could take the money in the safe, commandeer the firm, and tell Aleksei to get lost—but Aleksei trusted Ivan would not do this. As I pushed the point, Aleksei agreed that, should Ivan actually try a *coup d'état*, his bandits would stop by for a chat. However, Aleksei's frustration at my question suggested that he thought it ludicrous that Ivan, his friend, could turn against him.

For her changes to work, Denise needed more authority: she, not Aleksei, was there on a day-to-day basis. Aleksei decided that the only way to consolidate Denise's authority, to drive home the serious need for change, and to begin the transformation, was a public meeting to force employees to conform or to register their disagreement publicly, potentially incurring informal sanction. In autumn 1994 Aleksei created a "board of directors" (*soviet direktorov*)—inspired by the UN Security Council—consisting of himself, Sasha, Denise, and Ivan. Aleksei hoped the formal airing of complaints, blame, and solutions would rally Atlas around reforms. Aleksei said that, as he was now working at the chemical firm and would not be around day-to-day, they now had to take on collective responsibilities and decision-making. He decreed the *soviet* would meet every Friday afternoon, when leading employees would report to him. All *soviet* decisions were binding. Aleksei opened the first meeting by claiming forcefully that "we are working badly" and that they needed to improve work habits and organization. He focused on Atlas's strategies and new character. Henceforth, there would be greater attention to finding new clients, improving the firm's tools (office organization, computers, image), and altering work habits. Proposing new ideas was not enough. To light a fire under Ivan and others who might be inclined to take changes less seriously, Aleksei decreed that at each weekly *soviet direktorov* meeting, all members would report on the week's accomplishments and the status of ongoing projects. Denise agreed that the main reason for the board meeting was to nullify Ivan's contrarian status.

This first meeting set the tone and trajectory of change and demonstrated that Aleksei and Denise were in charge. Aleksei laid out Denise's agenda of professional work and image and formal rules and structure. Aleksei brought up one of Denise's current ventures, including purchasing a new computer and laser printer to improve the firm's image. Ivan showed a lack of enthusiasm, objecting that this was unnecessary and not how business is done in Russia, acting as if he didn't get it and could not understand the importance of the proposal. Aleksei promptly quashed this disagreement and resistance by telling Ivan openly and curtly to go along with the strategy—it was now formal Atlas policy. In this open forum of the Atlas "elite," Aleksei used his energy and authority to promote Denise's agenda as the normal future look and behavior of the firm. He cloaked Denise's authority in his own and made the new strategies normal *vis-à-vis* the previous abnormal behavior. With her authority visibly supported, Denise could begin plans for reform. The board of directors met a second time, and Ivan began to toe the party line. A third meeting took place without Aleksei—now too busy with his new business (he would not call any more meetings)—and ended after five minutes and no real discussion. Sasha was in charge. When he repeatedly asked, "When are we going to start this meeting?" others constantly shrugged. Having put Ivan in his place, Sasha and Denise were content to answer to themselves, leaving discussion with Aleksei for the occasional meetings at the office or elsewhere. Following Denise's lead, Sasha was also feeling somewhat more independent from Aleksei, and he did not want to be reminded of who had authority in these directors meetings. As it turned out, the board of directors became unnecessary. The initial meetings showed who and what logic were in charge.

To further consolidate her authority and reforms, Denise needed to ensure that new hires understood and followed the new principles of work and organization. Here she confronted legacies of networks and nepotism (*blat*) that in the Soviet era provided access to good jobs as well as reciprocity and trust. Through reciprocity one could ask for employment as a favor to oneself or someone in a network; as for trust, the unknown person might turn to the authorities or, after 1991, to the *mafiia* or tax police, with important information. Atlas was no deviant. Ivan was brought in because he was a friend who also had connections. Shura was hired because he knew rudimentary English and was a friend who needed work. Aleksei hired Lara as the firm's accountant, even though she did not know accounting, because she was a university acquaintance and was trusted. Aleksei would not trust the firm's books to an unknown outsider, no matter how qualified.[43] He helped her with her accounting work initially while she took courses; after two years she worked on her own. While Denise quickly won Aleksei over to her logic of hiring the best people, she clashed with Ivan when Atlas needed to hire more people in 1995. He demanded they fill the position with someone he knew and could trust. Denise did not trust that person's qualifications, and so she told Ivan that *he* would have to train her and be responsible for her work. Several days later Ivan backed down, claiming he had heard negative things about this person.

Through 1995 Denise's reforms started to take hold. She enforced schedules and procedures, and constantly interacted with employees. She had Aleksei's open backing, and she drew on her insider status and trust to build good working relations. Luck of timing helped consolidate her position and changes: she was an American, from the home of victorious capitalism, while it was still respected. By accident she tapped into post-Soviet transition culture's opposition of defunct socialism versus dynamic Western capitalism (although she did not use this dichotomy overtly). She *was* "the West" at Atlas and likely knew real market practices. She reinforced this image when harping on about "proper" business, citing how things were done in the United States but not in a condescending or nationalist manner. In Aleksei's representation of Atlas and change, Denise *was* American business. As I observed him in autumn 1994 and discussed Atlas, he repeatedly referred to Denise as the carrier of American business practices—he did not refer to such personal qualities as efficiency or will, but rather to knowing what a "normal firm should look like." He did not usually use stark good–bad dichotomies of transition culture to characterize American versus Russian work, and he noted positive aspects of Russian business. But American business was always positive: rhythm/lack of rhythm; discipline/no discipline; normal/abnormal routines. Finally, new clients were not young college students: they were middle-aged Western businessmen who also carried legitimacy. New business of organizing conferences for Western academics in Russia only helped. Atlas *had* to be "Western" and "market" because new clients took these totems seriously, unlike college students less likely to care.

In this milieu, Denise thrived, leaving Ivan to scramble for authority. In 1995 he claimed his role as co-manager was crucial: she introduced changes, but he helped her adjust and made those changes work. In this claim to local knowledge—how Russia really works—Ivan drew on continuities around him, e.g. persistence of bribes and networks.[44] Ivan was Soviet, survival tactics were Soviet—thus he thought he had legitimate knowledge and authority. Yet Aleksei countered with his own experience of more than one type of local knowledge. He denied Ivan alone understood Russian business and rejected Ivan's model of practice. Atlas needed discipline and clear enforcement of structured work. He was sick of Atlas's storming techniques, and authority was too soft: "until thunder roars, the peasant will not genuflect." Ivan was jaded and did not understand that things *could* change for the better—Aleksei had seen America and other Russian firms (such as the chemical firm) that adopted non-Soviet, "market"-like practices.

Americans can be incompetent, wearing away transition culture's sheen. Not so Denise. She augmented her status and authority through a double success: not only successful strategies, but also successful implementation of those strategies. Aleksei's new business dealt with American representatives of chemical companies who needed hosting. He suggested Atlas handle his clients, which Denise did, helping the chemical firm's business in the deal. Denise used contacts and expanded relations with the American Consulate to strike deals to host American consultants and retired businessmen working with Russian firms via aid programs. Denise changed both the client portfolio from students to businessmen and service suppliers, moving away from dormitories and previous hotels—attained via personal relations—to contractual relations with hotels that offered optimal quality and price for clients. By improving work *and* finances, Denise legitimated and consolidated her changes at Atlas—why go back when the new firms provided better wages, stability, collective identity, and normality? This success further augmented her legitimacy and standing in employees' eyes, such that she began to rival Aleksei.

Ivan could not defy the juggernaut, and tensions between him and Denise subsided—but he did not accept her view of the normal firm. Constant work to build the firm did not mesh with his subsistence logic. Even after 1996, as Atlas's future was looking up, Ivan still thought one needed only enough profit for a calm life: for food, for beer and bars, and for occasional purchases. He persisted, although more quietly and privately, to champion his local knowledge and its importance—and he continued to frame Atlas's recent history to his own advantage. In January 1996 Ivan told me, with no small pride, that he was of the old mentality. "Under the old ways I lived fine. I enjoyed it. I had no problem with that life."

Successful change: the new Atlas

The secret to Atlas's transformation was power-culture. From her experience and socialization, Denise had sufficient knowledge of intended practice to bring her designs to life. She created and used authority to inculcate change via claims and training—similar to the system Foucault found in modern organizations. Rather than create an atmosphere of confrontation, she created an atmosphere of collective endeavor—Ivan was the dissenter, rather than Denise the invader. Denise remarked that there remained occasional problems, but employees were proud of their collective. Discipline and formality were internalized; Atlas joined "normal" capitalism. She later noted:

> I constantly, constantly tell them and remind them that we are a team, that it is in the benefit of all of us that we work together, and that their future, their salaries all depend on how much and how well they perform and how they interact with each other…We have too small of an office to have those… micro-conflicts because it's a bad thing to have…

In the new millennium Atlas's structure and work habits remained intact. I revisited Atlas in 1997; it retained new reforms and vision, and was an entirely different firm from its 1991 incarnation. It survived and thrived because of a well-paying clientele (Western and Russian businessmen) and because its structure created effectiveness and maneuverability (e.g. moving to ticketing as core business by 1999). New faces joined and older faces left. By 1999 an *esprit de corps* developed— employees celebrated one year on the job as they celebrated birthdays. Denise proudly boasted her employees worked hard and professionally, meticulously following procedures and able to handle issues independently. In early 1999 Atlas hosted an academic conference, and employees worked late into the night for many days beforehand—quitting time was based on when tasks were finished, and no one complained. The collective was collegial, but there was less after-hours socializing—after work, everyone went their own way. Denise allowed birthday celebrations only for 30 minutes at the end of the day. Staff were professional on the telephone (courteous but to the point), and Denise forbade personal calls with mothers or partners except in emergencies, as this threatened the boundary between the personal and professional. All employees had offices with glass windows that made work visible, and Denise's office was next to the secretaries. There was little of past nonchalance: slow movement, aimlessly walking to take up time, slowly drinking tea and smoking at regular intervals, leaving for a haircut in the middle of the day, or playing computer games. (Ivan was the exception.) Even physical motions—going from one's office to the fax or printer, to other employees to discuss business, and occasionally to make coffee—were more efficient and, if not with a spring in their steps, at least fluid, not lethargic. They understood that at Atlas they were employees first, and that their jobs and Atlas were their first priority. As a demonstration, when I called trying to buy tickets for personal use in summer 2001, Pavel (who did not know me) said they only sold tickets to business clients for business purposes; he still refused when I dropped Denise's and Ivan's names.

Atlas once exhibited legacies of Soviet entrepreneurship: informality, identifying the firm with quick returns and provision (e.g. hiring friends or using funds for personal ends), resistance to formal authority especially by Ivan, lack of disciplined and structured procedures ubiquitous to markets, and innovation restricted to speculation or side trade. Denise confronted these, and her use of authority and legitimacy paid off. Not that this transformation freed Atlas from problems. The 1998 ruble crisis was a blow: businesses used their services less until 2000. Unlike other firms, which paid salaries in rubles, Denise maintained wages denominated in dollars (paid in rubles), so that the minimum $200 per month salary persisted—taking a bite from profits but maintaining loyalty of employees who, more often than not, were breadwinners supporting children, spouses, and parents. To support Atlas's health Denise turned her attention to organizing seminars and conferences to make up the difference, although in 1999 and 2001 she talked of closing up shop. (Before 1996 Denise harbored vague plans of returning to the United States for an MBA program.) As oil wealth healed the economy and Atlas's fortunes, the firm was successful enough for Denise and Sasha to invest in an apartment in an up-and-coming neighborhood.

There remains one footnote: Ivan. His role diminished and work habits declined over time. He no longer played a role in decision-making but was reduced to arranging train tickets and transportation and running the odd errand. He would occasionally show up late and hungover; his drinking worried Sasha and others who felt pangs of friendship. Ivan interacted less with them: Aleksei had his circle of friends, Sasha and Denise were living together and in 2003 had a child. Ivan withdrew to a circle of old schoolfriends. Denise predicted tension between friendship and work, when "something has to give." By 1999 Sasha's and Ivan's friendship gave way to professional duties—although Sasha had a nostalgic spot for Ivan until 2003. Denise was less tolerant: as Ivan's role diminished, he spent more time downloading anecdotes or playing computer games. She did not fire him because Sasha would not condone firing an old friend, even if he shared Denise's opinion. Tired of the work regime and his low status, Ivan left in 2003. Pavel, an Atlas co-worker, also suddenly quit, taking lists of service prices and clients and deleting files from Atlas's database. Soon after, Ivan demanded Denise pay him $40,000 for his share of the firm. Denise offered $10,000, which he refused. She suspected Ivan and Pavel wanted to open a competing firm—Denise could observe computer activity and noticed Ivan had done suspicious amounts of downloading. Denise and Sasha received phone calls from a stranger in Moscow who, in a tone implying this was not a courtesy call, advised paying Ivan the full sum. They refused. When Ivan stopped by the firm, Denise offered to take the matter to Aleksei. Ivan began to tremble and left forever. Despite tension between them, Denise, like Sasha and others, felt pity for him as someone who "lost his way"—a Soviet in the post-Soviet world.[45]

In many ways, this was a wonder to behold—I thought Denise would fail when confronting collective habits of Soviet work and business in an environment where norms were in flux. Entrepreneurship in 1994 still had an element of short-term gain and working in the shadows and through informality; formalized rules and norms were not taken-for-granted collectively or reinforced in institutions of education and business at that time. What was apparent later was how she successfully wielded authority to create hegemony—and how she did so unknowingly and unconsciously. Denise did not mention tactics of constructing power but instead framed her account of Atlas's transformation as creating natural organization. Atlas looked like a normal firm should look, and she was doing no more than being strict about following common sense. This might be the rub: if Denise thought she was creating a normal order, she did not come across as consciously wielding power. Could she be resisted if she was doing what was normal? Only Ivan framed opposition in terms of local knowledge about Russian normality. Rather than using power, she was warden and prisoner of capitalist normality's iron cage, inviting others to join.

Economists confused: the troubling case of Economics Inc.

In contrast to Atlas, Economics Inc. was a story of muddling through and problematic change that highlights problems of incomplete knowledge and problematic use of power. Misha, an economics professor in his late forties, founded Economics Inc. as an entrepreneurial venture into intellectual output. If anything, this was more original that Atlas: elite economists recognized the genius of the project, which ultimately failed because of a conjuncture of organizational incoherence and the bad luck of financial difficulties when creditors and employees decided to start demanding money owed them (not always automatic even in post-Soviet Russia). As with Aleksei, Misha had moral authority as organizational founder and could exercise "simple power." He faced shocks that awakened the need to change his idea of normal organizational behavior. Unlike Denise, Misha did not intuitively understand Fligstein's and Pfeffer's logic of organizational change as framing new normality and creating authority to implement it. Where Denise began by using discursive and narrative dimensions of power to alter categories and logics of normality—myth and mission of the firm—Misha did not engage either dimension, allowing and sometimes encouraging resistance and continuity of old practices. Where Denise applied the gaze of the wise, Misha stayed aloof; while he was an economist, he did not demonstrate business knowledge in practice (quite the opposite). Where Denise tapped into existing authority to build her own base, Misha, who began with authority, did not exploit this potential. Further, while Misha eventually recognized the need for change and devised initial plans, he himself did not articulate or defend clear new procedures, and it seemed he did not understand (or care to understand) the logic of potential new practices: we will now see our first case of decoupling between the levels of culture and knowledge in operation. In other words, the following narrative, contrasting Misha's story with Denise's, highlights Pfeffer's and Fligstein's insights about skills and knowledge, and the politics of framing and power within organizations.

Economics Inc. began fairly well, set in a potentially lucrative niche. In the early 1990s the Russian market was not yet flooded with economics and business literature; in bookstores one found compilations of laws (labor or tax law) and introductory economics texts. There was little on investment, financial evaluation, or Western accounting methods. Misha founded Economics Inc. to address this gap, and more generally to bring market logics to Russia through educational programs and literature, before Russian and Western universities began to set up MBA-style programs. Also, Misha had contacts with Western scholars willing to help with grant applications, to find outlets for selling literature abroad, or to come to Petersburg to lecture on finance and economics. Misha had contacts at the Ministry of Finance. Finally, Economics Inc. was in St. Petersburg, providing an enlightened metropolitan image in contrast to the "economically backwards" provinces or overly politicized Moscow. In short, Economics Inc. had a good market position. However, a recurring problem was the inability of Misha and employees to use this advantage, partly because of problematic decisions (more below), partly because of the inability of many staff members to put in disciplined effort to follow through projects. Much as at Atlas, organizational structure and practices were less than market-oriented or conducive to disciplined work or sustained innovation. Soviet practices and logics of welfare provision, resistance to disciplined labor, and cynical view of the organization's fortunes permeated, brought in by different generations of employees who had some socialization in Soviet organizations. Several employees and project managers complained that Misha had neither the knowledge to see the need for changes nor the resolve to implement them. Projects were haphazardly assigned, not supported, and when approaching completion sometimes brushed aside. Money was borrowed and spent without systematic consideration of costs and benefits of projects or actions. Lower-level employees worked lackadaisically, not concerned with quality or speed. Tea and smoking breaks were frequent, taken regardless of context (e.g.

an important job to be finished). People were not always in their positions (e.g. answering phones, running needed errands, etc.). Lack of authority and discipline hurt Economics Inc. and nearly led to its death in 1996.

Unlike Atlas, Economics Inc. had a fairly formalized structure. Employees had formal positions: head or assistant in the Foreign Relations Department (communication and projects with foreign colleagues), project managers and assistants for literature and courses, a "marketing" director, an assistant director, accountant, and secretaries. Formally the firm had two parts, one for publications and the other for courses on financial evaluation, banking and finance, etc. Yet real authority, structure, and meaning of work and the organization were confused. The main office illustrated the confused logic of organization and practice: the image of the main office was structured malaise and disorganization. The office was a large room in the corner of a public school. In the summer this had a quiet atmosphere, but sounds of children running and yelling were distracting at other times. Important data and documents on projects and procedures were in files organized willy-nilly in computers or alongside reams of draft documents and business newspapers. Employees' physical movements were a near-random distribution of the slow and lackadaisical and near-chaotic movement around the office or out to an economics department at some university or institute. Some employees would work halfheartedly at computers or desks, and then indifferently make and drink tea; others would work hurriedly and with aggravation over a sudden glitch in a project. Outside contacts involved in a potential or existing project would come in for a meeting and sit around waiting for Misha or the appropriate employee to materialize. Waiting for no explained reason was not unusual. Private conversations in corners and hushed tones revealed exasperation over egos, status, incompetence, arrogance, and the like.

To give this picture a precise human face, let us turn to a more important employee in 1994–5: Zhana, head of the foreign relations department. She gained her position not through qualifications but because she was the first hired for that department and was Misha's former student. She was supposedly skilled in Russian–English translation—although when I inspected one translation, I was bewildered by the mention of the famous economist "Kows" (bovine economics?) until I realized this was a letter-for-letter transliteration of *"Kous"*—the Russified form of "Coase," i.e. Ronald Coase. Zhana was often tardy and worked slowly even as important deadlines loomed. She was quiet, not because she was shy or aloof but because she simply did not display much verve. Her less-than-disciplined behavior complicated others' jobs. In autumn 1994, Economics Inc. ran a program on financial analysis, with one course taught by a British lecturer. Zhana and the foreign department of two other young women did not have lecture materials translated and organized as the lecture date approached. While joking about last-minute work, neither Zhana nor co-workers understood the lectures had to be printed in the same font and word-processing program to facilitate printing— they had not bothered to find out the details of their task beforehand. Resolving this problem necessitated rapid last-minute "shock work," much of which fell on the shoulders of a fourth woman (Inna) who worked part-time in the foreign department. She took the task seriously and worried that the materials would not be ready, the course would go awry, and the image of Economics Inc. would suffer. This was normal for Zhana and the foreign department; the ability and will to organize disciplined work were lacking.

Not all employees were indifferent to work or saw Economics Inc. only as a wage. A few—Inna and a handful of young men just out of university, and one easy-going woman in retirement—were careful with their work, but the absence of structure and rewards for competence disheartened them. They also felt the most powerless. The majority of employees had only a superficial sense of a work ethic or *esprit de corps*—their identification with the firm ended with some pride at being in a private organization on Misha's exalted mission of post-Soviet capitalist enlightenment. Internal rules and authority did not change behavior. As the "Kows" story suggests, quality control could be problematic. Zhana did not think much of the quality of her work, and there were no procedures linking reward to quality. While the content of outputs (literature, course lectures) was very good—probably because the lecturers and writers were competent and would see their names linked to their output—*organizational* work was slipshod, i.e. translations, course organization, producing and selling literature on time, drafting grant applications,[46] negotiating with potential clients, and the like. Secretaries were lackadaisical about duties and used access to phones, computers, and information for status and power *vis-à-vis* others—they might wantonly deny telephone or computer use to others who needed calls fielded or matters attended to.[47] Misha did nothing about this, even when other employees complained. Quality depended on the dedication of the particular producers themselves, not on any oversight process.

Misha was the formal head but did not exercise much authority—not unusual in the historical context. Economics Inc. began as a collective effort by university colleagues. Decisions on content of journals, what furniture to buy, and so on were collective. As activities expanded and Misha's managerial inability (shared by "assistant managers") emerged, this created problems. The ethos of "we're all friends who trust each other" hindered a structured division of labor and authority for running complex projects.[48] Sometimes others used Misha's authority for their own gain. In 1994 and 1995, the accountant occasionally dictated to staff and told Misha who could have what position or salary. Although it was outside her formal authority, she set the value of individuals and positions without investigating who did what. She rewarded favorites and used the firm's car and driver without reimbursing expenses. Misha never questioned her, despite employees' complaints of justice and costs. Her connections to an important bank needed for a key loan and accounts gave her some leverage but far from dictatorial status. Generally, complaints to Misha about Zhana, the accountant, and others produced little more than quiet grumbling; Misha gave no authority to project managers to discipline subordinates.[49] In short, he took no steps to structure labor, and employees inclined to work found themselves in a disheartening position.

Business practices

If problems with organization and work created only annoyance, there would be little to discuss; but these problems were coupled with Soviet logics of business and sales, affecting performance and survival. Tasks and procedures at Economics Inc. were disorganized and based as much on Misha's whim as on market considerations or appropriate tasks and skills. This reflected the organization's origins as a collection of local university academics who found a mission teaching businessmen and students about market economies. Decisions on production, purchases, and sales were collective, although Misha had the final say. The original task was to provide literature for high schools and universities—collections of essays and a journal on financial analysis and organizational practice, drawn from Western writings translated or summarized for readers. They used networks and moral claims (formal education as vital to post-Soviet transition) to get clients: educational institutes, schools, and enterprises. The Ministry of Education gave the journal and literature the status of "official textbook" (*uchebnik*), allowing state schools to use state money to buy them. This, with funding from the Russian state and Western grants, was initial income that helped Economics Inc. expand. One direction was training and teaching, especially intensive courses for teachers, accountants, and enterprise managers. The most ambitious was an autumn 1994 course on financial accounting that provided "tactical help" for managers and accountants who had to manage accounts and undertake investment as well as production. Other minor activities included lectures to high school students on basic economics.

Misha found a niche, less by actively seeking it than by a lucky coincidence of his own vision (teaching Russia economics) and a broadly perceived need for such education. But maintaining their position in that niche, by adjusting to competition and context, was another matter. As similar organizations developed in Moscow, subscriptions for literature and courses dropped. The Ministry of Education ended patronage, shifting funding to three Moscow organizations and ending "official textbook" status for Economics Inc.: schools could buy their journals only with non-state funds. As inflation made Economics Inc. literature more expensive, demand from schools sank. By 1993 schools and enterprises wanted journals and textbooks with practical knowledge, not the abstract theory that Economics Inc. plied. (American authors quickly outsold Russians in this area.) These shocks required adjustments, but Misha and colleagues were not prepared to take appropriate action. According to one former insider, pre-1993 business was easier because of less competition and schools and enterprises being hungry for *any* market literature or training. With narrowing consumer needs, financial constraints, and greater competition, Misha and company were paralyzed. To survive a more complex market, they needed appropriate skills to understand and react to the market environment—but they had only abstract knowledge rather than concrete experience of markets. Problems of personnel management hurt— low professionalism and discipline disrupted the timing of output and strategies of sales.[50]

One important event that illustrates work and business logics at Economics Inc. was the publication of a Russian–English finance dictionary. Misha took the dictionary project more seriously than others, but yet again he and staff were hampered by the lack of personal and institutionalized knowledge and market discipline. The goal in early 1992 was to grab the book market with a quality, comprehensive dictionary of financial and business jargon. There was as yet no quality Russian–English dictionary of that type, and even after 1995 their dictionary was among the best. The hope was to get it on the market quickly for Russians and Westerners.[51] Economics Inc. organized the writing and printing.[52] The printer offered a reduction in unit cost for orders of more than 100,000 copies. Misha thought this logical and ordered 100,000 copies to save on unit costs. He took out a loan of more than $100,000 from a Petersburg bank where their accountant had networks. A large loan and the chance to publish a quality dictionary ahead of competitors should have impelled organized work (or storming) and timely completion. Yet organizing and finishing the dictionary was a slow affair. Some who worked at Economics Inc. at the time remarked that Misha and staff did not cajole translators to finish their work quickly. Negotiations with the printer dragged, not because of disagreements but because Misha did not take them seriously enough to close the deal. Disorganized work by translators and staff delayed the dictionary's publication by almost a year, after which it was no longer the first of its type—as it would have been if the initial schedules had been followed. Competition cut into sales.

Despite problems of organizing production, the dictionary was produced at high quality. Yet writing and printing 100,000 copies was not *selling* 100,000 copies. Misha ordered 100,000 copies because of production cost calculations, when he had no reliable idea of how many he could actually sell or how to sell them. He and colleagues reasoned that this would take care of itself; there was no sales and marketing strategy. Some copies were sold, given away, or shipped to Western stores, but more than half sat for several years in storage until spring 1996. Sales consisted of occasional ads or calling institutes and firms to persuade them to buy the dictionary. I saw the dictionary in Petersburg's main bookstore only in early 1995. Negotiations to sell the book in the United States took two years, following a haphazard practice of calling or mailing small bookstores in major cities. I saw the dictionary in two small specialty books stores in Cambridge and Pittsburgh for $60. In Russia, the dictionary was priced at a constant dollar value of $15—a hefty sum, held constant for inflation, regardless of how it was selling.[53] In the end, the majority of dictionaries sat in storage collecting dust while the debt for printing threatened. The creditor bank, under new management following a bank run in late 1995, decided to pursue debtors, including Economics Inc. While the accountant managed to transfer Economics Inc.'s assets to another bank, Misha had to use networks to barter most of the dictionaries for the debt.

The dictionary story captures practices at Economics Inc. Misha did not understand or enforce organization, discipline, or procedures and logics that would facilitate responsiveness to external market signals, such as they were. He pushed projects but did not follow through completing them in a timely manner, and this logic extended to the firm as a whole. Misha would come up with an idea and assign it to an employee—but he would say little about its utility or purpose, what resources were available to support it, and to whom the project should be oriented. More than one employee ended up confused and angry as Misha waved aside requests for necessary details about orientation and support—leaving the poor employee wondering how important the developed idea should be and how much work should go into it. For example, Misha asked Inna to design two projects, one supporting academics studying in Russia, and one to support busi-nessmen (e.g. accommodations, databases, interviews at Russian firms). He saw American professors, graduate students, and businessmen flooding Petersburg, and he thought there might be a niche for such a service. Inna made trips to the library and information bureaux linked to the American Consulate and Chamber of Commerce to ascertain which Western organizations might be targets for the program. She desperately needed to know what services Economics Inc. could offer. Misha shrugged his shoulders and gave no answer. She turned to other managers, who also offered shrugs or commented that they did not understand the project. When Inna had designed the two programs and sent faxes to several American scholars and academic or business organizations, receiving lukewarm responses only from two, Misha suddenly waved off the projects as unimportant. This is only one example of how Misha would come up with a project idea that could, in theory, bring income—yet projects were always vague, did not take into account either the market (e.g. prospective clients, competition) or start-up costs. In the end, Misha became bored with these ideas and projects or became timid in the face of necessary additional investments of time or other resources for market research, and he let them die on the vine.

Despite slipshod organization, the firm could produce quality output—especially its dictionary and journals. However, quality without sales does not translate automatically into material gain. Misha was not ignorant of this—but neither he nor colleagues had a sophisticated grasp of how to tap market demand. Here we see the beginnings of the split between the superficial and fundamental levels of knowledge: proposing categories and tactics without fully grasping their manifestations in practice and how they link into other organizational routines. Misha looked to expand sales and avoid financial problems in 1993. To expand sales of literature and subscriptions to courses, he made a young graduate student the marketing director. He was given telephone directories and told to enter names, addresses, and telephone numbers of potential clients into a database. Other employees would draft letters on Economics Inc. products (courses and lit-erature). This graduate student soon quit, after a row with Misha about expanding marketing (which Misha rejected). This was as far as "marketing" got: calling up or sending out faxes and letters on products, or placing the occasional ad or using connections to journalists to run stories about upcoming courses. For the courses on financial evaluation, several women spent days calling assistant directors at firms and banks around Russia, running up phone bills, to interest them in courses. When employees traveled for whatever reason, Misha gave them tele-phone numbers of possible clients (schools, institutes, enterprises) and asked them to sell literature and courses. Yet he provided neither training nor strategies for approaching clients, nor enough information about products so that anyone quizzed could respond intelligently.

Most employees and some managers followed the parasitic-provisional logic of "firm as host," whose related practices might resemble torpidity or laziness, as some at Economics Inc. claimed. Collective events such as the annual New Year's party were well attended, and no one complained about the availability of tea, telephones, photocopying, or other services at the firm's expense. Employees complained of low or late wages, but there was only a weak sense of the need for collective belt-tightening and gearing up to improve work. Rather, employees used the firm for wages, resources, and résumés.[54] Such opportunistic behavior is not unique, but it was central to behavior at Economics Inc. Cynicism about Misha, the state of affairs, and the future, was manifested in tardiness, laxity, and general foot-dragging. Work was not coded as part of identity or a means to important and legitimate ends, but as a necessary evil. Zhana's behavior or that of others as I observed it was less laziness than ambivalence or resistance, depending on the situation: going through the motions rather than putting in disciplined effort out of fear or internalization of the goals and tasks of work. The way Zhana or others would listen to a command, slowly nod, go about work with occasional pouting or lack of energy suggests the kinds of resistance some scholars observe in peasant communities.[55] In the Soviet era, work was a duty,[56] and the Soviet legacy of passive resistance carried over into the market-building era. Identities, tool kits, and *habitus* did not change quickly; disorganized, undisciplined work of the Soviet era—an expression of resistance—continued into the capitalist era.

Much as Ivan linked normality to continuities in the Russian context, most employees' practices and assumptions at Economics Inc. persisted because of the inability of market logics to take hold around them. Why should employees think of productivity when networks provided sufficient revenues? Why should Misha think of discipline and organization when it was unclear how long Economics Inc. would survive because of the chaotic environment (tax laws, inflation, etc.)? More attention to organization, deadlines, and resource use would have aided productivity, set the foundation for better sales strategies, and helped Economics Inc. mediate financial problems after 1994. As well, the environment provided few positive or negative stimuli for change: taxes and inflation ate profits, and Misha used networks to avoid the punishment of debt. While Economics Inc. provided literature and courses on market finance and economics, this was abstract textbook knowledge, not knowledge of *how* to create a "market" organization. Economics Inc. was founded by economists who did not ask seriously what "market" structure and practices were or how to attain them. They provided formulas on financial evaluation but did not have access to market practices, as Denise had at Atlas and Aleksei noted in his experiences. Much like the state organizations where their offices were located (a school) or with whom they had relations (universities), Economics Inc. stumbled and muddled through business.

Attempts at change

By late 1994, sales and income declined—the beginning of a long period of financial difficulty, and unlike many larger Soviet-era industrial enterprises, Economics Inc. did not have various goods to barter (except publications, which they were loath to use in this way), and they were susceptible to monetary demands (taxes, rent, wages, overheads). Misha was unable to turn the firm around, and most employees did not pursue projects with vigor. Some journals or translations of Western economics came to completion, but failures drained Economics Inc. of time and money—worsened in 1995 by a decline in clients willing or able to buy literature or sign up for courses. Income from foreign grants was also drying up. Misha concluded that changes were needed to plug financial leaks and improve work. One solution was to devise new projects willy-nilly and apply for Western grants. Another was to increase discipline and control expenditure. Such measures came in summer 1995, when Misha adjusted formal internal organization. The foreign relations department was specified as four women, one of whom was also a project manager. A publishing division was created to more accurately reflect publication activities, and the people and positions were more formally specified. A marketing division was expanded—as once suggested by its first director—and now included several older women who staffed the telephones, calling enterprises to advertise literature and courses. Positions in the division dealing with courses were more formally defined. The chief of each division was accountable for costs such as use of telephones and photocopying. Photocopying and long-distance telephone calls were curtailed; anybody using a service had to log in the time and degree of use (e.g. how many pages photocopied). Misha legislated this scheme after complaints that funds were disappearing down a financial black hole, and that nobody knew who was in charge of any project or set of projects.

This did no good. Neither Misha nor colleagues examined data on telephone, photocopier, and computer use to discover who was abusing these services and draining money, assuming employees recorded their use. When I asked Misha if he checked this data closely, he shrugged his shoulders as if to imply this was not particularly important—but he did comment on the distressing state of finances. This stricter organization produced no tangible results. Zhana had more responsibilities, but this did not stimulate her or two other young women under her to take work seriously. Inna, the fourth in this "division" and who doubled as a project manager, consistently complained, sometimes in tears, about Misha's incompetence and the laziness of Zhana and others. In her description—which mirrored my observations—Zhana *et al* did what they absolutely had to do when Misha was around, but otherwise were "neither helpful nor useful," making her own work that much more difficult. The same was true for the literature division, where one young assistant director started out with some initiative and energy but eventually lost these, approaching his tasks with little effort or discipline. Before he quit, he spent more and more time away from the office with one of the women from the foreign department. Because Misha did not use observation, information, punishment, and reward to implement organizational changes, the reforms were superficial and did not have the same benefit as at Atlas.

Misha did not wield knowledge or authority to improve discipline or link employees to the firm. Work continued as before: little attention to detail and deadlines, followed by panic, storming, and lack of information.[57] His occasional presence in the main office did not help discipline and production. This was unfortunate, because Economics Inc. was not a total failure. They secured Western academic grants and produced good products despite scarce resources. There was some collective identity and goodwill. However, Misha did not actively use these. He let quandaries define and taint his authority. Many at Economics Inc. held him in contempt, although he retained authority as founder and manager. As finances worsened, he spoke in droopy tones of how "all is bad" or "things are not going well." If employees raised issues of strategies (e.g. concerning journal content or publication), he could be curt or show little enthusiasm. Nor did he wield punishment. He never fired anyone, and discussions with employees suggested he did not make examples of anyone to define "bad" work and buttress authority. If people left, they left voluntarily, tired of low or late wages, bad organization, or lack of a future. He did not use surveillance: if anything, Misha was *not* visible and did not actively interact to shape behavior. Often he either worked out of home or in an adjacent office out of sight and earshot of the main office, popping in only occasionally to check on some issue, meet a visitor, or make tea. When he was in the main office, he sat apart from others, perhaps in a corner, quietly drinking tea and reading rather than actively participating in work and watching over employees. This lack of visibility had two consequences. First, he could not enforce his own rules or create expectations among employees that they might be caught being lax. Second, his leadership image suffered: authority requires the leader be present in some form to remind people of stature.

The status of Misha's authority also suffered from paternalism. Like factory directors of next chapter, Misha felt he had to be paternalistic. The "welfare function" was limited by the firm's small size and resources (e.g. no dachas or medical clinic), but there were paternalistic rituals. Misha did not base hiring decisions on organizational needs or individual qualifications. Rather, he hired university or graduate students whom he knew needed work ("They need the money") and who came to him through networks. The assistant director and accountant were Misha's friends; members of the directorial board were colleagues. Project managers were former students or in employees' networks. This was part of his identity: not only manager but also almost head of a society to aid the unemployed. There were other rituals. Misha and several employees always made sure there was food and tea in the office. A New Year's party always took place, even in lean years 1995 and 1996. Food, bought with the firm's funds, was set out, as were champagne and vodka (more than twenty bottles), so the *kollektiv* could celebrate even as the institute tottered on the verge of insolvency and when most employees had been paid a symbolic sum or no wages for up to eight months. While this ritual was necessary to reinforce the sense of a collective united in duress, Misha did not exploit the payback: dependency and a sense of loyalty and reciprocity for prodding employees to work harder. Paternalism remained a duty.

By autumn 1995 the situation at Economics Inc. was bleak. Only the accountant and a few secretaries with personal histories linked to Misha received full wages or wages on time. Other employees left for greener pastures: a woman who played a key role in organizing finance courses; an assistant manager having an affair; the assistant director and Misha's friend, also the informal co-founder, left to work elsewhere as an accountant. In August 1995 a potential savior arrived. When Misha's friend and assistant director left, Economics Inc. advertised for a new assistant manager, and a former submarine captain was hired. His outlook was that the institute lacked discipline. We had a candid conversation about problems of organization and low morale. The Captain complained Economics Inc. was terribly disorganized, its employees unprofessional and undisciplined. When he tried to obtain information about a project or event or anything at all, employees referred him to each another, so that the Captain went around in circles. He complained that employees used telephones and the copying machine without thinking about how much money they were wasting. He soon made good on the policy whereby each user had to ask permission for photocopying or to make phone calls and record copies made or numbers called. But he was confident that the firm, with strict organization, could be turned around. He claimed, "there is money here," but the firm needed order to find and use it.

Misha now had a manager who could take the reins and turn the firm around: a Denise of sorts. However, the Captain did not stay long. Brought in to impose order, he was soon at odds with most employees—and, ironically, with Misha. Misha preferred a hands-off approach while at the same time issuing directives about his latest project ideas. (It is no small leap to compare his management style to the stereotype of Khrushchev and his hair-brained schemes.) If the Captain complained to Misha about particular employees, they complained to Misha about the Captain's demanding nature. Fed up with complaints, Misha set out to solve the problem—he did not support his new assistant, not giving much weight to his observations. Fed up with Misha's inability or unwillingness to take a firm stand, the Captain left. In retrospect, it is clear why he failed. Misha could not enforce his own badly designed measures, and he was unwilling to support the Captain's authority. Unlike Denise, the Captain was an outsider—he had not built up relations with employees beforehand, as Denise had—and he did not create strategic alliances—his relations with Misha were cool, unlike Denise's working partnership with Aleksei. Atlas employees were used to undisciplined work, but they also cooperated because they came from a general network pool. Economics Inc. employees came from non-overlapping network pools. They did not always cooperate and were not accustomed to the informal authority that Aleksei enjoyed. Aleksei and Denise projected the image of people with authority who were willing to use it. Misha had the opposite image, and so the Captain had no real authority behind him—when he tried to create a no-nonsense image, employees ignored or resisted him. When they argued with him, invariably Misha sided with employees—the opposite of Atlas. Finally, the Captain did not have symbolic capital enhancing his status or authority, unlike Denise. Of course, some employees at Economics Inc. did not care about the organization's health, especially those with jobs elsewhere (e.g. academics who worked on literature projects) or women nearing pension age whose husbands had jobs. Misha would have had to cull his workforce while actively supporting the Captain—but he was unwilling to do either, and it is unclear to what extent he actually understood that he needed to undertake these steps to improve work and efficiency.

An odd cavalry arrives: benefits of opportunism

At the end of 1995 the organization held its New Year's bash with a sense of foreboding that Economics Inc. would not survive 1996. One woman who left bitterly in late 1995 snitched to acquaintances in the Tax Inspectorate that Economics Inc. was not paying VAT on literature sales.[58] Economics Inc. nearly closed in 1996: tax arrears and late loan payments threatened bankruptcy, and staff were leaving because of low or late wages. Misha used connections in Moscow to reduce the tax burden, and dictionaries were bartered for bank debt. A core of employees remained, including Matvei, an economics graduate student hired in 1995 who ran the publications division after 1996. He found the work interesting and useful: he was writing an economics dissertation and could use the organization's literature and computers. As his responsibilities increased, Matvei brought in former students with the promise of experience instead of wages, and he made them work in an organized manner. By 1999 he improved efficiency at the publications unit. An organized person with varied interests and projects, including economic sociology and music, Matvei preferred results to muddling. From his economics training he thought in terms of efficiency, costs, and benefits. Undisciplined and unfinished work at Economics Inc. would cut into time for music or academic work. In short, Economics Inc. was a base of operations, and he helped introduce practices of discipline and market calculation.

Earlier I suggested opportunism is an insufficient foundation for market capitalism: simply jumping at opportunities for profit does not equate with building structures and procedures of rationalized practices and logics. In this case opportunism provided an unintended consequence: the "parasites" realized that a healthy host served their interests. Economics Inc. survived in part because Matvei and company improved work at Economics Inc. not out of loyalty, but out of opportunism *vis-à-vis* the organization and dedication to their work. This held the possibility that the opportunists' discipline and knowledge might dominate work there. However, this hegemony would have to rely on diffusion and status within—Matvei and company did not have the same power as Denise and so could not compel others to adapt their practices and discipline. Misha had changed little: he was unconcerned or unable to enforce discipline, and the only employees and practices that changed were those under Matvei's purview. Matvei commented that low pay was a problem—employees had no incentive for disciplined, competent work—but Misha's inability to discipline was important. In 2002 Matvei characterized Misha's managerial style thus: "He does not punish. He will tell someone, 'Oh, darling, you should work better,' when what he really needs to say is, 'Listen, bitch, get to work!'" (Matvei referred to secretaries and "grunt" workers, mostly women. Leading figures were mostly men.) Misha continued to demand employees work on many projects at once, leaving projects and wages under-resourced.[59] When Matvei and his group suggested it was better to focus on a few projects with a reasonable chance of success, Misha ironically answered that everything would be better if employees worked harder—a Soviet logic of throwing more labor at a project or storming. Matvei agreed with this assessment. Life at Economics Inc. continued as before: barely muddling through on what income could be generated and because enough employees remained to keep it operating. These employees tolerated low or late wages because Economics Inc. was their first job out of school or because they were near pension age, unlikely to find a better-paying job.

Matvei and his group took work seriously and realized that improving their host provided a stable base of operations for other interests—Matvei talked, sometimes tongue in cheek, of benefits of *homo economicus*. By 1999 they enjoyed decision-making status for important projects. Economics Inc. also acted as a safety net and kept them linked to academics. Some of them held second jobs as analysts at banks, and they wanted to retain links to the academic world. Others, like Matvei, preferred to remain as close to academe as possible and, given the difficulty of obtaining formal academic jobs, saw Economics Inc. as a close second. Academic jobs in Russia are tricky: low pay, corruption, job insecurity, the need for patronage to obtain work, and a dearth of openings. At Economics Inc. Matvei and others had academic work (organizing courses and literature) and could teach on an *ad hoc* basis elsewhere. Their working hours were flexible, and they were willing to put in fourteen-hour days to have three-day weekends or entire weeks off. Work on projects had white-collar status and looked good on résumés. They also found contacts at Economics Inc. with foreign scholars useful for careers and edification, and they worked hard to maintain a good image with the foreigners. This gave Matvei the chance to travel to Great Britain on business, although his real motive was see Scotland and listen to live folk music. Matvei and colleagues were also increasingly aware of competition from other publishers and MBA programs by Russian and Western universities. Misha relied on networks, but Matvei and company relied on their wits and energy to make the organization competitive.

Matvei and colleagues, like the Captain, saw potential at Economics Inc., and they were willing to put in work to keep the organization afloat. They took their work seriously enough to contemplate a *coup d'état* against Misha in 1999, although they backed down from deference to his authority as founder. Instead, they marginalized Misha in his own firm, much as Denise had done to Ivan. While he proposed projects, Matvei and others pursued what they thought important—projects with status, such as an updated version of the Russian–English finance dictionary, translations of key English-language economics work, and particular financial courses for Russian managers. They would sometimes work late into the evening—in 2004, Matvei spent so much time on the new dictionary that he set aside his music. Coming into the office on weekends to make sure a publication was making progress, or to ensure smooth operation of finance courses, was their norm. (I found it easiest to get hold of Matvei by phoning his work number.) Misha became dependent on them as well, and they ignored him when necessary.

Matvei and company were linked into transition culture by formal training in economics, which colored their arguments for discipline, quality, and competition. Meeting deadlines and producing quality work, within limits of diminishing returns, was logical to their economic worldviews. While they did not explicitly draw on transition culture's dichotomies, they did react against Soviet practices, partly because economic normality was also "anti-Misha." They saw a correlation between crisis or malaise and Misha's leadership. Some of them had been to the West and were building Western contacts; others studied finance and worked for Petersburg banks as consultants or internal analysts. Here they saw a correlation between strict organization, schedules and deadlines, efforts at quality, and rewards—although they also saw plenty of faults as well (e.g. use and abuse of informal networks in banks). These experiences contrasted to those under Misha. That is, they could draw selectively on experiences outside Economics Inc. to construct and justify strategies involving discipline and organization. Further, Matvei and company were younger, closer to a post-Soviet generation. To them and increasingly younger employees at Economics Inc., Misha and colleagues were the Soviet *nomenklatura* generation that could not guide Russia into capitalism. This was not an open claim, but it did slip out occasionally in informal discussions. Anti-Misha and anti-Soviet intermingled in presumptions of authority and legitimacy in constructing strategies and practices. This became clearer when Economics Inc. opened new offices in a nearby secondary school in 1999. Here Matvei and colleagues set up shop, renovating the interior and bringing computers, faxes, and literature. In the old office, which Misha frequented, work was still problematic. When Misha came to the new offices to hold a meeting, he still carried some authority and suggested new projects—but this was not his turf, and here he was a "counter-totem." Matvei could observe employees at the new site, and while he did not actively reshape them as Denise did, he did interact and sometimes demand. Employees at the new offices might not work Matvei's hours or show great passion, but they worked effectively. There were fewer tea or smoking breaks; telephones were answered, errands run, work handled routinely. Work was getting done—some of it difficult and time-consuming, such as the new dictionary. The renovations added to the feel of professional work.

Under Matvei's supervision, Economics Inc. undertook a second, greatly expanded version of the Russian–English dictionary. They had learned some lessons from the first experience, but other errors were repeated or came close to repetition. One lesson learned was that speed was of the essence—the dictionary had to be completed, with maximum control over distribution and profits. They planned to avoid the previous problem of trying willy-nilly to sell the dictionary abroad through less-than-honest distributors who really dealt in piracy. However, they repeated one earlier mistake: again basing the number of books to print on the printer's unit prices rather than projected sales. Again, they invested resources and energy compiling the new dictionary in all its complexity, with no regard for how the Russian and foreign markets would support it or how to distribute it. No probes were made about market capacity or what features the dictionary should have—this was decided by the producers' tastes.[60] For foreign sales, the strategy was to print the dictionary and have foreign publishers distribute it—even though foreign publishers often pushed their own dictionaries. Economics Inc. followed Russian publishing tactics: the organization designing the good produced it. This meant more income than royalties but also greater risks in the case of failure (e.g. higher debts because of greater outlays). They did not consider the Western approach—design the dictionary but let a publisher print, market, and distribute. This might gain only royalties and reputation but would lessen risks and use Western marketing experience. In fact, as the dictionary was coming along, the issue of distribution remained a constant, unresolved worry; the numbers to be printed were a non-issue. Only in early 2005 did Matvei and editors accept that Economics Inc. was too small, without sufficient resources or a distribution network for successful sales—but by then the end was near.

The end of Economics Inc.

By 2006 Economics Inc. was consigned to the dustbin of business history. After 2000, skilled employees were leaving for pastures with better prospects, environments, and wages. The organization's eventual death followed the same script as its earlier crisis in 1995–6, only this time Misha gave up the ghost of his creation. This was not an inevitable outcome due to inefficiency, market unworthiness, or enforcement of such market rules as profitability and debt repayment—these could have been circumvented yet again. The final act opened in 2001, when Misha decided on a massive upgrade of the dictionary—its expanded scope and size, and new electronic format, demanded a colossal investment of time, money, and manpower.[61] By 2003, Matvei rethought his own situation at the organization: as manager of this project, he could see the dictionary would be late and overbudget—again, due to weak discipline and organization that this time even he could not reform. Not wanting a "failure on his shoulders," he left Economics Inc. for work in another institution of higher education—although he did not abandon Economics Inc. entirely, and he participated in various meetings and retained good relations with Misha (characterized as father–son). In 2004 initial editions of the electronic version of the dictionary appeared. Yet Misha still felt unprepared to venture into the foreign market, and so he contracted marketing the dictionary to an outside firm. Quickly Misha faced a marketing problem: the dictionary would be at least $300 in the West (although with little real competition on quality), and the Russian market would not support the 1000 ruble price tag needed to cover costs. Again, the dictionary was a *creative* success but a *marketing* failure and albatross around the organization's neck.

To finance the project, Misha used relations with a well-off entrepreneur ("the Investor") whom he knew through networks to a local bank. Despite problems of budget and production schedule, the Investor continued to help Economics Inc. due to his friendship with Misha—and he even invested in a new project that would kill the organization. Misha's daughter's music teacher, a fan of a neoclassical Russian composer, had a musical manuscript he and European friends believed would sell well in the West. He suggested Misha add commentary and liner notes to the manuscript, print it on high-quality paper, and sell it abroad. Misha put together a business plan and realized the project would not be cheap: the translator was English and wanted a high fee, and the special paper was expensive. The Investor agreed to finance the project. The folio was produced in 2003 and sent for sale in 2004, but no one in the West was interested in it. Cost was one problem: the folio cost 1500 rubles to produce (to cover paper and translation), and the retail price of 3000-4000 rubles (mysteriously set) was too high for Russian sales. Musicians abroad were not interested in a folio that, it turned out, was not an original manuscript: it was the famous composer's orchestration notes for somebody else's music, not the composer's notes for his own famous work, and it had already been published abroad. The only people interested in this piece were Misha's daughter's music teacher and friends. Misha and the Investor had not investigated the market (or its lack) for this folio but blindly trusted the music teacher.

The dictionary and folio consumed resources and provided no payoff. By 2004 the Investor was moody and despondent about Economics Inc. and parted company with Misha, reducing funds for projects and everyday operations. Misha proposed or accepted small side projects (e.g. on education) for various foundations. These brought enough money only for immediate survival. Long-distance and other educational programs were winding down or faced competition from foreign and Russian business programs. Desperate, Misha went to banks with various ideas, and finally obtained a loan from an important bank—Misha knew the bank director personally and could use networks to save his organization, as he had done in 1995-6. In 2004 the bank loaned Economics Inc. three million rubles to publish the dictionary and translate business literature. However, the new literature projects provided only enough income to pay quarterly interest on the loan, basic wages, and rent and upkeep at the kindergarten whose premises Economics Inc. used for offices and workspace. The sum total of expenses—the bank loan, rent and electricity at the kindergarten, and general overheads—were greater than income. In 2005, Misha was paying interest on the loan and had neglected the kindergarten rent bill, which was now overdue. Desperate again, Misha went to various well-off entrepreneurs, trying to sell them Economics Inc. in return for funds to cover bills. No one took the bait, although Anatolii Chubais (Misha's acquaintance) provided $10,000, too little to cover debts close to $100,000. At the end of 2005, a foreign group bought out the bank. In a repeat of 1995, Economics Inc.'s creditor bank came under new management who played by the book: they demanded Economics Inc. pay up principal as well as interest on the overdue loan. To Misha's surprise and chagrin, they also started formal bankruptcy proceedings. Misha then went to his wife's son's friend, a lawyer specializing in closing bankrupt firms and hiding their assets.

As noted earlier, Economics Inc. was two separate legal entities: a school and a publishing institute. Misha had founded the school first, which then founded the institute. Later, Misha sold 50 percent of the school to Matvei and the Investor.

The institute in 2005, as in 1995, had copious amounts of literature in storage with potential market value up to twice the bank loan. Misha proposed that the creditor bank take the literature to cover the loan and interest, yet the new bank managers refused. This was an odd moment of Misha being more *homo economicus* than bank managers: bankruptcy proceedings were long and costly, and Misha was not negotiating good terms for handing over the literature—the bank would recoup the loan and interest *and* make profit without a struggle. Misha's new lawyer then used a well-worn trick to evade consequences of debt and legal entanglements, including arrest. Misha resigned as institute manager, and the board replaced him with an unknown woman registered in the Leningrad *oblast'* outside St. Petersburg, likely registered at an address where she never stayed. The institute now had a manager responsible for its debt whom the court would never find (for which the women received a token payment to play the charade). Matvei and the Investor sold the school to this woman for nearly nothing. This was key: if the institute could not pay debts, the court could legally turn to its founder, the school owners (now the woman, not Matvei and the Investor), for payment. At the end of the day, Misha, Matvei, and the Investor were no longer liable for debts. Misha could have sold the literature at reduced prices to an outside entity to keep these assets safe from bankruptcy, leaving the bank with bad loans and no assets. However, Misha decided "to play it straight" and let the bank take the literature in lieu of the debt.

By June 2006, Economics Inc. was gone. Misha was hired by friends at an established economics institute, founded by well-known economists who respected him and were jealous that he developed the idea of translating and teaching market economics literature before they did. (Misha clearly had a creative, entrepreneurial side!) While he continued to come up with new ideas, the bureaucracy at his new place of work was slow and muddled, leaving him feeling down (in Matvei's words). In 2007, Matvei and the Investor opened a new small firm to continue development of the dictionary, and Matvei continued to work part-time on its development.

Matvei claimed that the moral to this history was that Misha, the Investor, earlier managers at Economics Inc., and even he himself were "idealists and romantics" but not "professionals," at least when administering projects and bringing them to fruition. But Economics Inc. provides other lessons. One is that the market, via consumer demand, can signal weak fit between output and consumer tastes, but by itself cannot force change. And Economics Inc. was not a total loser.[62] Its products were good; Matvei *et al* were dedicated to quality work. Despite this, practices of production and sales made this quality producer nearly a value-destroyer.[63] Certainly barter and networks helped it survived as long as it did. The real issue was weak knowledge about how to sell or link production to the market—including something as simple as quantity to produce or how to price and distribute goods. In the absence of overarching enforcement mechanisms such as fields or bankruptcy, market-building was learning new practices by individual managers and firms and the institutionalization of new knowledge and logics in internal procedures and formalized relationships between firms or firms and consumers. Matvei and his group helped improve quality of work and output, but even they did not fully appreciate the marketing logic. Relying on competition alone did not drive change at Atlas or Economics Inc. Learning was more convoluted and important when broader marketing institutions—created and reproduced by actors with shared scripts and logics of market behavior—were inoperative.

Morals of the story: Atlas *contra* Economics Inc.

This chapter may seem at first glance to support textbook economics: the organized, disciplined firm is more successful than the less-disciplined (but innovative and creative) firm. Yet much more is at work. First, the meaning of "success" is not objective and eternal: it may be profit, market share, provision, or something else. Second, *how* both firms set out on their trajectories was more complex than textbook economics allows. This was a story of succeeding or failing to align identities and create collective interests, by navigating and using power-culture to shape narratives, discourse, meanings, practices, and *habitus*. A quick comparison is illustrative. Both firms produced quality goods and services, yet disorganization and weak discipline haunted them—threatening Aleksei and Atlas in 1994, Economics Inc. by 1995. A superficial conclusion would be that managerial capabilities matter—but *what kind of managerial capacities matter* in such a context, saying what about market-building? Ultimately, there was no model manager. The environment did not weed out the weak; it provided ambiguity rather than clear incentives, knowledge, or market enforcement. Its forces were deflected or mediated by networks or dynamics inside firms. Remaking organizational form and practice does not automatically emerge from or follow external forces. Were this the case, trajectories of Atlas and Economics Inc. would be reversed. Both markets were competitive by the mid-1990s, but Atlas proactively altered practices. By the middle 1990s literature on market economies was flooding Russia, and American and Russian universities were setting up MBA programs. If competition was not incentive enough, Economics Inc. faced desperate financial straits; Atlas had side activities and a steady income stream. Atlas had more incentives to be complacent—yet at Atlas capitalism took root.

There were key differences in tactics of leadership and reform that reinforce Pfeffer's and Fligstein's claims about political games and skill required for organizational change; this contrast also shows the importance of levels of knowledge, and that economic change is an organizational dynamic, rather than a pure organizational reaction to external demands. Aleksei and Denise provided Atlas with managers who understood the need for discipline and change; both had the will to incorporate changes. Denise understood the importance of authority, and she put it to use through formal procedures, observation, training, and interaction with staff, inculcating new procedures and meanings of work. Misha talked organization and discipline, but Denise actively used her status and authority to watch, train, and instill concrete routines, practices, and logics. If Denise was willing to observe, correct, and train employees, Misha was not. Most work at Economics Inc. went unobserved; Misha did not subject employees to a disciplining gaze or actively correct their behavior. In short, Economics Inc. did not have a central power actor (like Denise) able and willing to enforce change. Resistance such as Ivan's was not met head-on; Soviet-era practices of work and resistance continued unabated. Misha treated discipline as he treated projects: suggesting it as a good idea but not following through.

Denise and Misha pursued opposing tactics of authority. Denise facilitated change and rationalization by exercising control and cloaking it as building a normal firm. She did not just command, she coaxed. She did not punish, she trained. She created a positive collective identity. She talked to people and offered advice on personal lives and ambitions. She helped Shura pursue media work. She identified with employees as one of them (if first among equals). Resisting Denise meant resisting progress and the Atlas community. Only Ivan, of the original group, saw Denise's project as perverting Atlas's identity and logic. At Economics Inc., Misha facilitated resistance. The absentee manager, he provided opportunity for inefficient or rent-seeking behavior. If he did not care about projects he initiated, why should anyone else? Misha himself resisted imposing discipline and external discipline of competition and debt payment. He wanted to publish and organize courses but avoided the necessary coordination and leadership. He maintained a paternalistic, Soviet-style moral economy and organizational mission in which the firm was more than a community of disciplined, profit-oriented work. Paradoxically, if Denise created company identity and loyalty, Misha created an anomic work force that saw opportunity, not loyalty. His status as founder and director, plus connections without which Economics Inc. might fail, saved him from revolt in 1999. Only when individual interests and opportunity corresponded with organizational needs could discipline overcome resistance and inefficiency. In contrast to purposive, teleological change at Atlas, Economics Inc. muddled through. In terms of power, Denise created dependency (wages and work environment to be lost), controlled agendas and discourse (through Aleksei, controlling gossip), and gained hegemony (American status and transition culture, success). Misha provided little to lose, did not control agendas and discourse, and had little hegemony. Paradoxically, Misha was more *entrepreneurial*: he found a niche (business literature) addressing an important need (market strategies and skills). This was risky: Atlas could return to earlier clients or the shadow economy. Colleagues in Petersburg and Moscow in higher education were jealous of Misha for developing Economics Inc. He did not follow the formula; yet had he used old tactics to avoid bankruptcy, Economics Inc. would have lived on.

These lessons can help us understand change dynamics at industrial firms in the next chapter. Bureaucratic, vertically organized, state-owned, production-centered conglomerates became decentralized, horizontally structured, privatized holding companies. While the core processes are the same, stronger legacies, longer histories, and complex structures expand this chapter's lessons. These firms inherited more employees and managers, impeding coordination of change. All had work histories and deeply ingrained Soviet-era habits: social democracy (awaiting true fulfillment), paternalist provision, shopfloor identity, and resistance to outside forces (state or new owners). Ivan learned foot-dragging and Soviet work from university life and his railroad days. Kirovskii Zavod employees returned to Soviet legacies every day, reproducing them on shopfloors. Middle managers and employees had "local knowledge": they knew their jobs and were the best agents to enact change there. Formal law empowered employees with formal voice to discuss and vote on reforms that employees at smaller private firms lacked. The mission of the post-Soviet enterprise—profit, moral economy and community, or something else—was contested. Reforms unleashed a genie of contention.

3 Contradictions and conflict unleashed

Framing and contesting authority and enterprise restructuring

> For a while [enterprise relations] have a strange character, resembling relations between the former Soviet leadership with autonomous republics. On the one hand [the *kollektiv* has] full independence to decide its problems…On the other hand are attempts to decide the fate of the *kollektiv*…without accounting for the opinion of the *kollektiv* itself.[1]
>
> (E. Frolov, head of Sverdlov daughter firm Stankolit, on enterprise restructuring)

The post-Soviet transformation of larger enterprises was a story of variation and competition in creating new myths and narratives of the normal enterprise and pathways to the Promised Land. As hegemonic state power and Soviet ideology unraveled, managers and employees reshaped enterprises, begetting untold stories of reconfiguring principles and practices of structure and authority. The Sverdlov machine-tool firm and Svetlana electronics maintained structural integrity despite conflict, but were weakened. Structural changes at Kirovskii Zavod and Leningrad Metal Factory were less contentious; both firms survived. In 1993 Pozitron electronics fragmented into independent subdivisions. These firms had similar experiences: vague reform laws, financial crises, loss of East European clients, state as silent owner.[2] Variation emerged from contingent remaking of internal relations and fundamental shifts in meaning and principles of organization: the source of sovereignty, from employee collective (*kollektiv*) to managers and owners; the nature of property and authority, from class-based social property to private property; and the logic of the enterprise as producer of physical goods and welfare to producer of profit.

How do organizations change? What happens when myths and missions are open to change—and challenge? What are fundamental social forces of change and continuity? Russia's experience helps us address these questions by providing not only a context of radical change but also variation in change. Not surprisingly, as Gorbachev's reforms provoked the unraveling of the myth of the USSR as stable community,[3] economic reforms, in the context of democratization and discursive openness of *glasnost'*, facilitated mobilization in enterprises and unraveling of the myth of the unified, normal Soviet enterprise. This suggests that post-Soviet enterprise change was not entirely, if primarily, about seeking efficiency; and that it was not a story of interests alone, as these shifted when individuals and collectivities tried to figure out their places and identities in the new organizational schema. This was a search for normal authority, structure, and practice. It is no surprise that changes led to conflict, confusion, and variation.

This chapter weds insights from neoinstitutionalism (organizations as cultural entities), political sociology (power and framing), and Bourdieu (*habitus* and practices) to an appreciation of power-culture's multidimensionality to better understand organizational change. Fractally, firms are fields; practices and *habitus* contribute to the reproduction of *doxa* (organizational logic) and narratives, which in turn reinforce *habitus* and practices. Like broader structural change, organizational change requires a combination of shocks, and actors able to navigate the multiple levels of power and culture to learn, articulate, and enforce new organizational narratives and *doxa*. I continue to follow Fligstein's and Pfeffer's insights on organizational politics, which Melville Dalton noted less theoretically in his study of networks and authority.[4] Such political tactics are not isolated from power-culture, which will help us understand variation. *Vis-à-vis* culture, managers and employees could talk change, but the fundamental level of knowledge needed for radical change eluded many participants, leading to confusion and conflict over normal enterprise structure, practice, and authority. Tacit knowledge of running a new, decentralized system and handling accountability and conflict was weak. *Vis-à-vis* power, contingent policies and responses altered power relations in our three dimensions, breeding variation. In our schema, this is a *vertical → vertical/unresolved* power shift. Path dependency was a "liability of oldness," an ironic inversion of Stinchcombe's "liability of newness" in which newer firms face obstacles because they are unknown and have less legitimacy and weaker networks. Soviet-era enterprises undergoing reform were older and had more deeply entrenched rituals, informal relations, and interests. Contingencies—claims and policies proposed, by whom and when—also played a role.[5] Change was creative destruction.

Thinking about organizational change

Paradoxically, fundamentals of organizational change require more study. Russia provides an opportunity to examine the politics of fundamental organizational change: what happens when bureaucratic structures at the heart of modernity are subjected to restructuring. Accounts of organizational change privilege property, fields, and laws and do not adequately explore internal processes.[6] Economists define "restructuring" broadly to encompass any change in function—e.g. changing outputs or production processes—and assume structures shift frictionlessly and instrumentally with incentives. Implementation is flipping a switch and requires only managerial willpower.[7] But neat economic theory and closed-ended surveys cannot uncover processes and realities of change, such as the conflict and confusion this chapter documents. Political scientists often miss dynamics internal to firms, privileging classes and the state. Neo-Marxists claim enterprise structure and authority reflect dynamics of classes and capitalism, but they do not unpack the mechanisms behind such authority and ritualized meanings.[8] Organizational change takes a back seat to structures of broader capitalism. Economic sociology has been concerned more with relations between organizations, especially networks and the state.[9] In neoinstitutionalism, fields and states enforce new field logics that define a new organizational normality.[10] Isomorphic mechanisms (coercive, mimetic, normative) pressure managers to adopt new structures and strategies legitimate in an organization's field. Yet *internal* mechanisms by which change is legislated from fields or states are not always specified; real organizational practice might be decoupled from the superficial form, leaving organizational Potemkin villages in the wake of formal change. Frank Dobbin and colleagues showed how laws (e.g. Affirmative Action) become reality inside firms when human services have authority to enforce them, yet the micro-politics of *implementing* new power-culture and normality are invisible in these broad statistical analyses.[11]

Studies of post-socialist organizations have provided some important data and insights. David Stark's work on Hungarian firms undergoing initial reforms noted conflicts over social justice amidst reforms that used markets to counter bureaucratic failure.[12] Michael Burawoy, Pavel Krotov, and Kathryn Hendley noted how change in authority relations within and between firms degraded structure all around, creating speculative "merchant capitalism" and conflict between different actors inside firms. They did not push this empirical insight theoretically, however.[13] Inspired by social movement theory, Stephen Crowley compared radical coal miners versus passive steel workers in Russia and the Ukraine. Benefits in kind made steel workers dependent on enterprises; with higher wages, coal miners were less dependent. After 1989, cultural frames crept in: coal miners expounded socialist norms *against* the Soviet system. Yet Crowley undertheorizes power's dimensionality, does not address categories of meaning and authority, and at heart addresses sectors and not organizations.[14] Simon Clarke and colleagues carried out remarkable empirical studies of post-socialist/ post-Soviet enterprise change.[15] Yet despite rich data, their neo-Marxist framework restricts them. Enterprise change was about power and exploitation, but Clarke *et al* assume structure, even emergent, contains a fundamental fault line between managers and employees; they ignore other possible fault lines (e.g. between subdivisions) and why they might have had effects while others remained dormant. As well, Clarke and colleagues, like Crowley, treat interests as intrinsic from a reified structural environment itself in flux, i.e. myths of the normal enterprise, authority, identities, and interests. In his study of governance at two Czech firms, McDermott focuses on how network legacies and contingent uncertainty contributed to governance confusion, investment obstacles, and conflict, yet he elides categories and claims that are the politics of change.[16] Restructuring is a one-dimensional *instrumental* account of state, managers, and subdivisions trying to establish contracts and asset control. Enterprises become devoid of meaning and authority that bring structures to life. Yet managers and employees sought selves, positions, and boundaries (especially of the *kollektiv*) in a context in flux.[17]

Most studies of post-socialism and organizational change generally are not sufficiently embedded in power-culture to make sense of change and variation; instead they invoke static structure or managerial opportunism and without fleshing out broader processes of discovery and potential conflict from multiple normalities of practice and authority.[18] Post-socialism is about meaning as well as realizing power and interests; we are back to Kennedy's transition culture. Here I follow Tim Hallett's Bourdieusian work: organizational change involves reframing organizational meanings, narratives, and missions; and authority to implement new practices.[19] Further, as political sociology of social movements suggests, organizational politics wields material and symbolic resources through framing. These processes, which we saw in the last chapter on a small scale, expand in complex structures of large enterprises with more rules, roles, and people to coordinate. Soviet anti-capitalism, production-centered principles, paternalism, and vertical control came alive. Workers identified with enterprises, manifestations of Soviet socialism: "Kirovtsy" at Kirov, "Svetlantsy" at Svetlana. Enterprise paternalism reflected a Soviet moral economy of provision that bound employees via dependency and managers via legitimacy. Creating a capitalist firm meant remaking tasks, goals, *and* organizational meanings and logics. The post-Soviet *kollektiv* would obey shareholders and managers in pursuing profit and surplus value for shareholders, not welfare and justice for the *kollektiv*. Enterprise newspapers, absent from small firms, gave employees voice, as did reforms that let them discuss and vote on change. Closer than the distant Kremlin, these changes brought market-building and Russians face-to-face.

Pandora's box opened: the story of enterprise restructuring

First, let me recount the general story of enterprise restructuring. The vertical, centralized Soviet production association (*obedinenie*) was born in the 1970s when the state merged factories, R&D institutes, and shopfloors into vertically structured *obedineniia* to enhance innovation and economies of scale.[20] *Obedineniia* took many forms: "administrative," "production associations" (*proizvodstvennye obedineniia*), *kombinaty* (combines), and conglomerations of formerly autonomous enterprises. A "mother firm" stood atop vertical structure, administering and producing goods and lending its name to the *obedinenie*. Akin to vertical integration, proximity of direct interaction was supposed to foster cooperation between producers of similar goods or suppliers and producers, aiding efficiency and innovation.[21] Centralization and consolidation of smaller units decreased the number of firms under ministerial supervision, streamlining resource allocation and promising economies of scale. *Obedineniia* would facilitate innovation by bringing researchers and producers into proximity. Also, in Soviet bureaucratic politics, *obedineniia* could balance *glavki* or ministries, although the opposite actually obtained.[22] This structure came under strain when reforms increased enterprise autonomy and sanctioned blaming. These changes ignited *prikhvatizatsiia* of authority, as managers used opportunities to skirt price controls. This weakened authority, unleashed competing claims, and generated confusion and conflict over property control, decision-making sovereignty, and the goal of labor (profit or production).

Opportunity, shocks, and blame

Gorbachev used autonomy and socialist democracy to mobilize people and link their interests to socialism. Opportunity for change came in the 1987 law "On Enterprise," the 1988 law "On Cooperation," and the 1990 law "On Enterprises and Entrepreneurial Activity." Initial *khozraschët* (balancing finances) and *kooperativy* brought little relief. Managers then turned subdivisions such as shopfloors (*tsekh*), KBs (*konstruktorskoe biuro*, engineering-design division), and even factories into APs and MPs (*arendnoe predpriiatie*, rented/leased enterprise; *maloe predpriiatie*, small enterprise) with limited autonomy to set wages and to seek additional outside clients to boost income, encouraging responsiveness to the market (such as it was). For APs, shopfloor chiefs arranged contracts, and employees voted to confirm AP status. The AP paid rent for space and equipment and part of profit, filled *obedinenie* purchase orders before those of outside clients, and sometimes could privatize.[23] After 1992 managers used the MP form, with the mother firm as primary shareholder. One variation was the joint venture (*sovmestnoe predpriiatie*, SP), which gave foreign firms a foothold in the USSR and Russian firms access to foreign technology, know-how, markets, and hard currency.[24] Like APs and MPs, they were a panacea. After 1992 foreign firms turned to opening their own outlets or buying firms outright.

Restructuring fell on fertile soil. Managers claimed state-created firms were "unnatural," "monsters," "artificial creations" that "don't need to be around."[25] Decision-making authority belonged not to bureaucrats but to those who knew products and production. The director of chemical firm Krasnyi Treugol'nik claimed, "The present economic situation is such that it will be easier for smaller, more mobile enterprises [APs, MPs] to break free of crisis, as they have greater possibility to maneuver."[26] Svetlana directors hoped "structural *perestroika* of the *obedinenie* and organization of profit centers" would breed entrepreneurial activity. This fed another impetus for reform: managers were dependent on skilled employees who could leave for better jobs. Facing financial hardships and technological degradation, to maintain output managers used Soviet methods of labor-intensive production and maintaining the labor force.[27] Contagion and mimicry also drove restructuring, even if it impeded coordination of production. An example is from a Sverdlov employee's critique of reforms. MP income did not always come from new outside clients—MPs served traditional Soviet-era clients—and restructuring hurt performance if subdivisions subdivided further. Stankolit, a Sverdlov AP, restructured into smaller units for lathes and molten metal products, with no visible benefit as neither product earned as much as castings. American firm OTIS came to MP LenLik for mechanical reworking and galvanization. A castings producer, LenLik neither helped OTIS nor referred them to the proper shopfloor. Had Sverdlov retained structural integrity, administrators would have sent OTIS to the proper shopfloor. But "losses from our alienation, most likely, are greater than gains from initiating independent small enterprises. Initiative could have operated without factory fragmentation."[28]

Hidden in formal claims was a possible cunning motive for restructuring: shell games for profit.[29] With transparency and accountability weak, reforms enabled directors to act opportunistically. Mother firms obtained cheap deficit inputs from the state (raw materials or goods) and transferred them at low prices to shopfloors and APs—who resold them at higher prices to outsiders. In one case, a mother sold raw materials to daughters at $25 per kilogram, who then resold them for $60.[30] This tactic was widespread in the oil and gas sectors; to consolidate authority, oligarchs or majority shareholders (e.g. at Iukos or Lukoil) fought to reestablish control over daughters.[31] Middlemen daughters could skirt anti-monopoly laws restricting prices.[32] AP and MP expenses were charged to the mother's account, but profits stayed with daughters—the mother carried debt and held creditors at bay or went bankrupt, erasing debt. This made the shell game a tactic against outside ownership—a debt-laden mother firm was an unattractive purchase target.[33] Yet the shell game could backfire by unraveling enterprise authority and trust. If managers were confrontational with employees (blaming them for declining finances), employees could use shell games to accuse managers of siphoning enterprise wealth. Such increasing distrust could spur employees to leave the *obedinenie*. The chief of Svetlana shopfloor #88 called MPs "depravity." The mother paid overheads and for energy, and MPs retained profits.[34] Daughters were nominally independent; their cash flow could not easily be confiscated or traced to the mother, making them a means to launder money or hide income from creditors and the tax police.

Implementing the new firm: contradictions and conflict

Instigated to improve production or play the shell game, by 1992 restructuring—and related conflict and confusion—gained a life of its own amid financial crisis, panic, and oncoming commercialization and privatization. Decentralization unraveled power, and what seemed a simple response to bureaucratic failure was now contingent redefining, legitimating, imposing, and learning new *fundamental* organizational principles and practices of authority and structure. What helped make this process contentious was that employees gained voice from two sources. The first was the right to discuss and vote on managers and restructuring. The second was enterprise newspapers that took their mission of openness seriously. Organizational structure became a fault line, as decentralization made mother firm administrators and shopfloors seminal modes of interests and identities. Reforms were shopfloor-based, and discursive freedom empowered shopfloors and strengthened their symbolism. Journalists made shopfloors default actors ("shopfloor #88 believed…") and interviewed employees in that context. Discussions of restructuring and voting (voice) took place in shopfloors. Shopfloors might fight each other, not only managers. Thus, one important dynamic of change was whether employees framed shopfloor interests and relations *vis-à-vis* managers and other shopfloors as cooperative or divergent. This brought up the *kollektiv* boundaries: it could be the entire enterprise, including managers; it could be employees only, headed by unions;[35] it could be individual shopfloors, implying multiple collectives. But the *kollektiv* was sacred, and its meanings and boundaries created contention over who spoke in its name, defended it, and deserved its loyalty. *Kollektiv* sovereignty and authority spilled into social democracy inherent in reforms (employee participation in restructuring and privatization) and put relations of "principal" and "agent" under scrutiny: employees and managers both claimed to be the "principal," drawing legitimacy from the *kollektiv*. Managerial authority stemmed from bureaucratic position, historical elitism, and paternalism. With the lack of private property, the director was *de facto khoziain* (proprietor).[36] Workers' interests were employment, provision, and autonomy—paternalism and fulfillment of social democracy.[37]

Two structural-discursive issues could add to identities of difference and opposition: exchange between mother and daughters, and exchange between newly autonomous subdivisions within the same enterprise. The first was the contradiction between commanded profit-making and producing at low cost for the mother firm, and more generally between new rules and expectations. Daughters were expected to take initiative and responsibility for production, but managers at mother firms might impose plans and procedures. Elektrosila's autonomous daughters had to follow the mother's technical plan, yet "why, with economic autonomy and independence from the center, does the technical plan remain active?"[38] Another contradiction was the classic transfer-pricing problem.[39] Mothers demanded daughters maximize profit and minimize costs, but then required they make cheap goods for the mother (who charged cost plus profit for services). Transfer pricing dovetailed with employees' fears that managers were abusing enterprise structure. Krasnyi Treugol'nik managers claimed "not a single production unit works in isolation from other links of the large technical chain" and warned decentralization was "breaking ties between subdivisions" and "burying the *obedinenie*." Yet one subdivision left the *obedinenie* over transfer pricing.[40] The second structural-discursive tension was between individual subdivisions. If one shopfloor improved performance, others felt pressure to match it, and those offended by ratcheting might not provide successful MPs with materials. Another issue was coordinating, facilitating, and enforcing exchange and payment between shopfloors. This was fundamental—the actual organization and execution of shipping and paying for goods and services between subdivisions. Each MP had its own interests and its own problems; setting up transfers of goods and payments was more problematic than setting up prices, which were negotiated by the MPs themselves. Internal exchange occurred against the backdrop of restructuring, and problems of exchange contributed to the blame and claims about restructuring overall. However, because exchange was closer to everyday work than more abstract (if important) debates about ultimate authority, its disputes were often more concrete and sometimes brought up independently of other restructuring issues. While the issue of sovereignty blazed, employees and managers, and employees of different subdivisions also debated over who had to produce what for whom, and on what legal grounds (contract)—i.e. practical debates as well as abstract.

The heart of tensions over intra-enterprise exchange was accountability and conflict resolution in the new structure. In the Soviet structure (as in capitalist firms), some subdivisions produced inputs for others. In the past this was covered by bureaucratic structure—even when one subdivision might complain about late or low-quality shipments from another, ultimately all costs were covered, and the chief issue was whether a subdivision was held accountable for late plan fulfillment because of tardy supply. In the post-Soviet enterprise, subdivisions worked on a contractual basis rather than through bureaucratic coordination—horizontal, not vertical, relations. In the new "institutional design," managers did not set up mechanisms for sorting out blame, enforcing contracts and accountability, and resolving conflicts arising from misunderstandings or violations of internal contracts. In other words, decoupling emerged between horizontal autonomy and accountability in theory and practice. In theory, giving shopfloors autonomy and responsibility was not difficult; but creating a new system in practice was difficult, as actors moved from bureaucratic accountability and control to a contractual system whose practice managers and shopfloor employees did not understand. The result was conflict, unless enterprise managers retreated from reform and reimposed central control. Subdivisions could come to blows over pricing unfairness, low quality, or shipping delays. Such tensions made it clear that the new normality had not been achieved and that the enterprise was still abnormal. Also, such contention was more possible fuel for blame and claims driving enterprise conflict. Employee–manager relations could be frayed; once relations between subdivisions frayed as well, an enterprise faced the threat of collapse from its own emerging, contingent contradictions.

One flash point for conflict was enterprise paternalism. Paternal dependency supported managerial authority, legitimated socialism, and was seen by managers as duty.[41] This included provision—cafeterias, food from the firm's collective farm, medical and day care, shoes—and property such as *pansionaty* (summer dacha resorts) and apartments. As finances shrank, directors traded employment and services for nominal obedience, sometimes providing cheap bartered goods employees could sell on the side in lieu of a money wage.[42] Workers at one lathe-making firm were entitled to a half-liter of milk daily and a machine to warm their hands. An assistant director complained of too little money to provide what they *should* provide; there was no ill will about the obligation.[43] As finances worsened, managers could flout labor law to dismiss workers, and many asserted that only profitable shopfloors would survive. Yet this contradicted paternalism, and managers had difficulty closing subdivisions and for a time laying off workers, especially if paternalism was part of an implicit pact to keep employee shareholders happy.[44] Kirov director Pëtr Semenenko warned subdivisions of market punishment, yet fewer workers were let go in 1993 than in 1992: "from the point of economics and organizing production, we needed to fire around another thousand people."[45] One instructive example comes from shipbuilder Baltiiskii Zavod. Employees suspected managers took enterprise property to rent or sell; they framed objections in moral terms and social property, i.e. laborers' rights. The flash point was enterprise *pansionat* Ol'shaniki. Employees valued it for summertime rest, but it could be a cash cow for Finnish tourists. V. Shershneva, wife of general director Viktor Shershnev, rented the *pansionat* to independent firm Otdykh-Servis. When employees voted Shershnev out of office, Shershneva lost her job as *pansionat* director, but friendly state officials transferred Ol'shaniki to Otdykh-Servis.[46] The trade union filed charges of misuse and illegal property transfer; some employees shut off Ol'shaniki's electricity and water. When union representatives went to the *pansionat* to inventory property, Shershneva threatened them and refused to turn over keys. *Pansionat* employees claimed a busload of Baltiiskii employees and managers harassed her and staff. Baltiiskii managers later transferred the *pansionat* to a private firm offering employees cheap rates.[47]

Resolving contradictions and authority

The transformation of structure and authority reached its peak with commercialization and privatization—the former setting up formal organizational rules in preparation for selling shares—and then ebbed. Much as ethnic mobilization receded as an "event,"[48] enterprise change and conflict fed each other and receded together. Initial reform unraveled enterprise structure, but commercialization and privatization meant institutionalizing relations, including locating sovereignty outside the firm (shareholders). In this context, managers scurried to guard authority against outsiders and employees through a combination of luck and tactics in power's three dimensions. Managers could use what opportunities they had to legislate and frame new authority against the backdrop of crises, uncertainty, and the inevitability of new market rules. Sometimes an exceedingly problematic firm could splinter into independent components, with less contentious shopfloors remaining together under managerial oversight—sparing managers the need for pacification.

In the first and second dimensions of power (resource and discursive power), managers enhanced legal control of material resources and used dependence and emerging ownership to constrain empowerment and conflict. Some managers who attempted limited restructuring or included control measures (share ownership of daughters) could recentralize by fiat. Others reorganized mother and daughters into holding companies (*kholding*) that often reassembled the original *obedinenie*. Some did both: reorganizing subdivisions as daughters with the mother as a majority shareholder, gaining agenda-setting (discursive) power; and then privatizing mother–daughter combinations as a *kholding* and formalizing managerial control. Employees might be shareholders, but as employees they were subservient to new formal authority that again gave managers final decision-making authority, even if daughters retained financial responsibility and limited production autonomy.[49] Also, employee shareholders had difficulty coordinating action. Svetlana employees asked where all 40,000 employee shareholders would hold the annual meeting—in the city's sports stadium? Creating the *kholding* was not easy—employees wanted to know the impact of the *kholding* on work, authority, and accountability—but managers were helped out by perceptions of interdependency. Shopfloors and subdivisions starved for resources or clientele could work for successful subdivisions; those in dire straits might survive working for clients in the *kholding*.[50] This legitimated the *kholding* sometimes, although the *kholding* could exacerbate confusion and conflict, given problematic manager–employee relations.

In the third dimension (narrative power), continuing crises created trepidation, disillusionment, and disempowerment; managers played on these. Internal conflict and low wages ("too low to buy a sausage") reduced morale and left labor forces of pensioners ("thank God for pensioners, what would we do without them?") or lesser skilled workers with few options.[51] Global capitalism contributed to rebuilding vertical authority for size and capacity: "We did not set out to destroy the large state *obedinenie*, but rather to transform it to unite advantages of small business and of a large company. You remember an American teacher's oft-repeated phrase: 'To compete on the market globally, the enterprise should be large.'"[52] Once-vilified Soviet "monsters" now lowered risk and maintained capacity. Imbuing paternalism with a market logic could aid managerial authority and justify releasing employees or closing daughter firms. Kirov's Pëtr Semenenko mixed traditional and market paternalism, defending his firm by finding patrons such as Caterpillar and maintaining employment as best he could, while applying market logics such as putting weak daughter firms through bankruptcy. (Independent daughters were easier to close than shopfloors that were legally part of the enterprise.) Managers could also play on fears of outsiders and frame privatization and change in such terms: future threats from the state or from foreigners or New Russians buying the enterprise to sell it for scrap.[53] Opportunistic managers were a known evil. If successful, this could strengthen incentives for unity and reintegration.

One tactic was to redefine paternalism to include finances and survival. Another suboptimal tactic was to let subdivisions wither on the vine, with no income and workers leaving, and instigating four-day workweeks or extending the annual month-long vacation. Yet even in 1995 and 1997 managers told me it was immoral "to throw workers out on the street." The general director of a Petersburg furniture factory explained why he could not shed extraneous labor to reduce costs: "I know these people. They are my people. I worked alongside them. I cannot simply throw them out. They have families. I cannot do this."[54] Overall, "maintaining the labor collective" (*sokhranenie trudovogo kollektiva*) was a common priority,[55] and "not rarely, enterprises in an extremely difficult financial situation were more ready to withhold wages than reduce personnel."[56] Not that paternalism was always contentious or problematic. Petersburg's October Railroad continued to invest in the construction of housing and maintain its labor force and "other social issues."[57] The company supported its House of Culture (*Dom kul'tury*), which continued to organize dances, places of rest, concerts, and the like. Using their labor or funds, the House of Culture repaired most of its furniture, physical structure, and so on.[58] Social provision could turn up in seemingly Western firms. Beer giant Baltika maintained a sports center and dental clinic, which one manager defended as natural: when I suggested letting employees be grateful they had well-paying jobs, he responded that social provision was a proper part of normal organization.[59]

Variation: trajectories of restructuring

Lurking in this story was variation in processes and outcomes, in which change was an outcome of dimensions of power-culture and practices of legitimation and contention. As state control weakened and property regimes and fields had not developed, decision-making power devolved to enterprises and managers. In contingent negotiations and responses, innovations from law and events interacted with *habitus* of vertical authority, collective identity, and passive resistance. Because restructuring is remaking authority relations, our dimensions of power should be key to variation, and I propose the following schema using our dimensions of power (resource power, discursive power, narrative power). *Resource power* as axis of variation is the degree of autonomy or dependency between managers and employees and between shopfloors. Paternalism, which made employees dependent on the firm, weakened as new private firms provided alternative livelihood for engineers and skilled laborers, and as enterprise finances worsened— although managers continued to offer some provision. Structural interdependence between subdivisions or between daughters and mother could strengthen shared interests and reduce conflict. This was weaker in electronics firms and research-design divisions that lived on creativity, although sector is not a perfect predictor of conflict.[60] A final form of resource power was procedural control. Soviet-era control worked through bureaucratic structure; decentralization gave shopfloors autonomy, and managers did not apply decentralization uniformly. Some were cautious, others more daring. We see this dimension in operation when actors make claims with data about the necessity or reality of interdependence or autonomy; when enacted policies and practices follow a logic of dependence or autonomy; or when complaints emerge (e.g. one internal supplier abandons a partner, who cannot survive without this supplier, because it can choose new partners).

The *second dimension* as axis of variation was liberalization of discourse and radicalness of rhetoric, including blaming. The greater the decentralization of power and the more radical managers' rhetoric and demands, the greater the potential for contention when managers and employees stake claims to authority, autonomy, and normality.[61] With *glasnost'*, newspapers reported managers' and employees' claims. The more radical these were, the greater the likelihood oppositional identities would emerge. This dimension was not entirely dependent on the first. Enterprises with weak internal interdependence could hold together if discourse created community and unity *vis-à-vis* the outside world or an internal enemy (e.g. top managers). Thus, second-dimensional change depended on how managers implemented change (facilitating shopfloor autonomy and voice) and how employees used opportunities. This dimension could close if enterprise newspapers faced financial hardship or managers regained agenda control; privatization also altered voice. We see this dimension in operation with changes in the number of positions articulated; tone of claims; and degree of effort actors put into making and supporting claims about a particular position—the more often a manager must take a position and expend effort expounding it, the greater the discursive autonomy.

The *third dimension* of variation was perceptions and expectations of empowerment, normality, and others' motives, located in narratives that changed as events challenged perceptions of a possible new social order.[62] We can ascertain this by examining content of employee responses. With low interdependence, liberalized voice, and radical rhetoric, employees rethought authority and expectations of relations, including trust or distrust. Contingent responses could create expectations of distrust or compromise, identities of difference or commonality, and views of power as zero-sum or non-zero-sum. Confrontational managers risked intensifying division and distrust.[63] Responses could then be ritualized as studied trust and united identity or as studied distrust (ritualized accusation and suspicion) ended only by enterprise break-up or one side's victory, e.g. managers able to disprove or co-opt employee claims. Employees could use social democracy to support supremacy of labor, production knowledge, and *kollektiv*. Managers could use emerging capitalist logics of sales or knowledge of coordinating activity to justify authority. Employees could blame managers' policies for crises; managers could blame employees' inability to sell output. In these constructions, the *kollektiv* was sacred but vague. Managers and employees could make claims about its boundaries and who spoke in its name. We see this dimension in operation in logics of claims, explanations, and descriptions of situations—not just categories and tone, but how these were linked in one articulation, and how logics of articulations were linked. We also see this dimension in actors' claims or predictions about future events: what will happen with the fate of a shopfloor, enterprise, or *kollektiv*, for example.

Culture as well helped legitimate power into authority. Open discourse meant new categories and models of normal organization could be proposed, with their logics of power and autonomy. This led to culture's second a role in this story. At the tactical/superficial level, enterprise reforms involved varying degrees of decentralization; this meant not only granting autonomy to shopfloors, but also redefining just what normal shopfloors were supposed to do, and how to do it. Superficially, this meant redrawing enterprise organizational charts (as in the Kirov factory's newspaper). Having a new schema was not the same as having the knowledge to create practices and make changes operational. One problem in particular was creating concepts of responsibility and mechanisms for assigning blame and punishment in cases where enterprise subdivisions came into conflict— for example, for not paying bills or not shipping purchased goods on time. This could create confusion and conflict, and disillusionment with the reform project of decentralization—feeding back into contention over enterprise structure, with employees now at each others' throats. (This contributed to conflict and enterprise collapse at Pozitron, the last case in this chapter.) This is where culture links back to changes in power: less decentralization and reform, less articulation of new models of normal organization—and less chance for the contradiction between superficial and fundamental levels of culture to flare up.

Timing of changes was also important to changes and outcomes. Ironically, managers who took the chance to restructure quickly and early paid a price. Pre-1992 reforms took place in the heyday of mobilization from below. Social democracy had greater currency, enterprise newspapers were enthralled with *glasnost'* and published regularly. Employees had more voice to discuss and vote on change. Empowered early and told clearly they were autonomous and responsible for faults but not always success, employees turned discursive fire on managers as finances deteriorated and signs of shell games emerged. Other managers retained authority by delaying change and MP creation until privatization formalized shareholding in daughters and curtailed employee voice. As the cliché goes, slow and steady won the race.

A case of limited, controlled change augmenting managerial authority and avoiding conflict was Leningrad Metal Factory (Leningradskii Metallicheskii Zavod, LMZ). Managers opened more than twenty cooperatives after 1988 but quickly saw problems. Employees accused cooperatives of reducing productivity by working for outside clients or using cheap inputs as subsidies. Co-operatives also contradicted LMZ as a unified entity. The flash point was co-operative Okhta: critics accused it of neglecting core production, charging high prices, having low discipline, and not delivering goods or payments on time. Okhta's leaders responded that producing for outside clients was their job and criticized centralization and irrational distrust of co-operatives.[64] LMZ managers closed most co-operatives for low productivity or not "justifying themselves," and they were conservative with AP/MP creation.[65] Their alternative was to restructure within vertical authority by turning self-contained "mini-factories" into administratively independent subdivisions *without* financial and strategic autonomy. There was no mention of employees voting on these issues.[66] LMZ managers thus limited employee voice and defended their authority and enterprise structure. In rhetoric, the sanctity of a unified enterprise and structural integrity remained. Blame and accusations were aimed at cooperatives, not employees. General director Shevchenko also framed restructuring and identity *vis-à-vis* external threats of outsiders buying and asset-stripping LMZ. Employees did fret over this and called for mobilization against the state and "external influences," such as *mafiia*: LMZ belonged to the *kollektiv*, not outsiders.[67] Interdependence persisted, discourse privileged structural integrity, and restricted use of APs reduced employee voice. Shevchenko did not make radical claims for restructuring, place the onus of performance on employees, or set up confrontations. In 1998, this unity facilitated employee support against an outside threat in a war for enterprise control (cf. Chapter 5).[68] Only after privatization, when managers had stronger legal support, did restructuring begin. Financial, commercial, and planning activities were handled by one unit, technological services by another, "administration of production" by another, and so on. The goal was not forcing subdivisions to face the market but "creation of a more centralized, concentrated system to administer production."[69]

Restructuring elsewhere was more complex (cf. Figure 3.1).[70] Discursive power (*x*-axis) varies from timid to radical rhetoric and liberalized discourse and agenda control.[71] Material power (*y*-axis) varies from full interdependence to full autonomy/ decentralization. Soviet vertical authority, quadrant I, favored managers and the state who controlled provision, coercion, and discourse. This is *consolidated vertical authority*. Workers had little real voice; resistance was passive; firms showed

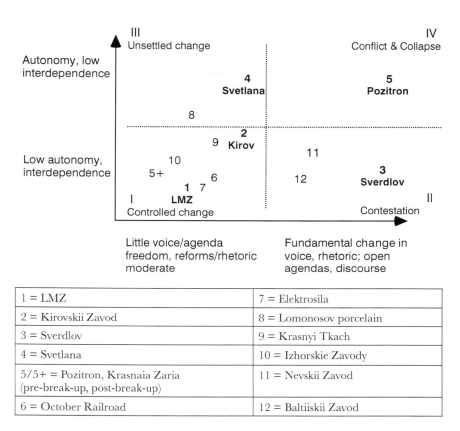

Figure 3.1 Variation in enterprise change

1 = LMZ	7 = Elektrosila
2 = Kirovskii Zavod	8 = Lomonosov porcelain
3 = Sverdlov	9 = Krasnyi Tkach
4 = Svetlana	10 = Izhorskie Zavody
5/5+ = Pozitron, Krasnaia Zaria (pre-break-up, post-break-up)	11 = Nevskii Zavod
6 = October Railroad	12 = Baltiiskii Zavod

little change. The remaining quadrants are different forms of *unresolved authority*. Theoretically we could see *consolidated horizontal autonomy*, although as a rule this did not occur because financial crises, conflict, and the inability of managers and employees to devise workable relations and rules of horizontal autonomy forced reconsolidation of authority. In quadrant II, expanded discourse and high interdependence, we expect tension if employees and managers frame identities and interests *vis-à-vis* distrust and opposition. Yet interdependence mitigated contention. Quadrant III enterprises had weak interdependence but weak voice. With a radical second dimension and weak interdependence, quadrant IV had highest contention. After extensive reading of enterprise newspapers, I evaluated these dimensions for Petersburg firms.[72] Post-privatization firms usually returned to quadrant I for reasons noted earlier. Because of contingencies, graph positions are *potential* conflict. Changes in the first two dimensions allow complex, contingent interactions, expectations, and claims. Sverdlov had more conflict than Svetlana. Svetlana managers negotiated with employees, creating compromise. Sverdlov managers tried to retain vertical authority, shifting blame to shopfloors—a game employees sniffed out, creating studied distrust; interdependence held it together.[73] Radical restructuring, low interdependence, and managers speaking patronizingly for the *kollektiv* and claiming knowledge status created studied distrust at Pozitron. Contingent responses led to break-up.[74]

I chose three cases of variation (Table 3.1). The *x*-axis is radicalness of rhetoric and degree of shopfloor voice and agenda control, and the *y*-axis is institutional and structural independence (daughters' freedom, production dependence).[75] For *controlled change* (I), Kirov (and LMZ), managers contained challenges by constraining change and challenge, by altering paternalism and practice. In *contested change* (II)—the case of Sverdlov—conflict overcame cooperation and control. Contradictory identities predominated; contingent responses fueled studied distrust. Interdependence and institutional control maintained integrity. In *unsettled change* (III)—the case of Svetlana that I refer to in passing[76]—interdependence was weak and identities began to diverge, but rhetoric and discourse favored cooperation. In *conflict and collapse* (IV), weak interdependence and radical rhetoric created distrust and autonomy. Employees could leave for other firms, and new laws allowed subdivisions to privatize independently. Managers lost control over the dimensions of power, and conflict spiraled out of control.

Controlled change: Kirovskii Zavod

Famous Petersburg enterprise Kirovskii Zavod—producer of tractors, tanks, pipes, machine and metallurgical output—shows managers reacting to initial risks, controlling the pace and degree of change, and holding the firm together. Historically the Putilov Works until renamed after Sergei Kirov, Putilovtsy were the more radical of Petrograd's 1917 proletariat; under communism its workers were Leningrad's better-skilled and higher-paid. It was a proud firm whose fortunes declined with the collapse of the Soviet economic zone and conversion to civilian production. In restructuring, management–employee relations were strained and there was blaming, but neither side framed relations in terms of absolute distrust and contention. In this process, General director Pëtr Semenenko maneuvered power-culture processes, not only to hold the firm together but also to reframe post-Soviet Kirov and its paternalism to support managerial authority and to include a market logic. Paternalism no longer meant automatic provision of job or goods; it meant providing enterprise health via patronage or market tactics, and survival.

Restructuring began with *khozraschët*, co-operatives, and elections of shopfloor and factory managers[77] (even if internal elections offered little choice or transparency).[78] This replaced Party activists decrying obsessions with money or low "culture" (*kul'turnost'*).[79] In 1988 twenty co-operatives opened,[80] but Kirovtsy voiced criticism and distrust of co-operatives as unfair competition, parasites receiving subsidies, or managerial scams. One shopfloor chief claimed: "Any co-operative is theft from the state and honest laborers"[81]—an ironic complaint, given that the state subsidized Kirov. Legal independence put co-operatives outside

Table 3.1 Cases of enterprise change

	Controlled discourse and identity	Open, contested discourse and identity
Weak structural interdependence	Unsettled change (III) Weak interdependence, radical restructuring. Limited discursive freedom. Expectations of some contention but possibility of unity. Managerial authority, firm structure survives amid claims & blame. Confusion, contradictions between levels of culture break out, contribute to contention. (Svetlana)	Conflict and collapse (IV) Weak interdependence. More radical rhetoric, open agendas (shopfloor voting, discussion). Narrative of blame, distrust, and empowerment. Diverging interests/identities, ritualized distrust. Managers lose power. Confusion, contradictions between levels of culture break out, contribute to contention. (Pozitron)
Structural interdependence	Controlled change (I) Interdependence, weak restructuring. Discourse controlled after initial changes; rhetoric moderate; little shopfloor voice. Narrative of managerial paternalism and rhetoric of *kollektiv* unity. Organizational integrity and managerial authority persist. Confusion, contradictions between levels of culture muted. (LMZ, Kirov)	Contestation (II) Production interdependence (initial or later survival tactic). More radical rhetoric, open agendas (shopfloor voting, discussion). Narrative of blame/distrust; employee empowerment offset by dependence, finances. Confusion and discord. Authority retained, but with friction. Weak foundation for further integration. Confusion, contradictions between levels of culture break out, contribute to contention. (Sverdlov)

popular redress for perceived injustices, a privilege many employees wanted.[82] This led to broader criticisms. One journalist noted of shopfloor elections, "the feeling did not end that there was a kind of confrontation between workers and the administration."[83] Two gulfs emerged: between co-operatives and non-co-operatives, and between employees and managers. As a factory newspaper reporter noted at a 1989 roundtable, "Workers repeatedly met with managers of another level" yet were "not well informed" on enterprise health and restructuring and had "little faith in tomorrow." Employees wanted to take the initiative, but managers imposed market reform by fiat, contradicting market *and* social democratic logics. "Where is administrators' initiative?" one representative asked. Others discussed justice and provision (e.g. *pansionaty*). Older specialists claimed they worked out of enthusiasm and patriotism, which managerial propaganda still assumed: "administration, trade unions, and party organizations are working according to old methods."[84]

As employee distrust began to build, general director Pëtr Semenenko shifted rhetoric. At an August 1989 meeting with shopfloor 350, he referred to an "unordinary" political-economic environment of "democratization with non-legality (*bezzakonnost'*) and absence of restraint (*vsedozvolennost'*)." The Soviet administrative structure and *means* of production had to change:

> Through natural *khozraschët* and full independence of concrete production [and] economic and financial autonomy, we can sharply change the situation of our affairs...All necessary subdivisions need to be turned over to production. What functions will remain with the *obedinenie*? First of all, social and other important functions, such as guaranteeing technical rearmament and capital construction. It is also possible to transfer energy supply for production, enterprise security and others, without which normal functioning of the productive mechanism is impossible.[85]

In summer 1989 some shopfloors faced a labor shortage, and democratization and shopfloor autonomy were not bringing in employees and investment.[86] Semenenko admitted *khozraschët* was a mistake.[87] Shopfloors needed financial and production autonomy; *obedinenie* administration would withdraw from everyday decision-making and support infrastructure. This met with general approval, as it would allow shopfloor chiefs to raise wages; some complained Semenenko should have done this from the get-go.[88] Kirov's railroad shopfloor was its first AP; in 1989 Prokom was Kirov's first MP. By 1990 six more MPs were born, followed in 1991 by three MPs, one SP, three APs, two independent joint-stock firms, and one limited liability partnership.[89] Shareholding underlie many daughter firms (APs and MPs), helping managers framed the process as profit for employees, whose shares would entitle them to profits: "you will receive a free present of a value that will always bring income to you and your grandchildren."[90] This also provided the means to maintain managerial authority over the decentralized structure.

Employees did not ignore the substance of reforms, and criticism emerged with paternalist and social democratic overtones. A representative of the Leningrad

Council of Collectives noted that privatization and commercialization were more about productivity than employee well-being. A close reading of the new charter (*ustav*) revealed the state would initially hold 68 percent of shares; land, equipment, and social property (e.g. *pansionaty*) remained under state control. One engineer claimed this would not attract investment and demanded clarification of state responsibilities, concrete production goals (types of tractors), and procedures to guard democracy and minimize investment risks.[91] Stories of confusion within Kirov echoed these criticisms. The railroad subdivision AP was immediately "thrown into the water." Purchase orders within Kirov dropped, supply problems rapidly deteriorated, and the AP could not fulfill planned targets. It received a 5,000 ruble prize from the state in 1990, yet Kirov's accounting department had not passed on a single ruble.[92] Managers were quick to pick up on these perceptions. Rather than ignore them or deflect blame to employees (which would be disastrous at Sverdlov and Pozitron), managers acknowledged problems to save the legitimacy of restructuring:

> Judging from these transformations in relations between the *obedinenie* and organized firms…we did not have experience, business accounts, understanding of laws. For example, co-operatives founded in 1988 were far from capable of work efficient or useful to the *obedinenie*. Thus, the number of co-operatives founded by the *obedinenie* was constantly reduced. As a result, [co-operatives] either shut down operation or changed their type of activity, broke their business ties with the *obedinenie*, and the *obedinenie* in its turn removed its institutional support.[93]

Managers now devolved fiscal responsibility and expanded Kirov's boundaries: with the *obedinenie* "Kirovskii Zavod" was now the *kontsern* (concern) "Kirovskii Zavod," made up of the Kirov *obedinenie*, Transmash (in the Tikhvin suburb), and the KB Transmash.[94]

Managers did not frame restructuring as easy panacea. The head of Kirov's property fund, Nikolai Miroshnichenko, claimed destatization was difficult in the absence of a working market. Employees were active participants, and naturally "there cannot and will not be absolute coincidence of interests" between shopfloors and mother *obedinenie*—but this need not lead to conflict. Being relatively up front, managers tried to deflect fears of scams. Daughters would have *obedinenie* representatives on boards of directors to enforce the enterprise charter. Miroshnichenko also noted that *obedinenie* managers retained final authority. New daughters were on enterprise territory; the enterprise charter was the final say.[95] As 1991 ended Kirov was seeking new structure and its place in broader fields; confusion and nervousness were real.

Constructing the post-Soviet Kirov

Financial hardship, negative experiences with initial restructuring, and inevitable privatization and its uncertainties gave managers incentive and opportunity to employ new frames of meaning to moderate decentralization while maintaining managerial authority. Finances and privatization allowed managers to use the threat of enterprise closure to reduce potential squabbling between managers and employees, and between employees themselves. It allowed managers to justify reducing paternalist provision, including overemployment and welfare provision. The result was survival of a hierarchical enterprise structure with devolved financial responsibility.

In 1992 commercialization and upcoming privatization spurred Kirov managers to find optimal enterprise structure. Disagreements between Kirov and the RSFSR Ministry of Industry ensued, although the Ministry soon vanished from decision-making.[96] As Kirov faced financial crises, managers and experts worked through laws and documentation. Employees discussed privatization, managers merged or split shopfloors and rearranged lines of command (e.g. in production and supply). This included merging material-technical services into an energy-electricity division, which would account for expenses rather than assume someone else would cover them. They would also adopt a new system to charge for services, with payments every ten days rather than once a month. Yet Semenenko admitted restructuring was incomplete: MPs and APs were not yet legally independent until commercialization.[97] This did not stop restructuring, and in 1992 30 independent factories and complexes were created: the tractor factory, metal preparation factory, consumer goods complex, specialized machines factory, machine-building, and even accounting, labor and wages, and "white-collar" services.

Commercialization (reforming enterprise structure for privatization) and privatization became central to the restructuring narrative. Kirov managers were quick to prepare appropriate plans, demonstrating they were in charge (aiding managerial authority) and adding legal support to managerial prerogative—in contrast to events at Sverdlov and Pozitron (below). Kirov managers created new fundamental rules of structure and authority that privatization would further consolidate and that *both* market and paternalist rhetoric would justify. Formally, they drew up the formal charter (*ustav*) in preparation for commercialization. The *ustav* covered general characteristics of the firm, legal status, basic activities, administrative procedure, and procedure for ceasing industrial activity.[98] Technically, the labor collective had the right to examine and approve changes in the charter, to make decisions about share offerings, to decide on social benefits for the *kollektiv*, to regulate activities of political parties on enterprise territory, to approve estimates of profit expenditures, and to select a labor council (*soviet trudovogo kollektiva*, STK) to work with the administration. Thus, managers legally maintained existing authority while throwing a sop to employees. Further, rather than shut down discourse or radicalize it through extreme changes and claims (as at Sverdlov), Kirov managers took a moderate route: embracing change and embedding it in survival claims. Semenenko legitimated shareholding and privatization as the only way to improve finances, and thus to maintain support for employees (paternalism). Further, as shareholders, employees would see the need to improve productivity and would accept restructuring as necessary to survival.[99]

At a spring 1992 labor conference, employee representatives were curiously inactive, orating more on general politics than details of commercialization and privatization. Semenenko and outside consultants proposed taking the first route of privatization (25 percent of shares for free) rather than the second (51 percent at full price)—this would leave more capital available for investment in modernization. Employee representatives disagreed; outright employee ownership was a better incentive to productivity.[100]

In August Semenenko expanded restructuring to keep authority in the hands of upper managers and the mother firm. Subdivisions and factories became "self-financing complexes" responsible for balancing budgets but with no control over distribution of property and restricted resource control.[101] Each factory or complex had an account but not independent legal status; only Kirovskii Zavod, the umbrella-like mother firm, had such legal status. All interactions between subdivisions would be regulated by the mother—including resolving disputes between shopfloors, although this did not work perfectly in practice. Semenenko also ended short-term rent, once the basis for co-operatives and APs and a means to avoid Soviet-era wage ceilings and expand employee control, which had become a flash point of conflict. Semenenko thus sought a middle ground between radical decentralization and vertical authority. Market logics dictated the former; many Petersburg firms pursued more radical restructuring that complicated structural integrity and entangled privatization with politics of enterprise authority. Semenenko's middle route adopted both market and bureaucratic logics. Forcing financial responsibility on subdivisions would foster adaptability necessary to survive an unstable environment. Central management and the mother firm would provide basic economic, accounting, and energy services, and would police conflicts between subdivisions. The central administration would control the use of property, opening and closing financial accounts, and appointing subdivisions' managers—implicitly depoliticizing the enterprise in favor of technocratic management.[102]

Semenenko received discursive help from rising claims by managers, shopfloors bosses, and factory newspaper reporters that subdivisions could not survive independently: as one newspaper headline put it, "We need to survive together." The combination of economic shocks (losing income when political networks to Moscow did not provide sustenance) and initial production and sales autonomy led various shopfloor chiefs and workers to see advantages in retaining interdependence. Commenting on restructuring amid economic chaos in 1992, one shopfloor chief noted that "many shopfloors morally were not prepared to display initiative." By retaining integrated structure, subdivisions could help each other, especially if some had fairly secure income streams.[103] There was some wider sentiment from below supporting unity. A survey of several "complexes" (divisions) showed that "in not a single [complex] did the desire to leave this [single] legal entity emerge...Already today, rental firms [APs] that had left the structure of Kirovskii Zavod have made known their wish to return..." *Who* answered the survey was not mentioned.[104] Of course, not everyone was happy. The head of the machine-tool group complained that the accounting department, remaining with the main administration, was no longer servicing subdivisions' needs, such as fulfilling documents: "I do not know how this badly-thought-out step was initiated. This is hardly the way to handle serious economic issues."[105]

Through 1993 commercialization continued and privatization plans were submitted to the city property commission. Kirov now included 51 entities.[106] Keeping all shopfloors and subdivisions on one account would be a nightmare; decentralization to "profit centers" was the "correct path." A 1993 McKinsey study cited some subdivisions where restructuring had neither disturbed "technological links [or] or cycles" nor produced noticeably negative results. At the top was Semenenko and five assistant directors: the main accountant; assistant director for social services (cafeterias, dormitories, *pansionat*, stadium complex); assistant director of personnel relations (personnel, security, KGB "First Department"); assistant director for economics and finance (planning, finance, legal and property departments); and assistant director and head engineer (responsible for several shopfloors and enterprise construction). Several factories answered to the general director.[107] This new schema created some confusion over roles and relations between subdivisions. Reorganization into mini-factories "complicated…the general production situation at Kirov [and] relations between shopfloors of different productions," because of low-quality supplies or shipment problems between shopfloors or mini-factories.[108] The head of energy supply, handling electricity payments to electricity utility Lenenergo, complained that previous payment procedures "were not perfect," but new procedures "were worse:" they included contractual relations between this subdivision and clients, and payment was in two parts, one based on cost of electricity without concern for subdivisions' energy expenditures.[109] Another shopfloor boss complained that titles were changing, and it was unclear who had what duties:

> …the assistant director for production preparation became chief of engineering-technical services. His functions remained the same, but not quite the same: now he fulfills work by contract concluded on all aspects of work that support work of the corpus…There was an assistant director of production…he became an assistant director, whose functions are practically the same duties of a director—in essence he is my double.[110]

Kirov managers understood the strains and called for clarification of subdivision relations, although they did not doubt such changes were necessary to survive market competition.[111]

Semenenko also strengthened his position with a "temporary provision" in the charter that created an administration (*pravlenie*) to run Kirov when the board of directors was not in session or between shareholders' meetings. This gave him authority in such decisions as setting general factory policies in accordance with decisions of the board of directors; preparing wage, labor, and hiring policies; choosing candidates for administrative positions; deciding questions of rent, sale, or exchange of Kirov property; preparing business deals, whose value was not greater than five percent of the previous year's financial turnover; recommending decisions for the Board of Directors on sales or rental of property more than ten percent of enterprise value, expenditure of capital from the reserve fund, calling emergency shareholders sessions, changing the *ustav*, distribution of profits, and conversion of shares from privileged to normal.[112] While strengthening manager authority procedurally, Semenenko *et al* did not neglect the discursive aspect of authority: not closing it down in Soviet style, but not ratcheting up radical rhetoric, accusations, and claims. Rather than act as cocky superiors *vis-à-vis* employees, they took a conciliatory, paternal approach—framing authority subtly as deserved not through position (blatant superiority) but because of hard work and knowledge. Kirov's logic of organization shifted as managers gradually framed policies to emphasize market survival via profit. Once restructuring commenced, factory newspaper columns read, "So many rumors have hit our ears," such as "one of the goals [of restructuring] is the need for new sources to feed the excessively inflated administrative apparatus"—which head economist V. Skatin rejected as against existing rules.[113] The factory newspaper brought up issues and confusions of reorganization, but managers discussed them openly, creating paternal benevolence playing on Russian and Soviet traditions. Managers also cited the fate of the USSR. One of Semenenko's assistant directors noted, "one might get the impression that the factory [Kirov] is falling apart into pieces. This impression is mistaken. The factory [Kirov] has been and remains a single whole. Only it has the right of legal status."[114]

Kirov managers made sure to get space in the enterprise newspaper to reframe social democratic and paternalist logics of Kirov's mission, identity, and organizing principles. Democracy, never trumpeted at Kirov, was secondary to income; paternalist provision meant enterprise survival, not cafeterias. That is, Semenenko *et al* used the surrounding crises *and* paternalism; they could not rebuild the USSR and its welfare system, but they could provide capitalism with a paternal face.[115] Financial shocks and the stereotype of global capitalism were an impetus and justification for the new firm, "the goal of which, as world practice teaches, is creating profit centers inside the [company]."[116] While autonomy and restructuring included "new forms of democratic administration," still "all democracy will be subordinated to the strictest demands of efficient working of capital."[117] Part of the new logic was to make daughters "structures that could sufficiently, operationally reorient to producing goods with current sales." Some shopfloor chiefs latched onto new discourse to propel restructuring—reorganization was not just fiat from above. Aleksandr Moskalenko, chief of a shopfloor stamping metal for tractor components, moved his shopfloor to *khozraschët* and independence. His 110 employees earned, not received, wages; he fined them ("punishment by the ruble") for labor infractions. He exemplified benefits of restructuring and was a counterweight to shopfloors whose "low culture" or "uncultured" work habits hurt Kirov prestige and efficiency.[118] In this logic, some daughters reduced employment to a minimum necessary and charged managers and chiefs to produce for market niches.[119]

Financial shocks induced change and provided justification to change the logic of enterprise provision, trading full social provision for financial health. While he found it "very painful to talk about this theme," Semenenko noted that he might have "to reduce sharply the expenses of the social provision complex"[120] and moved provision to a market basis. Rather than a general enterprise fund covering social expenses, Kirov would sell its services to employees at market prices.[121] Local government would provide some aid, but this only defrayed costs of core services (e.g. medical care, children's provision). Kirov managers turned over kindergarten complexes to the city. Kirov's dormitories, which housed 7,000 people (only half of whom worked at Kirov), required too much investment. The manager of social provision was at pains to show that nothing was *sold*— social property was Kirov's.[122] The trade union demanded the enterprise have an ambulance after the city ambulance could not respond to an employee's sudden heart ailment. Kirov once had an ambulance, but in 1992 Semenenko reduced Kirov's medical transport. Kirov medical personnel were woefully underpaid, as labor reductions did not require investment.[123]

Employment was not spared. By November 1992 Kirov succumbed to a four-day working week,[124] and employees were being let go or were leaving. Kirov had 5,194 fewer employees than in 1991, although managers claimed the majority left for "natural reasons" (retirement, army service, other jobs), and fewer left in 1992 than in 1991. Managers wanted to retain skilled employees but understood they had "to turn away from stereotypes and habitual decisions" and rethink strategies of finance, production, and personnel.[125] The company could provide "internal loans" to shopfloors and daughters only if the debt could be repaid. While some daughters were not doing well (e.g. the tractor factory and turbine division), Semenenko was pleased that subdivisions with independent accounts had improved production and balances. Returning to a five-day working week meant shedding superfluous labor. To make this easier on subdivisions, central administration would decide whom to dismiss. Semenenko added that only 1,995 employees had been let go in January–July 1993, although 1,000 more jobs could have been cut and managers tried to move redundant labor elsewhere in Kirov, e.g. to repairing roads, roofing, or façades, or to other more difficult work, e.g. in the steel division.[126]

Restructuring did not bring immediate relief, which led to moments of tension and a strike threat over wages in 1993.[127] Employees maneuvered within limits set by rules, external shocks, and Semenenko's new enterprise. Yet managers' tactics were working: a combination of discipline and negotiation, addressing employees' concerns but admitting hard decisions such as changing paternalism. Like employees, managers also worked hard to improve sales and win contracts with wealthy clients for Kirov profit. Despite confusions and tensions, managers and employees constructed a post-Soviet Kirov with less paternalism and more market discipline but that retained solidarity. A telling sign of the shift in enterprise logics and power comes from the enterprise newspaper. While restructuring, privatization, and internal relations were prominent from 1990 to 1994, after 1995 the predominant theme was sales—plans for new goods or attracting new clients—or Kirov's finances. Daughters were discussed in managers' reports of Kirov's health; fulfillment of output plans, debts and income, issues of quality and production were reported regularly in meetings between managers and the press. Semenenko praised and criticized daughters—but managers, caring for Kirov, made sure discourse centered on profit and survival.

Post-Soviet Kirov

In 1994, Kirov was a joint-stock company—managers referred to Kirov not as *"obedinenie"* but as "AO" (*aktsionernoe obshchestvo*), "the company." By 1995 Kirov journalists and employees looked on daughter APs and MPs as survivors. Reflecting on restructuring, Semenenko noted that "integration of Russian firms on the basis of voluntarily created unions [was] one of the preferred paths for exiting economic crisis." The creation of *obedineniia* in the 1970s was reversed into decentralization in the 1980s and 1990s, but this created problems. One was the initial euphoria of freedom, when managers felt they could set prices and produce as they saw fit—an illusion quickly dispelled as sales declined in the 1990s. Another was that various enterprise subunits needed each other to survive. By 1993 Kirov was made up of more than 70 different structural entities, although by 1995 there was consolidation and the number of daughter firms dropped to 24.[128] Semenenko admitted that shareholding and privatization had given employees little except share dividends. Mass employee participation in choosing managers and decision-making was problematic—too many people were involved, and the firm needed one responsible *khoziain* (owner). By 1995 Promstroibank and Rosneft were major shareholders, squeezing out employees. Semenenko claimed he favored internal democracy, not through votes or campaigns but via structural decentralization and participation of the labor collective trade union.[129]

In 1997 Kirov celebrated 200 years of life and five years as a joint-stock company.[130] Semenenko hailed Kirov as "pioneer" embracing the market. New meanings (property, owners, shares) encountered early problems; it took many meetings with employees and union representatives to explain privatization and benefits of privatizing as a single entity. Managers at other enterprises wanted "absolute independence, i.e. to take a piece from the 'cake'…and conduct their own developmental policy," but they appreciated and copied Kirov's integrated structure. By 1997, most daughters had gone through the difficult "survival" stage, when "everybody worked inefficiently." Now effective work was crucial to survival, and managers of underperformers were replaced by those "able to adapt to the market." The shift in discourse was complete: oriented to profit, balancing income and expenditures, expediting daughters from financial crisis, and efficiently using resources.[131] Financial health, profits for the *kollektiv* rather than shareholder value alone, justified reorganization and managerial authority. Production and income allowed post-Soviet provision—no income, no provision—and central to new social provision was a timely, reasonable wage. "Social defense" of employees remained a goal, and expensive provision such as vacations would come later.[132] Even the labor force changed: from over 20,000 employees in 1990, to 8,500 by 1999, with many laid off, gone elsewhere, or retired.[133] Commensurate with this shift, a daughter's life depended on earnings. To save Kirov, Semenenko was ready to create, merge, or liquidate daughters. Such daughters as Universalmash, Unikom, OPEK, or other underperformers might be consolidated or restructured until the right organizational formula was found.[134] Daughter firm Kirov-Energomash faced bankruptcy, and her managers spun off three profitable subdivisions (Reduktor, Atomenergo, Ikar) as ZAOs (*zakrytoe aktsionernoe obshchestvo*, closed joint-stock company).[135] In 1998 the property of bankrupt daughter Kirovremstroikompleks, which had done "firefighting" repairs, was sold at public auction. The director, in good cheer, admitted his division was never profitable, and other private firms did the same job at lower cost. All 66 employees were sufficiently skilled to find work.[136] Even profitability was no savior: ZAO Reestr was profitable, but legal changes required additional investment for registration, and managers decided it was cost-effective to close it.[137]

Semenenko maintained authority and held the enterprise together, projecting paternalism and bringing in business from General Electric, Gazprom, and the city. One analyst noted, "Semenenko is a very fortuitous mix of traditional Soviet director and market industrialist…Thanks to his Soviet habits, he was able to keep the plant from falling apart through the difficulties of the last 10 years."[138] Semenenko said he understood employees' reactions in the early 1990s: resistance had a "psychological character. People who do not understand things entirely said that the director was taking apart the enterprise and breaking it up into pieces, and that nothing will come of this." Overcoming this required intense propaganda work at meetings with union representatives and employees. He was successful because he wielded both administrative and engineering knowledge—knowledge of how to run Kirov and how Kirov operated.[139] The 1998 ruble crisis hurt sales and finances for most Kirov daughters, while some—Petrostal' (steel exports), Splav, KirovTEK—overfulfilled output plans.[140] Restructuring helped managers see *how* the ruble crisis affected Kirov and how to further reorganize (including post-1998 mergers and concentration of capital).[141] The crisis also shifted blame to Moscow, another boon to managers. (Semenenko received additional support when Yeltsin's government decided to use American aid money to purchase John Deere tractors. That Kirov had survived August 1998 and now had to unite against unfair American competition further aided the sense of enterprise community, with Semenenko at its head.[142]) Whether from luck or skill, Kirov managers managed to navigate the currents of power-culture and harness it; even if no longer the pride of the city, Kirov survived.

Contradiction and conflict meet interdependence: Sverdlov

This case demonstrates interaction of discourse, structural interdependence, framing, and studied distrust. The Sverdlov machine-making enterprise (maker of castings, lathes, and machine-tool components), an *obedinenie* with pre-Revolutionary roots, was crippled by conversion from military production, loss of clients in the former USSR and East Europe, and competition. Restructuring only added to the pain and hindered innovation and production. Rather than wait for privatization or after as at LMZ or Kirov, general director Viktor Pokasiuk moved early and quickly to apply AP and MP reforms. He cajoled employees to use reforms to work independently for better wages—and he was quick to criticize. Pokasiuk initially blamed enterprise hierarchy for hindering efficiency and innovation, but then turned on employees. Yet an astounding degree of discursive openness via the factory press and endless manager–employee meetings gave shopfloor bosses and employees the capacity to mobilize and counter-criticize as finances worsened. Managers and employees framed oppositional normalities: managers accused employees of irrationality, employees accused managers of incompetence and intrigue. The panacea of restructuring became a curse, and Sverdlov mirrored Russia's conflicts and confusions.

Innocuous beginnings to end of innocence

Sverdlov's reorganization began with *khozraschët* and *kooperativy* (co-operatives), and Pokasiuk blamed their failure on employee mentalities, not managerial practices or the Soviet economy. In his December 1989 New Year's address, Pokasiuk claimed reforms failed because popular mentality "was not prepared to accept even *kooperativy*."[143] Employee interests had to be linked to better performance and work habits, e.g. ending equal wages in brigades. An assistant director commented, "So far there are very few who would say, 'Comrade general director, I am ready to work in a new way.'"[144] Something radical was needed: the *arendnoe predpriiatie* (AP).[145] In early 1990 AP rules were published, enticing discussion of restructuring.[146] A former Sverdlov brigade and shopfloor boss claimed AP status linked employees' interests to enterprise performance via autonomy to set output and pay norms.[147] Employees traveled to Bashkiriia to observe APs in action; this legitimated APs, although some doubted they added much value.[148] On July 26, 1990, the *raion*-level Soviet of People's Deputies authorized AP status for castings shopfloor PDO-2: Stankolit, Sverdlov's first AP, was born after a long bureaucratic ordeal. First MP Reserv was soon born from a ten-man brigade of shopfloor #30.[149] According to Stankolit and Reserv chiefs, morale and work incentives improved.[150] An enterprise economist and assistant director claimed this would create economic dynamism as in the United States and Europe.[151]

To Pokasiuk shifting autonomy and responsibility to employees was vital to survival: "Reorganization…is directed at improving administration and administrativeness of the *obedinenie*, and…at deciding questions of actors' economic attitude both to the means of production and its product." In the feared economic downturn, when Moscow was planning a tenfold drop in capital investment, shopfloor employees had to respond to new realities in which "only those who can put out machines and who can bring in buyers will survive."[152] APs would also tap *nalevo* work (work under the table). If employees worked *nalevo*, demand beyond official state purchases existed and could be tapped for the enterprise: "That which shopfloors do today *nalevo*, they will do in a legal manner, hiding nothing…The idea of any reorganization arises from the need to restructure administrative work such that [the new system] united goals of the *obedinenie* with the goal of each worker, to arouse interests in each person in attaining goals of the entire obedinenie." This would help Sverdlov retain skilled employees as well.[153]

Reorganization was not limited to efficiency and wages. Financial autonomy meant devolving authority to employees, and the issue of enterprise democracy appeared. The head of the economics department suggested that a restructured Sverdlov be run democratically by an administrative board made up of AP/ MP directors and union representatives. Pokasiuk protested: "No democracy should interfere with production. There should be army discipline...What kind of 'democratic path' can there be if the market dictates conditions?...A single person should make decisions. The aim of administration is to *discuss* how quickly to decide this or that problem." Pokasiuk noted an inverse relationship between "results" and numerous meetings and debates—empowered voices and shopfloor democracy. To a question about further discussion of restructuring at the upcoming labor collective conference, Pokasiuk answered, "We don't need meetings. They lead to one thing—criticism. That is bad and should not be. Problems will be discussed by collectives of future MPs. Discussions in general— no one needs them."[154] Pokasiuk supported decentralized decision-making for immediate production issues, so shopfloors could "quickly reorient themselves, quickly restructure themselves" more efficiently on their own instead of waiting for orders. Yet ultimate authority would remain with him.[155]

Two views of normality were forming: managers claimed the right to rule from organizational position and superior knowledge, and employees cited reforms and shopfloor democracy. In defense of managerial power and shopfloor accountability, economics director V. G. Koriakin used Soviet and global logics *à la* transition culture. Sverdlov's current structure was like a collective farm (*kolkhoz*). The new normality meant APs, MPs, and undefined "market" relations, with central administration ultimately in control and shopfloors making immediate production decisions. Thus, criticism of reform was abnormal. Koriakin mocked: "The less a person knows, the simpler it seems to him to solve economic problems. It seems simple to solve everything, but nothing is done because our administrators are fools and lazybones." Socialism's stable prices and work were abnormal, and disagreement was a deviation from common sense.

> The majority thinks partitioning the *obedinenie* will destroy the enterprise and that this will be an economic catastrophe. Public opinion is accustomed to stable prices and that we will not move to a market. Opponents talk of how we once turned out more and better lathes, and so why think up [MPs]? Studying foreign experience, we confirm that abroad there is constant reorganization linked to the market. As the market changes, production changes. If firms do not reorganize, they go bankrupt...Many questions are decided at the level of *obedinenie* management, but they will be delegated directly to MPs...Issues of general *obedinenie* development remain with central administration, and issues of interrelations between MPs and development will be transferred to [MP/ AP chiefs].

Not everyone trusted Pokasiuk or shared his confidence. In shopfloor meetings employees questioned his claims about problems, blame, and solutions, and they began suspecting managerial intrigues behind crises: managers wanted to gain the lion's share of profits or were hiding corruption or incompetence. AP restructuring smacked less of market-oriented transition than the command-administrative system, directed from above. Many believed managers were reorganizing the firm to create more places for administrative personnel, to improve perks, or to control property and deprive employees of what was rightly theirs. Others believed restructuring would "destroy the *obedinenie*, annihilate the enterprise [and] be an economic catastrophe."[156] Some employees firmly believed lack of accountability and transparency let managers hijack restructuring; the solution was openness and shopfloor democracy.

By 1991 employee voice grew louder with a liberalized enterprise newspaper and voting rights over changes. In a February 1991 meeting of managers and employees, Pokasiuk had to defend and legitimate policies. He claimed employees, not managers or the state, drove AP and MP creation. These promised higher salaries and easier supply and sales via direct relations with other APs/MPs. Restructuring would save paternalism: Sverdlov could not provide apartments or goods, but employees with good wages could provide for themselves. (Still, in 1991, Sverdlov managers used hard currency reserves to buy Lenwest shoes and bartered for video equipment.) Pokasiuk also invoked the specter of unemployment: "The administration…is not planning firings, but I do not exclude this [possibility] at [APs and MPs]."[157] At a March 1991 roundtable Pokasiuk noted: "the idea of any reorganization arises from the necessity of restructuring administrative work to combine goals of the *obedinenie* with the goal of each worker." Calling for patience—there was no single model for independent shopfloors, and laws were weak—Pokasiuk claimed Sverdlov "gained serious positive experience—what was being lost, why it was being lost and why *khozraschët* relations did not work." He reiterated that shopfloors wanted independence, reorganization was "from below," and mother firm directors and MPs were redefining relations along the way. He even called the *obedinenie* an artificial state creation unifying diverse shopfloors by decree; legally it "no longer existed" and needed a new charter.

Stankolit boss Frolov answered that restructuring hurt performance. Pokasiuk was right earlier, that reforms let employees work for themselves, but the context had changed. Shopfloors were swamped with restructuring and its bureaucratic documentation, and now had to seek supplies and sales. There were too few specialized services to handle legal and bureaucratic issues or save subdivisions from "wasting time on internal organization." Also, not all shopfloors should be APs/MPs. Some services were necessary at low cost for APs and MPs to make a profit, especially if they sold goods to other shopfloors at low prices. If Stankolit charged Sverdlov low prices, Sverdlov should reciprocate. Sverdlov head engineer E. V. Kriukov backed Frolov; restructuring was breaking the *obedinenie*, harming shopfloor relations and cutting needed services. Restructuring turned a *kollektiv* into a collection of actors oriented to individual gains rather than a collective good, as some AP and MP leaders had already warned: making small firms independent hurt such necessary services as supply, research and quality control, accounting and selling, and so on, thus "burying the *obedinenie*." Pokasiuk rejected Frolov, claiming the real problem was unclear agreements between Stankolit and clients.[158]

Other emerging issues were trust, managers' real aims, and corruption. Union representatives accused Pokasiuk of using restructuring to marginalize them.[159] A roundtable planned for September 26, 1991 did not occur when management representatives did not show.[160] Later, one assistant manager claimed reorganization was not "dogma" but "orientation" for adapting to new economic realities. Others disagreed: new authority relations were confused, and Sverdlov hovered between decentralization and vertical authority—managers wanted power without responsibility, but shopfloors would get responsibility without power. A shopfloor boss complained that restructuring, like past reforms, was imposed from above via administrative means. Some shopfloors were internal monopolists; with autonomy they would raise prices and hurt others' competitiveness. Another shopfloor boss complained that reforms from above gave shopfloors responsibilities without real autonomy. Shopfloors should take on AP/MP status only on their initiative—a comment contradicting Pokasiuk's claim that employees drove change.

In late 1991 relations between divisions were more contractual and horizontal,[161] but MPs were in trouble: "it is not worth hoping for growth in production output (to raise wages)."[162] Restructuring created confusion, higher wages for managers, supply problems for shopfloors—but no improvement. Employees began to suspect managers, and Pokasiuk took a hard line on restructuring, discipline, and autonomy within vertical authority—shopfloors would take blame for problems, and the firm would take credit for successes. Distrust now took root in discourse.

Rebuilding post-Soviet Sverdlov

Timing and content of pre-1992 discourse had significant repercussions. Quick adoption of decentralization and radical reform rhetoric and implementation increased employee voice and counter-claims. Pokasiuk championed a restructured Sverdlov as a collection of independent daughters whose failures led to crises. This rhetoric of blame, instead of moderate rhetoric of a united manager–employee *kollektiv*, created a fault line between all-knowing managers and less-than-responsible employees. But discourse was open. Employees countered that managers' intrigues were destroying the *obedinenie*, and that their privatization tactics—mother and daughters privatizing at the same time but independently—would make Sverdlov a weak confederation with persistent legal and symbolic identities of separateness. Financial crisis exacerbated oppositional identities, and criticisms of restructuring became yet more contentious.[163] Stankostroitel' employees complained the mother paid late and fixed the books to make the daughter appear to lose money; yet Stankostroitel' accounted for one half of Sverdlov's output and income.[164]

An illustrative case of new claims and fault lines was at shopfloors #32 and #38. In 1991 managers proposed uniting them into an AP, and as per their right employees held a conference to discuss the plan. A charter had been adopted, a director appointed, a bank account opened, and several workers moved from the *obedinenie* to the proposed AP. At a follow-up conference in early 1992—a formality of collective approval—a majority of employees voted against AP status. One boss railed that employees "don't understand how they will benefit" and Pokasiuk argued that there was no alternative, but in the previous six months opponents had mobilized support against the plan. Employees suspected management's motives: "the growth of administrative personnel and the lack of correspondence between several leaders of the *obedinenie* with duties they occupy." These employees feared that "as a result of the transition to rental form and organization of small firms, only the administration, and not workers, would be winners." The proof was that bosses raised their own salaries after AP or MP status was achieved regardless of performance, violating the principle of wages based on profits. "The principle of 'wages should be earned' has so far only been declared [and not enacted]." As further proof of a con, those against AP form mentioned that workers did not know terms of AP rental contracts.

We should be wary of conspiracy theory in this debate. One employee claimed MP "Uslugi" paid the mother 68 percent of its earnings. No one could confirm this, and another AP boss believed the mother received only 17 percent of their earnings. Of course, "in the end, the matter is not figures but trust," of which there was little. Numbers alone were less convincing than general discourse, loaded with cynicism and distrust of managers' real motives. Workers at AP Stankostroitel' claimed numbers of administrative personnel had grown several times, and that "creation of an AP changed practically nothing either in conditions of labor or wages." Stankostroitel' employees knew of no plans to address financial crises, and workers at shopfloors #32 and #38 had no faith that managers had contingency plans. Worker Iu. Stoliarov claimed managers would privatize the *obedinenie* as individual AP/MP units, leaving workers not with real property but with "empty shopfloor boxes and machines." Few believed otherwise: as one worker said before a vote on AP status, "all is clear: again they are deceiving us. Let's vote against it." The reporter suggested, "It is possible that independence and renting are a good idea. Only organizers [of this idea] did not succeed convincing people of this—they did not have enough arguments. Perhaps they were 'shy' about showing their cards to outsiders?" Managers provided little on plans for surviving financial crises, on privatization and the role of the mother firm *vis-à-vis* MPs/APs, on wage procedures, and on benefits of APs versus *obedinenie* unity and structure. Yet managers' rhetoric of transition culture, framing restructuring as Western, legitimate, and inevitable, crept in: "The West lives—and lives well—by the laws of the market. And we cry about guarantees, forgetting that conscientious work of all should be the single guarantee."[165]

Worsening finances and privatization exacerbated employee–manager tensions in 1992.[166] Finances dictated path #1: enterprise economists and 80 percent of Sverdlov's workers decided path #2 was too expensive, even if shares acquired were non-voting. Some MP bosses claimed privatization path #2 would keep the *kollektiv* together, even if it meant loans and debt.[167] By late 1992 enterprise relations were agitated by news that Sverdlov would not privatize as a single, multidivisional entity, but as a *kholding* of independent subunits and mother factory. Some feared inevitable bankruptcy, breaks with supply partners, rising costs for the mother's services, or being sold to outsiders. Pokasiuk stressed *obedinenie* solidarity and the wisdom of his plan:

> We are seeking ways to overcome contradictions. Leaders and collectives of leased enterprises, aiming for full economic independence, in reality have not yet realized they can survive only in the *obedinenie*. They are forgetting their enterprises' work has greatest effectiveness only *in the obedinenie*...and they know and trust *only the obedinenie*. One should not forget that loans we receive are given *to the obedinenie*, that energy we use is regulated *through the obedinenie*.[168]

In 1993 the *kholding* was mother factory and more than 30 "legally independent subdivisions" linked in "a single productive chain," with "production organization oriented to the previous structure at the *obedinenie*."[169] A possible shell game, this kept alive manager–shopfloor fault lines and tensions of independence versus control—as witnessed in contentious debate, at a March 1993 labor conference, over wages, internal exchange (late shipments, defective materials), and social provision. Up to 100 million rubles of prepaid purchases remained unfulfilled due to lack of material and labor, and union representatives blamed managers: decline in demand began before 1992, managers should have had survival plans, and turning Sverdlov into APs and MPs hurt production.[170] Ongoing privatization brought different normalities and interests into sharp relief.[171] Employees were anxious to know their fate, but managerial silence bred rumors. One was that AP Stankostroitel' would privatize independently. Managers wanted path #1; Stankostroitel' leaders wanted path #2 to give employees control. At a Stankostroitel' conference, Pokasiuk said AP independence would hurt Sverdlov, and KUGI[172] would forbid it. Some claimed Sverdlov was falling apart, so why not privatize independently? Others believed privatizing together meant bankruptcy together.[173] Suspicions over privatization grew with managers' contradictions over the *kholding*. Managers talked of strengths of decentralization and its impulses from below, yet restructuring was limited, and the *kholding* would keep authority in the center—old wine in a new bottle.[174] Evgenii Frolov made this comment on mother–daughter relations:

> For a while [relations with the mother factory] have a strange character and resemble relations of the former Soviet leadership with autonomous republics. On the one hand is full independence to decide problems that can become general if casting production stops. On the other hand, there are attempts to decide the fate of the *kollektiv*, which for three years has been an independent enterprise, with no account of the opinion of the *kollektiv* itself.
>
> This has especially come about with the appointment of the first assistant to the general director, E. A. Grishpun, who considered himself as having the right to decide on his own both questions of privatization, ignoring, by

the way, even the opinion of members of the privatization commission, set up by an executive order of [Sverdlov administration], and questions of the unification of enterprises of the lathe-making complex…[175]

As 1993 progressed, finances and productivity dropped, fears swelled, and distrust between managers and shopfloor grew as Pokasiuk attempted to shift accountability to employees and claim managerial superiority via knowledge and organizational position. Employees asked why MP workers initially forbidden from participating in privatization could do so now that they had threatened to privatize independently. If subdivisions privatized independently, would employees receive shares in places where they worked earlier?[176] Top managers scrambled to regain the discursive high ground. Deputy general director Efim Grishpun pleaded to keep politics out of production.[177] Privatization debates were best left to elections or demonstrations; laws must be followed and Sverdlov must remain "a unitary organism." To Grishpun, "*kholding*" was just a legal buzzword. Most APs and MPs had privatization plans by October 1992, and KUGI apparently "understood that they should not break up [Sverdlov]." Grishpun tried to undercut workers' claims, using survival to justify privatization and market normality.

> Opponents [of privatization] always say, "This is our factory." They are mistaken. This is not our factory, it is the state's factory. The state is the property owner. Wages are ours…The state is *khoziain* [owner] and hired us…We are all its hired employees…The state as owner of [profit] simply turned over the right to use profit. Many do not understand this point… The main goal of privatization is to attract capital, including private capital, for investment…No one turns over their money just like that. Why should someone give the Sverdlov factory a present of [capital investment]? [The investor] wants property rights. That's normal. *The whole world lives that way.*[178]

Yet distrust over restructuring persisted, articulated in a 1994 petition at a meeting of managers and union leaders. Workers' representatives asked the factory newspaper to examine social provision, sales abroad and at home, and factors hindering production. Drawing attention to problems of trust and accountability, they demanded publication of "concrete documents" relating to "collapse of the *obedinenie* and who is at fault for this," specific steps for improving Sverdlov's finances, and how work and authority would be organized. In response, Pokasiuk held a meeting with managers and shopfloor representatives and denied Sverdlov's collapse:

> You ask, "Why is the *obedinenie* falling apart and who is to blame?" Let's think about what we mean by "falling apart." That it is divided into a host of small firms, or that we don't have purchase orders, or something else? Stankolit and Stankostroitel' employees who voted to create APs are *kollektiv* members and believe that they work independently…I today stand on those same positions and do not think the creation of APs or MPs is the collapse of the *obedinenie*.

Thus Pokasiuk shifted blame away from management. The number of administrative personnel was increasing at subdivisions, not the mother. The most important job was "to sell lathes, to receive money for them. And here there is only administrative work." One head technological engineer retorted that "you will find before you two or three people" responsible for enterprise collapse—a reference to Pokasiuk and company. A laboratory boss and union representative asked for proof that APs and MPs brought in money. A "veteran of labor" noted that if years of work were planned out in socialism, in capitalism the firm lived day to day. The AP/MP experiment was a mistake—newly independent shopfloors and other subdivisions were producing less and real wages were dropping, when they were paid at all. Pokasiuk answered that the newspaper was providing inaccurate information, skewing perceptions, and stirring up a certain type of blame. Problems with salaries, he said, were the fault not of managers but of individual MPs and APs.[179]

By April 1994 St. Petersburg's KUGI approved Sverdlov's privatization and plan for a *kholding* of mother firm and several daughters.[180] Assistant director Grishpun broke the news, but his speech did not ease fears. He admitted it was unclear what constituted a "controlling packet" of shares or who would own it. It was possible that Rosstankoinstrument, a company based on the former Ministry of Machine-Building and Tool Industry, might gain 10 to 20 percent of Sverdlov shares that "will allow enterprise administration from Moscow, as earlier." Grishpun was not sure KUGI would allow this. Two months before the July 1, 1994 deadline, necessary documents for voucher privatization were not ready—the fault of managers and KUGI, he admitted. Grishpun ran into trouble when he announced that the mother firm and a few APs would privatize together, but legally independent SPs and MPs would not. One employee implied this was a managerial double-cross. Had shopfloors refused autonomy, they would be part of the mother and could participate in privatization—but Sverdlov management discussed this aspect of restructuring only with shopfloor managers, not employees. Other workers chimed in that something was amiss: some MPs had been in the Sverdlov mother but now were not and could not participate in privatization— why, if they were once a mother firm subdivision? Again, employees articulated distrust in managers who did not explain restructuring and privatization.[181]

In May, similar arguments resurfaced at a labor collective conference. Pay and social provision—whether they would be provided and correspond to inflation— dominated discussion. Pokasiuk claimed Sverdlov would do its best to meet obligations, but finances made this difficult; he blamed the state and economy. Evgenii Frolov again was chief critic. The trade union "ceased to defend laborers' rights and interests," and Sverdlov was steeped in incompetence. A. E. Taranchuk, head of MP Uslugi, attacked the union for doing little work. A technician claimed the union had stopped Taranchuk from privatizing a Sverdlov *pansionat* for himself. Not all shopfloor bosses disagreed with Pokasiuk, and some attributed blame to employees and shopfloor bosses. Iurii Shafranskii, whose modest success as manager of MP Universal justified restructuring in a loose confederation, claimed that not everyone who understood "independence" lacked "legal and economic literacy" or suffered "inertia of thinking." Universal understood how to use autonomy to improve finances and production and "not to be a parasite on the *obedinenie* 'body.'" He did concede that "some centralization again might grant a positive effect."[182]

On June 21, 1994, KUGI approved Sverdlov's plan to privatize as a *kholding* of mother (Sverdlov) and five daughters. The *kholding* owned shares in daughters, which "guaranteed administration of a single technological process of preparation of our basic output". Not everyone was enthralled: some opponents threatened legal action, but Grishpun ignored them and asked them to be literate if they employed their favorite tactic of sending letters to directors' homes. (Note the arrogance.) Perfect justice was impossible, and managers had not committed gross violations for personal interests. Privatization and new organizational structure were unveiled in September 1994.[183] Managers announced Sverdlov would privatize as a loose confederation of autonomous sub-entities in *kholding* form—combining independent and joint privatization.[184] To survive a market needing only 40 percent of Sverdlov's capacity, the *kholding* would be "squeezed" to optimal size, with unnecessary property sold for capital. This would retain "technological chains" of production—not closing shopfloors of crucial output, and keeping as many employees as possible, with social support to balance adjustment pain. This was possible if Sverdlov privatized—a state-owned Sverdlov could not sell unnecessary shopfloors and property.[185]

As 1994 ended, Sverdlov remained deep in crisis. Pokasiuk blamed "low qualifications," although he attributed slow enterprise *perestroika* to "all of us. Our thinking, our habits, our fears..."[186] In 1995 ultimate authority was with shareholders and managers. Enterprise discourse closed up. Shopfloor meetings were rare. Enterprise journalists focused on crises, sales, and finances rather than employees' views. Even employees interviewed talked more of survival than managerial intrigues. Finally, interdependence mitigated fault lines; if employees and shopfloor bosses thought badly of managers, they thought worse of outsiders, especially the state.[187] The *kholding* was a *kollektiv* of daughters and subdivisions desperate to survive.[188] Those who once valued independence now saw it leading to ruin; subdivisions and daughters traded autonomy for security in the *kholding*, even if internal sales were below market prices.[189] Yet despite the stress on survival, independence and accountability did not disappear. Privatization as a confederation rather than as a unity kept manager–employee fault lines alive. This contrasted with Kirov—earlier and more radical restructuring created divisions at Sverdlov that privatization could not heal. Pokasiuk did not employ paternalism as creatively as Semenenko. He referred to provision in broad terms and included it in labor agreements, but he did not try to change the nature of paternalism. Nor did he land major outside patrons, and as Sverdlov slid into crisis, he had no halo of success. Put differently, Pokasiuk did not employ framing to unite the enterprise around common identity, mission, and authority. He played a cruder political game that bore bitter fruit.

Even if conflict died down after privatization, the Sverdlov *kholding* was not a happy community. One top manager revealed in July 1997 that he had devised a scheme to deal with malcontents and underachievers who were not up to snuff or lacked "proper" attitudes. Sverdlov would be reorganized into a *kholding* plus an independent, outside group of profitable or potentially profitable daughters. The *kholding*, which included subdivisions and MPs with little chance of market survival, would go bankrupt and take bad daughters and all Sverdlov's debts with it. In a different interview one week later, I asked two assistant directors at an electronics firm about this scheme. Laughing at Sverdlov's presumptions of ingenuity, both responded that Lenenergo had discovered the plan and warned this attempt to legally wipe out electricity debts would lead Lenenergo to shut off electricity to *all* Sverdlov. The Sverdlov manager said nothing of this in the interview, and Lenenergo had made the threat several *months* before our interview.[190]

The Sverdlov that made lathes and industrial equipment did not survive long. Bank St. Petersburg, to which Sverdlov owed 180 million rubles in 2002, went to court to force repayment and received 50 percent of Sverdlov's shares and enterprise property; they began to organize a closed joint-stock company (ZAO) to make money in equipment repair. In September 2003 Russkii Dizel' pressed bankruptcy charges against Sverdlov over a 1.5 million ruble debt. Sverdlov survived this, but in early 2004 Lenenergo sued Sverdlov and shut off electricity over debts of approximately 362 million rubles, hurting independent firms on the premises as well as Sverdlov and daughters. Assistant director Grigorii Zomba was investigated for fraud and misreporting Sverdlov's insolvency (in his interests and those of an unnamed third party). By 2004 Sverdlov was in bankruptcy, and in 2005 had sold the brand name of its lathes to a Kirov daughter. Outsiders purchased some of its buildings to construct a business-center.[191]

The ties that bind are breaking one by one: studied distrust, conflict, and collapse at Pozitron

Fundamental change in resource and discursive power risks conflict because multiple actors gain autonomy to act and articulate, and confusion or contradiction can facilitate mobilization and resistance, distrust, and politicization. If managers' and employees' contingent responses involved polarized positions, distrust increased; further events or snowballing claims could push an enterprise over the edge and break it into component parts—bad for productivity and not an intended outcome of reforms. Pozitron illustrates this dynamic of "studied distrust," ritualized enmity, and contradictory interests and identities creating conflict. Of all firms I examined, Pozitron had the most heated conflicts over reorganization and authority. Interdependence was low—subdivisions produced for outsiders as well as each other—and managers and employees thought they could go it alone. As at Sverdlov, restructuring began before 1992 and was accompanied by radical rhetoric and blaming. Managers claimed authority and status and shifted responsibility to shopfloors— but they lost control of restructuring and discourse and could not frame normal structure, identity, or paternalism in terms conducive to unity and managerial control.[192]

The Pozitron *obedinenie* was born when the state united different factories in electronics R&D and production of tuners, radio and television components, and military goods.[193] The first wave of restructuring began with moderate change.[194] In 1989 managers of the Pozitron mother gave member enterprises financial autonomy—*khozraschët* and MP functions without formal MP legal status. (Some feared *khozraschët* indicated crisis already brewing.) Vikond, a subdivision created in 1972 as a special laboratory to design such electronic goods as black-and-white televisions for export to East Europe and the UK, was the first to be reformed on January 1, 1990. As it supplied Pozitron brothers Mezon and Kulon and earned hard currency from exports, managers gladly accepted the change.[195] Kulon followed suit. Asked if he feared foreign competitors, Kulon's director said he feared competition from Pozitron subdivisions. Yet agitation was emerging with decoupling between new organizational *structure* and *knowledge of practices*. Questions emerged about financial transfers, who owned what, and what accounting techniques would be used for payments. If Kulon left Pozitron, some feared the latter would be left without finance.[196] When Girikond, Pozitron's scientific-technological R&D institute, went on *khozraschët*, troubles began. Her manager decreed that Girikond was an MP, and her internal subdivisions would not get MP status, which would disrupt accounting, resource control, and coordination. To some this went too far. A member of Girikond's Labor Collective Council felt reforms were adopted "without considering the institute's interests." In response, managers cited a labor council conference that had not taken place, and their actions—including transferring Girikond's property—contradicted the institute's charter and violated the idea of Pozitron as unitary entity.[197] Kulon's general director claimed these fears were groundless rumors; by law Pozitron had to be a unitary enterprise. This led to debates on Pozitron as an *"obedinenie"* or "enterprise" (*predpriiatie*)—the former an association of entities and the latter a legally independent entity.[198] The battle over centralized control of services and decision-making versus autonomy was on.

Top managers, especially general director Iurii Blokhin, used financial autonomy to attack subdivision managers, who in turn blamed the state and the environment. Accounting for debts and who owned what capital was the first source of confusion and tension—which emerged quickly at member factory Viton in early 1991. Aleksandr Pan'shin, then Viton's director, faced accusations by Blokhin that Viton held the largest chunk of Pozitron debt—whether Blokhin was setting up a shell game is unclear—and that not everybody was handling autonomy well. Pan'shin admitted Viton's performance was disappointing, but he blamed political, macroeconomic, and legal "cataclysms." Further, to foreshadow future conflict, the suggestion that Viton leave the *obedinenie* emerged in 1991. Pan'shin claimed to prefer a unified Pozitron: "I need the *obedinenie*: I need Kulon, Mezon, Rekond, the institute, I need our machine-shop base…and other enterprises in the *obedinenie*." Only Blokhin talked of the *obedinenie* weakening when he accused subdivisions of causing troubles—akin to "blaming a child for having grown up and continuing to grow," something "good parents do not do."[199]

Blokhin's reorganization of control spawned suspicions. He wasted little time framing financial dilemmas as employees' fault. VCR production was not bringing in hoped-for income. The new VCR-producing factory was legally independent but located at the *obedinenie*, which confused employees about its status and use of profits. Despite promises of VCR profit, Pozitron employees would not see immediate wage increases because, as Blokhin noted, "There is no money because we work badly." When journalists disputed this, Blokhin replied that "it is not easy to work independently, and…we are not able to work independently." Without citing concrete data as asked, and admitting their workforce had overfulfilled plan quotas for the first quarter of 1991, he said that Kulon had gone farthest accepting responsibilities and adapting to disciplined market work.[200] Less innocuously, Blokhin gained general directorship of Girikond and thus control over its property. Girikond was central to Pozitron research, and employees and managers understood that in electronics, research and innovation was the key to survival.[201] As at Sverdlov, between managers' lectures and actions, employees began to suspect a con game.

Workers believed restructuring would increase profits and wages—and finance and wages intermingled with justice and moral economy, which emerged with a vengeance in 1991. Chief of Rekond's shopfloor #1 petitioned for financial autonomy but was turned down. One Pozitron economist explained the refusal thus: "Viton was built on profit of shopfloor #1 and of Kulon"; shopfloor #1 had a more pressing function beyond profitability because of amortization and supply relations. Pozitron managers claimed the shopfloor would not survive independence, especially the higher prices they would have to pay for raw materials supplied by monopolies and *obedinenie* services such as supply and electricity. Also if autonomy was not restrained, then every shopfloor, even every brigade, would want independence, and in the "chain reaction" the *obedinenie* would break apart. In contrast, shopfloor workers considered themselves competent enough to deal with these tasks. Leasing arrangements were ideal at the start; but the goal of independence was to make work interesting and profitable. These employees found themselves branded as "separatists," even though they claimed no intention of leaving the *obedinenie*.[202]

In a chain reaction, Pozitron was fast becoming a complex of financially autonomous MPs and subdivisions. By October 1991, Girikond itself had eight autonomous subdivisions. Employees paid close attention to independence, especially to its effect on wages, social provision, and for whom they would work (MP or Girikond). In late 1991 these issues did not yet raise rankles, but employees were starting to ask questions.[203] As well, journalists were asking these questions of Pozitron managers, and printing employees' and managers' viewpoints. Discursive power was opening up, just as material power was transformed by restructuring. In late 1991, as issues of social property, independence, and provision continued to arise, narrative power was being breached. This was not inevitable in 1991, but contingent responses of employees and managers in 1992 made the circle more vicious. The most problematic case, which set the tone, was the relationship between Pozitron and Viton. In 1991 and 1992 voting was under way for Viton's general director. Employees chose Georgii Kichigin, former shopfloor chief at local enterprise Ferrit.[204] Pozitron general director Iurii Blokhin preferred Pozitron to remain a unitary enterprise under his control, but many employees and division bosses articulated distrust of him. Kichigin put autonomy into practice and ran head-on into Blokhin, fueling further distrust.

Pozitron–Viton conflict centered on exchange. A combination of confused intra-enterprise exchange, absence of mechanisms of conflict resolution and accountability, and a context of distrust fomented conflict. Confusion in intra-enterprise exchange acted as proof that restructuring meant incompetence at best, theft at worst. Viton and the Pozitron mother produced televisions for export, a point of pride and belief in superior output.[205] In 1989 Pozitron set up joint venture Vit-Frans with French firm Slava.[206] Pozitron imported French television parts, assembled them, and exported them to France. In 1992 Viton, the assembler, could not meet output obligations when inflation crippled finances. Kichigin claimed Pozitron owed Viton 80 million rubles for televisions assembled, but Blokhin disputed this, adding to broader distrust.[207] Blokhin admitted relations between Pozitron and Viton were abnormal and that Kichigin's behavior hurt Viton's finances. He tried to help Viton's *kollektiv* by firing Kichigin. By law Blokhin did not have this authority, and Kichigin enjoyed the support of Viton's employees. Claiming Kichigin did not answer for faults, Pozitron managers asked Petersburg KUGI to fire him. Blokhin downplayed personal enmity: "as general director I am worried most not by [Kichigin's] fate but by the fate of the factory *kollektiv*." Blokhin's case was not absurd: Kichigin was not a feeble victim of intrigue. The Viton collective decided to create a potentially lucrative joint venture (SP) with South Korean firm Daewoo, but this required merging Viton with the SP. Kichigin withdrew Viton from the project, claiming Pozitron did not want to share profits and was forcing the merger. Thus he kept Viton out of the deal to maintain Viton's autonomy. Blokhin was asked if the *obedinenie* did not want to share power and profits with Viton and wanted full control instead. Blokhin's response: "If you're talking about me, then I as general director have one desire— to help the *kollektiv* to hold out in this difficult time, to create hopeful supports for Viton. Just this—this is the goal of creation of the joint venture." The bitterness persisted and added to rising contention.[208]

By the end of 1992 conflict over reorganization expanded from exchange and debt to privatization (should Pozitron privatize as a whole or as independent entities), managerial competence, and Pozitron's fate. A fierce dispute erupted over Viton in public rather than behind closed doors, where compromise could be negotiated. Viton's head technician fired the first shot, demanding more managerial transparency so that workers would have facts, not rumors. He claimed Viton should be healthiest in all Pozitron—it never made military products—yet it had serious financial and organizational problems (e.g. five different general directors in nine years). At his election Kichigin promised a 12 percent increase in production; the reality was a 31 percent drop relative to the first nine months' in 1991, and employee lay-offs. Prices for Viton's goods were rising slower than inflation, but sales were falling. The technician blamed Kichigin and

Blokhin for being incompetent, self-interested, and perhaps corrupt. The only solution was for shopfloors to leave Viton. Other workers supported Kichigin and signed a statement blaming Blokhin for Viton's problems and scandals. They were afraid he would dispose of Kichigin by *kompromat*, misinformation, and pressuring union leadership to annul Kichigin's contract. To employees Blokhin clearly wanted an industrial empire, not Viton's well-being: "*obedinenie* leaders...want to commercialize Viton by Blokhin's scenario, consisting of the *obedinenie* headed by him, and [for him] it is extremely unprofitable to allow independent privatization to occur." They were satisfied Kichigin's actions would ensure profit and raise wages; thus they wanted independent privatization and freedom from the *obedinenie*. Of course, not everyone trusted Kichigin. Shopfloors #15, #16, and #23, with more than 600 employees, felt the privatization commission's work was insufficient and Viton's financial situation unsatisfactory. These shopfloors distrusted Kichigin and decided to privatize independently of Pozitron *and* Viton.[209]

Distrust between *kollektiv*, Kichigin, and Blokhin worsened. Viton's labor conference (September 23–5) debated privatization, and the initial suggestion was to make Viton a closed joint-stock company (AOZT, restricting sale of shares) and take privatization path #1, free privileged shares and discounted additional voting shares. Also at issue was how to find investors who would not radically alter Viton's work. However, presidential decree #721 gave shopfloors 715 and 716—the main shopfloors for VCR production—the right to privatize independently. The chief of shopfloor #715 implied that an enormous problem was that intrigues created distrust of managers. Kichigin claimed Viton's finances were normal; shopfloor experience contradicted him. Further, Viton's business plan had no concrete forecasts or plans on VCR production or where VCR workers would go should production end. Shopfloor #715 boss claimed there was no mention of VCR production in the first draft of the business plan; the second draft noted 25,000 VCRs for 1993. Pozitron managers told him #715 would produce 60,000 VCRs for 1993 and should have the capacity to make 80,000–100,000 VCRs per year. Additionally, the second draft suggested a new VCR model, yet #715 had yet to receive technology to produce it. Finally, the VCR price in the second draft was raised from 23,000 rubles (approximately $60) to 41,000 rubles, yet employees' wages were unchanged.[210] The chief of #715 said, "No one wants to give us time...We have serious grievances against the leadership." Three claims in particular were noted. First, there was no reliable information on enterprise finances, yet managers claimed everything was okay—only to be contradicted by two commissions that claimed Viton was badly off, and by everyday experience in 715, where production of "devices" (*pribory*) had slowed to far below the 6,000–7,000 they could produce per month. Second, abnormal relations with suppliers hurt production. "Why did we get a ribbon-stretching machine from Voronezh significantly more expensive than [one] from [other] Novgorod factories?" Third, preparatory work on privatization was sloppy and employees were not informed about details of other choices and strategies. Thus, shopfloor #715 wanted to leave Viton. Loath to lose these key shopfloors, managers delayed the vote on privatization to let tempers "cool down."

Events at Girikond were also dramatic, especially over privatization.[211] Through 1992 employees were increasingly worried about future structure, property, and work. Employees were bothered by increasingly complex relations with other subdivisions *and* within Girikond, which had twelve MPs of its own. Earlier Girikond financed all subordinate units. With constant decentralization, subdivisions had their own accounts, breeding conflict over who owed what to whom. Social property also entered the fray: one employee complained that Girikond employees had to pay 115 rubles for a pass to the Mechta *pansionat* built by Girikond and Pozitron together; but Pozitron employees had to pay only 25 rubles. Blokhin claimed this reflected how much Girikond contributed to expenses, i.e. Girikond was not providing enough subsidies. Finally, alarm grew that "outsiders" would buy Girikond, deprive employees of rights and employment, and sell assets, leaving an empty husk.[212] Girikond's working relations with other Pozitron members worsened, especially with Rekond. Research and development institute Garamond earlier had split into Girikond (research and development) and Rekond (production). Now their relations were unclear: were they partners coordinating development and production, or were they competitors producing similar goods (e.g. television components) for the same clients? Some concluded that restructuring hurt both, as both depended on each other—Girikond on Rekond for purchases, Rekond on Girikond for design. Each, now independent, focused on itself to the detriment of the other. Rekond's usual output was not market competitive, and they had no new goods to offer. Their leaders criticized Girikond for ignoring Rekond and entering commercial activities for which they were ill prepared: Girikond "leapt headfirst into commerce, while our production...has now been pushed aside into some third role." Girikond technicians and engineers responded they were occupied with "elementary survival," not commerce. Rekond wanted Girikond to design new products at its own expense, at which point the buyer would *then* pay for the newly designed product. Girikond managers wanted payment up front to cover outlays and development funds, which annoyed Rekond employees and soured relations.[213]

Girikond employees were not against privatization *per se*—two thirds of representatives voted for path #2—and the majority favored Girikond and Rekond privatizing as a single unit. Majorities at subdivisions with financial autonomy had little faith in managers.[214] But Blokhin, head of Girikond, argued in a speech *after* the vote on the institute's fate that Girikond should not privatize— knowing Blokhin's preference, delegates moved his speech until after the vote. If private, the institute would lose state subsidies, but it covered only ten percent of expenses by "its own economic activity." "Can the institute survive in a privatized condition? No. The institute will not. Can the *kollektiv* survive? Yes it can. If it will work at a different job." While Blokhin claimed concern for the *kollektiv*, Vladimir Lomasov, head of Girikond's union, claimed "the key task before the institute *kollektiv*...is to maintain the *kollektiv*, the institute's potential, and not to await administrative decisions on its fate, but with initiative to struggle for its preservation." Yet enterprise restructuring turned the *obedinenie* into "a collection of several legal entities" independently deciding on privatization.[215] This both hindered concerted collective action and created conflict over *kollektiv* boundaries and property. Employees and shopfloor bosses contended that property, especially *pansionaty*, was transferred illegally from member entities such as the institute or Mezon to the Pozitron mother. Blokhin claimed such property was transferred before privatization. B. Gelikman—with Blokhin and a third person, Girikond's ruling triumvirate—blasted employees and conference deputies for choosing privatization path #2. How would they obtain funds to buy 51 percent of shares and implement development plans? He had "no confidence that after privatization the institute will work better or live." V. Khalifman of the "sixth department" admitted employees thought Blokhin cared for them but was lying.[216]

Conflict over privatization spread throughout Pozitron's member factories. At subdivision Mezon, the preference was for path #2, with the *kollektiv* buying 51 percent of shares. One enterprise economist discovered that this would cost 139 million rubles—each Mezon employee would have to dish out 51,000 rubles, an unrealistic amount. The administration considered loans from banks or other commercial organizations, but this had a catch: Mezon would have to hand over 49 percent of its shares as collateral, leaving the *kollektiv* with two percent. Not wanting to part with the decision-making potential of shares, managers were forced to consider path 1—but remaining voucher shares could be bought by an outsider. Either way, the *kollektiv* could lose control. In the end Mezon employees chose path 1, with 25 percent of privileged/non-voting shares to the *kollektiv* for free, 20 percent to KUGI, ten percent to the "fund for joint-stock creation for the workers of the enterprise," five percent to the Mezon administration, and an additional 10 percent to employees. No doubt employees agreed to this plan because of a deal with St. Petersburg KUGI: the city would hand over control, but not ownership, of its 20 percent share. This left 25 percent of non-voting shares and 45 percent of shares, all voting, with employees. They had some control over their fate, although some feared KUGI, a state agency, might renege.[217]

Legislation gave Pozitron subdivisions the opportunity to use privatization to break free from the mother firm. Whether this happened was contingent on responses of studied distrust and ritualized contradictory identities. Distrust of top management was greater at Pozitron than elsewhere. (Not by coincidence did managers at electronics enterprise Svetlana study Pozitron to avoid a similar fate.[218]) One employee summed up the general mood:

> One side [employees] insisted on full clarity with future shareholders, especially outside investors. The other side [managers] aimed to avoid openness and to introduce investors immediately at the conference, so no one could come to grips with them. In this way the Viton factory could fall into private hands, in this way money of the shadow economy [*tenevaia ekonomika*] and *mafiia* structures is laundered today. This is why hysteria in Viton's *kollektiv* has swollen up. The scenario is simple, worked out even in 1937: there are enemies—intellectuals, renegades—there is popular anger, there is the screen against "the people," behind which the most monstrous crimes can be hidden.[219]

With interdependence weak and distrust strong, the Pozitron *obedinenie* broke up. In 1991 and 1992 it seemed financial problems could be solved only if *kollektiv* and *obedinenie* held together. Viton, Kulon, Mezon, and Rekond became independent firms. Viton went bankrupt. Kulon, once barely surviving on renting office space (a practice of firms unable to adapt),[220] had better luck after 2000, selling ceramic electronic components for 80 million rubles in 2001. Mezon made profit in 2004; Girikond, fully owned by Rossiiskaia Elektronika, muddled through.[221] A Pozitron core survived, living off Daewoo imports and sales of basic consumer goods.

Enterprise change: organizations and authority awry

These cases suggest forms of variation in enterprise change, and their stories are not unique. Some enterprises and *obedineniia* were closer to delayed or controlled change. Even in the mid-1990s, some managers' suggestions for rationalizing structure and strategy at October Railroad were rebuffed by state representatives out of bureaucratic inertia or by managers unconvinced of the need for change.[222] In 1991, entrepreneurs opened joint venture Evrosib-SPb to find and work with foreign or domestic partners through "direct contacts" (networks), organize documentation, follow up schedules, and handle customs issues. Some managers complained Evrosib "sat on the railroad's neck and enriched itself on its account," but Evrosib director Nikolai Nikitin claimed they were a useful middleman who earned money (11 billion rubles in 1993) and had trained personnel the Railroad lacked. Railroad experts blamed "the complicated system of administration in the sector, and the absence in administration of real economic and administrative levers to influence affairs at lower-level enterprises which have the same legal status as the railroad."[223] Shopfloor and line managers were skeptical that restructuring would improve finances.

In the early 1990s managers still hoped for quick recovery and hoarded labor, avoiding massive lay-offs; this allowed Soviet organizational principles to persist and gave employees leverage. By the mid-1990s, firms were fighting to survive. Increasing lay-offs and financial crises took the fire out of employees and made pensioners loyal for having a job and benefits. Skilled employees could find alternative jobs with better wages at small firms or larger employers such as Baltika or Coca-Cola and leave both deprivation and contention behind. Managers consolidated *de facto* or *de jure* share control after initial privatization, speaking for workers via proxy or owning shares outright. Many continued to stress paternalism, although some used crises to shed labor.[224] Privatization shifted voice and voting to shareholders' meetings, where managers set agendas, depriving employees of those shopfloor meetings where they set agendas and planned resistance. Financial hardship forced newspapers to reduce quality and quantity of output: from twelve pages to four, from every other day to every other week, with less coverage of conflicts and more of holidays and products. By the mid-1990s social democracy was weakened by the image of an ideology of older generations who had lost or would return to the police state. Finally, survival became more important than justice, now consigned to a luxury.

As noted earlier, alternative examinations of organizational change provide insights but also contain oversights or limitations. Economists do not even have power, culture, and conflict on their radar or in broad, vague definitions of "restructuring." Approaches in political economy, like those of McDermott and Crowley, look primarily to state policies, structures and networks (alliances), and material power; internal organizational dynamics remain underexplored. The capacity to articulate alternatives contributes to mobilization and empowerment, yet this dimension of power and enterprise politics does not emerge (although Crowley raises framing and ideology but without relating them to power's multidimensionality). Marxist-inspired approaches take power into account—conflict is on their radar—but mechanisms fixate on class. This is too crude to account for all organizational dynamics in operation; shopfloors were equally important. Hypothesizing variation in outcomes is also difficult when main processes are supposedly the same across enterprises. Finally, most neoinstitutionalism and economic sociology miss the shopfloor, privileging fields or using quantitative methods that miss processes of change and contention. If anything, this chapter is testament to earlier works that used ethnographic or similar methods and paid attention to dynamics of organizational interaction. This is the tip of the iceberg: operationalization of power and culture can be worked out further in future work, to clarify correlations between tactics and changes in power and culture, and processes of change.

Enterprises are structured power and normality akin to polities, with social movements and contention. Thus enterprise change is political, with its own endogenous processes of power and culture in addition to environmental effects. During radical change external factors such as fields or markets can break down, and internal processes of framing, negotiation, and conflict become paramount. Enterprise change becomes a story of contingent processes and tactics of framing and mobilizing over boundaries and mechanisms of power, resources, discourse and information, and perceptions and assumptions of normal practice. Part of the political dynamic was confronting legacies as "liabilities of oldness" and organizational "lock-in": not only old technology and networks, but also meanings of normality and legitimacy, *habitus*, and practices locking an organization into particular structural configurations. While legacies were difficult to disembed, change was possible, following contingent articulation and delegitimation. Paternalism was not initially attacked and hindered restructuring. Vertical authority reappeared in the *kholding*, now draped in market clothing. Many organizational theories lose enterprise politics because change is marginal or capitalist hegemony hides fault lines. But firms are not aggregations of governance structures or reflections of fields alone; managers do not follow strictures of profit maximization alone. Productivity and gain were proximal incentives for restructuring, but managers and employees were constructing and contesting normality along the way.

4 Innovation and confusion

Logics, practices, and strategies of sales

We did not know how to sell.
> (Tula entrepreneur, furniture maker, November 1995)

To learn, to learn, and to learn…to sell!
> (Headline, *Kirovets* July 2, 1993)

Fate was unkind to St. Petersburg electronics firm Neutron. This firm produced tuners and ceramic components, mostly for Soviet-style televisions and military goods—both collapsing markets. An assistant director there noted that his firm supplied a television assembler in Belarus. Managers continued this relationship, even though it was not profitable. The price spike in raw materials forced Neutron to raise prices; in response, the client reduced their purchases. Rising transportation costs, foreign competition, tariffs, taxes, customs delays, and delayed shipments and payments across borders aggravated production and finance for both, driving purchase orders down even more—but not ending the exchange relationship. There was an alternative: Neutron could sell to a *local* Petersburg television producer whose supplier was in Belarus. A Neutron assistant director claimed managers at both firms discussed benefits of trading with each other, but the idea went nowhere: as Neutron slowly died, "old thinking dies hard."[1]

Continuing our exploration of economic change, this chapter examines the adoption of new, fundamental assumptions, logics, and practices of everyday business, namely what to produce, for whom, and at what value. Some central issues are: *why* did Russian managers adopt marketing as they did (superficially), when the returns would likely be minor given immediate financial difficulties and in fact were minor as marketing divisions were created and went online? Why did Russian managers pursue a logic of production akin to the Soviet logic of the Plan: produce first, ask about selling later? In the financial crisis of 2008–9, American and British managers began reducing output and supply purchases and laying off workers, *in anticipation* of financial contractions. Russian managers in the 1990s, facing financial and other crises, did not systematically try to anticipate financial turbulence and plan accordingly. The post-Soviet response was not a *methodical* reduction of expenditures to optimize survival chances, but rather a desperate, often confused, attempt to maintain production for its own sake, to follow a survival logic that they knew—not a rational adjustment to a new financial context to optimize profits, as economic theory expects.[2] That is, Russian managers' post-Soviet responses were instrumentally "rational" only if we tautologically assume actors respond to institutional incentives (which reifies institutions and assumes their operation)—or if we unearth their particular logics of rationality. Freed from the state but needing money, why did Red Directors *not* copy financial entrepreneurs by playing the shadow economy and speculation for *accumulation*, not just immediate profit? Certainly some were rent-seeking: but why focus primarily on the firm's specific production? Why asset-strip rather than use this to speculate and invest into possible expansion—playing the entrepreneurs' game of money, rather than state subsidies and protection as the Red Directors' main lobby, Civic Union, did?[3]

To explore post-Soviet logics of normality, rationality, and practice, and their change (such as it was), I use a narrative of the *duality of marketing*: marketing as a logic of interpretation and practice, and marketing as transition culture myth and practice to signal legitimacy and normality. The first side of the duality is marketing as logic, with production subordinated to studying, addressing, even shaping demand for goods. This was a radically different logic of practice. Its adoption faced decoupling of superficial and fundamental levels of knowledge: creating marketing divisions or personnel versus incorporating the marketing logic into individual *habitus* and organizational routines. The other side of the duality is marketing as myth of normality. Russians tried desperately to discern what a normal post-Soviet economy was. Grasping at marketing in the 1990s was part of this attempt and journey, and as such it faced older narratives of the centrality of production, rather than sales and income *per se*, to mission and identity.

Myths, logics, practices: "marketing" and the art of trucking and bartering

"Marketing" emerged as panacea early in the reform process—but what is it? On the one hand, marketing is central to modern capitalism. Marketing is both specific tasks (surveys, ads) and rationalized processes to coordinate business activity. By providing a method for gathering and analyzing data, and relating them to business practice, it can provide competitive advantages for survival and growth.[4] While marketing's value awaits definitive study, it is not unimaginable that, like scientific endeavors, it provides added value. Max Weber saw rationalization as key to capitalism: double-entry bookkeeping helped make the economy calculable and controllable. Alfred Chandler saw rationalized gathering and analyzing of sales data (marketing, scheduling, accounting) as key to growth. To its champion Michael Porter, marketing is thorough, scientific systematization of business: rationally and rigorously constructing precise and consistent goals, using sophisticated procedures to measure and study demand and formulate production and sales goals.[5] This is not easy to learn. Russians' experiences illustrate complexities of adopting this new practice and embedding it as meanings ("sales," "value," "demand"), status (sales versus production), and routines. Such change was individual *and* collective, in managers' *habitus* and collective practices. This created a "double decoupling"—a gap between tactics and knowledge, and between knowledge and power. As this was horizontal power—the state could not enforce marketing on autonomous firms—reform depended on who had power and knowledge inside firms.

Narrating normality was also part of post-Soviet marketing. As post-Soviet enterprises' sales and finances collapsed and the Soviet system came under attack in the early 1990s, the search for post-Soviet normality was on (and continues). "Marketing" as panacea was part of the myth of normal Western capitalism. *Marketing* (as a Russian term) exploded in the business press as part of this conversion from Soviet *upravlenie* to market *menedzhment*. Russian managers embraced it problematically: learning and implementing marketing faced assumptions, knowledge, and practices long-entrenched in individuals and organizational routines and authority. Articulating "marketing" as the secret of success was part of post-Soviet enterprise change, whose contentious dynamics we have seen. Adopting marketing and reorienting practices of supply, production, and sales throughout the enterprise was a chase for post-Soviet normality and legitimacy, for new sources of finance and stability, for new values and organizational missions, and for organizational authority. This was quite the challenge. Russians could innovate, as conversion of industrial output in World War II showed; but rethinking overall logics and routines was a difficult challenge of shifting from Soviet logics of speculation and production to market logics of sales and finance. As one set of Russian scholars concluded, "in the transitional period it [was] difficult to expect enterprises quickly and painlessly to shift to market forms of economic behavior…[this was] a complex task, including evaluation of demand, choice of schemes of price-setting, developing strategies of competitive struggle."[6] Discourse and mimicry drove marketing as panacea, but limitations of knowledge and power, and contradictory Soviet logics of production and informality, meant managers imperfectly adopted procedures and logic—adding buzzwords or marketing divisions rather than altering practices. Directors reproduced Soviet practices until continuing shocks (e.g. reduced sales) forced change. The narrative of the post-Soviet firm was one of practices, power, and disappointment in the search for marketing.

In economic theory, strategies with optimal cost–benefit ratios are adopted; these might be influenced by production chain location, technological endowment, demand elasticity, and competition.[7] Yet such studies operationalize strategic change broadly, with little detail on *how* this occurs or justifications and logics invoked. Trucking and bartering is not a mechanistic, instrumental response to demand, laws, or taxes only.[8] Some analyses add skills and cohorts and address human capital as an impediment to change,[9] but *why* are these important? In the instrumental logic of economics, culture is absent. Rules (taxes, red tape) shape costs and action. For example, economists and political scientists invoke these to explain pricing and the shadow economy. Tax laws forced managers to use chains of semi-legal or fictitious intermediaries, to sell goods to a "live" firm that moved undocumented barter or cash to short-lived shadow intermediaries, who then paid for fictitious goods via bank transfers visible to the tax police. This avoided taxes based on real prices or differences between production cost (*sebestoimost'*) and average market value, which tax police used to create "profit" for taxation.[10] I do not dismiss this out of hand, but an explanation based on an instrumental fixation on costs risks tautology, as William Reddy demonstrated, and hides more than it reveals.[11] Taxes, like any rule, are games of power and practice that actors navigate. All actors faced these, but this did not produce a unitary response; nor did it have a role in marketing. Actors did not dwell on laws; they talked of *active* searches for new tactics and grappling with new methods of selling, producing, and interacting with "the market." Neoinstitutionalism invokes culture but does not examine either concrete content or meanings or generation of new practices and logics.[12] Isomorphism (mimicry, coercion, norms) is power, but dynamics of *adopting* new meanings and logics need more study. Neil Fligstein's "conceptions of control" are general guidelines of practice. How they filter into concrete practices and logics of everyday business, subject to reinterpretation and implementation, needs attention. Further, Meyer and Rowan note *decoupling*: change in outward appearances need not mean real change in substances of practices. Restricting analysis to an instrumental logic risks missing dimensions of power-culture such as decoupled learning.[13] Culture's multidimensionality (superficial/tactical versus fundamental/tacit) suggests that decoupling appears in radical change as a gap between these two dimensions (and perhaps resistance). Decoupling as reproduction of old practices in new form is more likely if wielders of power do not have the power, will, or knowledge to enforce change in culture's fundamental level. Some work on post-socialism stresses organizational hybrids.[14] Hybrids are unsurprising, but what occurs in the offices and on the shopfloors of those hybrids? Production as usual? Innovation? Decoupling? Post-Soviet marketing allows us to develop neoinstitutionalism's potential further.

"Normal" business: legacies and contingencies in meaning and power

Unlike in East Europe or China, where some inhabitants experienced market contexts,[15] Russians were socialized by 70 years of non-capitalist ideology, institutions, and practices. Soviet and market economies shared some traits (bureaucracy, reliance on technology), but ideology, vertical authority, and the Plan inculcated different procedures and practices of rationalization and organization.[16] Planning and production departments quantified and measured gross output and welfare, not profit-based cost-accounting. Vertical authority made managers orient tactics to state and suppliers, not consumers. Managers did not formulate goals but awaited plan output and shipment orders. Now they had to learn new logics, while justifying authority and status.

Logics of production and exchange

In an astute contrast of socialism and capitalism, Katherine Verdery noted two socialist economic logics.[17] The logic of the end-game is to whom organizations orient activity and strategies. In capitalism, consumers wield symbolic and economic power. Firms survive by appealing to consumer needs and fending off competition.[18] Sales and marketing shape production; firms aim to obtain income from market share, niches, and innovations. In socialism, state and suppliers wielded power of Plan and provision. Strategy focused on procuring supplies and negotiating the Plan, not sales, competitors, and consumers; and on acquisition skills and generating surplus inputs, rather than salesmanship and generating surplus value. In Verdery's second logic, differentiated consumers and sales personnel define demand—the former via preferences, the latter by revealing or shaping those preferences. In socialism, consumers had little power; enterprises shaped consumption by providing basic, generic goods to a mass public. Marketization was a shift in end-game logics, the firm's audience, and the meaning of production (addressing the Plan or consumers). To Verdery's schema we can add formality versus informality. Modern capitalism is formalization writ large; informality facilitates formal rules (e.g. casual meetings) or signals abnormality (corruption).[19] In Soviet and post-Soviet economies, informality was partly a response to state predation and bureaucracy.[20] Legal vagaries and contradictions gave tax inspectors and state officials (e.g. safety inspectors) a chance to elicit bribes.[21] Yet informality and the shadow economy were an alternative normality, cat-and-mouse games of state and society. This bred a contradiction: marketing was moving from shadows to formality, yet state officials' and managers' *habitus* reproduced shadows.[22]

Soviet institutions privileged acquisition skills, supplier authority, and identifying the firm with output and welfare. These required networks, political skill, and technical knowledge to dispute quotas or mobilize enterprise resources; they bred informality, hoarding, and last-minute storming. Directors were concerned with status, bonuses, and fulfilling targets while not ratcheting them upwards.[23] They knew of Western management techniques, but managers at one firm confessed they needed to learn more of economics, marketing, technology, and labor rights.[24] Hungarian and Polish entrepreneurs bemoaned the lack of training and admitted they needed guidance in analyzing markets and customer needs.[25] Market reforms implied shifting orientation from state and suppliers to consumers, from value inherent in production to value inherent in demand. This was not easy. Optimist managers saw crises ending soon and introduced innovations in output and organization faster than pessimists, who aimed to muddle through.[26] More educated managers and professionals seemed less fearful of change.[27] Managers' planning horizons (how long they expected to be in charge), perceptions of the firm (independent parts or a whole), learning style (via incentives or experience), and networks shaped degree of adaptation.[28] Further, perceived Soviet abnormalities (e.g. experiences of deficit goods or bad service) created a template for what change *should* be.[29] Yet this mapped onto tacit *Soviet* knowledge, logics, and practices, assembled and inculcated by everyday socialization in routines. Soviet-era firms inherited planning, pricing, and distribution departments; cadres' skills were Soviet. Marketing logics privileged autonomy and flexibility, unlike control legacies of the Soviet era and even earlier. Business scholar A. P. Prokhorov suggests the historical logic of Russian managers and the state is using control to obtain results; this did have results, such as building industry in the 1880s and 1930s.[30] Breaking out of this control model, to flexibility, competition, market autonomy, and sovereign demand, ran up against ingrained survival practices that, despite delegitimation, were still social reflexes.

Power and change

One approach to changing logics and practices is to select for and against certain strategies and practices through institutionalized practices of evaluation. Bankruptcy forces profit search to pay debts. Shareholding and evaluation of a firm's worth can enforce profit-oriented practices: shareholders demand higher share value and dividends, and evaluation determines performance and labels normality. Hence the importance of bankruptcy procedures and shares for developing economies: these select against non-market abnormality. In the early post-socialist period, enforcement mechanisms were weak. In the dimension of resource power, liberalization, privatization, and destatization weakened state control. Bankruptcy could not consistently enforce market behavior: it was a political bomb foiled by resistance tactics.[31] Special firms could obfuscate accountability by arranging documentation to close one business and open a new one before tax officials or creditors could seize accounts; creditors could not "pierce the corporate veil" to trace cash flows.[32] Such gatekeepers as fund managers or investment bankers were nonexistent or weak; the Russian Stock Exchange was a speculative site.[33] This meant learning had a more autonomous dynamic, and so creating marketing was both learning new logics and giving them status in organizational procedures: this was a potential challenge to status hierarchies privileging supply and production managers. Discursively, marketing enjoyed legitimacy, but this did not translate into its enforcement. Transition culture still competed with traditional practices not initially discredited, e.g. state subsidies or "directors' ethics" of fair pricing. Inside firms, managers could blame employees rather than learn new logics. Without hegemony, "learning the market" was about contingent decisions and outcomes, a decoupling of form and practice due to distance between tacit knowledge and new practices.[34]

An alternative to selecting *against* is selecting *for*. With private property, owners can try to enforce their knowledge or hire managers who display normal practices. As well, in theory, private ownership improves market responsiveness by encouraging efficient investment. Yet property alone cannot explain change trajectories,[35] except where foreign owners brought in managers. Tatiana Dolgopiatova suggests managers confident of survival were more likely to embrace change, not resist it;[36] others suggest private firms could continue traditional output.[37] Manager-run firms did not always change more slowly than those owned by outsiders: they might engage the market,[38] and they could gain from profitable daughter firms. Demonstrating market knowledge could convince new owners to retain them for local knowledge. Also, managers tried to learn *despite* property form.[39] Thus, our story is not one-to-one correspondence of property to practice, but how property intersected with knowledge.

Rather than continue to structure the narrative around explicit comparisons, I use an ideal-typical narrative made from several cases. LMZ, Sverdlov, and others responded to similar shocks and quandaries in a fairly similar manner. The previous chapter suggests why: in 1988–95 a defensive, managerial field community and logic were strongest, and much of learning marketing is about Red Directors. Further, focusing on Red Directors allows us to examine decoupling between two logics of economic action. Red Directors' similar Soviet experiences created a sufficiently common *habitus*, knowledge, and narratives. If restructuring had variations (Chapter 3), conservative reformers' approaches to sales (LMZ) were not unlike those of their radical brethren (Sverdlov). When the financial and state-centered field communities emerged with younger managers and owners, variation emerged; I address this later and in the Conclusion. My analysis turns to claims and narratives to unearth meanings and changes and stasis in practices and logics. Various managers and employees openly admitted economic distress. To justify tactics and authority, they discussed strategies and why. Claims and narratives were a means to maintain status and dignity in dire straits, as well as attempts to work out thoughts. Following grounded theory and extended case method to discern patterns of change, I trace these claims, responses, accounts, and justifications *vis-à-vis* perturbations of existing practices. This fleshes out how tool kits of meanings and practices underwent change *and* continuity, and how adaptation and implementation took twists and turns. What actors found important to talk about reveals perceptions of pressing issues, business normality, and presenting oneself in everyday life.

Many studies examine "success" (change or growth) as a dependent variable, but I dissociate it from "change." The two need not be linked automatically. Marketing, generational turnover, sector, property form, and finances could influence change and a firm's fate; but firms elsewhere changed structures without changing fates. "Success" as a judgment of that fate is part of the construction of normality.[40] Marketing was part of the narrative of success. Quantitative studies that examine productivity or lack of profit are part of the narrative of post-socialism, and they miss processes and obstacles of learning and discovery, including those that aid variation and similarity. This chapter addresses these issues thus far neglected.

Learning new logics of business: confusion, panic, and first change

While small stores could diversify if they saw demand for certain goods—a sports store near a dormitory where the author lived sold candy and beer as well as sports gear, and café owners used a standard menu—firms with high overheads (industrial enterprises, small firms in production or complex services) had more capital and employees at stake. Realizing the importance of sales came early, but its link to production was problematic. The timing of change varied: some managers learned marketing in 1993, others later, some never. Change was trial-and-error; fault for problems and new normality were seldom clear. Managers

Table 4.1 Dynamics of change in logics of business

	Pre-1992 (Soviet)	1st Phase (1992–3): Business as usual and first reactions	2nd Phase (1994–6): Second adaptations, beginning of marketing	Post-1996: 1. Progressive/innovation 2. Muddling through, decoupling 3. Retreat
Logic of business	Production logic. Fulfill plan, employment, legitimation of ideology. Informal practices crucial to supply.	Production-centered; sell what make. Increase profile to find solvent demand. Tap income stream. Informality crucial to sales.	Marketing simple: phone calls, copy prices; legitimation. Link with patron (oil/gas, foreign firm). Initial formalization of sales vs. informality.	1. Expanded marketing business logic. Play to consumers. Formalized sales practices. 2. Holding pattern (small niche, no real change) OR "patron"–client 3. Retreat to barter and virtual economy, shadows
Sales	Supply, acquisition skills > sales, salesmanship. Formal plan vs. informal shadow economy	Sell what produced. Flood the market for hopeful income. Maintain employment.	Rudimentary marketing = locate buyers. Decoupling possible here. Sell what made.	1. Formalized procedures. Produce what sells for best results. 2. Sell what made, some thought to demand. 3. Barter what produced; informality crucial tool, site
Demand	Assumed (state-driven)	Assumed initially Solvent demand	Market-driven, but market understood in simple terms	1. Complex, market-driven. 2. Niche or patron. 3. Virtual: network-driven.
Value	Set by the state, plan criteria and functions	Set by managers Unique production	Cost + profit formula	1. Complex tactics, markets 2. Copying, cost + profit 3. Barter, non-monetary
Survival	Plan fulfillment, political obedience	Make money to pay wages, supplies	Income for wages, supplies. Fragmentation: survival as stasis vs. survival as progress	1. Development; play for profit or market share 2. Stable income to get by 3. Subsistence
Change process leading to next phase	Blame: Soviet irrationalities, capital need. Solution: liberalize, flood the market.	Blame: state policies, employees/managers Solution: marketing	Blame: weak knowledge Solution: copy, learn. Power; individual learning shapes variation	

viewed the world through a production lens, but their responses marked out a basic progression.

Negotiating supply and blaming the command economy: 1988–1992

Gorbachev's unfolding reforms created initial shocks for change. Rather than strict Plan quotas, firms now had to fulfill explicit state purchase orders (*goszakazy*), after which they could pursue non-state clients. Firms were also supposed to balance their books (*khozraschët*). These reforms introduced early confusion. Managers had some autonomy to explore tactics beyond plan fulfillment; paradoxically, Gorbachev's reforms also reinforced Soviet categories and practices. If the Plan was no longer central, *goszakazy* maintained state centrality as the primary purchaser, hindering active market search from taking root. Soft budgets, paternalism, and production-centered categories persisted as well, reducing incentives to learn the market more quickly.

Given the ubiquity of state supply and the Plan, all managers faced supply bottlenecks of varying degrees—a common challenge that bred common perceptions of problems and opportunities early in economic reform. Supply problems worsened in the late 1980s as enterprise reforms disoriented coordination and exchange and income declined as state purchases and subsidies shrank (or disappeared via fraud). Managers turned to barter and to ministries or local organs for reserves.[41] By 1991 managers began to notice how sales, taken for granted under the Plan, became problematic.[42] At some firms, such as chemical enterprise Krasnyi Treugol'nik, there was talk of "crisis." As other firms raised prices, state policy fixed theirs. Finances worsened, and 1990 output was 75 percent of what had been planned.[43] Increased freedom to export was intriguing, but managers had too few cadres with necessary skills—the state had arranged exports, many from political deals and not competitive tenders. Without state support, LMZ managers saw that survival demanded increased exports, but one import–export division had only two cadres qualified to run the operation.[44] Other managers realized they needed new procedures to prepare for the market. Nevskii Zavod's general director told employees that survival demanded raising output, and one tactic was joining new associations and concerns.[45] In early 1991 Krasnaia Zaria telecom managers claimed survival required setting prices not from state lists but by negotiating with buyers and creating working groups to study market demand. However, even here the key criterion of health was how many goods subdivisions and shopfloors produced and shipped, which depended on internal restructuring, not rethinking enterprise strategy and function.[46]

In addition to supply bottlenecks, initial tactics in pre-1992 liberalization involved shell games and speculation. Co-operatives and daughter firms could use newly formed *birzhi*, commodities exchanges, for this. *Birzhi* were to help industrial producers and consumers independently exchange deficit goods. If the formal motive was encouraging efficient distribution, an informal *birzha* logic was the shadow economy and Soviet (bureaucratic) entrepreneurship: using formal rules for speculative advantage, such as obtaining cheap materials from the state and selling them at a profit or trading them for deficit goods at the *birzha*. This did not go unnoticed in a lingering Soviet moral economy: "That going on before my eyes took place under article 154 of the criminal code [against speculation]… Speculation went on: the sales of goods at prices exceeding price-list value, and even with the help of middlemen. True, speculation was called 'bargaining' and the middlemen 'brokers.'"[47] Paradoxically, while the new *birzha* could ease supply bottlenecks, it also created more space for the shadow economy and facilitated speculation without encouraging innovation and production of value.[48] *Birzha* and early reforms encouraged continuity in the logic that supply was the biggest problem; solve this, and an enterprise's output would find purchasers, as seemed to happen with shell games and the *birzha*.

After 1991: the double dilemma and first reactions

As the Soviet economy began disintegrating in late 1991, Yeltsin and reform architect Yegor Gaidar introduced radical changes for January 2, 1992. The reform cornerstones were liberalization of price-setting and sales, privatization, monetary reform (reducing ruble overhang, introducing hard budgets), and increasing discipline via restructuring and bankruptcy.[49] Destroying the state-centered Soviet economy was the political rationale; the economic rationale was that reduced subsidies, liberal exchange, and privatization would encourage competition and force managers to improve efficiency, innovation, and productivity. Managers were not always opposed to this. Soviet-era planning and state coordination had created bottlenecks, overproduction, and inefficiencies.[50] *Goszakazy* did not ease supply problems or improve income. One assistant manager noted how it made little sense to evaluate output by kilograms produced; worth had to be in terms of use and money. Two assistant directors agreed; their firm had no idea for whom they produced. All conceived of capitalism as anti-Soviet: targets set by the market rather than the state, production with constant rhythm.[51] Now managers could trade at prices and with clients of their choosing, although some were uneasy.[52] Managers also focused on supply and assumed sales and income; experience suggested supply would be *the* nightmare in 1992.[53]

Soviet-era networks (work, Party, education) were the new basis for sales, providing partners and trust.[54] Managers and entrepreneurs maintained some older relationships for benefit and justified networks in material terms. As the commercial director of an electronics firm noted:

> If earlier the centralized distributive system was in operation—[everything went] through ministries and supply networks, although there were direct ties through factories—today none of this remains…We established direct ties with suppliers from whom we wanted to receive materials and technical goods…Basically, experience from work helped me [reorganize supply]. For a long time I had many already-worked-out ties with other enterprises. I knew [people in] practically all the regions in the former USSR…I knew

these people well, my colleagues—commercial directors. And, continuing this system of direct access to suppliers, it is easier to agree with them on all problems [of supply]…That unneeded [state] distributive organ fell away—it really bothered our work—but for us nothing more really changed. All the firms with whom we were connected are the same—the same suppliers of materials, the same suppliers of technical supplies.[55]

Note the last lines: nothing changed except the absence of the state; no stepping back to examine whether tactics were not optimal. Unsurprisingly, this firm had problems learning marketing. Yet not all managers were content. Optimism became anxiety as budgets tightened in early 1992 or subsidies ended up in private banks. State purchases fell, especially for military goods, depriving firms of income streams. The Soviet collapse estranged trading partners in different republics.[56]

From shocks and responses, a double dilemma awaited. First, with liberalization managers reduced purchases, but not to the extent they could have; and traditional suppliers could raise prices or sell to competitors or non-traditional buyers, ending some partnerships.[57] This was unsurprising given Soviet overproduction, but it had a knock-on effect managers did not foresee: purchase orders dropped all around. LMZ lost previously assured supply of metal inputs and had to use their own resources.[58] Surveys revealed that enterprise managers supported liberalized exchange if *only they* could raise prices and choose partners; when all had freedom, all suffered.[59] A commercial director at above-mentioned Neutron claimed that, after post-privatization break-up of their *obedinenie*, their firm cut back on purchases from former *obedinenie* brothers. To raise funds to pay wages, energy, and supplies, managers used loans from pocket banks or private banks, but these came with interest and were finite. Managers had to turn to sales—not a crucial task in the Soviet era, thus leaving managers unprepared. As scholarship on the Soviet economy has shown, Soviet-era managers were adept at working in shadows and through networks to obtain supplies (i.e. through the *tolkach*, Soviet-era employee who worked informal networks for needed supplies), speculate, or play Plan politics.[60] When state-run hospitals rejected his medical equipment, one manager lamented that he could not locate alternative buyers, as he had "neither channels nor skills for such activity, and there were no corresponding specialists at the firm."[61]

As managers sought narratives of blame and solutions, one common tactic was to return to traditional partners and "business as usual," buying inputs and producing outputs as if the end of the USSR was surreal.[62] Facing a tight budget in early 1992, firms continued to place orders for raw materials, industrial machinery, components, etc. Price-setting was cautious: managers based prices on production cost plus a minor mark-up to avoid the image of *spekuliant* (speculator), a powerful Soviet-era moral, anti-capitalist category that still carries weight.[63] As some partnerships were of long duration and between managers linked through informal relations, raising prices violated informal codes of reciprocity and fairness—what one scholar dubbed a "directors' ethic."[64] This constrained price hikes until late 1992, when survival forced managers to raise prices.[65] (Russian scholars contributed to discourse by framing this behavior as *Soviet*—do not maximize profit at the expense of long-term partners.) This does not mean directors held prices to Soviet-era levels, nor that they held down prices for all clients; they were selective. As inflation hit, Russian managers were not always prepared to raise prices with familiar clients. This was clear in how they arranged contracts: some managers felt that, despite rising prices for electricity, water, materials, and even wages, raising prices for familiar clients was risky. One assistant director for sales at a lathe-making firm related their (1995) experience with pricing and contracts:

> We worked for a year—and then we understood that life dictates several different problems, and we needed to introduce into [contracts with a purchaser] new points and to foresee this or that situation…At first we did not have this point [in the typical contract]: when the prices for materials go up, when expenses for energy or heat rise, the seller has the right to reconsider raising the prices of the castings. Life prompted us to do this…

She added that most buyers reacted calmly to the need to raise prices. Everyone faced inflation, so raising prices to cope, rather than to improve profits, was a response to a common problem and a legitimate tactic—within limits.[66] Even as managers left some partners, Soviet overproduction meant other traditional partners remained and new clients emerged. Producers produced—if someone wanted the good, there was demand. This "business-as-usual" contradicted Gaidar's early hope that tight budgets would make firms spend wisely. If anything, in early 1992 managers remained most concerned about obtaining supplies at reasonable prices, or at all.[67]

Business as usual led to the second dilemma. Managers continued to order and produce—but at some point in the chain of production and sales, no one could pay for the finished good. The choice was barter or no payment. A tractor maker produced tractors for a state or collective farm, racking up debt for inputs; when the farm could not pay, the tractor maker could not pay suppliers. Stocks of unwanted goods and debt then piled up. Managers had misjudged (if they had ever investigated) potential demand. Further, with the absence of bureaucratic money or subsidies, firms bought and sold on inter-enterprise credit—the buyer would take goods and promise to pay later. When one firm could not obtain payment to pay its debts, its creditor could not pay *its* debts. The resulting "inter-enterprise arrears crisis" or "solvency crisis" (*krizis neplatezhei*) and "sales crisis" (*krizis sbyta*) threatened Russia's economy. Now they discovered that many buyers could not pay. Post-Soviet managers were damned no matter what they did.

Examples of continuity and business-as-usual abound. One was Kirovskii Zavod's K-20 mini-tractor. Conversion from military production and reduced state purchases of tanks forced Kirov to increase attention to tractors. The K-20 was a 35-horsepower mini-tractor for private farmers, a *fermerstvo* only emerging— yet Kirov managers felt 60,000 K-20 tractors per year met potential demand, despite the 800,000 ruble ($4,000) price tag.[68] Although this seems nonsensical in hindsight, when the number of individual farmers barely reached 100,000, the mini-tractor was a point of pride; in the crisis year 1992, a factory newspaper headline read, "The K-20 does not want to surrender."[69] The supply manager did not believe low demand was a systemic issue—Kirov's unique "tractors have and will have demand"[70]—and in 1993 the Kirov newspaper cited a McKinsey report that the market for small and medium tractors was better than for large tractors.[71] While the state encouraged the K-20, managers went ahead full steam even though they could have resisted passively and put the K-20 on a slow track. It emerged a rudimentary analysis of Baltics farming in 1990 was the sole basis for the K-20 design. Asked for an economic analysis, one assistant manager gave a long reply on the K-20's *technical* traits.[72] But a lesson was learned: "we must turn out only so much equipment as is demanded. In connection with this, corrections to the tractor output plan for 1992 were introduced and the 1993 plan has been worked out, that is output is calculated precisely for that volume that can be realized in full."[73] Kirov was not alone in focusing on traditional goods and assuming demand. The state of affairs at electronics firms Svetlana was no better. Declining sales there sent managers and employees into despair,[74] especially with the news in 1993 that an American firm refused to sell Svetlana's goods at prices to their liking.[75] Yet Svetlana continued to produce what was ordered. Even by 1994 the state and others had not paid Svetlana; familiarity with insolvency by then makes one wonder why such agreements were made. Daughter firm Svetlana-EVP produced six billion rubles of crockery that sat in storage.[76] As bad as the situation seemed at Kirov Svetlana, there was still hope they could generate income from non-military output such as steel, piping, tractors and related components and similar output (Kirov), and various electronics components and consumer goods (Svetlana). Other firms had less maneuverability and older technology. Lathe-maker Sverdlov continued to focus on lathes and associated goods (e.g. castings), even through they lost traditional East European and former Soviet trading partners. In 1992 military and state purchases tailed off, and for February–April 1992 Sverdlov's debts grew from 27 million to 60 million rubles, although insolvent buyers owed 53 million rubles. By June debts increased to 124 million rubles. Only 97 lathes and machines were sold in January–June 1992, compared to 127 in January–June 1991.[77] Electricity and heating costs increased massively. Had this not happened, Sverdlov would have paid 18 million rubles for electricity; but energy costs jumped from 9.5 million rubles for January–May 1992 to 25 million rubles for June–December.[78] General director Pokasiuk freed employees to expand income, and they set about doing what they knew best—making lathes—which provided little but additional debt in the crisis economy, even though output reductions reduced expenses. Military-industrial clients reduced purchases by 92 orders, more than expected. Sverdlov earned more than they spent, but more than half of expected sales did not materialize—lathes were made for buyers who could not pay.[79]

As enterprises suffered the impact of business as usual, declining payments, and rising input and energy costs, managers decided to test the state's commitment to hard budgets in a game of chicken. Some analyses claim that, armed by a tacit agreement with employees and local politicians, managers used inter-enterprise debt against hard budgets.[80] Voluntary associations lobbied for subsidies and tax support, not always with success.[81] By late 1992 inter-enterprise debt threatened the economy: debts of 800 billion rubles in March 1992 had ballooned to 3.2 trillion rubles by July. As a temporary measure Central Bank head Viktor Gerashchenko cleared some debt by issuing credits.[82] Yet this "political chicken" analysis assumes too much collusion by too many managers. It was also a massive risk for risk-averse managers. Business-as-usual may have had political chicken as an *outcome* or hoped-for *solution* to arrears—but it was not the only motive. When the game got serious and Gerashchenko responded, many firms were already in trouble. While the state did continue some subsidies via purchases, they were insufficient to cover debts. Along with this was moral outrage. At Leningrad Metal Factory (LMZ), managers and employees complained that their key supplier Izhorskie Factories continued to ship defective castings.[83] Where were market responsiveness and the realization that in a market, prices and quality conform to supply and demand—which LMZ managers and employees assumed would benefit them? Echoing this, a production manager at Svetlana complained that breaks in supply lines led to a 25 percent fall in production. In the Soviet era Svetlana suffered late or low-quality supply, yet supplies arrived. After liberalization and the end of the USSR, their Ukrainian watch parts supplier "dictated" what they would supply and how. Ironically using entitlement rhetoric, a supply chief complained that, with the state out of the supply picture, Svetlana lost its "rights to supplies" and was at the mercy of suppliers' "extortion."[84]

Identifying the firm with production rather than finance remained strong—else why not adopt a financial logic and shut down unnecessary production? Logics of production and paternalism were not openly blamed. According to one survey, maintaining the labor collective was more important than finances: managers waited for employees to leave rather than lay them off.[85] Managers did not code inter-enterprise debt as due to their own strategies: "a huge unpaid debt run up by a Russian firm should not necessarily be taken as an indication of poor management. Because the accumulated debt has grown out of proportion…and became a commonplace in all industrial sectors, debt performance has become separated from the business performance of the firm."[86] That clients kept ordering goods was proof a firm's goods had high quality and demand—yet purchasers could not pay. From electronics firms to producers of lathes, steel, and tractors, one sees a confidence in output and such refrains as "Our products are as good as those from the West." Russian buyers *were* in a financial crunch: clients such as collective farms wanted Kirovskii Zavod's tractors but could not pay. Svetlana's calculators, televisions, and electronic devices were losing to foreign competition or had no market. Shocks of rising energy costs plus declining demand and payments arrears made money important, yet debt was only becoming a market signal. Other managers felt that their technology and human capital locked them in a particular sector: LMZ managers felt they were trapped making heavy equipment for electricity production, but even electricity monopoly EES could not afford purchases.[87] In this context, managers blamed the state for disaster; firms were innocent victims who would prosper were enough money in circulation. As one manager for prices and expenses lamented: "We have, quite frankly, a country of paradoxes. There should be money, but there is none. Not at all!!!"[88]

Frantic responses: just make it and sell it!

Even with the double dilemma, the Red Directors' production logic dominated practices and justifications, in no small part because Red Directors still had enterprise authority.[89] In 1991 Svetlana general director Gennadyi Shchukin claimed his firm *overfulfilled* targets and was not in crisis. Real problems were lack of a financial plan, weak laws, and price liberalization.[90] After 1991, finances became a problem, but activity was still coded in terms of production. In December 1992 Shchukin discussed Svetlana's condition in terms of output and plans (overall plan fulfilled by 75.4 percent, consumer goods by 100.8 percent). Several months and a new director later, output was still percentage fulfillment, not income.[91] In 1994 Kirov discussions were in terms of production targets.[92] Sales remained the selling of what was made, and production was driven less by market dynamics than enterprise politics or survival. Even rudimentary marketing research reflected confusion. KamAZ managers claimed market research suggested producing 200,000 autos for 1993, when only 5,000 had been ordered and paid for in advance. Agricultural organizations and farmers ordered 26,000 tractors; only 3,500 were actually bought.[93] Watching finances drop and debts climb, managers and employees looked frantically for blame and solutions. Managers berated shopfloors to find new goods and earnings, blaming them for declining sales and income. Shopfloors blamed macroeconomic instability, not quality or productivity.[94] Managers understood survival depended on cash or barter from sales, which now took precedence over supply. Barter in fact became an important survival strategy, by which firms could pay off part of their debts and wage arrears.[95] Another shift in strategies and categories came as managers began to distinguish between "demand" (*spros*) and "solvent demand" (*platezhesposobnyi spros*)—the ability to pay—and they increasingly emphasized solvent partners and competitive output. This categorization remained problematic—"many managers highlighted that consumers very much needed their products, but buyers 'simply did not have the money' to pay for them"—yet managers were aware payment was important.[96] Value was still coded *vis-à-vis* production, but managers were paying more attention to pricing—within limits of fairness to traditional partners.

Desperate tactics: flood the market

"Flooding the market" was an important and widespread survival tactic in which the "market" was an arena of exchange where buyers and sellers would somehow meet and equilibrium would arise. When business as usual and staying with tried and true output failed, managers turned to flood the market with anything their shopfloors could possibly make. The part of our story demonstrates an interesting hybrid of Western market and Soviet production logics and decoupling: adapting Western business rhetoric superficially (addressing market demand) while not implementing the logics and practices that would make the rhetoric organizational reality. On the surface, managers began thinking in terms of markets of consumers and differentiated needs and tastes; they also realized they needed to produce for consumers who could pay. Yet the way to tap into this market was not to study demand but to apply existing skills to production: rather than discern what consumers there were and what they would buy and alter production accordingly (even if it meant abandoning one's business identity),[97] managers applied production skills to widen output in hopes demand would come to them.

There was some variation in the extent to which managers embraced widening output to flood the market in hopes of finding buyers. Electronics firms (e.g. Svetlana) as a rule could produce a wider range of consumer goods and components; their engineers could tinker with their technology to produce glassware, dishware, and vacuum tubes from the same basic technology. Firms in heavy industry and engineering output were more constrained, although in the Soviet era they too had to produce civilian goods and so had some skills and technological capacity for maneuvering. Yet there were only so many variations of lathes that Sverdlov could make. Despite this variation, what is fascinating is how common this response was, even across firms with different degrees of maneuverability in output. While technology could impose limits on how far managers could flood the market, most subscribed to the strategy. As well, managers more likely to engage radical restructuring—as at Sverdlov and Pozitron but also Svetlana electronics—were more likely to embrace flooding the market as a desperate measure. At LMZ, on the other hand, new measures of sales and production were muted, just as restructuring had been.

Given decoupling and the difficulty of altering thinking and practice overnight, it is no surprise that "survival programs" for solving crises demonstrated change *and* stasis. Some firms, such as Sverdlov, formulated more comprehensive programs. Ambitious if vague action points included "specification of demand for lathes in the domestic market and for export," better economizing, preparing production of "non-traditional goods" such as woodworking machines and lathes for railway and tram rails, and creating a marketing division. Employees questioned whether financial calculations proved measures would work, and some daughter firms noted that more had to be done inside the enterprise.[98] As an assistant manager at Stankolit noted, Sverdlov had to help its daughters financially, or else they would demand payment up front from other shopfloors for purchases. KBs (*konstruktorskoe biuro*, divisions for designing new products) desperately tried to devise new goods, yet too few lathes were being sold. One shopfloor chief bemoaned that the four-day week hurt morale: "the worst is when a person is at his work place and has no work." Responding to the mood and guarding his position, in 1993 Pokasiuk enacted a "stabilization program" little different from the earlier survival program.[99]

Other firms' survival plans, if less systematized, were grounded in the production logic and faith in their work. The tactic was to unleash a flood of goods in hopes of finding consumers who could pay. This strategy had affinity with enterprise restructuring: autonomous MPs would devise, produce, and sell new goods to paying customers or to traditional clients.[100] Not only did firms flood the market with traditional goods—Kirov tractors, Elektrosila turbines, Svetlana light bulbs and glassware. KBs also designed and MPs produced new goods.[101] "New lathes—new possibilities" reflected Sverdlov's hopes new designs would tap demand. One KB and partner shopfloor designed and produced woodcutting lathes they claimed had a market.[102] Given troubles in the timber sector, this project was probably not successful. LMZ showed pride in their engineers' many patents for unique designs that, some claimed, "brought LMZ a significant economic effect."[103] Engineers at engineering and heavy industry firm Elektrosila refined electronic meat-grinders and vacuum cleaners, deficit goods that should have demand.[104] One Elektrosila KB boss claimed, "[We make] tools...without analogs...If you ask an economist today if department #70 is profitable to the factory, from the majority you will hear, '[that] production is loss-making...' [but] Elektrosila...has profited from our work."[105] It did not strike him that designing does not mean income and survival, although he used a market claim: our goods make a profit, even though economists say that the design department itself is overall a loss-maker.

One example of Soviet logics and flooding the market is from electronics firm Svetlana. The Soviet logic meant coding output value via inherent properties, and electronics firms were susceptible to fixating on uniqueness to justify investing willy-nilly in new goods. Managers and employees believed their goods were inherently exemplary despite low demand (clearly distorted by reforms). The logic of production and unique output was reinforced by Svetlana's history of making unique military goods; but military purchases shrank after 1991. The chief of shopfloor #88 stated that in 1991–2 civilian goods had gone from zero to half their output. Defense production was easy: make the good and the state will buy it. With civilian production, "you need to seek a buyer, to know the situation on the market and to be able to know the multitude of things not familiar to us earlier." Now the shopfloor had to learn "how to trade" as well as produce and obtain inputs.[106] Svetlana managers and shopfloor bosses used uniqueness to defend status and justify flooding the market. Shopfloor bosses cooed that their goods "had no analog," were high-quality, and had demand.[107] Unique products included a ceramic boiler that boiled a pot of water in 36 seconds, a telephone distinct from German imports, thermostat components for small freezers, hand-held video games, alarm clocks, and decoders.[108] Special lamps were on sale in the competitive American market that demanded the high quality Svetlana managers claimed they easily achieved: "the name 'Svetlana' is well-known there." The sense of panic and pride in producing *something* was strong in 1993 and after: Chinese goods were cheap, but Russian goods were better—even Americans knew that.[109] Even in 1999 such rhetoric and logic survived, seen in a *Vestnik sviazi* (*Communications News*) demand to support domestic telecommunications firms that had "developed the production of contemporary telecommunications technology...that by their characteristics can compete with foreign analogs on the Russian market."[110]

Managers also took to the skies, traveling to expos and trade fairs (*iarmarka*). Like the *birzha*, these were sites where buyers and sellers congregated. Some Petersburg firms hoped such exposure to a larger group of potential clients would raise sales. Fabric producer Nevskaia Manufaktura (née Krasnyi Tkach) made some sales at a 1992 trade fair and a 1993 household goods exhibition in Moscow.[111] Fairs and exhibitions expanded dramatically in Russia: from 397 in 1991 to around 1,600 in 1995, most in eastern Siberia or central Russia. Local governments supported larger exhibitions (e.g. Petersburg's LenExpo, the Siberian Fair) to aid local firms. Firms also used fairs to gauge demand, and often general directors themselves or their immediate subordinates directly represented their firms.[112] In autumn 1992 Viktor Pokasiuk and colleagues traveled to China, India, Italy, and the United States,[113] and in 1994 to exhibitions in Hanover and Beijing, which marketing director G. A. Zomba filmed for employees. The film showed Sverdlov's best lathes, but shots of Chinese lathes "brought the audience back to reality" and drew disparaging contrasts.[114] Kirov too took to the high seas for sales. As early as 1989 Semenenko made exports a top strategy and sent managers into the world when Kirov gained export rights, but an unpleasant realization dawned: international giants looked on Kirov as a small partner with cheap labor, not an equal with creative input. Kirov's trade subdivision learned employees and managers had to show "professionalism"—knowledge of how to sell, set up contracts, and work with banks—that did not come easily. "In new conditions we continue to use our rusty, stiff, ill-suited but habitual, worn-out mechanism [micromanagement]."[115]

Coding value: sales and pricing

Decoupling of rhetoric and practices, manifested in flooding the market, appeared in discourse and practices of setting value. Price-setting was not oriented to finding supply–demand equilibria. It was also hampered by incomplete information on production expenses (materials, energy, wages), giving pricing a random quality.[116] In June 1992 a Svetlana employee expressed frustration with current pricing: "So far [the sale] of *obedinenie* products occurs to a large degree blindly." Who decided the price for a good sold in different locales, e.g. Tula and Vladivostok? Pricing now required more information and analysis, and the market had to be studied— but how?[117] While some state-owned firms still had to fulfill state orders at prices around production cost, they could also sell to employees and to private traders. By law state-owned firms had to sell some goods, even for individual consumers, to state-owned retail networks in 1992. Some firms, such as Elektrosila, sold goods to their own employees below production cost, according to the assistant director for prices and expenses:

> ...selling meat grinders to our laborers, we first set the goal of saturating the consumer market, especially Elektrosila employees, at a price which at present practically does not cover even production expenses. And when this meat grinder enters the market, of course the price will be higher. It will be something between...expenses and demand.[118]

Slowly managers started thinking that prices might come from market demand and not costs alone or dictation by the producing firm (which many managers hoped for after liberation from state control). As one manager put it in 1992, "We have to be ready to sell a lathe at that price which the purchaser proposes, and curtail the expenses of its production."[119] Discussing how chaotic relations between subdivisions raised the price of the final product, one Kirov manager claimed profitability should be based on the final product, and prices for parts and labor from each subdivision would be set as part of this overall whole.[120] By 1993 and 1994 managers claimed that pricing decisions had to be based on "the market" itself.[121] Yet what exactly was this market, and what was it demanding? Without knowing a product's supply–demand equilibrium even inexactly, actors latched on to analogs. Results of a survey of small businesses from winter 1993–4 suggest that entrepreneurs followed three strategies. In order of popularity, they were setting a price that recouped expenses and provided "normal" profit, selling lower than competitors, and orienting prices to those of analogous goods.[122] The first, the "cost + profit" formula, was also popular at industrial firms. Several managers told me that they set profit by determining costs and then adding a mark-up, perhaps of 10–15 percent for the more modest, 20 percent for the more ambitious.[123] In the third method, managers might orient prices to others' similar goods or follow quotations for goods taken from indices in trade publications.[124]

Most methods had a logic of survival or superficial adaptation. Partly this was due to decoupling, but other factors added to the challenge of learning. Financial crises made it difficult to discern which tactics would work, creating panic over new strategies. Initial concern with supply rather than sales, based on previous experiences and the assumption that market reforms would automatically improve sales, soon dissipated. The feeling that post-Plan autonomy, in contrast with previous subordination to state and Plan, would give producers a superior position and better profit masked possible financial threats. We cannot deny the influence of tax law, although overreliance on taxes to explain sales tactics, including pricing via the cost + profit formula, is a mistake. The December 27, 1991 federal law "On tax on profit of enterprises and organizations" set a rule to assess profit tax. If a price was above production cost (*sebestoimost'*), use the difference to tax "profit." If the price was below production cost, use the difference between production cost and market price. To stop tax fraud, a 1992 amendment stipulated that state-owned enterprises could not sell below production cost— managers might declare a formal low price for goods but sell them informally at a higher price. It also improved tax revenues by creating profit where there was none, reinforcing pricing rigidity and non-monetary exchange. It also inhibited inculcation of marketing logics of sales and valuation. However, strategies and discourse were too convoluted and imbued with a sense of journey to be reliant on taxes alone. Despite tax law, cost + profit was a popular tactic—why? This conformed to Soviet value methods and was an easy way to set value. If the state's drive to collect revenue inhibited inculcation of market principles, it was joined by persistent practices and superficial knowledge of marketing logic.

Adaptation and enterprise politics

Internal enterprise authority could hinder adaptation; given the dynamics we saw in Chapter 3, it would be surprising if it did not. Adopting a new logic and imposing it on employees could face resistance if an enterprise were politicized. Such was the case at Svetlana electronics. Even before 1990 employees complained that, despite increased enterprise decision-making autonomy, "in the enterprise itself (at least ours) administrative methods remain unshakable."[125] In response, in December 1992 director Gennadyi Shchukin moaned, "not everyone understands that you need to work in a new way" and that change occurred "very slowly" because "there still lives the old approach to formation of plans: make a report and then put the good on the shelf."[126] The assistant director of personnel moaned:

> Our [shopfloor] bosses need to study. They need to break stereotypes of economic relations. They have a weak understanding of "economic freedom." There are few who have the desire to sit down with pencil in hand and count how much something will cost and how much it will return in perspective. They don't want responsibility for decisions.[127]

Paradoxically, an older shopfloor chief agreed: "I am against the market. I am not ready. The majority at Svetlana...are people who are older, sturdy, patriotic, tough. We lived that way for seventy years. We were brought up that way, and we cannot reconstruct our psychology overnight."[128] In 1994 an assistant director ranted that employees had not adapted to the new world.

> ...for more than a year we are shareholders, but where is our feeling of ownership? It does not appear automatically...A [new] strategic direction is opening up new lines of production. Yes, for this we need money. But we do not even know what to open up. Let's suppose that we get money, we need to put that into work. But into what kind of work? So far this ideology is at work: there is no money—there is nothing to think. We need to think! We need to seek out purchasers...We achieved economic freedom we dreamt of. Our hands are freed, but we continue to look up [for state aid]. And we put responsibility for all our difficulties only on the government. Of course, we have many questions and claims towards them [e.g. unpaid purchases]...To point to the government and wait for help from it is an empty exercise. We need to act ourselves...[129]

As we saw in Chapter 3, claims to knowledge and normality were part of the battle over authority and enterprise restructuring. These quotes from Svetlana were among the more pointed in this context, although this was far from the only case of such discourse. Sverdlov's marketing experiment should be seen in the context of internal battles: Pokasiuk claimed managerial authority on the basis of knowledge; if marketing did not work, his authority was undercut, unless the real fault was shopfloor employees unable to produce quality goods or unable to help marketing by devising new goods. This also suggests that adaptation would be most difficult in enterprises where restructuring was most contentious. As I discuss later, Sverdlov, Svetlana, and Pozitron did not fully adapt to the new marketing logic; ultimately, Sverdlov went bankrupt, Svetlana entered a larger electronics *kholding*, and Pozitron (post-break-up) treaded water until a younger set of managers applied their skill set to constructions demands in the era of oil wealth.

Muddling through marketing: a new idea and its adoption

In 1993 and 1994, power-culture dynamics forced managers to continue refining their business logics and practices. Managers began to feel the weight of a new capitalist hegemony of transition culture, transmitted through media and financial practices. Managers could ignore debts so long as bankruptcy was inoperative or bankers did not recoup loans. As banks reduced loans and younger banking experts focused on investment value, money dried up. Bad experiences with past practices and financial hardship prodded managers and shopfloor chiefs to ask if their own practices were the problem. Balancing income and expenditures began to dominate decision-making,[130] but this begged the question of *how* to do so. Some managers were relatively proactive as it became clear the state would not ride in to save them. Realigning services was one tactic. Demand for October Railroad services dropped. One client reduced daily shipments from 65 wagons to 24 by 1994; others reduced shipments by two to three times, and employees noted fewer "informal shipments." The culprit was convenient, cheaper trucking. Managers reduced rates by 30 percent, and container traffic improved by $600,000.[131] In addition to realigning services with demand—seemingly straightforward as an individual tactic, but as we are seeing, less so as a developed logic of business organization and practice—some managers were turning to a survival tactic with a Soviet spin: finding patrons to fill the state's former role. While this tactic created dependency similar to that of the Soviet era (dependency on the state), it also meant survival, and perhaps the chance for investment and learning. In 1991 LMZ sought German firm Siemens for lucrative joint work, a partnership they and Elektrosila would court throughout the 1990s.[132] Svetlana received some profit from joint ventures with Americans who distributed Svetlana goods, such as special television lamps, in the US.[133] Kirov courted Gazprom, Caterpillar, and General Electric; this gave "Western experience of restructuring the organization of work."[134] A deal with Caterpillar via joint-venture Nevamash contributed income and image. As managers of Kirov's steel laboratory noted, "When other contractors found out we were making steel rolls for Caterpillar, it was the highest mark of authority…"[135] Kirov managers sensed the value of oil and gas and set out to make piping and processing equipment. They talked of using UN humanitarian aid to make baby carriages, which had unmet demand of 300,000 units per year. In 1994 Semenenko lobbied the city for funds to make buses; later they signed a deal to supply lathes to automaker VAZ. Except for gas piping and tractors, these were new products.[136]

Foreign and some Russian consultants and publications (e.g. *Kommersant*) began to talk about new categories and models of survival and success. In addition to "privatization" or "auditing" came a new panacea: "marketing." One Kirov shopfloor boss lamented, "[We] do not have a real marketing service or intelligible advertisement...no stimulation of sales, no planning of produced goods assortment." In response, Kirov managers created a group to work with McKinsey and the European Bank of Reconstruction and Development to determine future plans and design an information system. An Elektrosila manager noted, "earlier we only heard a word such as 'marketing,' and now we are beginning to undertake it closely."[137] Yet embracing the panacea did not mean learning and inculcating it in practices and organizational procedures.

In the beginning was the word...

Marketing departments spread like contagion by 1993. At Svetlana, one of the first to discuss marketing was V. G. Vil'dgrube, director of the firm's trading department.

> We never thought the time would come when it would be difficult to sell our goods. That problem did not exist because we were a monopolist for a range of goods and because for certain periods demands by various types of consumers was not satisfied...To live well there are two paths: either change the form of seeking partners, including foreign partners, or begin producing what we can sell...A whole range of our products do not have demand. But often that output does have an application, we just need to find out where...Then this problem arises: the sales service cannot turn their attention to all possible consumers...This work, the search for buyers, demands a large number of people...who take on the work of recommending our goods, knowing where we can sell them...This task, of course, demands good attention to advertising, particular engineering knowledge, knowing the technical parameters of our goods and their potential, to convince the potential buyer to buy it and to understand what the buyer wants...

Note the end: marketing as reaching out to buyers to explain and sell a good. A rudimentary first step was recognizing consumer power, but the link to production changed little. "Marketing" as used by the journalist was propaganda, preparing necessary documents, and word of mouth.[138]

If some at Svetlana talked vaguely of "marketing," managers elsewhere implemented it quickly but in vague form. Managers, journalists, and employees at weapons producer Arsenal learned "marketing" was unavoidable. In the dictionary, this was a capitalist practice of actively studying and acting on market demand to improve sales; an encyclopedia noted marketing was systematic administration of production to maximize profit. Producing quality goods was not enough; Arsenal had to link goods to the market. Thus, managers set up a marketing department and external relations department (*otdel vneshekonomicheskikh sviazei)* and in 1992 provided computers and refurbished an office for receiving foreigner visitors. The first task was seeking investors for a "social development" program and to help open these departments.[139] Yet even this discussion was in terms of freedom to advertise and expand links to foreign partners. Further discussion of "marketing" was in usual jargon: "analysis of the market situation... analysis of market demands towards quality...analysis of competition...analysis of prices."

Other firms quickly opened "marketing" divisions, but this did not mean marketing was entrenched. At telecom firm Krasnaia Zaria, which opened a marketing division in 1992, enterprise economist Andrei Petrov articulated his narrative in a full-page article on "new methods and forms of manufacturing and economic activity used in economic systems worldwide. Marketing has a special place..."[140] In a powerful demonstration of transition culture, Petrov invoked Peter Drucker and Philip Kotler, who taught the firm should produce and expend only what was necessary, as a homemaker prepares only that food needed for a meal. Krasnaia Zaria marketing employees would "find out what kind of goods, at what price, with what characteristics, in what quantity and where to find potential buyers, and then to decide whether to organize production." This required "a systematic approach to organizing and administering enterprises," including devising new goods, identifying equipment to make them, setting up sales and distribution, and actively seeking buyers rather than waiting for them. Petrov admitted marketing was not just sales *(sbyt)* but ideally made sales tactics redundant, as goods would fit consumer needs: "If earlier sales faced the task of realizing an already-produced good, in the work of a marketing system one needs to produce that good which will be bought." This was not easy: "Introducing marketing requires not only structural changes of the administrative apparatus, but also changes in the consciousness and psychology of leaders' behavior at every level." Qualified cadres were scarce; after so much reform employees might cynically see marketing as "panacea for all misfortunes."

> To work for the needs of the consumer, we need not only new equipment, shopfloors, departments, finances, materials, and the like. A deep restructuring *(perestroika)* in the psychology of every collective of the enterprise, from leaders to workers, is needed. And the task of the leadership is to create these conditions. Such large changes cannot occur in one moment...if this is not done, the enterprise will still end up needing to start over.

Alas, a combination of global competition in telecommunications technology and conflict and collapse at Krasnaia Zaria (the *obedinenie* followed nearly the same trajectory as Pozitron) denied the firm more united capacities of technology and human capital.

In October 1992, Viktor Pokasiuk decreed a marketing department into existence at Sverdlov. In contrast to Arsenal, Sverdlov created its marketing and sales department *(otdel po marketingu i prodazham)* by merging existing departments for contract relations, sales, information and ads, and external relations. New marketing director Grigorii Zomba claimed this was a long but necessary process: "the service is supposed to give the initial command [to produce] and in return secure relations with the consumer. Otherwise the unforeseen circumstance might occur when, for example, the *obedinenie* works beautifully, but no one needs its products." He believed marketing required knowledge—he read on marketing years before and signed up for an intensive marketing course taught by a University of Massachusetts professor. His aim was "to achieve a sharp increase in the income for goods on sale" by maintaining sales in domestic and foreign markets and pushing traditional and non-traditional goods. He claimed his department was successful, although the real added value was unclear. He rejoiced at purchase *orders*—actual income and solvent demand were another story. The enterprise journalist expressed skepticism: certainly a single department could not solve all Sverdlov's problems! Zomba admitted this was only one part of success, but they had obtained purchase orders.[141] One senses marketing was a new façade over business as usual and enterprise conflict—marketing was not well integrated.[142]

Nearby LMZ followed suit. Marketing director Aleksandr Kobalev took credit for improving LMZ finances. Marketing needed a suitable office for meeting clients. Kobalev raided the patent office for advertising staff and took commercial and market analysts from other areas. Again, marketing meant an office and technical skills—not a logic of business and departmental relations. Kobalev praised his people and blamed production for setbacks: "production does not possess sufficient flexibility for rapid reorientation to other profitable and deficit products, buyers for which the marketing department found." As at Sverdlov, his optimism seemed misplaced given solvency problems and was not without irony. His goal was to convince traditional clients to buy traditional goods, i.e. electrical stations already using LMZ's output. Marketing was selling what LMZ produced. Kobalev contrasted this to the strategies of Siemens, e.g. fêting Russian journalists at exhibitions of Siemens technology. There remained much to learn.[143]

Incomplete adaptation

Managers continued to feel the pressure for change from media and consultants: "marketing" was normal, Soviet/Russian practices, including adopting *marketing*, were suboptimal.[144] Ongoing crises lent weight to this view, and by late 1992 and into 1993 more managers came to view marketing as a totem of normal business: as one Elektrosila manager noted, "To experiment with product output without relying on studying the consumer market is very dangerous."[145] By 1994, Western advertisements flooded Russia: Snickers, Pizza Hut, Reebok, and the MMM investment pyramid (1993–4) using flashy television ads and the lead actress of popular Mexican soap opera *Simply Maria* to target Russian naivety with promises of 1,000 percent yearly interest on investment.[146] Yet marketing as practiced in transition culture's homelands is more than this: it is systematic study of potential demand to devise strategies. Russia did not have a vast reserve of marketing experts, nor did firms have funds to hire foreigners. Some Russians had marketing knowledge.[147] In-house analysts at a voluntary association of St.

Petersburg bread firms set up sophisticated business plans.[148] Andrei, a former industrial psychologist, set up a consulting firm that ran management seminars (e.g. on negotiation games and problem-solving) and did marketing studies. Small firms in furniture and food retail contacted him on optimal sales quantities and prices for coffee and a telephone directory. He produced marketing reports based on survey data and analysis showing how many people would buy these goods at what price. The result was a Bell curve: at a high price few would buy, but a middle price maximized profit.[149]

There was the occasional director who saw the greater logic of marketing and the need to learn its tacit knowledge *and* incorporate it into organizational practice. At Baltiiskii Zavod, infamous director Viktor Shershnev (1988 to 1992) brought a marketing department into existence in 1992. Successor Oleg Shuliakovskii realized one could not create marketing by decree.

> We again have a vivid lesson in what a marketing division for a western firm is. It is a serious structure occupied with analyzing the economic as well as the political situation in the banking sphere and so on, which helps the firm make an evaluation of necessary construction of this or that type of ship in the next five or ten years…We do not have anything like that. In fact we are at zero or close to zero in creating this service.

Shuliakovskii admitted that bad experience of a tanker contract with German clients taught them to use trained lawyers and construct realistic contracts and sales strategies. He noted sadly: "We have to admit that we work very badly, in all aspects of our activity. It became this way not today, and not yesterday. The roots are long and deep. I have to say that by our evaluations today of labor expenses, delivery time for our ships, and quality we lag behind the leading European firms by around twenty times. Not two, not three, but twenty." He tried to deflect blame from the state: "little depends on who leads us. We must reject the thought that a new, kind, intelligent tsar will appear and turn everything around." In an unusual departure from bragging about output, he admitted Baltiiskii ships were not as efficient as competitors'.[150]

Learning curves and levels of knowledge complicated the implementation of marketing. Superficial knowledge of "marketing" as surveys is not tacit knowledge and practice of marketing. Opening a marketing department is not adopting a marketing logic. The head of marketing at the firm Polieks said: "at the start we could not even understand what was demanded of us." Book and courses helped, and managers studied input costs for regions. Marketing was cheap supply or making a database.[151] Elsewhere there was vagueness and simplicity. Marketing at Elektrosila included studying potential domestic buyers and their solvency, possible exports, and coordinating production and sales to determine output quantity.[152] Few details were given—significant, given the detail provided on privatization and restructuring. Sverdlov managers discussed a "unified marketing network" in 1992 and 1993 but took serious steps only in May 1994, after an assistant director traveled to the United States and managers met representatives of the

International Executive Services Corps, an outfit that brought retired American managers to Russia for consulting, reinforcing transition culture's hegemonic categories. They took steps "to perfect marketing" and to arranged a distribution network and servicing department (*distribiuterskaia set', servisnoe obsluzhivanie*), but they admitted marketing "must be understood at a higher level."[153]

The initial lack of knowledge was reflected in how firms implemented marketing. Functions associated with marketing—pricing, sales and production strategies, economic plans—were split among different departments with similar functions in the command economy. Most managers lacked fundamental knowledge of marketing and how to implement it. The director of St. Petersburg's October Railroad claimed cadre training was the "key to success" and lamented weak knowledge and too few market experts: "In conditions of a market economy, the first and foremost goal is raising qualifications and improving the system for preparing cadres."[154] A marketing service could propose to the client not a "maximum sum" for services but a satisfactory "optimal sum." Assistant transportation director A. Golubchenko was more critical still. The Railroad did not properly serve its clients, and the Railroad still followed non-market practices:

> So far no one has analyzed [losses]. The irony is the meaning of such new categories as "market" and "competition" come to us with difficulty. We sit and wait for clients, just as before. A delivery agent comes to us, and we immediately throw a colossal sum...prices, additional fees, payments for all sorts of additional services. The potential consumer of transport services is disillusioned and leaves, our conditions do not satisfy him.[155]

One joint-venture manager noted that "selling well requires additional specialized employees knowledgeable of market structure, with links to information, oriented to world prices."[156]

In May 1993 Railroad managers gave in to requests from a younger assistant manager described as "mad over marketing." By 1994 marketing was supposedly the reason that the Moscow subdivision was the only subdivision with increased traffic—although the popular Moscow–Petersburg rail line might have helped. Consulting services, services for obtaining hotel tickets, and new payment methods to avoid arrears were marketing's helpful additions.[157] As one assistant manager noted, "The [marketing] division appeared first of all to try to find solutions by *non-traditional* means that would lead the thinking of these or other bosses in a contemporary direction..." Yet marketing worked best only for one subdivision, and setting up marketing had not been easy. One manager blamed managers' and accountants' weak knowledge: "those on whom everything depends...were raised in such a way that with all their might they try not to produce anything new, they stubbornly hold on to principles inculcated in the 1950s and 1960s."[158] One manager admitted marketing was not developing fast enough. The use of computers for service and data collection would help, but only if directed by marketing logic—but his "agency" did not have a specialist trained in marketing! Other plans included a system in which passengers could purchase a ticket and other services (e.g. hotel reservations) all at once. In 1995 ticketing window #44 handled some hotel reservations and ticket purchases together.[159]

Directors did not always implement marketing advice. One study of machine-building firms in the Far East revealed in 1995 "a low degree of adaptation… to conditions of economic reform." An analysis revealed restructuring followed whim, not rigorous analyses.[160] Managers copied each others' policies and structures as legitimate solutions to common problems and signals of competence. Yet copying a form does not mean implementing its logic: firms might adopt fashionable strategies and organizational forms, yet these are superficial, with little real impact on practice. Given the difficulty of fundamental cultural change and difference between Soviet and market logics, we might expect post-Soviet decoupling from marketing. As one Russian scholar noted:

> The psychological factor has great meaning for older generation directors, who are oriented in their activity to fulfilling tasks issued from above. Their main goal is to get their labor collective to realize proposed tasks; the problem of sales of produced goods is not of the highest importance for them. Therefore, the necessity of creating new goods with demand is put by these directors into second place. The primary strategy is walking around the offices in Moscow with the goal to convincing the government to buy products that are obsolete or even not needed in previous quantities. The main argument in such visits is, "I have a labor collective of several thousand. I need to feed them."

When directors of enterprises understood the impossibility of continuing the output of old products and tried to begin producing new goods, they ran into the problem of studying the needs of consumers, but they had neither the needed number of specialists at the firm, nor independent marketing services for the solution of such a problem. Russian industry still had not acclimated to the rule "produce that which will be bought, and don't sell that which you make."[161]

Despite the new marketing hegemony, the marketing narrative did not automatically, instrumentally, translate into real practices. The culprit was decoupling: adapting surface images but not deeper logics and practices, for which initial implementation of marketing provided a clear case. Managers could claim to adopt marketing, but this did not mean everyday practices corresponded to sophisticated methods and procedures of ideal marketing. I return to the case of a St. Petersburg electronics firm, whose commercial director cited earlier (p. 136) claimed little changed after 1991. This logic of weak change was echoed in their experience with marketing. In 1993 Baker and McKinsey visited the firm and recommended several strategies. The first was to restructure their store. Like other electronic firms, this firm had a store for radio and electronics parts. The commercial director whom I interviewed added a section to sell alcohol, sausages, and food—someone seeking a television part could now buy vodka and salami, a snack after trying to fix the television. The Americans suggested they sell their own products, along with electronic imports through a deal with an Asian firm, at the store. The firm followed this advice; in 1995 I visited the store and saw Asian calculators and VCRs, Asian and Russian televisions, foreign refrigerators, and Chinese fur coats. The Americans also suggested opening a marketing division. This task went to the assistant director for quality. In early 1995 the division consisted of him and a few graduate students competent with spreadsheet programs. The students would read electronics trade journals and visit electronics stores to discover competitors' prices, to set their own accordingly. This was the extent of marketing—no detailed studies of potential markets or sales and production strategies, or alignment of production with market demand. I probed further and less subtly if this was all. Did the marketing division study market segments to come up with a strategy for targeting sales and maximizing income while minimizing losses? Did marketing involve studying alternative sales and production strategies—e.g. selling other goods such as imported fruit juice, if this would be profitable? Were marketing work and analyses integrated into decisions about production so that the firm would know just what to produce, rather than just trying to sell what had already been made? He responded that they did only what he described: collecting price information. Marketing was not integrated with production or any other part of the firm's activity.

Petersburg shipbuilder Almaz followed a similar logic of sales and marketing. To scholars who studied the firm, Almaz management had no clear goals and strategies for orienting production and sales; the firm was still "product-oriented"—"production is the core function at Almaz, and it is strictly ruled by the Production Department which co-ordinates the material flow, the production and the quality control in the different workshops in the company."[162] While institutions were changing, personnel were changing more slowly, resulting in a "lack of market thinking" due to the "lack of qualified business economists and marketing personnel." Almaz survived when the shipbuilding industry slowly improved in the later 1990s, and the firm attracted powerful shareholders who helped inject financial investment in the firm. The machine-tool industry also had to change strategies, not only to survive but to overcome past legacies, such as overspecialized production that made it difficult for individual firms to diversify output and concentration of production in large firms. One recommendation for this sector was "to organize marketing services and to subordinate to them the work of engineering and production services, the activity of whom necessarily had to be undertaken together with purchasers." Additionally, firms in this sector needed to diversify their output and adopt the corporate form.[163]

Much of the problem was in the disconnect between marketing and activities of design and production. One observer suggested that

> formation of production strategies at industrial enterprises so far is to a large extent chaotic. First, at the majority of enterprises studied, [managers] do not understand the necessity of priority development of the assortment of goods [i.e. diversity]. This especially concerns production undergoing military–civilian conversion, which lives at the expense of preferential credits. As a result the enterprise [engages] in development and preparation of production of a set of goods not related to each other. In this there is no feedback between the producing and engineering-design subdivisions and departments of sales.

As a result, neither a preliminary analysis of an optimal level of output (break-even analysis) nor a sorting-out of reasons for failure in development of new types of goods is done. Even at more efficient enterprises a contemporary economic mechanism for administering creation and output of new products is absent.[164]

The production paradigm still dominated. In 1994 discussions over Svetlana's near-collapse, an assistant manager of MP SED-SPb claimed, "We know that objectively our output was needed yesterday and is needed today. It will be needed long in the future."[165] Specific output, not market results, remained the criterion of worth; business selling what was made. Most managers I interviewed did not appreciate marketing's full logic or challenges of integrating design, production, and marketing. Despite prodding, managers stated that marketing was researching prices or basic advertising to sell what was made. One 1994 survey of 30 general managers showed understandings of business plans, investment, and planning. Managers who claimed to follow "strategic" planning had horizons of two or three months. For 82 percent of firms, employees worked out business plans, although 60 percent had no special training. Half focused on production, 39 percent on restructuring, 36 percent on investment, and 31 percent on marketing. They also claimed marketing was most important basis for success, ahead of tax stability and investment.[166]

Organizational dynamics could hinder implementation of marketing. People invoked logics and practices in organizational structures and procedures. Enterprise restructuring shifted responsibility for sales and income to shopfloors, leaving managers with incentives to *portray* themselves as competent. Larger enterprises inherited Soviet planning and economics departments; as staff moved from these to marketing, they took previous skills with them. Yet cadres with some skills did not guarantee marketing logic operated in procedures. Note how most quotations here reflect status: assistant directors of economics or engineering, general managers and shopfloor bosses, not only marketing directors. At firms where I interviewed, marketing/sales directors were in secondary positions; assistant directors for economics/planning or production still had decision-making status. Marketing was a small group with out-of-the-way lodgings and staffed by younger individuals, not always in production or sometimes only recently hired, of short tenure and low status. In firms where I did multiple interviews, I met the head of marketing only at a specific request; directors passed me on to others with status, i.e. production, planning, supply. Andrei Petrov, marketing director at Krasnaia Zaria, clearly saw this problem. Other enterprise employees and managers would have to accept marketing's status, for one task was "correcting" shopfloor work and "choosing strategies and tactics of enterprise behavior."[167] In some cases, marketing and related services were not only low status; higher-up managers blatantly ignored their recommendations. At some banks, young economics graduates worked out plans and suggestions about loans, yet higher-up managers gave out loans based on networks or politics.[168]

Over time decoupling led to production–marketing hybrids, especially if they aided survival by discovering patrons or helping firms stay afloat without fundamental change. Telling data come from a March 1997 meeting of the International Directors' Club.[169] Managers discussed payment arrears of 400 billion rubles, plus 300 trillion rubles in wechsels (*vekselia*) and ersatz money in 1997. Directors blamed taxes and state arrears, solvable with low interest rates, state payment for purchases, and clearing interfirm accounts. Asked what *they* could do to ease arrears, managers cited barter, followed by marketing (without being clear what this meant) and using wechsels or prepayments. Yet despite marketing's importance, it was surprising that

> given the general admission of the great or very great importance of the problem of non-payments, almost none of the survey participants considered it necessary to create their own special groups or subdivisions with the main goal of seeking solutions to the problem. Practically no one even considered it important to bring in analysts or consultants.[170]

Despite claims of marketing's importance, few managers in this group took it seriously. When asked to brainstorm solutions, the consensus was "change in ideology and psychology of administrative personnel with reorientation [from production] to sales." However, five firms in good shape blamed state insolvency and "the inability of many enterprise managers to work in accordance with market demands." Were payment arrears cleared, these managers would invest in equipment and marketing; but the majority would use income for operating capital and wages.[171]

Muddling was neither stasis nor fundamental change. The next few pages briefly discuss marketing at Kirovskii Zavod in the latter 1990s. General director Semenenko admitted *bona-fide* problems of learning and implementing marketing logics. Experience with higher-status foreign partners was one shock; most managers had limited market experience and once believed they could sell goods and dictate prices to Western buyers. But Kirov was not hopeless; he offered himself as proof of learning, even if his was the language of producing particular goods, decentralization, and patronage.[172] Tractors were central to its identity; while the firm produced only one-fifth of its potential, it kept trying to sell, focusing on production and quality using imported components and using dealers (*dilery*) for distribution.[173] One assistant director claimed it was "difficult to find financial means to rework new technology for all our models." One tactic was overlapping projects for economies of scope, e.g. a tractor and bulldozer that shared components and production processes. Kirov managers looked to Australian and Canadian markets, but research revealed shipping costs hurt competitive pricing. Foreign competition intruded: Czechs preferred John Deere tractors. Kirov increased its studies of possible demand:

> The marketing service receives data and handles goods sales, and one task is creating networks of dealers and agents to sell equipment…The KB is busy

studying the market and kinds of equipment to make, whether it corresponds to standards and demands of the consumer market in Russia and beyond. We are strengthening these two services now and working actively with them. A second direction…is creating new equipment, based on results of work by these services…

There was new urgency to marketing: ruble appreciation *vis-à-vis* the dollar and inflation drove up Kirov dollar prices so that a $25,000 tractor in January 1995 cost $42,000 one year later.[174]

Competition, transition culture, and stable managerial control (cf. cf. 3) aided introducing marketing with some impact at Kirov. In summer 1997 the assistant director for sales and marketing, a younger man in his forties, told me how marketing staff analyzed data on potential Russian and foreign clients to tailor output and prices.[175] While such work was circumscribed—it focused on output that Kirov could realize through existing production technology—his department did have an important say in overall production and sales policies, although it did not dictate them. More important for his marketing staff was nurturing relations with clients, especially long-term partnerships as a safety net to complement the search for possible new clients and output. His description of Kirov's marketing stood in contrast to marketing at other major Petersburg firms in 1997, such as a local poultry processing FPG, a machine-tool enterprise, a furniture producer, members of a local industrial association, and local production-centered associations Rosstankoinstrument and Stankoinstrument. (The former united machine-tool firms, including Petersburg's Sverdlov.) One analyst likened the corporate structure of these last two to early voluntary associations (Chapter 5) based on networks. They did not coordinate members' activities, and the production logic of "make what you know and look for buyers" persisted.

Marketing and sales logics spread unevenly throughout Kirov's complex structure; the break with the past was incomplete. Profit came from simple reckoning of what people bought. Vadim Adamovich, manager of Kirov's "TNP Factory" (consumer goods), noted the best-selling goods were summer or garden goods, sports equipment, and electric shashlyk (shish kabob) machines. Staff studied prices of analogous goods and reduced their prices to compete. He noted:

> Of course we are all children of our time and learn as we go along, and because we were born in another time there is much we do not know. The word "marketing" is new to us, sometimes incomprehensible, but it is necessary to work with the market seriously, to study it, to react to consumers' demands. No one can answer how that is done, and I do not know either, despite having two economics degrees…[Our marketing] is small, two people. They study marketing seriously, and we don't distract them with other tasks.[176]

Profit was small, wages late, provision underfulfilled. In January–February 1997, TNP fulfilled only 41.5 percent of its plan, although they did not consider seasonal variation of sales. (If only they could sell beer on Kirov grounds…) Output remained key to identity and strategy: "significance [of tractors] for Kirovskii Zavod is difficult to overstate. Despite other earnings, financial health of our entire enterprise depends on conditions at…Petersburg Tractor Factory."[177]

Uncertain hegemony: power and market knowledge decoupled

In 2002, as a stronger ruble made imports cheaper and WTO entry promised competition, minister Aleksandr Braverman asked Russian producers to take marketing seriously to improve competitiveness. He noted how a gas station chain manager used marketing to improve income by over ten percent. The Russian Union of Industrialists and Entrepreneurs agreed and asked the Russian Marketing Association to study the use of marketing audits for capitalization.[178] Yet one account of Urals firms noted how marketing was badly understood. These managers relied on networks for sales, copied others' tactics, and focused on subsistence rather than innovation. While marketing training improved (although Russia still needed its own schools), managers did not or could not incorporate that knowledge into practice. Organizational politics played a role: production and sales managers had higher status. Many marketing functions were spread across departments—price-setting in the financial-planning department, goods profile in sales, product design in production, brand work in advertising. Managers who tried to use marketing found sales still required networks and bribes. Some marketing experts claimed a "civilized" and "rational" ideology of "business-to-business" relationships, based on marketing logics, would take hold if managers broke with tradition and refused to use networks and favors— not something widespread or easy. Dearth of skills and organizational and managerial obstacles to incorporating marketing logics persist.[179] Oil wealth rewarded adopters, muddlers, and retreaters alike.[180]

A popular image of the 1990s is corrupt managers undermining reforms and using shell games, barter, and looting because this is what they knew or they wanted to asset-strip.[181] I do not deny this happened, but this is only one narrative. Managers could set up daughter firms and use marketing to augment ill-gotten gains. Yet *habitus* kept Red Directors from learning the market to enhance gains. Because of the multidimensional nature of power-culture, the story of marketing demonstrates change and continuity, through continuing organizational routines and perceptions and practices.[182] Primary rhetoric changed from plan fulfillment, to finding buyers, to finding solvent buyers, to marketing. Yet managers did not always adopt new logics. Two ways to correct decoupling are enhanced opportunities to learn and to reorient organizational structures; and forced market exit. The first requires actors with knowledge who can enforce learning. Market exit, economists' preferred method, requires gatekeepers (brokers, lawyers, politicians) with power, knowledge, and will—not easily legislated into existence. In exploring woes of the machine-building sector, Russian scholars made eight suggestions; the first was that "at every enterprise market services must be organized and work of engineering and productive-technical services, whose activity ought to be run jointly with consumers, be subordinated to them." When state control weakened, no new organizational logic entered the vacuum.[183]

This chapter's goal is not to deny that technology, sector, capital hunger, or tax and other laws can affect strategy and performance; I aimed to move beyond a one-dimensional instrumental logic of economics and institutionalism to examine *how* they matter and are refracted through power-culture's dimensions and dynamics in change. Decoupled learning, and contradictions between old and new hierarchies of knowledge, impinged on adaptation. I have also shown another dimension to post-socialism's narrative of "success" and normality: creating new categories and practices, and problems of adopting practices commensurate with the narrative. Russians moved from Plan hegemony to marketing hegemony; success was profit *obtained in a particular manner* (added value through marketing). Multidimensional power-culture challenged implementing the narrative, which required knowledge of a supposedly natural, normal practice. If anything, by readily accepting marketing, Russian managers were less aware of its mythic side. Marketing as mode of scientific analysis and organization has potential gains, but as panacea it blinded Russian managers to the enormity of change needed in everyday practices and logics. Implanting marketing in organizational logics and practices might improve performance, but it is no cure-all.

This was especially true if others played by different rules. Economic theory assumes competition and consumer power make market logics hegemonic; yet what if logics are *not* shared? One example was a group of Petersburg chemists. They rented part of a chemical factory for their production, which included chemical ingredients for shampoo sold to an Italian company, ingredients for cosmetics, and a special powder for trapping water molecules to absorb water for cleaning up industrial sites, removing water from pits, etc. Publications, patents, and certification showed the powder to be efficient and biologically safe. It could be added to sausage to retain water content, improving profit for sausage-making firms: if sausage is priced by weight, water loss hurts profit. Local sausage-maker managers accepted the chemists' health certifications and agreed that using the powder was rational, but no one bought it—not because of price or other fears, but because they were not interested. The chemists said this was a recurring problem.[184] "Success" was embedded in collective logics. Being a market actor was not easy.

At the outset I suggested that one explanation for pricing, informality, and the virtual economy is taxes.[185] My account does not discount the impact of taxes or other laws on practice—but it also points out that taxes are far from the dominant explanatory variable. Within the context of tax laws, there was plenty of room to maneuver. If draconian taxes create incentives not to expand sales by much, why embrace the new marketing logic to improve finances, when retreat or muddling through are alternatives? Formal tax law forbade industrial firms from selling goods below production cost and allowed tax assessment based on a good's "market price" (set by a complex formula) rather than sale price (if below production cost).[186] Tax assessment could be based on prices for analogous goods and services, if that value was higher. But tax laws, like other laws, depend on how officials enforce them and how actors react (evade or adapt). To leave explanations at taxes misses the development of logics and practices that evidence makes all too clear. There are five reasons why taxes need not be the primary explanatory variable. First, pricing is only part of sales strategies; even the virtual economy is more complex than reactions to taxes. Second, court challenges and tax law changes relieved some pressure, and the 2002 tax code eliminated assessing profit tax on anything but profit (difference between price and production cost).[187] Yet this did not deter firms from continuing to use "cost + profit," despite its limitations. Third, tax-based incentives did not prevent managers from being flexible with "profit." For many Russian managers, the profit mark-up was the focal point of marketing and pricing. Fourth, managers I interviewed never used taxes to justify this formula, even though they complained loudly about taxes. Taxes might drive exchange underground or hurt investment, but it did not seem explicitly to determine sales strategies. They talked vaguely of "cost + profit" as how things were done, even when I suggested alternatives.[188] Fifth, formal tax *law* was not always *practice*, given chances to bribe, negotiate tax assessment, or pay for goods "by briefcase."[189]

Returning to an opening theme: in 2008–9, American, British, Japanese and other managers socialized in modern capitalism methodically (not "objectively") studied financial landscapes and instituted survival plans that involved gradual cutting of costs in labor, purchase, and production. As we have seen, Russian managers circa 1992–3 had methods and methodologies inspired by Soviet-era logics that survived, papered over by "marketing" and then oil wealth. Yet change was not impossible, and the crisis of 2008–9 shows an interesting mesh adaptation of market logics and reemergence of 1990s logics. Facing severe financial constraints again, some managers and owners cut expenditures by reducing output and laying off workers—although one senses from business reports that they were less methodical than Western comrades.[190] Wage arrears, barter, and desire to keep skilled employees, familiar practices in the 1990s, returned to managerial tool kits.[191] Paternalism migrated from firms to state populism. Yet, given the rise of state-centered empires, one wonders about further change in logics and strategies—is a pseudo-Soviet logic of production and militarization returning?[192] Putin brought in neither Red Directors nor demonstrable entrepreneurs to run Kremlin champions; he brought in bureaucratic allies. In the 1990s state economic involvement was problematic; now only a handful of analysts (writing in foreign-owned publications) question whether state champions can produce wealth via efficiency and innovation.[193] With oil wealth, propaganda, and political power Putin's regime is constructing a hegemonic counter-narrative of national power based on natural resources rather than Western-style capitalism—a counter to previous transition culture.

5 Fields of battle

Power-culture, property, and remaking fields

The genesis of Russian capitalism requires its own theology. Its creator and original sin are one and the same: privatization.[1]

Property and governance are central to neoliberal market reforms, but their creation and consolidation require legitimation and reification of power and risk contention over new normality in authority and practice.[2] In post-Soviet Russia, the first battle over normal authority and practice was managers versus employees; the field of battle then expanded to managers versus owners and shareholders, and then oligarchs versus Vladimir Putin's *siloviki*. This last act opened with the showdown between Putin and Mikhail Khodorkovskii. Khodorkovskii's oil giant Iukos embraced Western transparency and business methods. Rich and restless, he funded political parties and hinted he would leave business for other ventures. Seeing him as a threat, *siloviki* used *kompromat* (tax fraud material) to arrest him in October 2003. In December 2004, state-owned Rosneft took Iukos's main division Iuganskneftegaz in lieu of tax debts. This grew into a grander process: in 2005 state-owned weapons export monopolist Rosoboroneksport began accumulating metallurgical and industrial firms. Its daughter Rostekhnologiia (Rossiiskaia Tekhnologiia), run by Putin ally Sergei Chemezov, became the main engine of this state empire. *Siloviki* were on the move for property and the master field of power.[3] Putin's state elite created a new narrative of normality: a technocratic state elite running property empires to rebuild the economic order and claiming greater wisdom, capacity, and authority than civil society. That new normality and the actors who championed it faced a supreme challenge in the 2008 global meltdown: could the new *dirigisme* allow Russia to ride out the crisis and ultimately prosper, or would it lead to conflict over scarce resources and injustice (a *siloviki* fear)[4] and entrenchment of state elite power at any cost?

Privatization was central to policy discourse and analyses,[5] which too often fell into the one-dimensional trap of privileging instrumental rationality and assuming rational cost–benefit calculation of interests and tactics is behind scrambles for wealth and power. Yet this does not ask where interests and tactics come from, how actors framed and justified tactics, and how frames reshaped struggles. Why should the initial positions of Red Directors and oligarchs persist? Why did Red

Directors keep acting like Red Directors and oligarchs like oligarchs, when sticking to their guns risked failure (Red Directors in the 1990s, oligarchs after 2000) and joining the winning team even as a subordinate could bring gain? To cite power and wealth as motives risks tautology: *what shaped perceptions of interests, identities, and normal actions?* An easier path would have been for Red Directors, state officials, and financiers to split the pie and divide and conquer, as did many East European managers and owners.[6] An important answer is that Red Directors, oligarchs, and officials were competing to remake core myths and logics of economic normality, the master field of overarching logics, and statuses. The end of the Soviet order and radical reforms unleashed competing claims of normal property and governance, and oligarchs or *siloviki* not only rewrote laws but also became totems of normality other actors were impelled to follow (narrative power). Consider the contrast to field dynamics elsewhere. American fields shifted with new laws or crises (the Sherman Anti-Trust Act, Great Depression), but new logics retained fundamental core tenets: centrality of private property and a relatively autonomous economy. Privatization in Britain and Mexico involved states selling property and altering regulatory frameworks, while Russia's story is *rewriting* the very rules of the game.

We are moving from micro-practices to broader collective practices and framing, but power-culture and practices *fractally* remain crucial and act one organizational level higher. In Chapter 1's schema, power is *vertical (→ unstable horizontal →) unresolved*, with competition over conceptions of normality. Different actors (Red Directors, financial entrepreneurs and oligarchs, state elites and officials) began with initial relational positions, *habitus*, capital, knowledge, and interpretations of normality. To make sense of change—from early pluralism of logics to domination of oligarchs and then *siloviki dirigisme*—and to make sense of the dynamics and forms of conflict, we have to move beyond power politics, laws and policies, and interests alone. Merely to posit alliances and desires for gain cannot explain *patterned* alliances and conflict—these remain taken for granted. We have to look at *how* opportunities, policies, interests, and normality were perceived by actors. This returns us to power and culture. We also must note that the consequences of actions, especially conflict and consolidation, had profound effects beyond the mere creation of new property empires and elite alliances. The winners were demonstrations of a new normality of policy and practice, even if the legitimacy of such normality was unstable.

This chapter has one methodological caveat: given high stakes of property and the field of power, close data on elite networks and deliberations are dangerous to collect. Being a player or having access to this data could lead one to jail (Khodorkovskii) or death (Vladislav Listev).[7] Yet this does not mean we should ignore this topic; we must use expedient "Kremlinology," scouring existing data to pierce byzantine façades. I bring new data on some aspects of field change (financial-industrial groups) and embed derivative, secondary sources on oligarchs and *siloviki* in the framework for a new way to think about property.[8] Limits or errors are grist for future research.

Rewriting the game: property, governance, and fields in flux

The predominant narrative of market capitalism gives prominence to property ownership that provides incentives for efficient investment and resource use, creates civil society, and binds the state.[9] In neoliberal discourse, privatization is a magic bullet; the economics narrative of post-socialism was little different initially.[10] Later analyses noted political struggles over property, yet these require more embedding in emergent processes and logics of power-culture and normal organization and practice.[11] Privatization was not only redistributing resources (carving the pie); it was socially reconstructing economic meaning and authority (what kind of pie and how to make it). This requires we examine who constructs what myths, meanings, and narratives related to new boundaries and rules of economic communities. We have some insights on which to build. In a seminal work on East Asia, Gary Hamilton and Nicole Woolsey Biggart showed how economic structures mimic frames regimes use for legitimacy.[12] David Stark and László Bruszt invoked fields to explain post-socialist policy and privatization,[13] although they say little about change *and* continuity or about conflict.[14] Neoinstitutionalism, seemingly well-placed to take analysis further, requires some correction, and fortunately Bourdieu left several tools. Fields are arenas of power and conflict over norms, status hierarchies, and rules of capital. The key field is the "field of power" or "master field" of elite organizations and actors that, through homology, provides a template for lower-level fields.[15] Remaking property directly impacts the role of the state and distribution of authority, engaging reconstruction of the master field. Russia's story was not one of fine-tuning field rules, boundaries, and authority; it was remaking their essences. In this process, historical legacies acted in two ways. They could be immediate templates of post-Soviet relations; and contenders could propose *opposite* logics as normal. Also, the past survived as the Soviet *habitus* and provided tools, rationales, tactics: for managers, defending enterprises and production; for financiers, promoting the myth of capital's inevitable and inherent superiority; for state officials and *siloviki*, defending national interests that market reforms could harm.

Scholars of privatization address resource power and might hint at discursive power and agendas, but they miss narrative power and the scramble to stake out material and symbolic positions and remake power-culture.[16] In the Soviet system, fields were organized around ministries and local *glavki*. The ideology of Party supremacy, production, and paternalism justified centralized control, tempered by informality and patronage. Reforms altered resource access, and control of firms and fields moved from ministries to managers and owners. Following privatization, managers might obtain proxy control of employees' shares or buy them via holding companies. Lobbies such as the Russian Union of Industrialists and Entrepreneurs worked alongside clans and state-business networks that became nodes for mobilization and agenda-setting. The narrative dimension of power was structured by transition culture via discourse, influence of insider "reformers," Western advisers, and aid organizations who framed private property against abnormal socialism.[17] The initial battle was managers and employees and their welfare narrative versus financial elites and their narrative of markets and private property's superiority. In mainstream media, economic capital, state as neutral referee, and fair property distribution dominated. Critics attacked reform *processes* and Red Directors as "Soviet" holdovers or thieves. Putin later laid out a narrative of Russia as hydrocarbon power with a security elite rebuilding the nation.[18]

Habitus, capital, relational position

In Chapter 1 I suggested actors' *habitus*, capital, and logics of practice, created by initial positions and socialization, provide lenses and resources for interpreting and reacting to crises and opportunities. This does not mean stasis; yet as these groups confronted each other, their logics of practice and organization seemed to calcify. Red Directors saw a lack of protection for production; oligarchs saw the need for stable property rights and freedom to invest; *siloviki* and state officials saw weak social order benefiting only elites. Red Directors had a *moral economy* of local organization and defending output; money was a means to this end. Their capital was networks of supply and politics, and local knowledge of production. Financial entrepreneurs, especially oligarchs, followed a *profit economy* of money, a logic and identity learned in the Komsomol and Party; economic capital was their tool, and their identities centered on manipulating resources (rubles, people, Party property). This was not surprising, as they began their careers on the margins of production as Party activists and engineers. While Red Directors viewed Gorbachev's reforms with conservative suspicion, younger entrepreneurs saw opportunity. State officials were in a confused state in the 1990s. Their logic and legitimacy formally was defending the public good, and their currency was political capital of law and *kompromat*.[19] Informally, state officials' logic was *prikhvatizatsiia*, personal use of state authority for status or gain—an outcome of Brezhnev's "little deal" (position as secure bailiwick in return for loyalty) and weak accountability. Yeltsin's logic was creating the new in opposition to, and destruction of, the old. This meant state officials followed Soviet-era logics while trying to make sense of new laws and logics (destroy that order and support a new market they did not understand). This left officials weakened and unable to use coherent meanings for normality and legitimacy, until Putin linked these seemingly disparate strands: officials gained status and rewards by reining in the economy for *siloviki* state authority. Money was useful if it benefited the ends of state power and national prestige; after 2000 Putin *et al* would not ignore the financial gains to be made from oil wealth, which they redistributed to create a state populism that they then turned into political legitimacy.

Role of the state

Through policies and such organizations as the State Property Committee (*Gosudarstvennyi komitet po imushchestvu*, GKI), the Russian state set out to remake both property relations and its own structure and role. Three models of state–economy relations were available. One was the Anglo-American model, implied in 1990s reforms: the state as neutral referee enforcing rules articulated in public arenas (but by whom?) to facilitate and regulate the market. In the second model, that of Europe and East Asia, the state participates actively as first among equals but respects economic rights (e.g. property). In both models, states regulate for public welfare via due process; property is state-supported, institutionalized autonomy and competing authority. The third model is the state above property and even law, subordinating the economy to state and regime. Tsarist patrimonialism and Bolshevik revolutionary justice, versions of this model, were a powerful legacy embedded in state officials' assumptions and practices. In contrast to Western reciprocal elite–subordinate obligations, Russian and Soviet state–society relations were pseudo-colonial: exploitative, distrustful, antagonistic. Tsarist and Soviet states were not beholden to law: "rule by law" rather than "rule of law" was the norm, with law a politicized appendage to state rule. Linked to this was studied distrust: state officials' assumptions and formal rules that private actors would cheat, and popular assumptions that state claims were a façade for exploitation.[20] This hindered creating an economy with the state as guarantor of rights and recourse, subordinate to law. One result was the tenuous security of private property that could be lost if officials decided to apply their interpretations of the law, as they saw fit, to prosecute businesses.

Organizing property

As Moscow's grip weakened, managers, financial elites, and some state actors went into action. Initial structural locations and *habitus* created different interests, identities, logics of normality, legitimacy claims, and resources. Managers (insiders) were wary of reforms; they saw Kosygin's reforms fail in the 1960s. They justified authority via paternalism and production and aimed to fortify the autonomy of Brezhnev's "little deal." In Soviet socialism, directors as Party-state agents had legitimate *use* of property, but not ownership.[21] Controlling shares after privatization meant entrenching autonomy from outside control; as proxy shareholders managers continued logics of production. Even under outside ownership directors accepted owners' rights to residuals that the Soviet state once expropriated. New Soviet entrepreneurs and financiers began as organizational subordinates or outsiders, sometimes in the Komsomol. With no direct memory of earlier failed reforms, they were less wary of opportunities; as they were not managers, they had less to lose. Rather than challenge managers, they went into the shadow economy and emerging market, using organizational resources to speculate. Their logics and justifications were markets and money; their resources money and networks to reformers. Property and shares meant control over decision-making and capital. State officials, especially in the security apparatus, lost status in the late 1980s and 1990s, especially when Yeltsin split the KGB into the FSB and other components. Their basis of authority had been security. *Siloviki* and officials had to withdraw to local arenas, e.g. "First Departments" watching enterprise secrets, arranging local use of state funds.

These logics were manifested in financial-industrial groups (*finansovo-promyshlennaia gruppa*, FPG), collections of industrial and financial organizations centered on a holding or finance company.[22] Three forms and logics of FPGs emerged: a production-centered "Defensive" FPG, a diversified, finance-centered "Financial" FPG, and a state-centered FPG. Each mirrored their creators' logics: Soviet managers (Defensive FPGs), younger financial entrepreneurs and elites (Financial FPGs), and state elites (state-run FPGs).[23] Each addressed a perceived risk: supply and support (Defensive FPGs), investment (Financial FPGs), and national interest (state FPGs). Defensive FPGs were voluntary groups pursuing defensive tactics of lowering risk and uncertainty, providing mutual aid, maintaining trading relations, and defending production and paternalism.[24] Financial FPG principles privileged accumulation and investment, with ownership centered on a financial organization and daughters to avoid anti-monopoly laws. Private bankers invested profits from currency or other speculation into privatized firms. They organized FPGs to consolidate property governance and diversify gains to lower risk. The third FPG emerged as state elites accumulated control over property through appeals to security. Principles of production and Brezhnev-style patrimonialism merged with awareness of rents. Thus, three logics competed: sector-based voluntary groups for production and welfare; state-centered empires based on networks and bureaucratic power; and empires of diverse firms producing for profit. These logics grew out of legacies and contingencies: initial social locations and *habitus* and responses to opportunities, which kept shaping groups' perceptions of normality and claims to legitimacy.

While no periodization is perfect, I suggest field logics followed rough stages. In the first (1988–94), Red Directors, new financiers and bankers, and state officials fumbled for policy models and justifications. Defensive and Financial FPGs emerged and coexisted, with local officials favoring the former and federal elites caught in between. In the second stage (1995–8), an alliance between elite financiers (oligarchs) and the Kremlin boosted Financial FPGs. Conflict between managers and financiers heightened in the second stage of privatization. An important policy was the loans-for-shares scheme, where the state sold its shares in potentially lucrative natural resource firms in auctions rigged for finance allies. The Kremlin–oligarch alliance enforced a finance-centered logic, with fields crystallizing around Financial FPGs; Russia might have become South Korea. Yet this arrangement rested on an unstable foundation. In the third stage (1998–present), the ruble crash and privatization scandals weakened Yeltsin and financial elites. Putin and *siloviki* came to power, using *kompromat* (compromising legal materials), prosecutorial powers, and state property empires to impose a new order of technocratic nationalism framed as "dictatorship of law," using state-owned firms as vehicles for power.

Table 5.1 Fields and property

Aspect (logics, framing)	Defensive FPG	Financial FPG	State-owned empires
Clan; interests	VPK/industrial (Korzhakov, Soskovets); defending production and survival	Finance clan (Chubais); accumulating profits	Yeltsin: Gazprom clan; personal gain via state Putin: *siloviki*; augment state power and security
Principles of authority and governance	Managerial knowledge and position. FPG control holding company through shareholding.	Shareholding, money, finance and market knowledge; state allies, dubious procedures. Clash with managers, minority shareholders.	State authority (legal and material resources). Indirect control through *kompromat* threat.
Normal economic activity; central totem	Secure production, supply, paternalism. FPG as security blanket.	Profit-centered FPG secures and coordinates investment. Elite-led capitalism, state distributes and guards share ownership.	Consideration of profit and welfare, but national security crucial. FPG as vehicle for state influence.
Risk and uncertainty; solutions	Uncertain rules and supply; reinforce and structure supply through FPG coordination	Return on and of investment; diversified holdings and shareholding to control decision-making	Loss of state control, security (of development, state power, control of strategic resources)
Templates, inspiration	Soviet ministries and *glavki*	Multinational corporations, Japan/South Korea models	Version of Soviet control without micro-management.
Property	Enterprise shares in holding company, whose shares members own. Property as claim to residuals.	Central holding company owners shares in members. Property as decision-making authority.	Property as claim on residuals and decision-making, subject to regime's formal/informal demands. Less sacred than state.
Role of the state	Local governments facilitate Defensive FPGs. 1990s: state policies after FPG emergence	Yeltsin's regime supports, policies follow oligarchs' initiatives. Putin's reins in/attacks.	Yeltsin allows personal empires; Putin reins them in as vehicles for state power.

Opportunity and necessity (1988–1994): reorganizing post-Soviet fields

The end of the command economy weakened the field of power, and managers and financial entrepreneurs began staking out positions and justifying logics of normal property, governance, practice, and status, and seeking organizational means to defend or advance their logics and *habitus* as normal to defend and augment gains and position, reinforcing their own legitimacy. Managers created voluntary associations and Defensive FPGs, and financial entrepreneurs created private banks and Financial FPGs; both reflected a "moral economy" of production and national security versus a "profit economy" of shareholding and profit. For Red Directors, whose Soviet experiences inculcated a conservative operating logic,[25] reforms meant autonomy. Mikhail Khodorkovskii noticed this: while he eagerly used reform opportunities, his superiors and other managers had seen "reforms" come and go and were inclined to fortify autonomy rather than make money.[26] As managerial authority, production, and paternalism were sacred, privatization was legitimate if it defended production.[27] Managers' main defensive tactics were obtaining shares to guard against outside challenges, and designing voluntary associations and Defensive FPGs for mutual aid. Financial entrepreneurs were less encumbered by Soviet experiences and saw liberalization as chance to profit. Initially they did not command state resources but could convince patrons for seed money. With no perceived responsibility to employees or production, they made profits as "institutional entrepreneurs" playing the margins of legality, using Party-state resources to speculate with currency or deficit goods. If managers used paternalism and production for status, financiers used global capitalism and transition culture, especially money. Local state officials joined managers, helping create Defensive FPGs to maintain earlier functions coordinating supplies and funding. Federal officials were caught between the camps; initially, Kremlin clans were still well-balanced, and despite vague rhetoric of hard budgets, liberalization, and privatization, there was room for different models of state–economy relations.

From such rudimentary interests, practices, and reactions, competing logics emerged. This was possible in part because of the opportunities afforded by a privatization program that did not have a narrow, focused structure and that was not strictly enforced by the state. In the first stage of privatization, three paths of initial privatization were possible. In the first path, employees and managers (insiders) received 25 percent of shares *gratis* and could obtain an additional 10 percent at a reduced price. This was not so popular because it did not give insiders initial majority shareholding. In the second path, which employees and managers were more likely to favor, employees had first crack at 51 percent of a firm's shares (priced at 1.7 times their nominal value). The third and least popular path involved buyout of the enterprise, as approved by employees, with the promise of investment. After this first round of privatization, employees usually held the majority of shares, with a significant block still with the state. Workers often gave managers proxy rights; but they could sell shares, and potential buyers found ways to coax them to do so. While there was as yet no developed stock market, this did not mean shares were inaccessible. Shares were a potential tool for power; what remained was clarifying property rights and the wielding of governance, and how legitimately to organize property holdings.

First steps: from ministries to voluntary associations, from Party to private banks

In the Soviet system fields centered on the state bureaucracy, embodied in ministries and local-level *glavki* that coordinated distribution, production, and enterprise functioning. This provided one template for post-Soviet industry. If ministries and *glavki* formally disbanded or changed with the end of the command economy—losing direct control of enterprises—their essence survived as voluntary associations (*assotsiatsiia*) and Defensive FPGs. In contrast, financial entrepreneurs began with private cooperatives or banks and networks outside the production sphere, e.g. to Party cadres, other entrepreneurs, and so on. Rather than rely on a preexisting model of relations and functions, they had to build new organizations and follow a vaguer foreign model of finance and business. In this early stage privatization supported managers and employees, indirectly aiding the manager-centered logic—insider privatization was the regime's attempt to make privatization palatable. But even in the last years of the USSR, managers used initial autonomy to restructure relations in sectors, mimicking state ministries and *glavki*.

Voluntary associations

The unraveling of the Soviet economy gave Red Directors both opportunity and necessity to buttress their local organizational positions. While they worked on their own enterprises, they also looked to local and national partners in their fields, others who from their Soviet experience were in their networks and with whom they shared a common logic. To address collapsing state investment and supply and to guard production and authority, directors in the same sector came together in such groups as concerns (*kontserny*), associations (*assotsiatsii*), and cartels (*kartely*). In the Soviet period, industries were organized in national ministries and local *glavki* according to output—heavy industry, electronics, textiles, etc. This was a model that managers and local elites understood and could create from existing networks, and so ministries and *glavki* were the template for new associations. From 1987 on, with freedom to act and worsening supply and finance, firms in the same *glavk* maintained ties through *kontserny* and *assotsiatsii*. Various associations sprang up in St. Petersburg's industries: engineering, heavy industry and military production, bread, furniture, and foodstuffs. The main rationale for creating associations was not to rebuild centralized control but to create "mutual aid societies." Most voluntary associations were confined to sectors in which managers were linked through networks and shared production identities and interests. In 1991 17 *obedineniia* and enterprises and 33 "legal entities" formed electronics *kontsern* Farada to attract investment and sales, end supply problems, coordinate business relations outside the USSR, and distribute output.[28] In 1992 St. Petersburg's Military-Industrial Corporation (*Voenno-promyshlennaia korporatsiia*) included Pozitron, Impulse, Red October, the Kalinin factory, Promstroibank, newspaper *Sankt-Peterburgskie Vedomosti*, and Eldoradio. The two largest contributors of start-up capital were the Military-Industrial Investment Company (founded by the Ministry of Defense) and the Military-Industrial Exchange. Its goal was to aid conversion to non-military production, but some members feared it would subordinate Petersburg firms to Moscow. Others asked why important military enterprises (Kirovskii Zavod, Elektrosila, Arsenal) did not join, although they were in RSPP (Rossiiskii Soiuz Promyshlennikov i Predprinimatelei, Russian Union of Industrialists and Entrepreneurs). The association raised initial capital but disappeared after 1992.[29]

One important group was the Association of Industrial Enterprises (Assotsiatsiia promyshlennykh predpriiatii), founded to organize Petersburg's military-industrial enterprises, coordinate supply and sales, and lobby the government.[30] When these goals remained unfulfilled and the state was unable to deliver, the Association turned to fostering ties between member firms and financial institutions. It provided data on member firms to potential foreign partners and investors, and provided data for members on each other to facilitate cooperation. The Association shared the spotlight with RSPP, whose Petersburg branch (Soiuz Promyshlennikov i Predprinimatelei Sankt-Peterburga) sported more than 80 members from heavy industry and finance. This voluntary self-help group lobbied regional and national governments, sought investment capital, provided lawyers and a defense fund for members under official investigation, and encouraged ventures with foreign firms. It could not sanction members but only consult or act as arbiter in disputes. When I asked about policing against internal opportunism, the president's response was genuine surprise, as if he never thought of this. The Union did not pursue active public relations—odd, given Red Directors' image as thieves. When I asked about implementing such a policy, he thought and said that they simply did not pursue this.[31]

Another important association for this chapter was future Defensive FPG Energomash, born in summer 1988 as one of the first two Soviet concerns. Legally an MGO (*mezhotraslevoe gosudarstvennoe obedinenie*, intersectoral state production association), Energomash united eleven enterprises, four institutes, a construction agency, and a KB that produced electricity generation machinery. These were Petersburg's elite: Leningrad Metal Factory (turbines), Izhorskie Factories (atomic and conventional electrical generating equipment), Zavod Turbinykh Lopatok (ZTL, Turbine Blade Factory, turbine components), Elektrosila (electrical generators and switchgear), Nevskii Zavod (turbines, pumping sets, castings), Znamia Truda (vale and rotary equipment), and Sevkabel (cables, wires).[32] The original goal was to support exchange and production relations between firms, improve productivity, and pool capital to invest in development (e.g. repair or new construction, research and development). Enterprise autonomy persisted; neither MGO nor members answered for each other's liabilities.[33] Contradictions soon surfaced. The MGO faced the old problem of supply of deficit goods and bureaucratic red tape,[34] and tensions emerged over coordinating supply. While members agreed to pool resources, individual firms preferred to use allotted capital for themselves, defeating the collective purpose of the MGO and threatening some members with worse debt.[35] In 1989 pocket bank Energomashbank was born, and to improve sales and supply Energomash set up joint commercial services.[36] Energomash later added specialized daughter firms to service energy equipment, handle import contracts, and obtain and distribute deficit supplies. Energomashbank was especially crucial for "obtaining monetary resources necessary to credit MGO enterprises"— although LMZ and Nevskii Zavod managers feared this would lead to inefficient banking practices. Energomash also worked out a scheme to standardize quality control and credentials, although it is unclear if this was put into practice. In 1990 members' debts increased, much of it to Energomashbank.[37]

Associations seemed promising in the late 1980s as a safe means to pool resources, seek capital and Western contacts, and distribute gains. Some did evolve consulting functions to complement lobbying work. A Petersburg voluntary association organizing 18 of St. Petersburg's 22 large bread factories was originally founded by economists with links to the bread sector. They were asked to draw up privatization plans and later to provide economic business advice, at which point they decided to found the association as a non-profit organization to bring together and advise these bread-making firms. By the mid-1990s the bulk of the association's work was arranging mutual aid, marketing studies, and organizing wholesale and retail bread outlets.[38] Yet they also faced pitfalls that plagued other voluntary associations, such as free riding. In the bread-makers' association and RSPP, collective decisions were non-binding; members could refuse collective policies, depriving associations of resources to mobilize for specific goals. The lack of real political organization also hindered their real formal influence, especially after the failure of Volskii's Civic Union in 1993 elections. By 1995, associations were being overtaken by FPGs and consigned to providing various services.

Rise of financial elites

The rise of Russia's private banks is fairly well known; but we need a better grasp of context and processes at work, beyond the usual story of networks, laws, and financial shocks. I add *habitus* and practices these financiers gained in early experiences of education and first jobs, which were then strengthened by their post-Soviet successes and embedded as logics of new property empires and fields. (Given that many data about biographies and tactics are still in the shadows, this analysis should be seen as an hypothesis for later testing, and as a systematizing of such data through a neoinstitutional interpretation.) Oligarchs, Financial FPGs, and the finance logic came from younger entrepreneurs who, as organizationally marginal and less able to supplement enterprise authority, used networks to play on the margins of laws and organizations to create niches and wealth. As entrepreneurs they innovated, but as Soviet entrepreneurs they were not *entirely* free of their Soviet pasts: innovations were more organizational and bureaucratic than technological or productive. Tactics ranged from currency and trade speculation to elaborate financial schemes, future models for loans-for-shares privatization or moving assets after the 1998 crisis. They used structural holes between parties that needed but did not know each other, such as automobile producers and customers, or organizations needing hard cash and those supplying it on a restricted basis. Another common thread was using others' capital (e.g. Party and state), sometimes a version of the shell game: setting up fictitious business plans or ventures, attracting money from enterprises or Party organizations, and using it for other purposes. A constant factor was using loopholes in laws and organizational procedures and speculating rather than adding value through production. Further, financial entrepreneurs used shocks to the Soviet and post-Soviet contexts in a different way from Red Directors. If the latter used opportunities to augment control of enterprises and to coordinate production so as to save it, financial entrepreneurs followed a *profit economy* and used opportunities in the unraveling Soviet economy and chaotic post-Soviet economy to speculate and feed their financial coffers. It was as if they loyally followed Marx's dictum about the logic of capitalism: accumulate, accumulate, accumulate. In so doing, they distanced themselves from Red Directors and linked themselves to the money-oriented transition culture of global capitalism.

Let us examine early formative experiences. Mikhail Khodorkovskii initially worked at a technical institute and was a member of the Komsomol (Party youth league), in which he gained access to Komsomol funds. With initial liberalization in small co-operative business under Gorbachev, he started out using Komsomol and institute capital to combine business initiatives and peculiarities of the Soviet financial system to make initial profit. One financial peculiarity was the difference between bureaucratic cash (*beznalichnye*), of which organizations had plenty, and rarer hard cash in hand (*nalichnye*) that the Soviet state was more loath to give out but which could create problems for managers needing to pay for work or supplies under the table—a more common problem with the rising trade in deficit goods at new *birzhi* (commodity exchanges) and use of *nalevo* informal work at enterprises (cf. Chapter 3). Using networks to enterprise managers, Khodorkovskii would obtain *beznalichnye* "start-up capital" or "investment" to fund fictitious research projects or the sale of products (e.g. software) which did not exist or were already developed. Enterprises would pay Khodorkovskii's "creative collective" in *beznalichnye*, and he would use his connections to the Komsomol, which was allowed to have both forms of money, to exchange *beznalichnye* for *nalichnye*. Along the way he took commissions to pay contacts, colleagues, and himself. Khodorkovskii expanded business by trading hoarded *beznalichnye* for timber, which he then exported for hard currency. He also imported computers, drawing on *beznalichnye* from institutes and organizations and transforming it into *nalichnye* at a profit. The crowning moment was creating private bank Menatep, through which state and Party money began to filter thanks to Khodorkovskii's connections and willingness to play with or ignore formal legal constraints on transactions in rubles or hard currency.

Aleksandr Smolenskii learned to use networks as a construction *tolkach*,[39] a skill he used to open construction co-operatives and Stolichnyi Bank. His first gains came funneling state funds into his bank for currency speculation. It was claimed he gained access to Central Bank funds through forged transfer orders, although it is unclear who did the forging. Vladimir Potanin, head of Oneksimbank, was a late-comer. In 1990 he founded Interros as a trading company, with start-up capital from 20 other organizations. In 1992 a major state bank faced financial collapse and urged customers to take their assets to Interros, which made $300 million. Potanin then founded Oneksimbank for import–export operations. For his most important ploy, he used networks to the state to organize a schema whereby customs duties moved through Oneksimbank, providing enormous operating capital for speculation or investment.[40] Boris Berezovskii began his rise to wealth as a go-between for AvtoVAZ and Fiat, an activity he institutionalized as LogoVAZ. As a middleman Berezovskii took AvtoVAZ cars on consignment, valued at artificially low state prices, and sold them at a mark-up. Storing gains in dollars, Berezovskii would stall ruble payments to AvtoVAZ so that inflation reduced his real debt. Using structural holes and maneuvering outside the state, he amassed a fortune that he invested in other dealings and shareholdings, e.g. in natural resources firms (aluminum, oil), aviation (Aeroflot), and media.

Profit was a central logic in emerging principles of Soviet entrepreneurs and financiers. Enterprises were sources of profit: how it was made was less important than its generation. That these actors exchanged different goods, jumped between activities, and worked out of financial organizations was a crucial material and symbolic aspect to practices: they were about money.

The emergence of financial-industrial groups

From voluntary associations and private banks came a new inter-enterprise structure: financial-industrial groups (FPG). Privatization was key to FPG emergence: property gave managers autonomy to join Defensive FPGs and owners the power to create Financial FPGs. In one economy, these two competing forms of organization were responses to uncertainty or opportunity (proximal motives) and ultimately clashed over the field of power and rules of the economic game. In the Defensive FPG, managers in the same or related sectors voluntarily united to guard supply, finances, production, and managerial authority. The Financial FPG involved a private bank or holding company running firms in various sectors to guard and expand investment rather than production *per se*. FPGs I examine here were domestic, although in 1996 tentative steps were taken to create FPGs across former Soviet republics.[41]

State and FPGs

The state initially provided little input into FPGs. In September 1992 assistant defense minister Andrei Kokoshin argued, "survival of Russian industry requires the strong fist of powerful companies, sectors, financial-industrial groups, heavy diversified holding companies." An October 1992 trip to South Korea reinforced this conviction: Russia needed "locomotives of industry" unifying production, capital, and state leadership.[42] By 1993 some analysts, officials, and elites agreed. Goskomprom (State Industrial Committee) floated FPGs as voluntary, vertically integrated structures with older managers in charge to support flailing firms. RSPP vice president Mikhail Iur'ev proposed compulsory and diversified FPGs with "stars" and "cash cows" and for which regional elites would appoint managers. Kremlin insider and Red Director ally Oleg Soskovets took up Iur'ev's logic, championing sectoral FPGs to replace Soviet-era ministries as "locomotives of the Russian economy."[43] In echo, some managers looked to FPGs as a cure for sharp industrial decline. In 1993 one general director claimed that

> an especially destructive role was played by a proposed conceptual thesis, according to which formation of an optimal structure of industrial sectors and effective division of investment streams are attainable only by a process of "natural selection" unfolding on the basis of providing full freedom of market-competitive forces. All reform practice shows that realizing this "paradigm" in our country brings full dismantling of much [industry].[44]

To apologists, the FPG was a multinational corporation: big and private was good on the world market.[45] Others in the state saw FPGs as coordination without state intervention. By 1993, with Soviet socialism and state direction still abnormal, some believed a core of private bankers would better coordinate economic activity and change, given the defection of qualified cadres from the state to the private sector. As firms clamored for subsidies to alleviate welfare costs, some high-level officials claimed FPGs would shift financial responsibilities to organizations whose cadres had better knowledge and resources, although the state could still bring empires to heel.[46] Also, by uniting potentially lucrative enterprises, the state encouraged private investment: the state would do the job of consolidating empires for private investors by providing already-prepared FPGs. This could also provide income to cover the state budget.[47]

Only when enterprises organized *de facto* FPGs did the regime act. A December 1993 presidential decree allowed registration of FPGs as firms with shares transferred voluntarily to one partner or an umbrella firm. An FPG could be created by the Council of Ministers; by voluntary agreement by all participants; or by consolidating share ownership by a central shareholder. However, the decree listed restrictions. FPG composition could not violate anti-monopoly legislation; gathering all steel-making firms into one FPG, for example, was illegal. A firm could not enter an FPG if the state owned more than 25 percent of its shares; banks and financial institutions could not own more than 10 percent of shares in any one firm. State approval was required if one firm had more than 25,000 employees or if the entire FPG had more than 100,000 employees.[48] The decree described FPGs in language of international competitiveness:

> securing structural reformation of the Russian economy, quickening scientific-technological progress, increasing export potential and competitiveness of Russian enterprises, increasing administrativeness of the national economy,

and introducing an active industrial policy…uniting material and financial resources of its participants to raise competitiveness and production efficiency, the creation of rational technological and cooperative ties, the improvement of export potential…the conversion of defense industries, and the attraction of investment.[49]

Analysts noted, "in no single country in the world are there such restrictions." Kremlin reformers may have feared monopolization if banks or managers had free reign.[50] Such laws did little to promote formal FPG registration, but *de facto* FPG creation persisted. Banks used daughter firms to avoid share ownership prohibitions; Defensive FPGs used cross-shareholding to solidify structure. Former *obedineniia* were potential FPGs-in-waiting, although this was more a superficial label than reestablishing coordination and possibly control between enterprises.

Defensive-Managerial FPGs

Following the moral economy of production and voluntary associations, Defensive FPGs were voluntary groupings of firms with a Soviet logic of coordinating production and exchange: they produced for each other or made similar products and were in the same ministry or *glavk*. As such, they were an organizational manifestation of Red Directors' *habitus*, capital, and operational logic: Red Directors had local positions in enterprises linked through production and supply, and they desired safety nets to guard their enterprise positions and production. The Defensive FPG was a logical outgrowth of voluntary associations and the managerial moral economy. This is especially clear in contrast to financial entrepreneurs and oligarchs: even in 1992 it was clear money could be made speculating on particular goods and resources, yet even managers who did speculate did not set out to expand that speculation or to institutionalize accumulation of profit. Unlike oligarchs out to make money, Red Directors took profit (even by asset-stripping) but did not direct efforts towards *accumulating and augmenting* it.[51] (Note how we saw some proof of this in difficulties implementing marketing.) The fundamental Defensive FPG logic was structuring property to pass the buck: to defend firms against outside control or accountability, and literally to distribute funds to support each other, as in a mutual aid society. Older directors used to state-centered planning saw risk in collapsing exchange and distribution, finances, and unsettled rules of the new economic order.[52] Exchange partners needed to group together to defend production and exchange of goods linked in production cycles, and so they rebuilt safety nets embodying production logics and relations—which world experience supposedly legitimated.[53] That Defensive FPGs were production-centered was hinted by an Oneksimbank top manager, Vladimir Shmatovich, who contrasted Oneksimbank's logic to that of Red Directors: "In several FPGs industrial enterprises lead, and there is a pocket bank that, giving enterprises risky and unsecured loans, sooner or later falls apart." Defensive FPGs were easy money for production despite demand—the old, abnormal Soviet philosophy.[54]

To build a Defensive FPG, participating firms created a holding company to which they turned over shares. Holding company shares were then split among FPG members, whose directors sat on the FPG board of directors. In this way the FPG would defend managerial autonomy and enterprise security. Comments by the director of a Petersburg bread factory are instructive. There was no formal bread FPG, but these firms united in a voluntary association to facilitate cooperation. While their sales provided sufficient income for survival and modest modernization, they lacked capital for substantive technological improvement. In a view of normality that he shared with other managers, this director rejected outside investment repeatedly on the grounds that "they will want something in return." It was clear he meant decision-making authority.[55] The head of a local Petersburg furniture FPG intimated the same. When I asked about pursuing outside investment, perhaps by entering a Financial FPG—dominant in 1997, when the interview took place—he responded quickly and forcefully that he did not trust "bankers," who, he claimed, bought enterprises only to squeeze them dry and discard them. Bankers did not share his production and paternalist values of advancing production and protecting employees.[56]

Former Party and state-ministerial elites actively aided creating some Defensive FPGs, using networks and the ministerial template: one tactic was to create a holding company in a voluntary association and transfer shares of participating firm to that holding company, creating an FPG. One such case was Fin Prom, created by a coalition of local state officials, enterprise managers, and the State Privatization Committee and made up of mining companies, real estate firms, a bank, and a trading company. Other cases were FPG Transmash, originally the Ministry of Heavy and Transport Engineering, and Konsensus, formed from the Soviet Ministry of Light Industry. Even without local state participation and aid, networked managers still used the ministry-*glavk* template, as in the case of PAKT (Primor'e region). As prices for materials, transport, energy increased and managers had to deal with taxes and economic uncertainty, PAKT managers decided that they needed an FPG to fulfill functions that formal and informal Party networks and structures previously discharged. Another such FPG based on pro-duction links was Progressinvest, in the timber business.[57] Similar logics underlie other local-level Defensive FPGs. Formally registered in 1995, Defensive FPG Doninvest (Rostov-on-the-Don) comprised six local enterprises in machine-tool and military-industrial production. Agricultural machine-tool enterprise Krasnyi Aksai was its real authority. As agricultural and military purchases dropped and brought flagging finances, the FPG was created to strengthen "technical links" between the firms, pool resources for investment projects, and improve output and efficiency. Doninvest was charged with arranging price policies, marketing procedures and strategies, and improving accounts and capital use. In its first year of formal life (1996), FPG output improved markedly (974 percent increase over 1995), mostly from a deal the FPG negotiated with Daewoo.[58]

An important Petersburg Defensive FPG was Energomashstroitel'naia Korporatsiia (EMK), originally MGO Energomash and founded on a former state structure and sector (Energomash *kontsern* and energy generation sector).

The *raison d'être* was the usual defensive posturing: the need to reorganize inter-enterprise relations in the wake of economic crisis and privatization. Where the original Energomash was Petersburg-centered, EMK, registered in Moscow in 1993, expanded beyond the city to include six of Russia's largest enterprises in energy machinery. Of original Energomash members, some Petersburg firms remained (LMZ, ZTL, Elektrosila), some were dumped (e.g. Sevkabel, Znamia Truda), and close working relations remained with others (e.g. Nevskii Zavod). Non-Petersburg firms included Belenergomash (Belgorod), Sibenergomash (Barnaul), EMK-Atommash (more on this firm later), and Uralmashzavod. Like its earlier incarnation, EMK was created "with the goal of joint decisions of production and sales problems and the attraction of investment" and to organize and support productive capacities of their sector throughout Russia. It would also act as "sales and marketing center" for members.[59] We will return to EMK later, for it provides a lesson on possible property-driven instability of the Defensive FPG. Other lesser Defensive FPGs in Petersburg included Tekhnoprom, formed in 1988 to organize Petersburg chemical firms, and poultry FPG Ptitseprom, uniting Leningrad *oblast'* chicken-processing enterprises. Both began as sector-based voluntary associations; cross-ownership of shares and authority structures were not entirely clear. Petersburg's first *official* (formally registered) FPG, Gormash-invest, included Petersburg firms Samson, Khlebnyi Dom, Petmol, and other foodstuff firms, plus VITA-bank and financial institution Lenstroimaterial. Petersburg's second formal FPG, Morskaia Tekhnika, brought together defense-industry enterprises with "secret" production profiles. Unlike Gormash-invest, Morskaia Tekhnika included the non-Petersburg *kontsern* Rosvooruzhenie and Inkombank.[60] Like many Defensive FPGs, these were mostly local, such as the furniture FPG—production and distribution networks were local, and integrated distribution and supply did not go beyond Petersburg.[61] Another example was a Petersburg chemical FPG: once the USSR's second voluntary association, it became a Defensive FPG to support production and research.[62]

Overall, Defensive FPGs did not follow one exact formula or format. Some concentrated primarily on one area of production and created their own banks—the model of AvtoVAZ or Magnitogorsk Metallurgical Combine. Others focused on a broader sector but had some outside interests and a clear mother company.[63] These groups did share a general logic of defending production and enterprise-managerial autonomy, sometimes consciously in contrast to financial conceptions of organization. After the formal interview, a manager and representative of Petersburg's chemical FPG mentioned earlier heatedly criticized bankers and Financial FPGs as bloodsuckers who drained Russia's wealth and cared little about production, educating a new generation of chemists and engineers, and maintaining Russia's competitive edge in chemical production and research.[64] Yet this logic of organization had two weaknesses. First, it ran against the tide of a transition culture that privileged finance and authority of outside owners and shareholders. Second, the emphasis on subordinating finance to production meant fewer investments in financial games (e.g. speculation), thus less profit for development. While the monetization of Russia's economy was far from perfect, money was becoming an important resource. Financial FPGs, oriented to profit and money, had a better fit with transition culture and this new totem of value, as well as with the rising stars sitting in the Kremlin.

The rise of Financial FPGs

The financial entrepreneurs' organizing logic and profit economy extended into Financial FPGs. After 1992 major commercial banks expanded beyond financial games with currency and treasury bills (GKOs, OFZs) to acquiring shares in privatized firms. Oneksimbank and finance company Mikrodin united as Interros and acquired shares by various means in such privatized enterprises as Norilsk Nickel or Moscow car factory ZiL (later saved by Mayor Iurii Luzhkov). Menatep, Al'fa-bank, and Inkombank invested in oil, confectioneries, and metals.[65] Komsomol experience gave these elites skills to manipulate finances and rules and use loose laws for gain; they could also apply market vocabulary to engage Western investors. They had sufficient capital to interest the cash-strapped state, and they had as allies some Kremlin insiders who came less from *nomenklatura* than from the Komsomol or other institutes. They conceived of risk primarily in terms of control of and return on investment, i.e. property ownership and governance. To managers of banks and Financial FPGs, enterprises were commodities to be bought and sold (via shares) through market means. Not the enterprise itself, but capital and shareholding were sacred. Note that despite this preoccupation, even genius, for informal financial dealings, these financial elites were not always effective managers. Some holdings (e.g. Norilsk for Interros) *lost* money when oligarchs took over. Only after 2000 did Khodorkovskii introduce Western transparency and business strategies, and this was the rarity.

These entrepreneurs and organizations built empires by obtaining shares through privatization auctions and the secondary market through a variety of means, usually indirect and difficult to trace formally. We will later see some ways they could acquire shares; given the weakness of formal stock exchanges, usually these involved complex use of daughter companies tempting employees to part with their shares for hard cash—no small offer when wages were low or unpaid for months on end. Banks such as Menatep and Inkombank needed to invest profits, revealing a logic of accumulation, not merely speculation and rent-seeking for its own sake or merely to sate the owner.[66] GKOs (Russian Treasury bills) were one means, but they provided no control over investment. Buying shares helped diversify risk, provided possible future profit (shares were cheap), and gave a means to control the use of investment. As Menatep president A. Zurabov noted, "in Russia it is still impossible to make financial investments without real control over the debtor…If we control management, the situation, capital streams, account transactions, and the like, then of course the probability of a return of such loans in order are higher than loans by a clientele on the side…"[67] Another answer to risk on investment was spreading risk around. The logic of Financial FPG Sokol reflected this perception: as one director claimed, "we operate on the principle of the submarine, where there are several compartments—this helps keep it afloat during difficult times when one compartment is suffering."[68] This aspect of the Financial FPG logic was partly the result of cumulative, contingent investment decisions. Menatep invested in firms with export potential so they could transfer those firms' hard-currency accounts to Menatep itself. Bank Rossiiskii Kredit initially invested in shares in order to engage in speculation, and found itself with a large number of shares in metallurgical enterprises.[69] Inkombank and Al'fa-bank focused on areas of quick return, usually foodstuff preparation.

Not all Financial FPGs were formally registered. Such incentives as tax breaks and state aid were vague, with no confidence of being fulfilled—a lesson learned from unfulfilled similar promises for small businesses. An important negative incentive was anti-monopoly clauses to avoid concentrating industries in a few hands. To avoid this, *de facto* Financial FPGs managers used ownership via daughter firms or intermediaries, making these FPGs complex webs of indirect ownership arrangements back to a central figure. Menatep followed this model. Menatep daughters would purchase shares and create a string of relations that ultimately led back to Menatep. As this empire grew, Khodorkovskii founded Rosprom in 1995 to administer holdings and moved important managers to it from Menatep. For several years Rosprom remained a holding company of several enterprises and FPGs (e.g. Russian Textile Consortium) and thus a *de facto* but not *de jure* FPG. In 1997 Rosprom and Iukos informally united as Rosprom-Iukos—formally both were independent, although they pursued joint projects and owners and managing personnel were nearly identical. Similarly, Oneksimbank and Mikrodin pooled resources into Interros in January 1995 to administer property holdings.[70]

Until 1995, managers, financial entrepreneurs, and state actors set out to safeguard positions or make gains, creating inter-enterprise organizational forms and logics along the way. There were emergent properties to fields that studies of politics or policies alone miss. Yet logics were not yet well embedded beyond concrete associations and FPGs because no group predominated outside them, in broader inter-enterprise fields or the field of power. There still was balance as actors focused on defending themselves. This would change as privatization proceeded and the stakes grew. If 1988–94 was a period of cautious exploration, 1995–8 was a period of conflict, as both camps realized they would need more property and power to defend themselves and that survival meant promoting their own logics in the corridors of power.

Uneasy fields: expansion, confrontation, consolidation (1995–1998)

By 1994 the three leading political camps were industrial managers (Defensive FPGs), financial elites led by Anatolii Chubais (Financial FPGs), and natural resources groups led by Gazprom and Prime Minister Chernomyrdin. In 1995 and 1996 these groups and their clans clashed over principles of privatization, shareholding, and governance; the stakes were not just local property but the overall field of power and its economic principles. Early privatization favored insiders, but the second stage favored elites with economic capital and Kremlin allies. In the contention over privatization, especially the rigged loans-for-shares program, and Yeltsin's presidential election, oligarchs, Financial FPGs, and finance-centered principles seemed ascendant.

Managers and owners tried to use formal laws to assemble FPGs, but laws were more catch-up than proactive and promised illusory benefits. In 1995 and 1996 Yeltsin issued additional laws, such as "On Financial-Industrial Groups" (November 30, 1995), defining FPGs as

> the aggregate of legal entities acting as founding and daughter groups, in full or in part having united their material and nonmaterial assets (system of inclusion) based on an agreement on creating a financial-industrial group in the goal of technological or economic integration, for realization of investment or other projects and programs oriented to the increase of competitiveness and the expansion of markets of sales of goods and services, to the rise of efficiency in production, to the creation of new working places.

FPGs were voluntary and contractual, but they were more than loose confederations. The founding charter would create a central company as FPG representative and "investment institute" to handle finance and investment, to organize members' accounts, and to account for transactions. An FPG had to have at least one bank and one producer of goods or services. Daughter firms could enter only with the mother firm. The FPG board of directors would include representatives of member firms. The new law incorporated both Defensive and Financial logics: voluntary creation and a stress on finance with restrictions. While there were still few real incentives for official registration, some FPGs did so anyway. From only five officially registered FPGs in 1995, by the end of 1996 Russia had 45 officially registered FPGs. "Hundreds" remained unregistered and a hundred had applications pending.[71] The formally registered FPGs employed more than three million in 1997, and included more than 700 non-bank firms in January 1997.[72]

Slow at first to address FPGs, the state was drawn in as privatization progressed. The 1993 Constitution strengthened the presidency, and Yeltsin continued to use decree powers over privatization. The Kremlin also remained a potent symbol, unlike the Duma: Yeltsin still enjoyed leadership authority even if a growing number of Russians came to loathe him. The struggle for meanings and structure of fields became linked to the Kremlin. In 1995, this erupted in the battle of clans over policy, property, and thus the master field. One person who commented early on this, in 1995, was American embassy official Thomas Graham. In an article for *Nezavisimaia gazeta* he categorized Kremlin clans according to economic positions.[73] The finance clan, led by Anatolii Chubais and his "Petersburg *mafiia*," included heads of major banks (Oneksimbank, Inkombank, Menatep) and reformer allies in the regime (Sergei Beliaev, Alfred Kokh). Oligarchs worked in this clan. Military-industrial firms (VPK, *voenno-promyshlennyi kompleks*) were represented by presidential aides and former cabinet members Aleksandr Korzhakov and Oleg Soskovets. The natural resources clan included Gazprom, Sibneft, and Rosneft and was headed by Prime Minister Chernomyrdin. The Moscow clan, headed by

Mayor Iurii Luzhkov, defended interests of the capital and Luzhkov's leadership. In the center was the "Family" clan of Yeltsin and his gatekeepers, daughter Tatiana Diachenko and presidential administrator Aleksandr Voloshin. The clan war came to a head in 1995 and 1996 over loans-for-shares auctions and the presidential election, visible in July 1996 scandals that ultimately cost Korzhakov his position.[74] Chubais and oligarchs traded property in rigged auctions for financial support for Yeltsin's campaign, and they reaped rewards after Yeltsin's victory. A 1996 cabinet reshuffle strengthened the finance clan: Soskovets was out and Chubais ally Boris Nemtsov was in. Chernomyrdin remained prime minister and Gazprom defender, but he was balanced by Chubais. Agrarian interests unraveled with the Agrarian Party's weak showing; Luzhkov's clan grew in stature.

The second stage of privatization was a key moment for clan politics, FPGs, and structuration of the master field. In this stage the state sold its remaining shares (often the majority of voting shares) in larger industrial organizations. The first phase was selling off small firms or assets. For larger enterprises, the state initially gave employees and managers first crack at a portion of shares to satisfy social democracy and legitimate privatization. Citizens could use vouchers to purchase shares—an attempt at public legitimation that brought little investment to enterprises or the state. Shares not sold off in this round would be sold in the second round at auctions or closed competitions for money, with conditions that buyers invest in their new purchases. Oligarchs mobilized to shape privatization to their interests. Discursively, they invoked the South Korean *chaebol* and Japanese *keiretsu* to legitimate centralized property empires,[75] and they used the negative image of communism to justify redistributing property to the "capitalist" financial elite. Anatolii Chubais, the mastermind of privatization, realized obstacles to his reforms by the mid-1990s and sought to block the reemergence of Red Directors and communists to bring down the final curtain on the Soviet past. Khodorkovskii claimed: "it became clear to everyone that big industry remained in the hands of the red directors, and if nothing happened, then they would bring the Communists back to power."[76] Fear of communism framed a new normality of private elites owning property, running the economy, and acting as counterweight to the state.

Behind-the-scenes negotiations resulted in the 1995 loans-for-shares scheme (*zalogovaia privatizatsiia*). Arranged by Chubais and Vladimir Potanin, this involved temporary transfer of state-owned shares in firms in exchange for loans to the state budget.[77] Firms involved were potential money-makers such as metallurgical conglomerates (Norilsk Nickel), oil firms (Iukos, Surgutneftegaz), and heavy industry (Perm Motors). Auctions were closed and used sealed bids. The winner had to invest a hefty sum in the firm and loan the bid amount to the state. If the state repaid the loan in a year, shares reverted to the state. For Chubais, loans-for-shares was an expedient means to building a working market: "the fact that [oligarchs] would be the forces supporting their own private property, that they would defend their private property, and that in the political process they would be, by definition, against communism and pro-reform—that was 100 percent sure."[78] In November–December 1995 competitors turned in bids and deposits, and Yeltsin's new allies won.[79] Inkombank, Oneksimbank, Menatep, and Berezovskii gained lucrative firms and organized them in a web of opaque ownership relations. Menatep gained oil giant Iukos. Oneksimbank won giant nickel smelter Norilsk Nickel and oil conglomerate Sidanko.[80] The state did not repay loans and required the oligarchs to sell the shares at auctions—at which oligarchs sold the shares to daughter firms under their control. Menatep daughter Laguna, which won Iukos, sold the shares to Menatep daughter Monblan.[81]

This auction and privatization of oil, gas, and aluminum firms bred scandal and conflict, as groups struggled over governance and gains. That auctions were rigged for oligarchs hurt the image of privatization, reforms, oligarchs, and Yeltsin. Some auctions created conflict between oligarchs: the sale of telecommunications giant Sviazinvest led to a clash between Berezovskii, Potanin, and Chubais. While Defensive FPGs did not always lose out, on the whole oligarchs and their FPGs expanded their empires and overall economic and political power. Finance had won; managers were left setting their houses in order or fending off triumphant oligarchs.

Consolidating Defensive FPGs: confusion and conflict at EMK

Lobbying efforts in the Kremlin did not provide Defensive FPGs with the desired support; the managerial clan was squeezed out of the Kremlin. This is not so surprising, given the better fit between oligarchs and Yeltsin's Kremlin (destroy the old, money as a central totem) and the oligarchs' better focus on the national level of politics and economy (in contrast to Red Directors' local knowledge and focus on their own firms). Managers were restructuring firms and had to consolidate relations with suppliers and FPG partners. Some Defensive FPGs became vertically integrated structures if one member sufficiently dominated or if members were sufficiently interdependent or focused on a narrow set of products. One example was the Magnitogorsk Metallurgical Combine (MMK). Like Kirovskii Zavod, MMK shed some superfluous labor and unprofitable work, but this violation of the paternalist credo helped it survive.[82] In other FPGs, structures remained loose and members defended independence, which could hinder integration and coordination.[83]

At Energomash (EMK), Leningrad Metal Factory (LMZ) attempted to guard autonomy and solidify supply relations with EMK brother Turbine Blade Factory (ZTL). Following privatization, LMZ managers used investment from share offerings to shore up control: they feared employees strapped for cash might sell shares, and coordinating employees for strategic voting was costly. On learning outsiders were buying LMZ shares in 1994, managers set up finance company Romeks-invest to buy and handle LMZ employees' shares: "those shares sold on the side will leave [LMZ control] and allow any outside 'capitalist' [to gain control]."[84] Romeks was framed as "us versus them," privileging insiders (managers *and* employees): "LMZ leadership, thank God, quickly understood this [outsider threat]."[85] In four months Romeks paid 617 million rubles for 771,000 shares, ultimately putting over one million shares (10 percent) in managers' hands. By law, Romeks now had to stop, although it was also out of money (the source of which was unclear).[86] In December 1994, the state transferred its shares to EMK, and managers obtained 116,000 more shares from a Western firm. By March 1995, 5,395 employees owned 22.64 percent of LMZ stock; managers owned 10 percent, EMK 32 percent, and offshore daughter Mardima 17.6 percent,[87] giving insiders and allies a majority.[88] Still, managers kept warning employees about selling shares: private firms waited outside LMZ gates to tempt those whose wages seemed inadequate. If LMZ dividends were low, managers claimed that share value would improve as LMZ recovered and the tax burden declined from 70 percent of profits.[89]

EMK owned shares in its members (who owned shares in EMK), yet this did not clarify inter-enterprise relations, especially when one firm set out to clarify and tighten relations. This led to conflict when LMZ turned to consolidate supply relations with ZTL, an important LMZ supplier (once part of it) and the single Soviet producer of blades for turbine and energy machine producers. After the first wave of privatization, foreign firm Stumhammer obtained 35 percent of ZTL's shares and began to change its output profile, threatening LMZ. In 1993 and 1994 LMZ, EMK, and Mardima acquired ZTL shares. Citing "national interests," they stopped Stumhammer from participating in a subsequent investment auction, in which LMZ and EMK gained the state's 20 percent share packet.[90] ZTL leaders were not happy: LMZ was an outsider threatening autonomy. An LMZ-led coalition of majority shareholders called an emergency meeting to appoint Valerii Chernyshev general director.[91] ZTL's board of directors, Soviet-era managers headed by Anatolii Gromov, voided Chernyshev's contract, but a shareholders' meeting a few hours later rehired Chernyshev and ousted the standing board. The result was "a Russian situation familiar to all, dual power (*dvoevlastie*)...an economic revolution with a seizure of power, and inevitable disagreements between two financial-industrial groups, and major shareholders carving up the pie, and simple ambitions of top leaders and 'generals' of LMZ and ZTL."[92]

These generals asked local authorities to declare Gromov's actions invalid. Security services were called to guard property; and employees spontaneously assembled at ZTL. In 1995 LMZ gave ZTL $1 million and agreed to invest $2 million more. LMZ director Shevchenko used shareholding and economic health to defend control of ZTL.[93] He claimed that Gromov and the ZTL board threatened investment plans. The new board would be "in conformity with the interest of shareholders, whom the board was obliged by law to represent adequately."[94] Gromov countered that LMZ had rigged the investment auction, and their $1 million "investment" was really payment for goods shipped a few months earlier. He also claimed Chernyshev used blackmail and threats to gain compliance and had overstepped authority by signing investment agreements with LMZ restricting exports. In sum, "all forces are aimed at turning ZTL into an ordinary LMZ shopfloor" that might not defend employees. Gromov was not against partnership with LMZ—"it would be strange to turn down a very big purchaser"—but he felt it his duty "to defend ZTL as an independent enterprise."[95] Ultimately, LMZ consolidated control of ZTL.

LMZ–ZTL conflict was indicative of Energomash's confused cross-shareholding structure; in 1997 EMK managers were unsure of who owned whom.[96] Despite LMZ's victory, manager-enterprise independence remained important to the Defensive FPG logic: ZTL's claims to independence were akin to LMZ's, only LMZ managers claimed to support supply to defend autonomy. To improve coordination, competitiveness, and profitability, EMK members had to address structure and authority—contradicting EMK's *raison d'être* and setting off conflict.

Financial empires and logics on the move: first confrontations and consolidating governance

While the second stage of privatization facilitated some consolidation of Defensive FPGs, this was the age of oligarchs and Financial FPGs. In their profit economy of normal economic practice and organization, economic capital—money especially but also shares in private property—was the main tool of business, and profit was the normal, legitimate goal. Their logic of normal business had the best fit with Yeltsin's Kremlin and general discourse in the press: they wanted to destroy the older economic regime, viewed the crisis in financial terms (inflation and liquidity), and saw salvation through privatization and a wager on the sober and the strong.[97] With superior financial resources, ability to engage transition culture, and strong Kremlin connections, the financial elite were poised for empire-building. By 1995 they had accumulated capital and were investing in privatizing enterprises (Table 5.2). Menatep's holdings, some in holding company Rosprom, included metallurgy, chemicals, textiles, foodstuffs, industrial and military production, and oil (Iukos). Oneksimbank's holdings with partner MFK were in natural resources and heavy industry: metallurgy, oil refining, chemical production, and aviation.[98] Gusinskii had his Media-MOST empire, with television channel NTV the jewel. Via LogoVAZ Boris Berezovskii expanded into media and automobiles (AVVA), and with protégé Roman Abramovich into oil (Sibneft), aviation (Aeroflot), and aluminum (Krasnoyarsk Aluminum Factory). If not unified, this elite shared policy interests. Table 5.2 notes these empires before 1998.[99]

Assembling Financial FPG empires meant more than buying shares: it meant making governance operative. This was potentially toxic: two sets of differing logics of authority and normality, which could in turn create contradictory interests, especially if conflict did break out between owners and managers. In theory, share ownership grants claims to residuals (dividends) and decision-making authority. Initially, managers swallowed owners' claims to residuals, but they were less willing to share power and legitimacy than profits. The key moment of governance was when new owners tried to change boards of directors before introducing reforms in business strategies and structures. Managers played such trumps as contradictions in privatization and governance legislation, claims to production knowledge and paternalism, attacks on financiers as a threat to national and local interests, and keeping new owners off the shareholders' register.[100] They framed outside authority and decision-making as a threat. Privatization and victories for new owners (oligarchs) gave force to new financial logics: *à la* the third dimension of power (narrative), one set of claims was victorious, the others history's losers. That victory relied on an alliance with the state; yet financial logics were not reified, as Putin would show.

Interros and Norilsk Nickel

The first confrontation of managerial and shareholding interests and logics was the governance war between Interros and Norilsk Nickel. Once Oneksimbank won the state's shares in Norilsk, Potanin set out to consolidate governance. In January the bank cited financial problems at Norilsk and demanded representation on the board of directors and an emergency shareholders' meeting to discuss strategies, finances, labor, and administration.[101] Norilsk general director Anatolii Filatov attacked Oneksimbank's claims: Norilsk had no financial difficulties and, like other natural resource firms, was profitable. Oneksimbank was using "financial distress" as a smoke screen to take over the firm, but Oneksimbank was only *holding* the state's shares temporarily and thus had no property rights or decision-making authority. Filatov cited a June 1993 presidential edict "On Distinctive Features of Privatization of the 'Norilsk Nickel' Concern (*Kontsern*)," by which only the state could appoint the board of directors. The board thus had rights to the state's shares. This edict came earlier and was still in force, overriding loans-for-shares. Further, Filatov claimed loans-for-shares was not registered with the Ministry of Justice and was invalid. Oneksimbank rebutted that the 1995 presidential edict "On the Order of Transferral to Deposit in 1995 of Shares Belonging to the Federal Government" let the state dispose of shares as it saw fit. Oneksimbank and the Kremlin also claimed loans-for-shares need not be registered with the Ministry of Justice.[102] In 1996 the Supreme Arbitration Court dallied, and Norilsk workers began a hunger strike over unpaid wages. Filatov blamed Oneksimbank for defaulting on a 50 billion ruble loan, which he suddenly found to pay wages.[103] In April 1996 Prime Minister Chernomyrdin obtained Filatov's "resignation" and transferred him elsewhere in the state. New director Vsevolod Generalov was an official in Roskomdragmet (Russian Metallurgy Committee), demonstrating the state's power in the conflict.[104] Norilsk and its accounts were transferred to Interros and an overhaul of management began.[105]

Yet a majority of shares did not guarantee control. According to Norilsk's charter, board members could not be replaced without state permission; thus, Oneksimbank's authority depended on the Kremlin. Oneksimbank also discovered Norilsk's previous managers played a shell game—a daughter company in the United Kingdom handled export contracts and undertook "strange deals" without Norilsk instructions. When Oneksimbank reworked export contracts, managers hurriedly concluded deals for lower prices or barter.[106] Interros faced Norilsk's enormous tax and wage debts, potential employee rebellions, and support for local infrastructure.[107] Clearing debts required restructuring, confusing the organizational schema and threatening bankruptcy.[108] Since 1993 energy debts to Norilskgazprom were enormous. When Norilskgazprom pushed for Norilsk

Table 5.2 Finance-based empires at their height

Oligarch	Mother organization	Important holdings
Boris Berezovskii (pre-2001)	LogoVAZ (weak center)	RusAl (aluminum), Aeroflot, Sibneft (oil); Kommersant publishing, Channel 1 (ORT) and TV6 (television), *Nezavisimaia gazeta*
Mikhail Khodorkovskii	Menatep-Rosprom	Iukos, Russian Textiles Consortium; various firms in chemicals, metallurgy, construction, food; Investments in ORT and Itar-TASS
Vladimir Gusinskii	MOST-Bank, MOST-Group	NTV (television), *Segodnia*, Itogi other print media; Ekho Moskvy (radio)
Vladimir Potanin	Oneksimbank (after 1998 Rosbank) Interros	Norilsk Nickel, Sidanko Oil (until 1998), Sviazinvest telecom (until 1998), NLMK metal combine, ZiL (automobiles), Perm Motors, Mikrodin finance, LOMO, other firms in oil, chemicals, railroad and transportation, exports; *Ekspert, Komsomol'skaia Pravda,* and *Izvestiia* (print media)
Aleksandr Smolenskii	SBS-Agro (fails 1998)	Investments in ORT and *Kommersant*
Vladimir Vinogradov	Inkombank (fails 1998)	Confectionaries (e.g. Babaevskii), investments in Magnitogorsk and Sokol
Mikhail Fridman	Al'fa-Bank, Al'fa-Group	Tiumen' Oil, various smaller firms in cement, chemicals, construction
Anatolii Chubais	EES (electricity monopoly)	National electricity grid, local electricity generation and distribution
Rem Viakhirev (pre-2001)	Gazprom	Domestic gas complex (reserves, extraction), banks (e.g. National Reserve Bank), media (e.g. newspapers *Trud* and *Komsomol'skaia pravda*, NTV and ORT television)

bankruptcy, Oneksimbank purchased it and replaced its top managers.[109] Local authorities demanded Norilsk pay debts to local government, and they confiscated $60 million worth of materials ready for export.[110] Support for local welfare continued to drain resources; while profits in 1997 improved to 1.4 trillion rubles, local support cost 1.5 trillion.

In August 1997 the state's shares in Norilsk went up for sale as per the loans-for-shares scheme; a consortium including Oneksimbank won the tender. Oneksimbank-Interros and the financial logic of fields won this high-profile test of property rights and governance—not unimportant in the context of the clearly rigged and publicly illegitimate loans-for-shares auction. Yet the victory was not inevitable. Norilsk managers also had legal arguments in their favor, and ultimately, Yeltsin's regime provided crucial aid. Despite financial problems, Norilsk remained the center of the Interros empire; it purchased foreign palladium producers and obtained Polius, Russia's largest gold producer, and South African company Gold Fields Limited.[111]

Menatep-Rosprom and Iukos

Consolidating governance of Financial FPGs often involved shady tactics.[112] Transfer-pricing, opaque monetary transfers, and quasi-legal moves against minority shareholders were expedient means to maintain cash flows and enterprise functioning. This happened once Menatep won control over Iukos in loans-for-shares. Quickly using Rosprom to consolidate governance over Iukos, Khodorkovskii faced a legacy of Soviet oil sector reforms, as real authority at Iukos was devolved to member enterprises. To bring together oil production, refining, and distribution, Yeltsin's regime created semi-vertical structures: Iukos, Lukoil, and Surgutneftegaz in 1992, Sibneft, Sidanko, and others in 1995. In these structures, mother firms owned 38 percent of daughters' shares, which made up a majority voting block (75 percent of all shares were voting); e.g. Iukos owned 38 percent of its most important subsidiary, oil producer Iuganskneftegaz. Khodorkovskii moved into oil in 1994–5, purchasing oil firm shares on the open market. With loans-for-shares Rosprom became majority shareholder in the Iukos holding company. In 1996 Menatep managers moved to Iukos, but Khodorkovskii had to consolidate control and coordination of cash flow and decision-making among Iukos daughters. With low liquidity and capital access and contradictory laws, managers and owners had to think of present cash availability to pursue substantial business. Opaque organizational structure hid cash from the Iukos mother and the tax police. Paradoxically, to gain control of Iukos, Khodorkovskii had to avoid transparency. Initially he made a show of force by sending security personnel to Iukos daughters to prevent theft of assets, oil, and money. Offshore companies helped control cash flow: oil was sold to offshore firms at low Russian prices and resold on the world market at global prices, with offshore profits safe from the state and daughters. Further, Iukos managers forced extraction daughters to sell oil to other Iukos daughters at low prices. As daughters' losses and debts grew, their share prices dropped—increasing Khodorkovskii's influence.

One obstacle to vertical reintegration was minority shareholders, especially those interested in speculation. One tactic was to exchange member enterprises' shares for a common share, requiring negotiating value of the share swap. New Iukos managers issued additional shares not to increase investment but to water down opposing shareholders' power. In 1999 Iukos issued additional shares bought by offshore companies linked to Iukos managers.[113] An inverse strategy was consolidating shares, e.g. from one million to one hundred. Minority shareholders were left with fractions of shares that were invalid (until changes in shareholding law in 2002). A third tactic was to obtain court orders confiscating certain blocks of shares and invalidating their rights. Khodorkovskii used this to gain control over Iuganskneftegaz: he found a judge to order confiscation of shares held by minority shareholders who opposed new share offerings (to water down shareholding power).[114] Protests came to naught; laws and courts aided such consolidation.

While much of this may seem to be rent-seeking or asset-stripping, this is not the entire story. Creating an integrated structure with the capacity to invest, consolidate, and promote innovation, effective production, and distribution required consolidating authority. As oligarchs expanded empires, they had to gain control of cash flow, decision-making, and assets. Given lower-level managers' resistance, speculative minority shareholders, and punitive taxation, oligarchs were acting rationally by manipulating property rights, governance law, and transparency. While the Rosprom-Iukos story was less visible in the media, it still contributed to the emergence of the financial logic of fields: yet another empire was consolidated, providing examples of successful tactics to augment governance and of the wave of the future as it seemed in the late 1990s.

Successful managerial resistance

Constructing financial empires could face resistance. Managers wielded rhetoric of a moral economy, but they needed allies with resources. These might be employee shareholders or local political elites best served by managerial authority. One such story of managers and employees versus financial elites was Menatep's failed "hostile takeover" of confectionery firm Red October. Red October profitably produced quality candy and held its own against imports, making it a good investment. In July 1995 a Menatep daughter announced a public tender for shares in Red October, offering employees nearly $10 per share (50,000 rubles, no small sum). Red October's managers saw this as a threat to their authority and countered with psychological warfare. Through loudspeakers at the firm, directors blared propaganda at employees, accusing Menatep of trying to gain control of Red October to shed workers, squeeze profit from the firm, and cast it aside.[115] Menatep countered that they wanted to modernize the firm, but the employees did not relinquish many shares.[116] Small wonder Russian directors did not raise capital through share offerings in the 1990s—it courted the danger of losing control. A state survey of large firms confirmed this.[117] Logics of authority and control trumped logics of capital investment and modernization.

Another case of successful managerial resistance was privatization of airplane engine producer Rybinskie Motors.[118] After initial privatization, Goskomoboronprom (State Committee for the Defense Industry) held 37 percent of Rybinskie shares (51 percent of voting shares). In 1993 General Electric and Gazprom joined forces: Rybinskie would produce airplane engines for GE and turbines for natural gas equipment for Gazprom. Gazprom ally Viktor Chernomyrdin authorized GKI to sell the state's shares to Gazprom, but others were interested—Perm Motors, with Pratt & Whitney, were also interested. Citing the danger of depriving Russia's airplane industry of this key producer, Perm Motors and the Iaroslavl' *oblast'* government (Rybinskie's home) pressured the Kremlin to stop the sale, and Goskomoboronprom joined the chorus. Rybinskie general director Valerii Anikin and his board of directors refused to give Goskomoboronprom representation at a 1994 shareholders' meeting. Yeltsin's administration accused Anikin of "improper relations" with workers and shareholders, and a Rybinsk city court declared his actions invalid. Managers appealed the ruling; Anikin ordered managers to disobey the shareholders' meeting. The regional GKI was told to replace Anikin with the head engineer, but Anikin fired the engineer; employees and minority shareholders supported him.

To complicate things, in April 1995 the regional bankruptcy agency declared Rybinskie Motors insolvent. Anikin resigned, and shareholders appointed Valerii Shelgunov director, but enterprise shares were now with the bankruptcy commission FUDN.[119] In August 1995 a FUDN official arrived at Rybinskie with "young people of athletic build" to convince Shelgunov to leave; but the Procurator ruled this move illegal. In September, FUDN prepared to sell the shares, and Chernomyrdin demanded the selling the shares to Gazprom. The Iaroslavl' *oblast'* governor, Perm Motors, and Goskomoboronprom cited state instructions to sell the shares to many buyers, not just Gazprom, and Duma representatives Sergei Burkov and Sergei Glaz'ev protested against the sale as a "serious blow" to Russian aviation (national security again); military-industrial ally vice-premier Soskovets chimed in with support.[120] In December 1995 Shelgunov said Rybinskie would challenge the sale in Arbitration Court, and Russian Chamber of Commerce experts noted that Rybinskie's 20 billion ruble support for local infrastructure made it only *appear* insolvent.[121] In January 1996 the Supreme Arbitration Court supported selling the shares to Gazprom, but nationalism butted in. As communist Gennadyi Zyuganov looked strong in election year 1996, managers harped on "national interests" and Rybinskie as "strategic producer" of engines for airplanes IL-62, IL-76, and TU-154. Rybinskie should remain state-owned rather than belong to an *American* firm. In October 1996 Yeltsin made Rybinskie a firm of "strategic significance," safe from privatization. This "saved the leadership of an inefficient enterprise."[122]

With the state a silent owner, Rybinskie remained manager-run. Managers had challenged privatization's validity and legitimacy using chaotic legislation and appeals to echoes of the Soviet moral economy. Interros defeated Norilsk managers not entirely because of superior arguments; they had courts and the Kremlin on their side. Rybinskie played out differently—the managerial logic intersected with "national interests" in an election year. Gazprom had the prime minister on its side, but in this case rhetoric won out. This case demonstrated that, despite limited access to money and the rhetoric of transition culture and global capitalism, the production-centered logic could resonate and be successful in some quarters. Finance was not entirely hegemonic.

State-run empires: Gazprom the firstborn

In addition to Defensive and Financial FPGs, a state-run property empire was emerging. Early on its contours are blurrier than after 2000; important state-run property included railways monopoly Rossiiskaia Zheleznaia Doroga (RZhD), electricity monopoly Edinaia Elektrichestkaia Sistema (EES), and natural gas monopoly Gazprom. EES would eventually be broken up (July 2008) and the Railroad remained focused on transport, but Gazprom would become the first instrument for the state's reclamation of economic power, and so I turn briefly to its status in the mid-1990s. Whereas the oil industry was broken up for privatization, the gas industry remained integrated as state-run monopoly Gazprom.[123] Gazprom's Soviet-era predecessor was created in the 1960s to integrate the gas industry. In its peculiar structure, member enterprises were linked via contract rather than bureaucratic verticality and were relatively free from ministerial tutelage—an oddity in the command economy.[124] In 1989 gas and oil ministries were united into a super-ministry headed by Viktor Chernomyrdin. In November 1992 state-owned Russian joint-stock company (RAO) Gazprom was born, controlling nearly all of Russia's gas industry, from extraction to transport. (Western-run Itera competed to transport gas outside Russia.) This gave Gazprom nearly a quarter of the world's gas reserves and a quarter of the Russian state's hard currency earnings.[125] While the state split up the oil sector into independent conglomerates and sold its shares in them, Chernomyrdin and Gazprom director Rem Viakhirev protected Gazprom from such a fate. Under Yeltsin, Gazprom was politically quiet. It participated in the virtual economy and earned hard currency for the state, although it had enormous tax arrears. But this slumbering giant was a potential tool for economic and political domination if leadership and will emerged.

Chernomyrdin entered the government in 1992 and Viakhirev ran Gazprom until 2001. The two formed a powerful duo, and under Chernomyrdin's patronage Gazprom and Viakhirev prospered. Gazprom was sheltered from all-out privatization and received special state funding and privileges. Privatization was restricted to avoid concentration of ownership in a non-state entity: Russian individuals (physical persons) were allowed to purchase shares, and then only up to three percent in any regional auction. Gazprom daughters and divisions could also purchase shares in Gazprom itself, maintaining control within the overall structure. Gazprom management reserved the right to refuse share sales to outsiders, and sales to foreigners were curtailed before Putin's regime allowed liberalization—only after the state gained a solid block that allowed it effectively to run the monopoly. In the 1990s the state's shareholding rights were essentially transferred to Viakhirev via proxy. Gazprom daughters were legally independent entities formed, owned, and run by the Gazprom mother. When its shares were floated on the market, Gazprom was unified, its daughters turned into functional subdivisions.

Gazprom managers later created or bought into Gazprombank, Imperial Bank, and National Reserve Bank and arranged partnerships with Mosbiznesbank and Vneshtorgbank. This made Gazprom a *de facto* state-owned FPG. To guard its productive capacity and independence, Gazprom expanded its empire to producers of important components, e.g. piping. Managers eyed Perm Motors and Rybinskie Motors, competing in privatization auctions for state-held shares, to vertically integrate and improve supply of piping and gas-refining equipment. Opportunities for further expansion would come after 2000, when Gazprom was the vehicle for state power.

1998 and all that (post-1998): Putin, *siloviki*, and post-Soviet *dirigisme*

In England, 1066 was a historical watershed, as William the Conqueror imposed a new elite and field of power. Whether 1998 will be so significant for Russia is open to debate, but Russia's trajectory did change. In the fluid master field, property rights were not embedded in rule of law or state–elite balance; they were secure if owners could use physical force (e.g. bandit-style "rent-a-thug") or state allies. Property's manifestation as authority was not sacred. "Rule by law," not "rule of law," was the norm. Carriers of financial logics, oligarchs, relied on money and political connections; losing these legs threatened their wellbeing. The August 1998 ruble crash and debt nightmares forced elites to dismantle empires and removed the halo of natural authority from them and Yeltsin's regime. These disruptions, with NATO bombings of Yugoslavia and the problems in Chechnya, embittered Russians and provoked nationalist sentiments. One group profited: personnel of the FSB (Federal Security Service), trained in the KGB, who staffed state bureaucracies. Disempowered under Yeltsin and left out of the redistribution of wealth, their opportunity came when Yeltsin named Putin as heir. As financial elites stumbled, state actors turned to use Gazprom, *kompromat*, and rhetoric of national interests. But not only oligarchs and *siloviki* faced challenges: Defensive FPGs continued to consolidate, generating conflict over governance. When the dust settled, the field of power had new drivers and *doxa*, oriented to state and security.

Contradictions of the defensive logic: opportunism and revolution at EMK

Conflict at Defensive FPGs was not inevitable. Groups with a dominant leader who did not abuse authority (e.g. Krasnyi Aksai in the Doninvest FPG) might encourage consensus.[126] Daughter firms at the Magnitogorsk Combine were sufficiently interdependent in steel production for stable authority. An assembly that expanded slowly, Magnitka became a hybrid Defensive-Financial FPG. A

Petersburg furniture FPG and poultry FPG were also calm; a central figure with key resources (money or networks) at the center provided for members.[127] However, when member firms were not minor, traditions of hard-fought autonomy and independent identity could set off the contradictory logics of FPG unification and autonomy. This occurred at EMK when general director Aleksandr Stepanov set out to centralize it and build a personal empire.

Once an official in the Soviet energy sector, Stepanov used ministerial connections to help EMK arrange deals with foreign clients, earning him a post as EMK assistant director. He also ran Mardima Company Ltd., registered in the Virgin Isles and possibly founded with Communist Party money.[128] Stepanov increased his power by having EMK issue shares to increase working capital; Mardima bought these.[129] As EMK members privatized, EMK and Mardima purchased their shares as well. EMK or a daughter would act as sales intermediary for member firms; rather than turn over sales income, Stepanov would keep half the sum to buy that member's shares. Stepanov also used financial trickery to build his empire. He would set up a daughter firm to milk his target enterprise of assets. Alternatively, he would gain enough shares in his victim to appoint a subaltern as general director to implement restructuring and drive the victim bankrupt. Stepanov would be named external administrator and transfer the victim's assets to a daughter under his control. His first victim was Atommash, driven to bankruptcy in 1995. As external administrator Stepanov created daughter firm and trading intermediary EMK-Atommash. EMK-Atommash set up a lucrative deal between EMK and a nuclear power station that made a large prepayment for goods. EMK used metal reserved for military purposes and prepared less equipment than agreed upon. The prepayment likely went offshore; EMK-Atommash, stranded with debt, went bankrupt. Stepanov turned to chemical combine Bor. As external administrator for the bankrupt Bor, he transferred Bor's assets to Energomash-Bor and left the debt behind.[130]

In 1997 Stepanov made EMK the exclusive intermediary for selling members' goods, extracting a commission of 14 to 30 percent of the sale.[131] This deprived the target firm of income to pay wages and debts and raised the price for the firm's goods, driving off former clients and adding financial woes. With income reduced, the target firm was usually close to bankruptcy. Formal complaints about debt payments, initiated by a Stepanov-run daughter, began the process. In 1997 Stepanov applied the bankruptcy trick to Petersburg firms, and he transferred their assets and employees' labor contracts to EMK. After a quick victory over ZTL, Stepanov turned on Elektrosila and LMZ,[132] but here he met resistance. Through EMK and Mardima, Stepanov had 58 percent of LMZ shares by 1998, and he installed Valerii Chernyshev as general director. Against Elektrosila he used EMK's majority shareholding status to ask the board of directors to replace general director Ravil' Urusov with Chernyshev. Urusov refused, complaining about EMK's exorbitant middleman fee and how EMK had yet to turn over 113 million rubles and $883,000 for goods Elektrosila had produced and consigned to EMK for shipment.[133] The board called for a shareholders' meeting to force out Urusov, but he and shareholder allies (including Energomashbank) petitioned the

Arbitration Court to stop the meeting.[134] Stepanov also lost control of some shares: in 1997 EMK and Inkombank finalized an agreement whereby Inkombank loaned billions of rubles in return for EMK-held shares as collateral. After the 1998 ruble crash, Inkombank's assets were frozen, including EMK's shares in Elektrosila. This let Elektrosila managers tie up enterprise politics with court challenges.

Real trouble broke out at LMZ. Chernyshev implemented rapid restructuring that, critics claimed, lost foreign hard-currency contracts and created losses of $200 million in sales for 1998 alone.[135] Two further events transformed discontent into rebellion. First, Stepanov pulled the bankruptcy trick on EMK itself. As Energomashstroitel'naia Korporatsiia—"EMK-1," registered in Moscow—went bankrupt, its assets would go to "Energomashkorporatsiia," or EMK-2, newly registered in Vel'sk (Arkhangelsk *oblast'*). They were legally unrelated—EMK-2 was fully owned by offshore company Dream Investments Ltd.—but names and personnel were suspiciously similar.[136] (The process was completed June 27, 2000, when a Moscow court ruled EMK-1 bankrupt.) Second, LMZ was to go bankrupt. Employees were suddenly told this when they were given the opportunity to resign from LMZ and to register to work at EMK-2. They had reason for alarm: LMZ's labor force had dropped from around 9,000 employees in 1995 to 5,000 in 1998, and 19,000 employees had been released from other EMK firms under Stepanov. On December 3, brigade leaders suddenly told employees that Chernyshev had agreed to transfer them from LMZ to EMK-2. Employees had to register their residence as Vel'sk as well, although they would be physically present in St. Petersburg. Some employees, trade union representatives, and sympathetic journalists saw this as a "second serfdom"—especially when Chernyshev withheld December's wages from those who refused to re-register or otherwise protested against the policy.[137]

This energized resistance by employees and the board of directors. Sales under EMK's direction dropped 30 percent in 1998; managers accused EMK superiors of incompetence. An LMZ spokeswomen said, "EMK is run by people who do not understand power engineering and were unable to ensure effective management of LMZ."[138] In 1998 Siemens, LMZ, and others started bankruptcy procedures against EMK-1 for withholding money from sales.[139] LMZ's board, which included Elektrosila's Urusov, a Siemens representative, and Energomashbank director Andrei Bykov, took defensive action and replaced Chernyshev with former director Viktor Shevchenko. Chernyshev turned off heating and water to LMZ, stopped wages, and had security keep Shevchenko off the grounds;[140] employees physically escorted him into LMZ. Stepanov denounced this attempt "to break up" and destroy LMZ, which only EMK could save.[141] Shevchenko and Bykov accused Stepanov of betraying goals of unifying the energy-equipment sector; rather than coordinate production, EMK was withholding payments for goods sold, closing production, leasing out shopfloor space for no reason, and ruining marketing services and relations LMZ and others had spent time and energy learning and organizing.[142] Stepanov called a shareholders' meeting to create a friendly board of directors and gain legality; Shevchenko, Bykov, and allies challenged this. Neither side had a solid 50 percent of shares, creating dual power at LMZ. Employees staged a strike and formed "human corridors" to help Shevchenko enter the grounds, and local police prepared to intervene.[143] Stepanov framed the conflict as strong, unified Russian industry against those who would wreck it for foreign interests (i.e. Siemens).[144] In a personal appeal in a local newspaper, he admitted Chernyshev 's managerial style and approach to people were not proper, and that he, Stepanov, had not paid enough attention to employees.[145]

Stepanov was not without defenders, and in the Petersburg media spotlight he had to frame his case. One justification for Stepanov's tactics was to improve performance and survive global competition. EMK aimed to reduce domestic competition and unite producers to provide clients with a "complete package" of goods to choose (generators, turbines, etc.). This required improving EMK's structure and production practices and reducing labor, which in turn required using offshore companies as "the traditional means to gain control over a company." Even bankruptcies and asset transfers at EMK had a rationale: EMK had many creditors, and it was natural to create a new debt-free EMK to leave debts behind. However, EMK leaders faced opposition, much from state ministries, who feared EMK would increase authority over member firms.[146] Other claims focused on Stepanov's attempt to combat lingering Soviet abnormalities, the most egregious being underemployment and producing goods with marginal returns and unimportant to core activity (e.g. making vacuum cleaners at Elektrosila). Unfortunately, control over these firms thus far was insufficient to impose stringent and painful restructuring.[147] While EMK managers were making hard economic choices, employees' meetings—a legacy of Soviet rhetoric and ideology and a last, desperate attempt to save inefficiencies—impeded progress to meet global challenges. Experience outside Russia—for example, in Polish firms—suggested that Stepanov's tactics were proper for a market context.[148] A related justification was nationalism: by increasing control over EMK members and transferring assets and authority to EMK-2, Stepanov would save Russian producers of energy generation equipment from Siemens.

The revolt at Elektrosila and LMZ spread to ZTL, where Stepanov was director and whose employees had re-registered with EMK-2. In late January 1999, ZTL's board of directors fired Stepanov.[149] Finally, Stepanov lost at his own game. Stepanov and Chernyshev led LMZ to bankruptcy to control LMZ's assets and pass off its debts—but creditor BNP-Dresdner Bank was quicker to begin bankruptcy proceedings. On March 10 LMZ was declared insolvent; the new director was S. A. Fiveiskii, young head of a consulting firm who had worked at Petersburg's currency exchange.[150] As LMZ and Elektrosila creditor, Siemens initially headed the creditors' commission but sold its LMZ debt to Interros.[151] Stepanov had subordinate V. Markin named LMZ's outside administrator, and Markin's personal consultant was Stepanov ally Tatiana Gramotenko. Markin quickly lost the official register of LMZ creditors (except for EMK). The Arbitration Court did not let this pass: they removed Markin and asked bankruptcy commission member Evgenii Guliaev to run LMZ.[152] Guliaev and creditors agreed to cover LMZ's debts by issuing 14 million additional shares.

This watered down EMK's shareholding, and via subsidiaries Rosbank and Balt-Oneksimbank, Interros bought the new shares to become majority shareholder. EMK challenged this in court but lost. ZTL's freedom was complete in 2000, when Energomashbank and EMK split after years of conflict. LMZ sold 34 percent of ZTL shares to Energomashbank, now a partner with Interros. Energomashbank took its ZTL shares into the Interros partnership.[153] Interros integrated these firms and others into its Silovye Mashiny (Power Machines) corporation; it then dropped bankruptcy charges against LMZ.[154]

EMK began as a prototypical Defensive FPG embodying Soviet logics of production, managerial autonomy, welfare, and moral economy that grew out of attempts to support Russia's industrial base. While Stepanov used EMK for his own wealth and power, this is not the entire story. Stepanov justified his actions by reference to transition culture (Soviet as abnormal), and under his leadership the focus of EMK shifted from managers and members to EMK and offshore firms—a logic resembling that of Financial FPGs. Stepanov's tactics were not unfamiliar to oligarchs; his rhetoric included efficiency gains, competition, and profit. Yet *hubris* got the best of him; he did not try to bridge the Defensive and Financial logics, as Pëtr Semenenko did bridging paternalism and profit at Kirov (Chapter 3). Employees and managers reacted via the moral economy of the Defensive FPG, although ultimately to save themselves LMZ, Elektrosila, and others under threat turned to Financial FPG Interros and ended up in Silovye Mashiny. Instrumental rules and interests were embedded in normal organizational relations. EMK survives with some member enterprises (e.g. EMK-Atommash, Chekhovskii Zavod). Despite losing LMZ and Elektrosila, Stepanov integrated what remained into a functioning group that continued engineering work and production for the energy sector.[155]

The state strikes back: Putin versus oligarchs and the fate of the field of power

Financial FPGs and logic faced shocks of the 1998 crisis and the coming to power of a new elite and the unfolding of a new *doxa* in the field of power. In August 1998 the state's debt pyramid collapsed, driving the ruble down five-fold against the dollar and hurting elites who invested in state debt as low-risk, high-yield speculation. Not all empires were hit badly—Al'fa-Group survived because of diversified investments and limited GKO investment—but others were less lucky. Inkombank and SBS-Agro invested heavily in GKOs and in other firms hit hard by 1998; Menatep and Oneksimbank faced bankruptcy. To save their empires, oligarchs used political networks and legal loopholes, including the inability to pierce the corporate veil and track assets, to transfer assets to debt-free organizations, leaving the older shell with debt. By 1998 Menatep personnel had moved to Rosprom or Iukos and assets to Menatep-SPb; Menatep proper defaulted on $1 billion of debt, much to Western banks Standard, West Merchant, and Daiwa who took 32 percent of Iukos shares as collateral but discovered assets were transferred offshore.[156] Oneksimbank moved assets to Rosbank, Interros's financial agent, although Potanin lost oil giant Sidanko and Sviazinvest for foreign debt. These empires might have regrouped, but politics intervened. After the pain of 1998, average Russians took out their anger on the oligarchs, Yeltsin, and perceived Western plots to emasculate Russia. To guard himself after leaving office, Yeltsin named Putin prime minister and then acting president. Untainted by oligarchs or privatization and framed as a disciplinarian, Putin could wield blame to use security, stability, and "dictatorship of law" to rebuild state and regime authority.[157] His political base was the military, security forces, and Edinstvo, less a political party than a makeshift group of coattail-riders and technocrats.[158] With Putin came *siloviki*, creatures of Soviet security services. Propaganda and secrecy, rule by law rather than of law, and selective use of *kompromat* for political ends were their principles.[159] Still, *siloviki* were not interested in micromanaging the entire economy, as this Soviet logic was thoroughly delegitimated and a logistical nightmare. Private property would remain within limits of laws as interpreted by the new elite and of national security as defined by that elite as well.

Given the secrecy of the security apparatus, discussion of *siloviki* is speculative. One analysis suggests this group is 6,000 people trained in the KGB-FSB and in positions of state power, especially "power ministries" (Internal Affairs, FSB). Some Kremlin *siloviki* are Putin (former FSB lieutenant-colonel), Sergei Ivanov (Putin colleague in the Leningrad KGB), Igor Sechin (deputy chief of staff, foreign intelligence, Putin aid in Petersburg), Viktor Ivanov (former FSB deputy director), Nikolai Patrushev (former KGB-FSB colonel and Putin colleague, FSB head), Sergei Naryshkin (Putin deputy prime minister, KGB training, Putin colleague), Vladimir Yakunin (head of Russian Railways, deputy prime minister, Putin colleague), Sergei Chemezov (Rostekhnologiia CEO, unclear background, links to Putin in East Germany and Petersburg), and Viktor Cherkesov (anti-narcotics operations, KGB since the 1970s).[160] To assume these players share ideology, identity, and interests is unwarranted, as Kremlin turf wars suggest.[161] Yet corporate unity and stability are striking in contrast to Western cabinets. Security, national status, a secretive, corporate structure, and remorse over the end of the USSR seem shared.[162] Order and control were clear in Putin's "power vertical," regional officials answerable to him; later reforms let the president appoint regional governors rather than risk local elections. Once in power, Putin and *siloviki* set out to remake state power, and as they turned to the economy and property, a *dirigiste* logic emerged.[163] While personal gain cannot be dismissed, it should not be assumed as prime mover: gain can follow myriad paths, and we need to understand what forces guide perceptions of "gain" and how to achieve it. Oleg Shvartsman, to whom I return later, noted varying agendas in the *siloviki* circle, but also a corporate identity and shared concern for state power: individual gain operated through a common *habitus* and collective logic I have dubbed a *political economy* of normality. This centered not on sober and strong (or loyal) private elites, but on state direction (though not complete ownership) of the economy for the cause of national prestige and security (rather than individual entrepreneurial profit and prosperity or defending labor and local production). While the command economy might have lost legitimacy and attractiveness, controlling the commanding heights in the name of national security and state power had not.

First steps: Putin / siloviki versus oligarchs

From the outset it was clear that to consolidate state power and implement post-Soviet *dirigisme*, Putin and *siloviki* had to deal with the oligarchs. Victory over the top oligarchs would not only reduce outside resistance; it would provide the state elite with the means to further augment state power. A pro-state strategy and attacks on competitors had precedent. Krasnoyarsk governor Aleksandr Lebed, with Berezovskii's backing, attacked aluminum tsar Anatolii Bykov to grab aluminum assets. Police raided Bykov's offices for documents and *kompromat* on Krasnoyarsk Aluminum privatization; Bykov went to jail.[164] Another *siloviki* prequel was a 1999 investigation for defrauding Aeroflot. Berezovskii fled to France and returned after a smear campaign ended state Prosecutor General Iurii Skuratov's career and the investigation. Key features of these events were conflict between state and financial elite factions, with *kompromat* and images of legitimacy as tools. Lebed and Skuratov were restrained, but Putin and *siloviki* had more will and capacity to perfect these weapons, in so doing consolidating state and regime influence over the economy. The first tool was finance: either *kompromat* related to fraud or pursuing debt and tax arrears. *Kompromat* and debt weapons were formally legal, but underlying them were extra-legal machinations. Vague and contradictory laws and *prikhvatizatsiia* ensured that most people in business had violated some laws. Rather than defending law as duty, officials and *siloviki* enforced laws selectively even while framing actions as law enforcement. Tax audits were targeted, not random or consistent: audits of Putin's enemies were more thorough and found serious violations, but were quick and clear for allies. The second *siloviki* weapon was using state-run corporations to purchase debt or shares of targets. The favorite early tool was Gazprom, which emerged from 1998 healthy: gas sales provided the state with stable revenue, and its authority expanded in the virtual economy. It had financial resources to take over competitors through mergers or exchanging property for debt.

To use Gazprom, the regime needed to strengthen its organizational control, and Gazprom became Putin's personal project from the first days of his presidency.[165] Rem Viakhirev had built a personal empire, with daughters owned or run by relatives and associates. Gazprom's charter made it difficult to oust the CEO; this required a vote of the board of directors, which Viakhirev controlled. In May 2000 a shareholder suggested altering the charter to make this easier, and Putin followed with a scathing critique of Gazprom's ineffective use of capital.[166] In summer 2000, soon after taking power, Putin replaced Viktor Chernomyrdin with his loyal subordinate Dmitrii Medvedev on the board of directors, and at the July 2000 shareholders' meeting, five of the eleven board members were Putin loyalists, and only four were Viakhirev allies.[167] (By 2007 eleven of the eighteen members of the board of directors were Putin's allies from St. Petersburg or the FSB.) In 2001 Aleksei Miller became the new CEO. Gazprom managers set out to expand the corporation and consolidate state shareholding, which required navigating the boundaries of legality and legitimacy *vis-à-vis* the international market. One area of concern was opening Gazprom to investors so as not to betray vows made to placate the international business community. While Putin relaxed restrictions on foreign ownership, he set out gathering shares to make the state the majority shareholder. With Gazprom under control and controlling enough capital to engage in acquisitions, the regime could recentralize economic resources.

To recentralize authority Putin *et al* turned against oligarchs.[168] The first target was media baron Vladimir Gusinskii. Gusinskii's media holdings, especially independent television station NTV, had made their name being critical of the state. This was a shrewd business move: dissent bequeathed some legitimacy and played to the lingering positive image of post-Soviet openness. NTV's criticism of the Chechen war did not sit well with Putin, and Gusinskii became the first target.[169] The attack came on two fronts: debt and *kompromat*. Gazprom loaned Media-MOST $473 million for 40 percent of Media-MOST shares as collateral, and was suddenly anxious to clear the debt by transferring the media empire to Gazprom-Media. After a police raid on Media-MOST in May 2000, Gusinskii was charged with embezzling $10 million. Gazprom-Media sued Media-MOST to recover debts owed.[170] In November 2000, Gusinskii transferred Media-MOST to Gazprom-Media and fled Russia; prosecutors issued an arrest warrant for asset-stripping and fraud. The next target was kingmaker Berezovskii. His ORT television channel launched attacks on Putin after his May 2000 inauguration. State control of ORT could aid framing discourse and expectations (the second and third dimensions of power). Putin restarted the Aeroflot fraud investigation, and Berezovskii was asked to give up ORT.[171] Roman Abramovich, Berezovskii's protégé on various investment projects (RusAl aluminum, Sibneft oil, Aeroflot), repaid his mentor by acting as intermediary with Putin, offering Berezovskii a pittance for his media and industrial holdings. For his loyalty to the regime, Abramovich gained Berezovskii's holdings except for ORT; mostly unknown before 2001, he soon became Russia's second richest man.

Importantly, Putin and company kept these holdings close to the state: rather than sell them to the highest private bidder—a natural tactic in a financial logic— Putin and *siloviki* retained these gains to enhance state control of discourse. This should have been an early sign that *siloviki* had a *dirigiste* operating logic, although whether they came to power with a well-organized plan is unclear. What was clear was that Putin was not the puppet the oligarchs assumed. After the attacks on Gusinskii and Berezovskii, the oligarchs requested meetings with Putin. An uneasy truce followed: *siloviki* would leave the oligarchs alone if they stuck to business and toed the party line.[172] This ended in 2003. The pro-Putin Council for National Strategy claimed oligarchs aimed to undermine the state and leadership.[173] In a 2003 meeting on state corruption and administrative reform, Khodorkovskii was openly critical of Putin.[174] Now annoyed and facing Duma and presidential elections, Putin and *siloviki* struck back. Some oligarchs were safe. Roman Abramovich provided services to Putin. Vladimir Potanin and up-and-coming Oleg Deripaska kept a low profile, focusing on business. Khodorkovskii was another matter. His empire was in oil, he hinted at future political activity, and his Jewish surname gave *siloviki* room for attack via covert appeals to latent anti-Semitism. Khodorkovskii was openly critical of the state,[175] but such confidence that served him well building an empire was useless against Putin. In June 2003 Khodorkovskii's right-hand man Platon Lebedev was arrested for fraud and murder. The oligarch himself was arrested for tax fraud. Investigators had plenty of *kompromat*: when Khodorkovskii announced in 2005 that he would appeal his guilty verdict, investigators responded that the Kremlin had enough charges to keep him long in jail. Khodorkovskii multiplied his woes by making Iukos transparent, aiding police raids for evidence of wrongdoing.

Putin and critics framed the contest in terms of stability and justice, and popular reaction was positive or ambivalent.[176] Oligarchs and the RSPP begged Putin to rein in *siloviki*; framing a defense *vis-à-vis* property would be difficult given rigged privatization, so the elite invoked stability: renationalization and capricious investigations would make investors nervous. In a open letter, the RSPP claimed, "The actions of law enforcement agents in the economy have often gone beyond the framework of the law recently, and in essence are being based on political expediency…An independent player on the economic field has been created out of these agencies with [an aim of] redistributing markets with the use of an entire arsenal of strong-arm tactics."[177] Prime Minister Mikhail Kasyanov, later an oligarch ally, called Iukos arrests "excessive" and hoped investigators would be "understanding" in their duties.[178] Independent media commentators criticized both Putin and Khodorkovskii for subverting the economy and rule of law. As former Kremlin insider Boris Fedorov put it, "Oligarchs used the law and the corrupt judges to their benefit for many years. They are now getting some of it back in their faces."[179] Anatolii Chubais also offered a warning over the Iukos affair.[180] The occasional commentator supported Putin's clampdown. Investment fund CEO William Browder, whom *siloviki* would later attack, said, "A nice, well-run authoritarian regime is better than an oligarchic mafia regime—and those are the choices on offer."[181] Interior Minister and Edinstvo member Boris Gryzlov claimed, "All the natural resources that Russia possesses belong not to some corporation, nor to any specific person, but to the people of Russia…And if some corporation took it upon itself to manage the resources, it does not mean that they can privatize our profits."[182]

During the ordeal Putin and company used "rule of law" to frame their actions. Initially Putin warned authorities to follow procedure carefully, but he also took the fight to critics. In late 2003 he stated, "Leaders of the Russian Union of Industrialists and Entrepreneurs have sent a message to me over the arrest of the Iukos chief, while several political figures have asked me to meet with them to discuss this issue…There will not be any meetings or bargaining over the activities of law enforcement agencies, as long as these agencies stay within Russian law." He also reassured the West, adding, "I understand the concerns of the business community, because any activities by the federal authorities start and end as a sort of campaign…I wish to emphasize that no generalized inferences should be made from this case, which will not set a precedent for other cases, and all speculation and hysteria over this case should end…" Former economics minister Yevgeny Yasin interpreted this as rejecting renationalization *and* projecting state power and as a declaration that "when we want to attack someone, we will do so. We will crush anyone."[183]

By autumn 2004 Putin admitted the state might take Iukos assets in lieu of tax debts.[184] *Siloviki* brought in Western consultants to value Iukos assets, and in December 2004 they used state-owned firm and vehicle of state power, oil firm Rosneft, to take Iukos's most important daughter, oil extractor Iuganskneftegaz. This deprived Iukos of its primary income generator. In destroying a successful Russian firm, *siloviki* demonstrated that the logic of state supremacy predominated. "Iukos" became the symbol for risks of resisting the state. *Siloviki* now had organizational and material resources (state-owned firms generating hydrocarbon profit) and symbolic power (image of a tight elite able to crush opposition and shrug off criticism). While this did not make them confident—witness the Kremlin's reaction to the Orange Revolution and farcical elections in 2007 and 2008—it did propel Russia towards state-centered power, with trappings of national status and security, that were well on display in the attack on Georgia in August 2008.

Russian dirigisme unfolds

As *siloviki* assembled state property empires, meanings and principles of the field of power, economic normality, and legitimate property use began to emerge.[185] This *dirigisme* had two sides: direct share ownership and a client elite of "Putin oligarchs." Direct state ownership of shares, combining a state-centered with private property, was limited: the state did not have capital to build state empires, and this risked Russia's image with Western investors, happy with political order and to make money from Gazprom dividends but worried by renationalization. Putin and *siloviki* left other empires in private hands, so long as private emperors toed the party line, be it investment in local social projects or acting as regional governor.

If Putin *et al* did not have a master plan in 2000, that they were developing an economic normality was revealed inadvertently by Oleg Shvartsman, head of FPG Finansgrupp. In a *Kommersant Daily* interview in November 2007, Shvartsman revealed details about such Kremlin economic operations as "velvet nationalization" and using Rosoboroneksport as a vehicle of state power.[186] Whether he was telling the truth or embellishing is hard to verify; the reaction against him was swift, including annulments of venture capital agreements with his investment firm and Rosoboroneksport's libel lawsuit against *Kommersant Daily*.[187] No surprise: Shvartsman revealed *siloviki* tools and strategies of power, including a web of financial relations:

> We are closely affiliated with certain political figures and manage their assets. We have relations with the presidential administration, and with his power bloc [*silovoi blok*, i.e. *siloviki*]…There are several Cypriot and other offshore companies. This is not leadership of the president's administration, it is

members of their families, high-ranking people. There are…*feesbeshniki* [FSB] and *esveerovtsy* [SVR, foreign intelligence].

FSB operatives devised this structure in 2004, linked to Igor Sechin and such "power ministries" as the Ministry of Defense and Ministry of Internal Affairs (MVD), "to incline, bend, torment, lead [oligarchs] to social [paternalist] activities." Despite victory over Khodorkovskii, other oligarchs had *siloviki* allies and defenders, making further attacks difficult. So the regime changed tactics: working with rather than oppressing oligarchs. One example was an alliance between state-owned Rosneft and private oil firms TNK and Lukoil to create Russian Oil Group.

Not all tactics to augment state wealth and power were so innocuous: Shvartsman nearly admitted that the state engaged in "raiding," although he preferred to use such terms as "greenmail."

> This is not raiding (*reiderstvo*). We do not take an enterprise, we minimize its market cost with different tools. As a rule, there are voluntarily compulsory tools. There is market cost, there is the mechanics of blocking growth, and of course various administrative means. But as a rule, people understand where we are coming from…

Where *mafiia* used violence to gain rents and property in the 1990s, the state used greenmail, debt collection, and cajoling minority shareholders against majority shareholders. The regime also used MVD veterans to analyze target firms' assets and weaknesses, e.g. to determine if "debt collection" was a viable tool for takeover. This also kept MVD veterans employed and not falling into criminal structures, as happened in the 1990s.

Shvartsman's interview reveals a hybrid of logics. *Siloviki* worked through courts and law but also used informal networks to draw in allies from security and state services around the country as an informal social movement. *Siloviki* used patronage as indirect property control: "clients" would act as *siloviki* wanted. Also interesting was Shvartsman's invocation of social interests: leaning on oligarchs to pursue "social activity"; creating state corporation "Social Investment" for "velvet nationalization"; using the political party "Union of Social Justice for Russia" (Soiuz sotsial'noi spravedlivosti Rossii). That is, *siloviki* justified field logics via a collective social good, not individual or market enrichment. Much as in the French economic logic, the state knew what was best for the nation; and the regime knew what was best for the state. *Siloviki* took this logic and used two avenues of practice to bring it to life in the new field of power and Russian economy: through formal ownership and organization of property; and through the assembly of a new oligarchy beholden to the state, a private elite as allies in following the new logic of fields.

State corporations

Field logics create the structure of the field and disseminate through it: organizational relations create field boundaries and structure, and their operation augments field logics that arise through discourse. After 2000, Putin and *siloviki* used claims (discourse, propaganda), legal and economic capital (*kompromat*, debt collection, oil wealth), and new property forms (state-led empires) to remake the field of power. While *kompromat* could intimidate opposition—after the Iukos affair Lukoil and Sibneft (oligarchs Alekperov and Abramovich) faced audits—*siloviki* exerted field power through formal property ownership in state-led financial-industrial groups, "state corporations" (*gosudarstvennaia korporatsiia*, also *federal'noe gosudarstvennoe unitarnoe predprüatie*, FPUG, federal state unitary enterprise). Oil and gas were initial targets; in Putin's second term *siloviki* organized national champions. In 2005 there was talk of the state buying engineering giant Silovye Mashiny,[188] and a report by the Center for Current Politics in Russia claimed *siloviki* hoped to take private energy giants Lukoil and Sibneft,[189] although the Russian Oil Group (Rosneft, TNK, Lukoil) became a functional equivalent. Some state corporations were set up to coordinate or revive troubled sectors. As decreased military sales and foreign competition hurt aviation, a state-led consortium, OAK (Obedinennaia Aviastroitel'naia Korporatsiia, United Aircraft Corporation), was set up to integrate aircraft producers MiG, Iliushin, Sukhoi, Tupolev, and Irkut (all but the last state-owned). Aleksandr Zurabov, a "Western-styled manager" who saved Aeroflot in the late 1990s, was tapped to organize OAK. Possible obstacles from minority shareholders were quickly overcome. OAK would force a change in production strategies, from the older commercial aircraft to a newer "Russian Regional Jet," and would improve efficiency and capacity to compete with Boeing and Airbus. The state did what the market had not: induced a merger to save a sector of national security and pride.[190]

An important national champion is Rossiiskaia Tekhnologiia (Rostekhnologiia), once a daughter of Rosoboroneksport. Rosoboroneksport was formed in April 2000 as the state weapons export monopoly. It organized several firms as helicopter producer Oboronprom, and in autumn 2005 it gained a majority of shares in auto giant AvtoVAZ. Under Kremlin direction, Rosoboroneksport managers gathered firms in metallurgy, machine-building, and production of goods of "strategic value" to the military (trucks, jets). Citing defense of strategically significant industries, by late 2006 the organization acquired or was acquiring direct or indirect control of titanium giant VSMPO-Avisma; Petersburg shipyards Severnaia Verf and Baltiiskii Zavod; and jet-engine manufacturers Saliut, Chernyshiov, Klimov, and Ufa Engine-Building Obedinenie. At one point there were rumors Rosoboroneksport managers wanted Energomash and truck manufacturer KamAZ. The organization changed its status to "state corporation" (*goskorporatsiia*) for production flexibility and social provision laws.[191] As Rosoboroneksport grew, the Kremlin reorganized the empire around daughter Rostekhnologiia. Putin ally Sergei Chemezov, a top manager at Rosoboroneksport, devised this project initially in 2003. Sensing the market would not aid heavy industry and that too much metallurgy was in private hands, Chemezov and the Kremlin set out to gather firms in metallurgy and heavy industry. Rostekhnologiia was registered in November 2007 to administer Rosoboroneksport's holdings in heavy industry and metallurgy; Rosoboroneksport later became Rostekhnologiia's daughter.[192] Disagreement emerged over the project—Ministry of Finance officials and the anti-monopòly committee were nervous—but on July 10, 2008 president Dmitrii Medvedev transferred 426 firms to the new empire.[193] The official goal was to create a state corporation (an open joint-stock company in which the state owned all shares) to develop high-tech industrial production and to systematize production and business development in strategic economic sectors. Chemezov's initial strategies included organizing the property into 24 military and seven civilian holding companies, to consolidate production and to prepare the way for IPOs.[194] Now *siloviki* had an industrial engine for state power.

Not all state-run enterprise groups were so active. State-owned FPG Kompomash, created in 1994, was 25 firms in 2000, in military production and medical or agricultural equipment. Member firms were debtors, making Kompomash a target for Gazprom or other poachers. Other sector-oriented, state-led dinosaurs did not have skills to optimize exports despite key markets (e.g. energy machinery to Southeast Asia). Rosstankinstrument and Stankoinstrument, a corporation and an association headed by Nikolai Panichev and including more than half of Russian machine-tool enterprises, retained 1990s FPG structure and logic: decentralized, maintaining internal support and autonomy, integrated more around Panichev than investment. In the bearings sector, two holding companies were organized in the late 1990s, but consolidation provided no noticeable returns, and sales relied on trading companies rather than FPG integration.[195]

Indirect state control: Putin's oligarchs

A new generation of empires and emperors followed, and they might be subtly combining the financial logic with an emphasis on sectoral production, rather than raiding diverse fields for speculative profits.[196] In this hybrid, status is linked to making one's mark via modernization and competition. Some examples are Severstal and Evrazkholding (steel) or Kakha Bendukidze's OMZ, in machine-building and heavy industry and including such firms as Uralmash and Izhorskie Zavody. The wealthiest Putin oligarch is Oleg Deripaska, head of BazEl (Bazevoi Element, Basic Element) and RusAl (Russian Aluminum). Deripaska's rise began in the aluminum sector, initially at KrAZ (Krasnoyarsk Aluminum Factory). In 1990 Deripaska was financial director for a trading company in aluminum; in 1993 he met Michael Cherney, a player in Russia's aluminum market who introduced Deripaska to his political and business network. In 1994 Deripaska took over Saianogorsk aluminum, and he and Cherney founded Sibirskii Aluminum in 1998. Deripaska and Cherney were engaged in struggles to control the aluminum sector.[197] British firm TransWorld and entrepreneur Kenneth Dart obtained KrAZ shares, but from 1995 to 1997 Oleg Soskovets (citing national interest) and KrAZ managers blocked their shareholding rights. Manager Anatolii Bykov and colleague Gennadyi Druzhinin ousted TransWorld and tried to integrate KrAZ, Achinsk Alumina Combine, and the local electricity producer to control costs and supplies. This local feudal arrangement was based on violence; Bykov intimidated managers in the state-owned Tanako holding company to oust state representatives from governing boards. Bykov's power and popularity were at their peak: managerial paternalism to employees and region made him a local Robin Hood.[198] Yet local governor Aleksandr Lebed became a powerful foe. After the 1998 ruble crash Lebed turned on Bykov. In 1999 the Ministry of the Interior, likely at Lebed's request, investigated Bykov for money laundering.[199] In 2000 Bykov was arrested in Budapest and lost his KrAZ directorship.[200] Via Sibneft and Siberian Aluminum, Berezovskii and protégé Abramovich acquired shares in KrAZ, Bratsk Aluminum (BrAZ), and the Achinsk Alumina Combine. Emerging aluminum overlord Oleg Deripaska lobbied the state to stop them on anti-monopoly grounds. Deripaska's Siberian Aluminum (SibAl) was a vertically integrated corporation formed around Saiansk Aluminum, Bratskii Aluminum Factory (BrAZ), and TransWorld.[201] Deripaska had shown managerial talents restructuring his firms and improving performance, and SibAl was Russia's largest aluminum consortium. He also had a powerful ally: Anatolii Chubais, head of electricity monopoly EES, reduced Deripaska's electricity prices to undercut competitors.[202] Rather than fight, Berezovskii, Abramovich, and Deripaska united their holdings as Russian Aluminum (RusAl).[203] By 2001 Deripaska and Abramovich were aluminum tsars, with Deripaska continuing his legendary devotion to the sector (it was rumored he regularly slept at the factory). In 2003 Abramovich sold his RusAl shares to Deripaska.[204] In 2006, Deripaska and Abramovich merged their empires— RusAl (Deripaska) with SUAL and commodity trader Glencore (Abramovich)— to create an aluminum giant. This paralleled metallurgy generally: mergers and consolidions of producers and suppliers, increased investment, and bringing up managers from within.[205]

Deripaska's tactics and empire have a passing resemblance to those of oligarchs, but there are differences. He began as an industrial manager, an insider. He built RusAl not from diverse holdings but following a logic of industrial production, and in 2001 he organized BazEl to consolidate his aluminum empire.[206] This made him closer to Kakha Bendukidze and Aleksandr Stepanov than Berezovskii. BazEl expanded other areas: GAZ (automobiles), Continental Management, electricity supplier Evrosibenergo (a KrAZ supplier), Aviakor (aviation equipment), Irkutskenergo, Soyuz Bank, the Ruspromavto automobile holding company, funds for education and science, and collective farms. While diversifying, his empire remained industry-based, with tacit *siloviki* approval.[207] He was not always successful—he and Abramovich failed to gain control of Ilim Pulp through the courts and State Property Committee.[208] Finally, Deripaska has not hidden statist, nationalist beliefs. One of his business ambitions has been to help restore Russia's economic and political status on the world stage, and he famously admitted that he was ready to give his holdings over to the state: "If the state says we need to give it up, we'll give it up…I don't separate myself from the state. I have no other interests."[209]

Contested construction: fields in flux

Contingencies of 1998, opportunities available to Putin and *siloviki*, and problems of oligarch legitimacy contributed to the end of the finance logic, as *siloviki* rode a nationalist wave to bring key sectors of the economy under state control, even if this triggered occasional fears and capital flight.[210] Barring radical regime change or economic collapse, state empires appear to be the way of Russia's near future. This logic has seeped into the regions. The new field of power now gave local state officials a stronger rationale for interfering or preying on local economies.[211] An example was the saga of Ilim Pulp. Deripaska had tried legal machinations to take over Ilim, and in August 2003 Ilim's offices were raided—but not at Deripaska's behest. Local-level *siloviki* were out for gain, enticing Ilim or Deripaska to pay to stop lest harassment continue.[212] This led analysts to talk of new, systemic Russian feudalism.[213] Private property on its own did not balance the state. *Siloviki* did not threaten *abstract* property rights. Claims of transparency and rule of law were signals to foreign investors decoupled from reality. Such was the *siloviki* logic of law: rather than routinely gather evidence for a case against law-breakers, officials *prikhvatized* state authority, collecting *kompromat* for their own use. The rule of law became a tool of law; property, rather than enshrined as a cornerstone of civil society and, like law, a constraint on the state, became a tool of *prikhvatizatsiia* in the battle for political power.[214] Its effects were felt below the field of power, by local-level state officials and smaller property empires out to consolidate holdings against competitors and establish their own property bailiwicks.[215] *Kompromat* and networks, not the rule of law, guided the 2008 transfer of power.

Battles over property do take place elsewhere, but post-socialist privatization was more than the corporate raiding or privatization of 1980s America and Britain. Corporate raiders did not so much invent new logics as apply existing laws to fulfill their interests; the outcome was a recombination of existing logics and the unfolding of something new but not radically different. In Russia the entire web of meanings of property, practices, and rules of authority and governance unraveled and coevolved, making this more than a battle over wealth. It is also too crude to see this as the continuing history of a strong state preying on society. Structural and cultural legacies of a strong state, weak civil society, and particular groups and *habitus* played no small role. Yet contingencies were at work; problematic laws and a weak state gave financial elites advantages that became *kompromat* for a tight-knit state elite to use to rebuild state power. This story is also more than instrumental power politics. Conscious motives may have been profit, power, or ego; proximal tactics came from laws and networks. Yet results of contingently using tools and tactics, in the context of *habitus* and tool kits, had emergent properties of building fields and logics that acted back on tools, expectations, and tactics. In the end, property regimes, governance, and field logics did not simply evolve from efficiency, elite competition, or formal laws alone. They were linked to expressions of normal strategy and structure— primacy of managers and production, of shareholding and finance, or of state and nation. Different FPGs and public articulations by their leaders were part of promoting and legitimating not only strategies but also frames and hierarchies: production skills versus financial knowledge and capital versus the national good. The question of what costs property addresses has multiple answers: loss of profit, or of enterprise control, or of the national economy (or at least its profitable sectors). The optimal structure of inter-organizational relations also has multiple forms and goals: diversification for general profit versus uniting firms in the same sector for defense, versus creating natural resource empires for state and geopolitical influence. Institutionalizing authority in property and governance, building empires and fields, and the resulting emergence of principles of economic behavior are a complex web of structural and cultural legacies and contingent struggles.

This chapter supports some neoinstitutionalist claims about fields and change, especially the role of shocks and the punctuated, not evolutionary, nature of change. The Great Depression undermined the manufacturing conception of control and the status of its field champion, Ford Motors; the ruble crash of 1998 hurt oligarchs' economic power and the normality of the financial logic and FPG empires. Putin and *siloviki* came to power and centralized the field of power around the state and the regime. This bred a hybrid logic, combining market aspects (shareholding, a money economy) with Soviet aspects (state centrality and national security). The first lesson for neoinstitutionalism is: even in radical change, contingent structuration of fields is a key process. Whether new field boundaries, structures, and logics take root depends on time and resources to consolidate control, and to provide material for justification and sanctification (e.g. enough success and time for propaganda to make field structures and logics seem to be keys to economic truth). The second lesson concerns competing logics, conflict, and victory. Field analyses see one field logic slide into another or see a unified field logic. Stark and Bruszt note one field logic for Hungary, another for Poland, depending on privatization policy. In Russia, different logics emerged amidst the same laws; when authority boundaries came into contact, exacerbated in the privatization free-for-all, conflict erupted.[216] These struggles were over normality and status as much as over wealth and power. The probability of competing logics correlates with degree of radicalness of reform and unraveling of economic foundations: the more controlled or moderate the change, the more likely one group and logic remain hegemonic. Field boundaries were also crucial to property conflict. *Siloviki* sought to regather property and expand boundaries of state-centered property. This was possible because they had guns and *kompromat* and faced a weak civil society; in *siloviki habitus*, state and nation were founts of normality and sovereignty that happened to resonate with enough citizens to legitimate the grab for property. In the end, Red Directors, oligarchs, and *siloviki* came from different backgrounds and had different tool kits and contents of *habitus*; they enacted these contents in different logics of property and governance. Taking content of culture seriously, especially of field logics and practices, we see just how *habitus* matters in a way neoinstitutionalism until now could not.

6 Conclusion

Lessons from the journey to the Undiscovered Country

This transition is going to take a generation.
(Middle-aged woman to another, standing in
line to pay a telephone bill, autumn 1995)

Jeff, quit it! You think we follow rational economic rules!
(Assistant director of a "slowly dying" Petersburg electronics firm)

In summer 2007 I returned to Russia to start a new project, but I could not avoid some ethnographic study of the continuing post-Soviet experiment. Were petrodollars and Putin's discipline changing Russia? In Petersburg and Tula, many people had more disposable income. Loans were more readily available, and more Russians drove used foreign cars and were buying apartments (the quality of which remains unclear). Consumer service improved after 1991, although my experience and acquaintances' anecdotal evidence suggest quality dropped after 2003. Putin seemed in control in the Russia media, although clearly rigged Duma elections in December 2007 and his increasingly strident bluster abroad makes one wonder whether the master has lost the plot. Tram lines laid five years earlier were ripped up and roads were repaired in record time for the June 2007 European economic summit—the old logic of Potemkin villages. Capital repatriation and oil wealth were followed by inflation, then by capital flight and economic shocks after war with Georgia. Corruption and red tape were endemic, it was unclear whether such state projects as nanotechnology were just propaganda and patronage, and the spirit of innovation might not have overcome the spirit of "easy money."[1] If the market transition was creating consumer society or letting entrepreneurs open stores, Russia has been on its way to the market.

But is this what economic change was about—consumer goods and flashy cars? Was this rebirth of a great power or erection of a façade and illusory wealth? There has been change, but after long, hard looks from 2007 to 2010, I believe even more in this book's claims. We still need to ask to what extent today's Russia resembles and differs from its Soviet parent, and why—no small question for social science. Has Russia had changed economically for the better if politically for the worse, or does Soviet-era "Muscovite authoritarianism" survive in a continuing focus on the military and the inability or unwillingness of post-Soviet leaders to create the rule of law?[2] With change came continuity, and the way to understand this is to dig into power-culture. And we need to turn that power-culture lens on our own narratives. Russia's story is ours. The welfare state has been under siege by new narratives of normality. In 2008 we saw where this led. We need urgent reconstruction of economic normality as we tax the earth's capacity to support a growing population and energy needs. Russians were told to change their practices; now we *all* must rethink economic normality. Are Americans ready for slower growth, less consumption, and a stronger state role? Will they sacrifice freedom of automobiles for public transportation? Is the future a permanent state of war over oil? Devising new policies from above is not enough: as Alexis de Tocqueville noted, changing race laws in America would not create new interracial practices automatically.[3] What are we to do?

Into the future? Possible variation in logics and practices

I have no crystal ball, but the theory and narratives might provide insights on what to expect. Business scholar A. P. Prokhorov was not optimistic about fundamental change of the Russian/Soviet command-control model.[4] Yet there was learning, generational replacement, and opportunities to observe non-Soviet logics in interactions with foreign actors.[5] The financial logic survived long enough to facilitate the arrival of younger managers more likely to understand transition culture.[6] This does not mean newly trained Russians were ready-made market actors; but less Soviet socialization meant less to unlearn. Organizational control also stabilized somewhat. New owners could bring in managers they evaluated as competent, especially with foreign ownership. Healthy demand could reward learning marketing. If demand was *too* healthy there was less need to adapt, and rent-seeking or speculation could persist. Weak demand could make it difficult for managers to discern if they were using marketing properly; decoupling could persist unchallenged, or learners could retreat into decoupling. Firms producing for end-users (e.g. consumer goods) and not locked into buyers were more likely to adapt.[7] Yet the new narrative fractured as *dirigisme* emerged, privileging state control of the commanding heights of resource extraction and industrial production related to military output, with market-oriented narrative and logics for the consumer market.[8] This *dirigisme* is not the full-blown Soviet system,[9] but given global demand for hydrocarbons and military goods, state corporations and Putin's oligarchs have captured markets. Rent-seeking and redistribution trump marketing for now.[10]

I return to the four change processes of Chapter 1 (innovation, continuity, decoupling, contradiction) to suggest trajectories of change.[11] The first is *market engagement*, with two wings: *innovation* and *integration*. These actors closed the gap somewhat between superficial and fundamental levels of knowledge by learning new logics, choosing personnel with requisite knowledge, and enforcing new organizational routines. Such firms more likely had younger or foreign owners and managers and were in fields with greater use of marketing. *Innovating* managers were more likely to use ideal-typical marketing to discover, provide for, and try to influence demand; creating value was key to strategies. *Integrating* owners and managers use marketing less to engage demand than to identify lucrative mergers and acquisitions and increase market share and vertical integration. The second form of variation is *market dirigisme*: state power and national security are coupled rent-seeking, and oil and gas profits are distributed to create dependency on the state. Legal restrictions on foreign investment in "strategic sectors" restrain competition.[12] However, such state-centered logics are not anti-capitalist *per se*, and we cannot discount recruitment of managers with Western skills.[13] The third form of variation is *market muddling*. This included Red Directors who adapted incompletely, faced tough contradictions, or serviced a narrow set of consumers. A common tactic was to use networks for sales and to muddle through (until the oil boom raised sales), or to latch onto patrons such as Gazprom.[14] The fourth form of variation is *market retreat*. Due to a combination of learning problems (greater decoupling), problematic labor skills or technology, or producing for a dead or hypercompetitive market, these managers turned to subsistence in the "virtual economy" of barter.

Market engagement: innovating and integrating

One useful example of this form is beer firm Baltika. While foreign-owned, most of Baltika's decision-making is by Russian managers, hired for innovative and organizational competence and answering to owners every six months.[15] In the mid-1990s Baltika had new technology; sales strategies meant it was Europe's second-largest beer brand by 2004, making Petersburg Russia's beer capital. Post-privatization investment played a role in success, but three other strategies were crucial. The first was establishing local distribution networks to reduce dependence on local sellers. This vertical integration was not without difficulty: Baltika's CEO complained they had to confront local laws forbidding the sale of Baltika. The second was producing sufficient quality to differentiate themselves from other brands, at low enough cost to gain market share. The third strategy, initiated in 1994, was to produce a variety of beers, all with a number (one to nine) and images and qualities corresponding to different consumers. These strategies made Baltika a success by 1997, helping transform Russians from vodka to beer drinkers. The 1998 ruble crash confronted the giant with a dilemma: reduce quality or price. Managers chose the latter to maintain market share and their image suffered. Some responses were rebranding or introducing new brands and buying Tula's Arsenal beer works to offer a new line of numbered brands of beer. By 2003 Baltika faced competition from specialty brews (Tinkoff) and mass-produced Bochkarëv. Following marketing logic and analyses, Baltika managers noticed some regions were loyal to local beer, so they withdrew sales there. Baltika constantly analyzed their image to devise new tactics, e.g. abandoning a "eurobottle" design or introducing a cheaper "Dal'nyi Vostok" brand.

Other firms were successful due to lucky breaks that aided physical and mental retooling, yet successful logics and routines could reach limits. One such case is

FOSp (Fabrika odezhdy St-Peterburga). Young general director Vladimir Mikheev, who took over in 1995, used profits from a lucky one-time deal with Germans to invest in new equipment. He set out to design and produce sharp-looking Western-style clothing and used Western-style ads to appeal to businessmen and professionals.[16] To control costs and distribution efficiency, he created a formal network, stores or sections within stores, to sell and advertise FOSp clothes. To improve sales and image, he bought a license to produce French brand Bruno Saint Hilaire. Yet Mikheev focused on production and immediate sales. Higher-end male clothing (business suits) was a deficit good, and Mikheev felt no need for marketing studies or a specific, alluring image for the firm and its creations. Marketing meant sales and distribution, but with increasing competition, growth required expanding the brand. Business analysts claimed FOSp required "applying effort not in the sphere of production and distribution but first of all in the area of marketing production," including new assortments of goods, developing their brand, and licenses for Western brands. A new patron—Baltika's top manager bought FOSp in 2005—raised hopes of new dynamism.[17]

Generational changes in elites also were at work. The next wave of oligarchs had a late-Soviet *habitus* from the Komsomol, universities (studying engineering or economics), and industries. The combination of production and economic or similar knowledge (e.g. mathematics) balanced an orientation to output or sector with appreciation for financial planning and sales. While earlier oligarchs used political connections to build empires and rent-seek, newer elites who came into their own in the late 1990s combined political acumen with post-Soviet experience—although to call them market entrepreneurs might be a stretch, as one study suggests their firms only marginally outperform those of other Russian managers and fair worse than foreign-owned firms. Improved performance could be due to political networks and buying firms already performing well.[18] Yet if they did not reject political tactics to gain and defend rent-seeking, they also focused on innovating or integrating holdings.[19] One example is Kakha Bendukidze and Uralmash-OMZ. A manager who worked his way up the ranks at Uralmash, his experiences and images of Western production and innovation suggested that the older model of one-shot, project-based relations between engineering and production did not create sufficient synergy. The Soviet and post-Soviet system of badly integrated engineering and production hindered innovation: Soviet enterprises and *obedineniia* were not engineering companies but were "production components," with managers looking for buyers rather than innovating output and sales or integrating firms to enlarge product ranges. Bendukidze consolidated and integrated OMZ to improve innovation, production, and orientation to consumers' needs. By increasing the number of firms and output in OMZ, Bendukidze allowed clients to "mix and match" purchases; he could provide clients with expanded purchase options and entire sets of equipment and services.[20]

If Bendukidze was an innovator, Oleg Deripaska was an integrator combining production knowledge with political skills to build and integrate empires in profitable sectors.[21] Known for sleeping at his aluminum factory despite health risks, Deripaska was dedicated to aluminum. His prime strategy was reinvesting profits to expand and consolidate holdings in Russia and beyond, creating an integrated global empire of metal extraction and processing. He also demonstrated savvy to discern emerging demand, e.g. cement for the recent construction boom and insurance. It is not clear to what extent he imposed fundamental changes in managerial practices, although some reports claim he introduced the "Toyota way" of business practice, focusing on human capital and careful organizational structure. As he noted, "We are trying to move from the principle of just buy and sell" and short-term horizons, towards more active plans "to rebuild production" and the country's infrastructure—admitting that the chief obstacle now was the lack of skilled managers capable of running such numerous and massive projects.[22] Less impressive (but not shabby either) is Aleksei Mordashov, head of steel firm Severstal.[23] Mordashov arrived at the Cherepovetskii Metal Combine in 1988 (leaving little time for socialization in everyday Soviet business) with a degree from Leningrad's Tol'iatti Institute in Engineering and Economics. At the Metal Combine he became head labor economist and head of planning—his *habitus* was being formed in finance as reforms began. In 1992 27-year-old Mordashov created and ran Cherepovets daughter Severstal-Invest, an investment fund that purchased a majority of shares in Severstal, as Cherepovets was renamed when privatized. This concentrated authority around Mordashov.[24] Cheap labor and cheap steel exports, especially to China, provided profit reinvested into production and expansion, such as acquiring two light automobile factories and consolidating them as daughter Severstal-Avto. In 2002 he created holding company Severstal-Group and with the help of British-trained managers expanded into coal, shipping, ports, piping for Gazprom, and timber; in 2007 and 2008 Severstal acquired steel factories abroad, including in the United States. He also encouraged a collective identity and paternalist loyalty.

Newer, smaller firms should be candidates for innovative change, although we cannot assume this all the time. One report in business journal *Ekspert* noted traits of smaller firms with niches, quality production, and output and profits growing at 100 percent per year until 2004. They gained control over production processes to improve quality and efficiency. Discipline reigned: employees followed dress codes, energy was economized, and shopfloors were clean. Rather than decide output blindly, these businesses studied consumers' purchasing capacity. One company, Interskol, focused on new construction technology they thought would have demand as construction expanded. Another key strategy was creating and controlling distribution through networks. Yet Chinese competition brought new challenges and turned attention to brand, a stable consumer base, and embedding innovation in organizational practices. Some firms analyzed export markets; others studied which goods optimized demand and minimized competition (e.g. the Zvezda toy-maker's model of the Soviet BT-5 tank). Others individualized output (e.g. construction technology). Attention to the market, maneuverability, and innovation helped expansion despite meager finances.[25] Yet given the complex processes of learning and implementing marketing, fundamental change remained slow and uneven.[26] For many, marketing remained price-setting via a strict "cost + profit" formula. This had limits: firms would lock into the lower end of a market to compete via price, but sales improved little. Even after August 1998, only a minority of managers heeded consultants' advice to move to a "consumer-driven" formula and make price dependent on what consumers would pay. This new method involved covering fixed costs with increasing throughput and optimizing several variables, especially consumer tastes and product prestige—a pricier good might bring in more profit even if fewer people buy it. A bread firm turned to this strategy; its output increased fourfold, even though its retail price was 10 percent above average. A sunflower oil producer exited the lower end of the market to compete with higher-priced imports; its income increased as better-off consumers paid for perceived higher status.[27] Still, business journalists bemoan passive approaches to sales or trivial research into product niches appealing to consumers with disposable income and creative tastes.[28] Oil wealth may allow inefficiencies and suboptimal adaptation; raising corporate loans was easier.

And consider this. Data on Russian auto sales come from reports of autos *shipped* to dealers; and dealers underestimate sales each year to avoid having cars in storage. This habit creates confusion for planning production. Dealers are used to having too few cars and buyers are used to waiting for ordered cars. Rather than devise accurate data analysis for marketing prognoses, auto dealers prefer the easier and eerily Soviet-style logic of waiting.[29] Mechel steel made record profits in 2004, but it was unclear how much was from new strategies or from selling cheap steel to the supercharged Chinese market.[30] Can these oligarchs adjust to changes in global demand and structure?[31]

Market dirigisme

State corporations and national champions are revealing their logics, but access to their managers is difficult in the Putin era. State corporations invoke control of natural resources and metallurgy to keep profits away from foreigners, and to create geopolitical advantage as global demand for raw materials rises. Managers of state giants are neither business people by trade nor Red Directors: their *habitus* is state service. For example, Putin ally Sergei Chemezov, head of state corporation Rostekhnologiia, worked first in a metallurgy research institute, then as state director for export operations (including monopolist weapons exporter Rosoboroneksport), and then as head of the state department for external relations. New state corporations are sector-oriented and sometimes quasi-monopolies: airplane construction (OAK, United Aviation Corporation), shipbuilding (OSK, United Shipbuilding Corporation), heavy industry (Rostekhnologiia). Each state corporation includes producers in that sector and key suppliers. Consider Rosoboroneksport and its daughter Rostekhnologiia, and begin with Rosoboroneksport's strategies *vis-à-vis* auto producer AvtoVAZ. Before incorporation into Rosoboroneksport, AvtoVAZ used tariffs and non-payment of taxes to survive. Managers paid attention to car models, although inefficient production and aging technology hurt. They had some success with the "Desiatka" model, and sales improved in 2005. Yet AvtoVAZ continued to face problems designing new models to compete with imports.[32] Takeover by

Rosoboroneksport did not fill analysts with confidence: Rosoboroneksport officials had no experience with auto manufacture. Initial discussions included changing suppliers and distributors, building a new factory, and increasing sales to military-industrial firms via Rosoboroneksport.[33] Some analysts claimed networks between Rosoboroneksport managers and Putin meant direct or indirect state aid,[34] suggesting a turn to import-substitution. Eventually the state sold shares to French firm Renault to bring in investment and market skills.

The crowning moment was Medvedev's formal creation of metallurgical and military national champion Rostekhnologiia. In a lengthy interview for business newspaper *Vedomosti*, CEO Viktor Chemezov explained the Rostekhnologiia project,[35] which foresaw "creation of vertically integrated holding groups" to concentrate state-led development of the military-industrial complex and strategic civilian industries, such as airlines and aviation, and turn Rostekhnologiia into a global competitor. The champion would internalize needed services, such as a typography firm to print up required massive amounts of documentation. It would provide the state control over strategic production, hinted at when Chemezov avoided a question about possible resistance from private investors: who cared if there were private shareholders, "most important is that state corporations provide control." This structure would connect firms linked in "production-technological chains" to improve efficiency, which also meant "an enterprise is profitable and its capitalization grows"—an interesting meld of Soviet logics of state control and production centrality with the market profit. This logic also governed which state-owned firms would enter Rostekhnologiia: heavy industry would aid military production, and inclusion of airlines would facilitate creating a competitor to Aeroflot. Transparency would not be comprehensive; parts of the budget were closed to scrutiny. Of course, the state might interfere. Chemezov complained of a directive from a state official on how to vote in one meeting that was counter-productive.

Chemezov's interview with an independent, Western-owned newspaper is telling. Rather than use Western jargon, Chemezov made a case similar to that for the Soviet *obedinenie*: consolidate firms in a production chain, improve efficiency, state control. Like his Kremlin patrons, Chemezov is more a product of the Soviet system than Khodorkovskii or Deripaska: a state-centered logic to rent-seek and integrate production rather than to address a bottom line, diversify, or add value. State-led empires are like some oligarch cousins—a means to accumulate capital from natural resources or other sectors (weapons) or to control a market sector. As these empires were assembled in the era of high hydrocarbon profits, it is unclear whether managerial *habitus* and organizational routines are imbued with enough marketing logic or market savvy and innovative flexibility for these empires to develop or reshape the market by creating value, rather than through monopoly position, high Chinese and domestic military demand, or state authority. Empire-building led to corporate debt, not capital investment—increasing rents for redistribution and political gain.[36] Further qualitative research into practices would be useful; even if state corporation managers *speak* the language of marketing and markets, the logics of practice may be different. What these empires will do should the global economy sink into long-term recession or shift radically given environmental concerns remains a story worth following. Tactics *vis-à-vis* the crisis and the state will tell much about change in Russia in economic practices and logics.

Market muddling

Some managers learned enough to introduce flexibility into production and sales to bring income to get by or even expand slightly; identification with primary products persisted, and marketing was still "sell what we make." These managers understood they could not rely solely on producing goods willy-nilly and hoping for buyers. Part of their adaptation was to seek niches and patrons and enter various deals as junior partners, or actively look for buyers in a smaller niche. One study from the later 1990s claimed managers were still conservative, did not admit the need to change, and were reluctant to use professional consulting.[37] Those managers willing to change might do so incompletely, creating unintended meshes of old and new—implementing changes slowly but surely, never quite dislodging the old logic. Sometimes an opportunity came along, and managers could put adaptation and learning on the back burner and concentrate on consolidating and coordinating production and supply for a new-found wealthy client. General strategies along this line included lobbying the state for projects or creating networks with Western and Russian giants (EES, Gazprom).[38] Some managers focused on internal restructuring and narrow links, essentially formalized networks, to specific partners and especially patrons with sufficient financial resources and fairly good chances at survival or prosperity in the medium term. Engineering giant Elektrosila turned to pre-Revolutionary owner Siemens,[39] a relationship that grew stronger when Elektrosila was integrated into engineering holding Silovye Mashiny. Under a younger, vibrant general director, Baltiiskii Zavod courted foreign buyers and, like fellow shipbuilder Almaz, aimed at the Russian military. Other firms expanded relations with local stores and businesses for a regional niche.[40] Economics Inc. muddled along as well, seeking niches and patrons, until Misha personally decided he'd had enough.

Svetlana electronics provides one case of muddling through. Producer of various electrical components for military hardware and medical equipment, small electronic consumer appliances, and lighting goods, Svetlana faced initial reforms in 1988 with enthusiasm but after 1991 quickly learned that they faced great challenges not just in post-Soviet adaptation, but even in survival. Svetlana was hurt by initial discord between its subdivisions, and later between a one-year general director and the employee *kollektiv*.[41] Svetlana's earlier "flooding the market" provided little real help, and in the second half of the 1990s managers shifted tactics.[42] First, they stopped flooding the market and focused on projects that promised reasonable income. An important component was strategic partnership with foreign companies. Svetlana also won some local projects, such as designing telephone pay cards with microchips. While Svetlana managers tried to fit employees' skills into market niches, this was as far as marketing went, and managers continued to think of their firm as a producer of electronics components, rather than expanding conceptions of what the firm could be. Targeting of foreign patrons was not so successful, and in 1997 Svetlana entered the *kholding* Rossiiskaia Elektronika, providing easy potential buyers. Pozitron's post-break-up story was not so different. In the 1990s Pozitron was left with a few small stores, some of which offered electronics parts (not always Pozitron's), and one that I saw in 1995 sold food. An early cash cow for survival was assembling Daewoo VCRs,[43] but Daewoo eventually turned to direct sales of VCRs. Eventually, Pozitron's managers withdrew into subsistence activities that generated enough income to keep basic subunits open, and when oil wealth entered the economy, Pozitron applied its technology and skills. Younger managers had taken over by the Putin area; with less *habitus* and identity in electronics, they could focus on niches where they had something to offer, e.g. advanced siding and window panes for home and office construction. Pozitron-Plast, a daughter dedicated to producing wooden and metal façades, frames, and similar output, opened in 2003.[44] Not all former Pozitron members were so lucky. Troublesome Viton's post-privatization independence was short-lived. When it left Pozitron, Viton was excluded from the Daewoo deal and was forbidden from using the "Pozitron" trademark. Unable to sell its VCRs, Viton went bankrupt in 1995.[45]

That muddlers were savvy enough to target well-off niches suggests a move away from the Soviet production logic but not a fundamental break with the past. Some who tried to adopt post-Soviet marketing found challenges too arduous and abandoned the experiment, returning to original output. General director Vladimir Vol'man of rocket manufacturer Novator recalled:

> Thank God people of the older generation remained—the basis for the KB's (*konstruktorskoe biuro*) collective brain. At the start of the 1990s we tried to produce civilian goods: we started putting out diamond rings, microwave ovens, nails…But, as we told then-chairman of the Russian government Viktor Chernomyrdin, who stopped by the KB at that difficult time, Novator always made weapons, and no matter what we did, it always turned out as weapons…

Realizing they could not compete with foreign consumer goods, they returned to what they knew—rockets, pistols, weapons—found a niche (rockets shot from torpedo launchers) and, with the help of the Russian state's efforts abroad, improved exports.[46] Production skills and state weapons trade, not marketing knowledge, saved the firm.

Market retreat

A last ideal type was retreat from market engagement to subsistence and survival. This behavior has been addressed elsewhere;[47] I include it as one form of variation this framework encompasses. A common tactic was using barter in the virtual economy; others included living off rents without active investment or market search. What these share is literally a retreat from engaging the economy and adapting production and sales to consumers, instead surviving in contingent exchanges providing enough money or goods to cover basic wages and expenses. These firms added little real value to the economy and often actively consumed value—but ironically, this group may have been market-savvy. Such managers understood survival meant abandoning pretenses of learning new logics: perhaps costs were too high or they could not find adequate outlets for output. Marketing might reduce inefficiencies, but it cannot save every firm.

One infamous form of survival was the "virtual economy" of barter networks to support production and employment.[48] Not quite the shadow economy, the virtual economy—so-called because value was in "virtual" terms (in kind) rather than "objective" money—was a social space in which managers of firms that did not produce profitable goods used networks with local politicians and other enterprises to exchange their unprofitable output not for money, but for other goods. Managers would set up complex barter deals to receive supplies, produce goods for more barter, and pay workers in kind or money (received in these complex transactions).[49] Rather than close their firms or risk bankruptcy, managers turned to the "virtual economy" of barter relations to obtain those inputs. A firm would enter into direct or complex barter chains, sometimes bringing in enough money to pay some wages in money rather than in kind. Local elites might support and even facilitate such barter to keep operative the local infrastructure that the stricken firm supported. Suppliers such as the railways or Gazprom would play along with the virtual economy for several reasons: if they did not make a profit, this still reduced their tax burden; it was a favor within networks of elites; and forcing such firms to pay was problematic, as assets could be hidden from formal accounts and beyond seizure. The virtual economy also fit with values for welfare and national security, as both supported local infrastructure and military-industrial firms that produced as much symbolic output (of Russian military strength) as market value. If enough actors engage in "perverse" behavior, it is inopportune to act differently. As managers engaged in barter, their suppliers, clients, and local political elites found it difficult to buck the trend.[50]

Subsistence and survival without adding much economic value followed other rudimentary, non-barter paths. Soviet-era firms could use one legacy, buildings and land, even if they did not own land outright. New private firms needed offices; older firms needed income. Neutron—the electronics firm whose story opened Chapter 4—went through financial distress and sales collapse. By 1999 it was renting office space in its best building, allowing it to avoid restructuring or rethinking strategies. The yearly shareholders' meeting hosted a desperate power struggle over profits from rent. Because managers had sunk little into "buying" the firm, rent was the only real income stream. Earlier sales practices could not address demand for goods. Had Neutron managers focused coldly on profit and adopted marketing practices, they might not have avoided their fate, although they could have softened the market's blow. What is certain is that fewer resources would have been wasted in desperate pursuit of income.[51] With new oil wealth, they can sell ceramic components to Russian electronics firms. While better off than Neutron, Pozitron stood on the border between muddling and retreat; oil wealth reversed its fortunes, although it is nowhere near its Soviet-era self. Other electronics firms relied on tax breaks and state purchases. While such firms might not actively destroy value, they use labor power, space, and other endowments that could be used in more productive ways. Market retreaters survived to propagate their logics and practices in a context where competition is not automatic.

Morals of the story: the road thus traveled, and where it might lead

After experiences of post-socialism, the 1998 Asian flu, and the 2008 global meltdown, we urgently need to rethink not only our social and economic priorities but also our models, and their relations to narratives. Heterodox economists and non-economists should speak up now. For my part, I end my journey with modest ideas on institutions, policy, and social change. To explain variation, social scientists evoke institutions, policy sequencing, and coalitions. We have exploited these variables, but a growing body of work in the tradition of Bourdieu, Foucault, Giddens, and others shows the need to investigate what underlies and to reject simplistic behavioral assumptions.[52] Saying something is "socially constructed" is not enough; we need to understand *how* social phenomena are constructed, deconstructed, and reconstructed. Power-culture's dimensions, *habitus*, practice and logics, and normality should be at the heart of new thinking. And if post-socialism is not to be forgotten or misused, we need to understand previous mistakes and move in new directions. Insights of economics and political science should not be disregarded, but like Newton's mechanics, they must be properly situated in broader social theory.

Power-culture, post-socialism, and social change

Post-socialism was not merely a story of getting policies right or wrong, state capacity and elite intrigue, or undoing structural deformations. Nor was it only material interests of managers, politicians, and clans. Nor was it reawakening a private sector (as in Latin America) or freeing peasants and inviting foreign investment (as in China). This was a revolution in which Russians sought identities, interests, and meanings. Initial scholarship framed this event as institutional design: correcting deformations with rapid policies to let market forces and civil society emerge. Had we applied political sociology of revolutions and contentious politics, we might have been careful with analyses and more appreciative of reconstructing fundamentals of power and culture. Generally, social change involves actors navigating power-culture's dimensions to shape discourse and articulate meanings of authority and normal practice. How actors do so, and their success or failure, is badly understood if power-culture is ignored or exogenous. We can cite Putin's legitimacy and oligarchs' illegitimacy to partly explain post-2000 politics—but this is *ad hoc* without considering power-culture's dynamics as underpinnings of structure and institutions.

A power-culture approach takes us beyond an oversimplified instrumental cost–benefit approach to show *how* shocks work and structure unravels. Simply citing costs, the failure of monitoring, or bank runs on state resources, while elegant, says nothing about how competing, alternative normalities emerged in the first place to challenge and overtake the old. The Soviet system generated contradictions that could not fully emerge until power-culture shifted. Gorbachev's reforms and resulting shocks altered power's dimensions. The state apparatus initially gave up some resources and then discursive control without introducing accountability and a new narrative to guide change. Had reform merely involved transferring resources from ministries to managers or regional elites, change might have been less traumatic. However, *glasnost'* and the social democratic nature of reforms opened up discourse and brought non-elites and employees into the reform process. Structural and cultural hegemony came apart, competing heterodoxies emerged, and the scramble over material and symbolic resources and solidifying heterodoxies as hegemonic orthodoxies (nationally or locally) was on—a story not so different from that in 1789 France, 1917 Russia, and 1910 Mexico.[53] In a sense, we know this about Russia (and East Europe and France)—and now we can give that pretheoretical intuition theoretical voice.

Let us put Russia alongside other examples of social change to see multidimensional power-culture at work. Implementing claims assumes actors know how those claims work in practice; otherwise, conflict and decoupling ensue. The Bolsheviks faced this: the peasantry was having nothing of Soviet power, and workers were not following the Bolshevik script as hoped. The new regime turned to Civil War practices of imposing hegemony through violence.[54] When Stalin unleashed his revolution from above, managers had to learn a new system of provision and production; even this faced resistance, contradiction, and decoupling.[55] More recently, the Russian system shared qualities with East European counterparts—plans and command economies, paternalist provision, economic crisis and socialist collapse—but to call all socialist firms, regardless of country, equally socialist is akin to saying French and American firms are essentially the same because they are "capitalist."[56] Differences include the degree of *de novo* creation of market capitalism, and here East Europe had the advantage of less time and generational cohorts under Soviet-style socialism as well as variation in degrees of experimentation with reform: from Hungary's NEM and Yugoslavia's experiments with decentralization, to a surviving peasantry in Poland, to more constricted systems in Czechoslovakia and especially in Romania. Further, the pathways of extrication from socialism varied, in particular degrees of institutional weakening and transformation, relationship with the European Union, strength and form of national identity (*vis-à-vis* the West and Russia), and political alliances and policies. Such combinations of similarity and difference make for exciting possibilities to examine power-culture, decoupling and contradiction, narrative framing, fields, and negotiation versus contention.

Power-culture, post-socialism, and economy

As Timothy Mitchell noted, the modern narrative of economies and development means an autonomous "economy" that follows its own laws—and this narrative has been challenged by evidence that economies are constructed and by economic shocks in Western economies and the global economy as of late. American leaders and public are considering what European leaders never forgot and Russian and Chinese leaders embraced: a state active in the economy. Yet American discourse still involves instrumental logics of analysis, centrality of the self-interested actor, and assumptions of competition and efficiency. We have yet to see a truly alternative narrative of normality, such as that Gandhi once articulated: a society where people discard pleasures and burdens of modernity.[57] Socialism was once an alternative, although it shared Enlightenment roots with capitalism and its Soviet form was not free of vices and dangers. We are not trapped, but to move ahead we must free ourselves from worn-out cognitive and behavioral models, assumptions of instrumental rationality, and letting methods be the tail that wags the dog.

Despite growing empirical, theoretical, and practical problems, economic theory remains in the epistemological saddle. Partly this is because some economic theory reflects reality: the need for capital through sales *did* encourage change, and on the surface Atlas seems a poster child for textbook economics. However, we cannot discount narrative power. Professionals with economics training are situated in key positions in Wall Street, the IMF, and elsewhere.[58] Who is interviewed about financial meltdowns? Economists. Which Russian university departments have the highest salaries? Business schools. As well, the market narrative has status by theoretically and methodologically bandwagoning on the natural sciences. In economic theory the state of nature is competition, rational action, and self-interest, a view made popular by Adam Smith and naturalized by Charles Darwin. This worldview may have essences of truth, but the jury is out on its degree of accuracy. Methodologically, economic theory, and some quantitative work in political science and sociology, tacitly draws on the legitimacy and status of the natural sciences, in which mathematical formulae, measurement, and non-textual representation imply objectivity: mathematical proofs have the authority of deductive, objective truth that lets policy-makers plug in values for advice. Sometimes this breeds *hubris*. According to master shock therapist Jeffrey Sachs, "The reason shock therapy—as they call it—didn't work in Russia…was because the policies were not really carried out. People who criticize my work don't read the data. They don't look at data because they are not interested and because, I am convinced, they can't read it."[59] This begs several questions. What are legitimate "data," and do they include power, politics, meanings, or learning? Why was it that "the policies were not really carried out"? If policies and designers cannot account for implementation, what is their use? More than a decade after the congenital problems of shock therapy became quite clear, Sachs still harbors illusions. He is not alone.

Central to much economics is growth, an issue I elide—and I suspect growth and economic organization are not so tightly linked and there is no single best path. Competition and growth were correlated in the United States, as were protectionism and European investment,[60] but other principles of economic organization—*dirigisme*, state-led import substitution, export-oriented growth, the command economy—created miracles at some times and nightmares at others.[61] Economic organization impacts growth, but other endowments can compensate.[62] Further, debates over sales and production, privatization, and enterprises were framed in terms not only of growth and efficiency but also of justice and normality. Perhaps "growth" should be exposed to deliberation: what should the trade-offs be between growth, justice, security, and social compassion? These questions are now central to political debate in the United States and European Union. Shocks of global warming, oil prices, and financial crises are not easily solved. A closely related issue is "successful" change. What is "success"? Survival? Profit or market share? A particular organizational ethos (e.g. paternalism)? Adding value? Denise had a general idea of success at Atlas: profit, good wages, and honest work. At Economics Inc., success was intellectual and pedagogical innovation; profit was only a means to that end. Post-socialism, then, was a journey to discover normal "success." We have seen different definitions, most starkly in Chapter 5 (field logics) but also in variations of organizational change and the challenge of marketing. To expand our understanding of policy formation and implementation, we must emancipate ourselves from transition culture and assumptions that such categories as efficiency and success are ontological reality. The economics approach to institutional design works best when power-culture foundations are not challenged and have a good fit with economic theory's logic. When that fit is weak, economics and its policies come into doubt. If economists read more Bourdieu and less Paul Samuelson, power-culture and *habitus* would be more central—and would wreck the elegant mathematical "proofs" of economic theory. But such a trade-off might be worthwhile.

Power-culture, post-socialism, and institutions

What insights has this journey provided about "institutions"? While most approaches examine elite politics of institutional designs, something funny happens at the micro-level: "institutions" as such disappear. Actors may use laws as signposts of action or appropriate legal categories; but private property, contract law, enterprise governance, and "money" operate as practices of gain, survival, and resistance. If anything, institutions do not beget practices; institutions *are* practices. To be socialized by "institutions" means learning via embeddedness in collective practices. Actors filter their environment and responses through tool kits of categories and meanings structured by *habitus*. From this come practices and logics that might reproduce what exists already or innovatively combine past and present. And from this comes power-culture, as managers or officials combine expectations and knowledge to structure discourse and its content, use of or reaction to material resources (e.g. firing managers or striking against them), and narratives of normality. This approach is appropriate to post-socialism and social change: how else to explain the corruption, seeming irrationalities, even chaos of the 1990s? Kremlin elites enacted liberalization, bankruptcy, and privatization; and unsurprisingly, such policies did not take root quickly or frictionlessly. This suggests an element of game theory at work. We could define "institutions" as power-culture-practice + game-theoretical expectations and interactions. Change occurs when the players realize the rules are not being enforced, make no sense, or do not exist. Some keep following old rules, others innovate new rules (for cooperation or individual gain). Some make attempts to impose their rules on the game, and if they can grasp discourse and resource mechanisms (practices in and of themselves), the game might be theirs. And here is the real challenge of radical reform and remaking power-culture: rewriting not only rules but also expectations that rules are normal and operative. We are used to thinking that resource power (money, violence) drives reproduction or change—but narrative power is no less important. How to get police to enforce laws? Make them expect punishment for insubordination; and create confidence that the narrative of normality is in fact an objective account of the normal, natural social world.

A related topic is institutional design. Assumptions of strong instrumental rationality oversimplify these issues. Sociologically inspired scholarship shows an appreciation of power and culture, discourse and narratives, and "events" in policy design and implementation. As well, behavioral assumptions of rational action need rethinking: *how* costs are embodied, articulated, and interpreted should not be assumed. The importance of knowledge, authority, and practice means institutional design risks contradictions between logics of existing *habitus* versus logics of new designs; decoupling between old knowledge and that required for target institutions; competition between versions of normality that emerge once design begins; and contention over authority that might shift in institutional redesign, especially if initial moments of reform unleash the genie of autonomy. To make sense of implementation we need to examine micro-practices of states and citizens. The tax collector and police officer, like managers and employees, are identities, to themselves and people they serve or exploit. What goes on in micro-interactions is what makes states, citizens, and policies what they are. This means we need more attention to the micro-practices of policy implementation and institutional emergence. Testing and developing power-culture models is always difficult, as it requires intimate detail of discourse and practices of multiple actors in multiple contexts. Access to relevant data in the shadows of the corridors of power will always be problematic, but we can use available historical archival data to construct more encompassing frameworks that could provide, if not prediction, then *sensitizing* concepts for actual use, much as is done with game theory today. Such sensitizing concepts might be a better approach to policy and institutional design than today's cookbook models.

According to Joseph Schumpeter, capitalism's dynamism is creative destruction that innovates and culls.[63] However, policies should not simply *unleash* creative destruction. Creation requires nurturing, as Peter Evans noted in his taxonomy of developmental states; the post-socialist challenge is creating these very structures and institutions of embedded autonomy.[64] If we open up power-culture's dimensions, we glimpse how nurturing creation against destruction is not easy. *Pace* Jeffrey Sachs, we see shock therapy failed by oversimplifying or making exogenous crucial social dynamics. Gradualism was more careful: post-socialist actors had to learn new rules, and reforms, especially privatization, had to be slower. Yet gradualist apologist Peter Murrell did not scrutinize learning and creating practices closely, nor did he question "institutions." Further, China and Poland, gradualism's poster children, had more intact dimensions of power. Polish reformers did not have to demolish the state to evict socialism, and they also had a relatively organized political base and initial legitimacy for reforms.[65] The Cultural Revolution sufficiently weakened power of the central bureaucracy, allowing Deng Xiaoping to negotiate with enterprise managers and peasant communal organizations; but he had enough state power to maintain social order.[66] In contrast, Soviet/Russian socialism was deeply entrenched; ideology and system still resonated with a large numbers of Russians, especially given legitimacy won in World War II. And the shadow economy and famers' markets (*rynok*) were less an alternative economy waiting in the wings than residues of *Soviet* economic practices.

Perhaps donor countries, the IMF, and the World Bank could have conditioned aid less on reducing inflation than on encouraging open deliberation over the post-Soviet narrative and then on disseminating new knowledge: not imposing a Western narrative, but aiding Russians and others in developing their own narrative and then aiding the transmission of appropriate knowledge. Funds could have been earmarked for sending younger entrepreneurs and managers abroad for internships—as USAID did in the mid-1990s, sending entrepreneurs to sister cities in the United States for five-week apprenticeships. Foreign schools could have opened programs to train businessmen through case-study analyses of thought-processes and contexts. Aid could have come with stringent demands for anti-corruption policies. Yet we should be realistic about gradual change: coevolution of economic institutions took decades and even centuries in the West. Perhaps Putin unwittingly grasped one lesson of development some scholars articulated in the 1960s: radical reform might be possible only through strong-willed, even ruthless, use of centralized power.[67] Lenin and Stalin understood that imposing the new Bolshevik normality would require force. Technocratic revolutions (e.g. 1980s Mexico) involved containing democracy to impose policy. Following the logic of power-culture explored here, it may be that fundamental change requires the exercise of concentrated power, less to contain reactions against the pain of transformations than to break older practices and logics. But before we celebrate applying concentrated power, let us keep in mind objections to the Hobbesian pact: the Leviathan might not use this power wisely.[68] Leaders are not immune to legacies or *habitus* or decoupled learning.

Power-culture, post-socialism, and economic sociology

Economic sociology and neoinstitutionalism provide powerful insights into how economies and organizations operate, but wrinkles related to power, culture, agency, and change remain. These subfields must be rejoined with political sociology, as originally under Marx and Weber. Adding political sociology, Bourdieu's analytic tools, and dimensions of power-culture can correct these oversights and push the envelope. Too often we see the battle from the generals' perspective, but the battle is won or lost in officers' and soldiers' actions on the battlefield. Power-culture's dimensions show *how* power and culture of fields, capital, and *habitus* play out. Elements of political sociology help account for change, especially framing and claim-making. Skills at mobilizing material and symbolic resources—economic and social capital (networks), frames of meaning and normality—were key to outcomes of challenges. Ultimately, fields, *doxa*, and capital involve contestation over status and authority, especially in the field of power. In Western societies, political alignments can rearrange aspects of field *doxa* on the margins, but fundamentally realignment is more likely in revolutions. As structure collapses, the dynamics of power and culture are unleashed in remaking institutions and structures; and power and culture have ordering principles that this book has tried to illuminate. One lesson from firms as fields and polities is that isomorphism, and power mechanisms generally, are political and should be treated as such with tools of political sociology. Fields may set general strategies and structures, but this does not mean automatic implementation. Mergers are one method for constructing field members and logics, but are they frictionless? Unfortunately, this question is not a high research priority, especially for economists but also for neoinstitutionalists. Further, these power-culture dynamics work fractally, across different levels of social organization simultaneously: privileging one level of analysis is dangerous, unless we can demonstrate mechanisms by which that level of analysis is hegemonic. If fields weaken, managers are game-changers. As we have seen, managers were in a strong position to impose change if they could control discursive and resource power to shape narratives and expectations. Successful tactics included creating images of normality and invincibility, or latching on to external sources of power. Managers at LMZ and Kirovskii Zavod did not unravel resources and discursive power enough to bring harm, and they navigated power-culture to manipulate terms of discourse and relations of resource control.

The Russian case also suggests that neoinstitutionalism, when accounting for power-culture and framing, can contribute to the understanding of hegemony. Social hegemonies are aggregates of interfield and intrafield discourses, interactions, and practices that work game-theoretically and from which narratives of normality emerge as field leaders, challengers, and political elites situate themselves and stake claims and academics, experts, and journalists observe and try to make sense of the scene. Game-theoretically, we see why fundamental change is not common and requires shocks: we individuals watch each other and fear retribution for exclaiming that the emperor is naked. To play it safe, we mimic claims and practices, even if we dislike them, do not believe them, or are ambivalent about them. And so hegemonic meanings persist: we do not always question for fear that this will show a maddening collage of webs of meaning and power that, even if robust, seem quite fragile. Perhaps symbolic interactionists were right all along; in his anthropological work, Bourdieu came close to saying something similar. To elide these complex webs of power-culture manifested in discourse and practice is like studying chemistry and eliding quantum mechanics: our knowledge remains incomplete, perhaps dangerously so. For the sake of those who have paid the price for social scientists' sins of omission and commission, we should elide these social forces no longer.

At journey's end

When I began this journey, I sweated over defining "market" and "market economy." While OECD or other organizations and scholars use prefabricated definitions and measures, these are preconceptions, categories, and narratives taken as reality—like economics itself, they are trapped in their own rhetoric. Each era takes its time and knowledge as "closest to God." Hoping for progress in knowledge is not *hubris*; but reifying knowledge and linking it to status lets the tail wag (or throttle) the dog. This is exploring an Undiscovered Country— unknown, mysterious, towards which adventurers boldly set out, using others' tales and marking a trail as they go along. It is inexact. My goal has not been to redraw the map but to rethink how maps are drawn. Economic theory and political economy made important points about states, laws, and costs, but something deeper remained. Until we get to that level, such manifestations remain subject to *post facto* and *ad hoc* rationalizations. We are doing complex chemistry without understanding quantum mechanisms: too much theory focuses on macro- and meso-levels (classes, states, organizations) without paying enough attention to micro-level dynamics. Rational action will not do: we are instrumentally rational in some contexts, ritual or emotional in others. Social scientists must push the envelope to radically rethink "economies," "societies," and human interaction.

One problem may be methodological and theoretical dogmatism. We must avoid being scholarly drunks in the streetlight, using data or theory only where we feel safe and can allow each other to look. Models serve as heuristic devices or metaphors; but human society and its theories are conditioned by time and place. We should examine our intellectual homes before we rearrange those of others. Perhaps in the future, when Russia's Undiscovered Country of social change (and those of East Europe and China) has been better explored—and from batteries of empirical data our cherished theories, from neoclassical economics to economic sociology, lie scattered in a shambles like so much debris—this warning of theory and reality will be a lesson of this contemporary Great Transformation. One hopes that then—when yet another generation has been sacrificed at the altar of social experimentation—real learning will begin.

*   *   *

If my intellectual bond is with political and economic sociology, my personal bond is with Russia. As Russians have gone on their journey of discovery, I have gone on mine. Russians have known displacement and pain, and with bravery and bitterness pressed on. From the inception of this idea to its conclusion, I moved between cities and countries; saw an apartment burn down; endured the insanity of British academic bureaucracies; and grieved the loss of my first-born son Mitchell. Russians and I have grown in this process, but at what cost? One wishes wisdom—or at least experience—was less painful, with less loss. I hope the next years are kinder. And perhaps this is the most powerful lesson. Structures, stability, freedom, and life all die, but hope remains—invariant and universal, indestructible and unchanging, as we all make our journey to the Undiscovered Country.

> I beseech you in the bowels of Christ, think it possible you may be wrong.
> (Oliver Cromwell)

> It is cold in the scriptorium, my thumb aches. I leave this manuscript, I do not know for whom; I no longer know what it is about.
> (Umberto Eco, *The Name of the Rose*)

August 1993, Princeton–March 2010, St. Petersburg

Appendix

Participant observation

For participant observation, I selected Atlas (a tour firm) and Economics Inc. (a publishing house that also ran seminars and courses in finance). They were founded at the end of the Soviet era (Atlas) and the beginning of the post-Soviet period (Economics Inc.). Personal contacts provided access to these firms, and the personal trust arising from these contacts allowed me to ask pointed questions and get honest answers. Interestingly, the two firms differed on many important points, allowing for contrast between a case of successful change (Atlas) and muddling (Economics Inc.). I observed Atlas in July 1991, February–July 1993, August 1994–February 1995, randomly in 1995, and in the summers of 1999 and 2001. I observed Economics Inc. August 1994–December 1995 and briefly in the summers of 1997, 1999, and 2001. During observations I watched processes of daily business life: problems that arose and how they were categorized; discussions and debates, and language used, over various issues; relations of power (who said what, whose opinion became policy); confusions and conflicts over practices and claims; and to what extent change took root (i.e. whether new ideas became real practices).

Interviews

These were in-depth, open-ended interviews with managers and entrepreneurs, from large industrial enterprises to small private firms. They ranged in length from forty minutes to four hours, and were conducted in December 1993 and January 1994, October 1994–January 1996, July 1997, and July 1999. (I do not cite all eighty interviews. However, much of the empirical chapters draw on these interviews aggregated—e.g. claims, impressions, and issues they revealed.) Most subjects were in St. Petersburg; a few were in Tula, an industrial city south of Moscow (in the list below the place was St. Petesrburg unless otherwise specified). General themes included exchange (contracts, sales and supply strategies, problems and changes in previous strategies), value (price-setting, criteria of valuation, investment and debts), and production (labor issues, technological problems, mistakes and changes in strategies). Interviews were kept flexible, to allow me to follow up on "hot issues" for each informant and to use interviews as "micro-histories" of change and learning.

- ArtEnerg: consultant in charge of market search and concluding exchanges (for money and barter) for a division of Energomash; July 1997.
- Association of Industrial Enterprises: President of the Association of Industrial Entrepreneurs (private voluntary association); July 1997.
- Bank1: high-ranking specialist in an important Petersburg bank; January 1994.
- Beer-1: financial expert, Baltika beer enterprise; July 1999.
- Beer-2: assistant manager, distribution and sales, Baltika beer; July 1999.
- BreadAssoc-1 and BreadAssoc-2: main executive for non-profit voluntary association of 18 of 22 Petersburg bread factories, undertaking marketing and other studies; June and July 1995.
- Brkda-1 and Brkda-2: assistant director at large firm manufacturing construction materials; January 1994 and December 1994.
- Broke-1: brokerage and investment dealer (who then left to import fruit juice and to work in an investment firm); December 1994.
- Carpart-1: director and owner of small firm specializing in mechanical parts for cars, other machines, and electronic goods; December 1995.
- Chem-1: owner and director of small private chemical firm (designs various chemicals for shampoo, water absorption, etc.); June 1995.
- Chem-2: general director of large Defensive FPG uniting various large chemical enterprises in St. Petersburg; July 1997.
- Chem-3: director for chemical importer; September 1995.
- Chem-4: financial director for private chemical importer; July 1999.
- Cloth-1: general director and president of board of directors for medium-sized (200 employees) privatized clothing-making factory; July 1997.
- Consult-1 and Consult-2: two young marketing and strategy consultants, one of whom had formerly worked with a prominent American consulting firm; January 1996.
- Cosmo-99: former sales director for branch of Western cosmetics firm; July 1999.
- D-Com: commercial director of Petersburg trading firm (consumer durables) and former commercial directors of Economics Inc.; November 1995.
- Elec-1: assistant director of economics and assistant director of international sales of an electronics firm; July 1997.
- Extinguish: assistant director for fire extinguisher producer (subdivision of larger firm undergoing restructuring and privatization); July 1999.
- HomeDir-1 and HomeDir-2: owner and assistants of small private firm for cottage construction and sales of home appliances. Manager was in local Communist Party and became a middle-ranking city official; November 1995.
- KhF-1 and KhF-2: general director of medium-sized (over 200 workers) bread firm; July 1995 and August 1995.
- Kr/Mrkt: marketing director for member factory of a St. Petersburg *kholding* involved in machine and tractor building; July 1997.
- Ku-1/1 and Ku-1/2: assistant manager of an electronics firm; January 1994 and December 1994.

- LawConsult-1: two young professionally trained lawyers working in private sector, often involved in privatization and tax issues; January 1996.
- Lmbr-1 and Lmbr-2: managers of a Petersburg lumber exchange; July 1995 and August 1995.
- MechGood-1: small business owner specializing in mechanical household goods and auto parts; November 1995.
- Nik-1 and Nik-2; high specialist in a major private bank; December 1995 and July 1997.
- Psk-1: general director of a machine-making enterprise; July 1997.
- Ptit-1: general director of poultry-processing factory and chairman of association of Petersburg poultry-producing factories; July 1997.
- PtSb: marketing director for small private firm importing higher-priced German household products for upper end of Russian market; November 1995.
- Rom-1 and Rom-2: engineer (second-highest ranking) for rocket-making division of heavy industrial enterprise; Tula, November 1995 and July 1999.
- Rom-2: 30-year-old computer expert opening small software business; Tula, November 1995.
- Rozh-1 and Rozh-2: owner/director/expert for personnel firm in management training (role-playing, game-playing, seminars) and marketing studies; October and November 1995.
- SevFurn: general director and president of the board of directors of the main firm for a furniture-making conglomerate; July 1997.
- Tar-1 and Tar-2: entrepreneur with history as *birzha* broker, commercial agent, sales manager; September 1995.
- Tula-café: Tula entrepreneur formerly in the café business; Tula, September, 1995.
- Khlebpik-1 and Khlebpik-2: private entrepreneur in making the machines for bread-making; June and August 1995.
- Rail-1: assistant economics director, St. Petersburg October Railroad; March 1995.
- Tula-mebel: owner and manager of small private furniture-making and furniture-assembling enterprise; Tula, November 1995.
- Union of Industrialists and Entrepreneurs of St. Petersburg: president of the Petersburg branch of the All-Russian Union; July 1997.

The following interviews were with managers in an electronics enterprise.

- Pz-1: general director and assistant director for marketing; February 1995.
- Pz-2: assistant director for marketing; February 1995.
- Pz-CDir: commercial director; March 1995.

The following interviews were conducted with the general and assistant directors of a lathe-making and castings firm.

- Stnk/Gendir-1 and Stnk/Gendir-2: general director; November 1994, February 1995.
- Stnk/Sa-1 and Stnk/Sa-2: assistant director for sales, March 1995.
- Stnk/Prod-1 and Stnk/Prod-2: assistant director for purchases and production; March 1995.
- Stnk/Ec-1 and Stnk/Ec-2: assistant director for economics and planning; March 1995.
- Stnk/T-1 and Stnk/T-2: head engineer; April 1995.

Enterprise newspapers

After *glasnost'* became policy, enterprise newspapers exploded in discussions of topics such as enterprise relations, managerial strategies, problems, and even historical issues such as the Terror. The quality and depth of reporting varied. I tried to cross-reference claims and information. Through accounts and interviews with managers, shopfloor bosses, and employees, reporters presented accounts of strategies, problems, and conflicts. I analyzed accounts, claims, and rhetoric of enterprise conflict, power and restructuring, production and sales strategies, and actors' various perceptions. I examined newspapers for more than twenty large enterprises. The bulk of material I use comes from ten that provided sufficient material and variation for analysis. The name of the newspaper is followed by its enterprise.

- *Baltiets* (Baltiiskii Zavod—heavy industry)
- *Elektrosila* (Elektrosila— electrical generation equipment and goods)
- *Izhorets* (Izhorskie Zavody—electrical generation equipment and goods)
- *Kirovets* (Kirovskii Zavod—heavy industry)
- *Krasnaia zaria* (Krasnaia Zaria—telecommunications electronics)
- *Krasnyi tkach* (Krasnyi Tkach—textiles)
- *Krasnyi treugol'nik* (Krasnyi Treugol'nik—rubber)
- *Leningradskii stankostroitel'* (Sverdlov—heavy industry)
- *Maiak* (Positron—electronics)
- *Molot* (Nevskii Zavod im. Lenina—heavy industry)
- *Svetlana* (Svetlana—electronics)
- *Turbostroitel'* (Leningradskii Metallicheskii Zavod—turbine and other heavy industrial production)

Notes

Introduction

1 According to Levada Center (a fairly independent research group), one third of Russians lived in poverty up to 2005 http://www.levada.ru/dynamicabed.html. In July 2007 over 40% of Russians had problems obtaining basic foodstuffs or elementary goods www.levada.ru, July 30, 2007).

2 Aleksandr Dubrov, "Prezumptsiia vinovnosti," *Rossiiskaia gazeta*, April 30, 2008; Clifford Gaddy and Barry W. Ickes, "Resource Rents and the Russian Economy," *Eurasian Geography and Economics* 46 (2005), 559–83; William Tompson, "A Frozen Venezuela? The Resource Curse and Russian Politics," in Michael Ellman (ed.), *Russia's Oil and National Gas: Bonanza or Curse?* (New York: Anthem, 2006), 189–212. By late 2005 Gazprom's foreign debt was $33.1 billion, Rosneft's $12.2 billion, and electricity monopoly EES's $5 billion; the return on investment in physical capital and infrastructure is lower than a scan of data suggests. Boris Nemtsov and Vladimir Milov claim $16.6 billion of Gazprom's debt came from buying non-gas assets and importing natural gas from Central Asia for domestic demand. Nemtsov and Milov, "Putin i 'Gazprom,'" *Novaia gazeta*, Aug. 28, 2008 www.novayagazeta.ru. On corporate debt and defaults, see Marina Tal'skaia, "Zreet urozhai defoltov," *Ekspert*, Sept. 8, 2008.

3 Julian Cooper, "Can Russia Compete in the Global Economy?" *Eurasian Geography and Economics* 47 (2006), 407–25. The World Economic Forum gave Russia low rankings for competitiveness in institutions, financial markets, goods market efficiency, and business sophistication: *Global Competitiveness Report 2007–2008* (http://www.gcr.weforum.org/, Sept. 1, 2008).

4 Pekka Sutela, "Economic Growth Remains Surprisingly High," *Russian Analytic Digest* 38 (April 2, 2008), 1–5.

5 Ol'ga Evseeva and Aleksandr Zadorozhnyi, "Ekonomika i finansy: investitsionnaia politika Udmurtii," *Ekspert-Ural*, Oct. 30, 2006; Mikhail Malykhin, "Rossiiane tratiat zria polovinu rabochero vremeni," *Vedomosti* Feb. 4, 2009. Lina Kalianina *et al*, "Tseitnot," *Ekspert*, Nov. 27, 2006, claim light industry and middle-sized business will face hard times.

6 Kathleen Smith, *Mythmaking in the New Russia* (Ithaca, NY: Cornell University Press, 2002).

7 Cf. Gerald A. McDermott, *Embedded Politics. Industrial Networks and Institutional Change in Postcommunism* (Ann Arbor, MI: University of Michigan Press, 2002); Clifford Gaddy and Barry W. Ickes, *Russia's Virtual Economy* (Washington, DC: Brookings, 2002); Steven Solnick, *Stealing the State* (Cambridge, MA: Harvard University Press, 1998); David Woodruff, *Money Unmade* (Ithaca, NY: Cornell University Press, 1999); Juliet Johnson, *Fistful of Rubles: The Rise and Fall of the Russian Banking System* (Ithaca, NY: Cornell

University Press, 2000); Andrew Barnes, *Owning Russia: The Struggle over Factories, Farms, and Power* (Ithaca, NY: Cornell University Press, 2006).

8   Some political economy conceptualizes "institutions" as structured rules and processes, not unlike "organizations," e.g. Peter Hall, *Governing the Economy* (New York: Oxford University Press, 1986).

9   David Woodruff, "Rules for Followers: Institutional Theory and the New Politics of Economic Backwardness in Russia," *Politics and Society*, 28/4 (2000), 437–82.

10 John Markoff, *Abolition of Feudalism* (University Park, PA: Penn State Press, 1997).

11 Jack Goldstone, *Revolution and Rebellion in the Early Modern World* (Berkeley, CA: University of California Press, 1991).

12 Peter Berger and Thomas Luckmann, *The Social Construction of Reality* (Garden City, NY: Anchor Books, 1967), 58; Anthony Giddens, *The Constitution of Society* (New York: Cambridge University Press, 1984).

13 Berger and Luckmann, *Social Construction of Reality*, 55.

14 Karl Polanyi, *The Great Transformation* (Boston, MA: Beacon Hill, 1944); William Reddy, *The Rise of Market Culture: The Textile Trade and French Society, 1750–1900* (Cambridge: Cambridge University Press, 1984); Max Weber, *General Economic History* (New Brunswick, NJ: Transaction Books, 1987) and *Economy and Society* (Berkeley, CA: University of California Press, 1978); Richard Lachmann, "Class Formation without Class Struggle: An Elite Conflict Theory of the Transition to Capitalism," *American Sociological Review* 55 (1990), 398–414.

15 On "economies" as social constructs, see Timothy Mitchell, *Rule of Experts: Egypt, Techno-Politics, Modernity* (Berkeley, CA: University of California Press, 2002).

16 Following Iurii Lotman, Tim McDaniel argues that post-Soviet discourse was rejection of the past for a new normality. McDaniel, *Agony of the Russian Idea* (Princeton, NJ: Princeton University Press, 1998).

17 Elaine Weiner, *Market Dreams: Gender, Class, and Capitalism in the Czech Republic* (Ann Arbor, MI: University of Michigan Press, 2007).

18 Cf. Ted Hopf, *Social Construction of International Politics. Identities and Foreign Policies, Moscow, 1995 and 1999* (Ithaca, NY: Cornell University Press, 2002).

19 E.g. see Robert Wade, *Governing the Market* (Princeton, NJ: Princeton University Press, 1990); Alice Amsden, *Asia's Next Giant* (New York: Oxford University Press, 1989); Gary Gereffi and Donald Wyman (eds), *Manufacturing Miracles: Paths of Industrialization in Latin America and East Asia* (Princeton, NJ: Princeton University Press, 1990); Alice Amsden, Jacek Kochanowicz, and Lance Taylor, *The Market Meets its Match* (Cambridge, MA: Harvard University Press, 1998).

20 Robert H. Frank, "Rethinking Rational Choice," in Roger Friedland and A. F. Robertson (eds), *Beyond the Marketplace: Rethinking Economy and Society* (New York: Aldine de Gruyter, 1990), 53–88; Charles Perrow, *Complex Organizations: A Critical Essay* (New York: Random House, 1986), ch. 7.

21 Janos Kornai, *The Socialist System* (Princeton, NJ: Princeton University Press, 1992).

22 David Lipton, Jeffrey Sachs, Stanley Fisher, and Janos Kornai, "Creating a Market Economy in Eastern Europe: The Case of Poland," *Brookings Papers on Economic Activity* 1990/1 (1990), 75–133; David Lipton, Jeffrey Sachs, and Lawrence H. Summers, "Privatization in Eastern Europe: The Case of Poland," *Brookings Papers on Economic Activity* 1990/2 (1990), 293–341; and a symposium in *Journal of Economic Perspectives* 5/4 (1991). The "gradualist" alternative did not assume institutions emerge automatically, yet it also elided culture, power, and practices. John Marangos, "Preventative Therapy: The Neoclassical Gradualist Model of Transition from Central Administration to Market Relations," *Carl Beck Papers*, 1604 (Pittsburgh: University of Pittsburgh Center for Russian and East European Studies, 2002); Peter Murrell, "Can Neoclassical Economics Underpin the Reform of Centrally Planned Economies?" *Journal of Economic Perspectives* 5/4 (1991), 59–76.

23 Amos Tversky and Daniel Kahneman, "Judgment under Uncertainty: Heuristics and Biases," *Science* 185 (1974), 1124–31, and "The Framing of Decisions and the Psychology of Choice," *Science* 21 (1981), 453–8.

24 Douglass North, *Understanding the Process of Economic Change* (Princeton, NJ: Princeton University Press, 2005). Even economists who address cognition view "economies" as autonomous social sites: John N. Drobak and John V. C. Nye (eds), *The Frontiers of New Institutional Economics* (New York: Academic Press, 1997).

25 Yoshiko M. Herrera, *Imagined Economies: The Sources of Russian Regionalism* (New York: Cambridge University Press, 2004), ch. 2, critiques economists' outdated views of cognition.

26 Viviana Zelizer, "Beyond the Polemics of the Market: Establishing a Theoretical and Empirical Agenda," *Sociological Forum* 3/4 (1988), 614–34; John Lie, "Sociology of Markets," *Annual Review of Sociology* 23 (1997), 341–60.

27 James Millar, "From Utopian Socialism to Utopian Capitalism," *Problems of Post-Communism* 42/3 (1995), 8.

28 Paul Ingram and Karen Clay, "The Choice-within-Constraints New Institutionalism and Implications for Sociology," *Annual Review of Sociology* 26 (2000), 525–46; Oliver Williamson, *The Economic Institutions of Capitalism* (New York: Free Press, 1985); Robert Bates, *Essays on the Political Economy of Rural Africa* (New York: Cambridge University Press, 1983); Hernando de Soto, *The Other Path* (New York: Harper & Row, 1989); Herbert Simon, *Administrative Behavior* (New York: Wiley, 1945); James March and Herbert Simon, *Organizations* (New York: Wiley, 1958). NIE assumes the state makes laws meaningful without asking *why* law works anyway. Patricia Ewick and Susan Silbey, *The Common Place of Law: Stories from Everyday Life* (Chicago: University of Chicago Press, 1998).

29 For an NIE-inspired view of the post-Soviet state, see Jerry Hough, *The Logic of Economic Reform in Russia* (Washington, DC: Brookings, 2001).

30 Cf. Stephan Haggard, *Pathways from the Periphery* (Ithaca, NY: Cornell University Press, 1990); Peter Evans, *Dependent Development* (Princeton, NJ: Princeton University Press, 1979) and *Embedded Autonomy* (Princeton, NJ: Princeton University Press, 1995); John Zysman, *Governments, Markets, and Growth* (Ithaca, NY: Cornell University Press, 1983); Valerie Bunce, *Subversive Institutions: The Design and the Destruction of Socialism and the State* (New York: Cambridge University Press, 1998).

31 Jeffrey Frieden, *Dept, Development, and Democracy* (Princeton, NJ: Princeton University Press, 1992); Joseph Blasi, Maya Kroumova, and Douglas Kruse, *Kremlin Capitalism. Privatizing the Russian Economy* (Ithaca, NY: Cornell University Press, 1997).

32 Michael McFaul, *Russia's Unfinished Revolution* (Ithaca, NY: Cornell University Press, 2001).

33 Cf. Weber, *Economy and Society*, vol. 1, pp. 24–6 and 85–90.

34 Paul DiMaggio and Walter Powell, "Introduction," in Walter Powell and Paul DiMaggio (eds), *The New Institutionalism in Organizational Analysis* (Chicago: University of Chicago Press, 1991), 1–38.

35 Cf. Humphrey, *The Unmaking of Soviet Life: Everyday Economies After Socialism* (Ithaca, NY: Cornell University Press, 2002), ch. 8.

36 Douglass North, *Institutions, Institutional Change, and Economic Performance* (New York: Cambridge University Press, 1990); William Roy, *Socializing Capital* (Princeton, NJ: Princeton University Press, 2007).

37 Douglass North, *Structure and Change in Economic History* (New York: W. W. Norton, 1981).

38 Cf. Paul Starr, *The Social Transformation of American Medicine* (New York: Basic Books, 1982).

39 Conflating *institutions* with *institutionalization* and *reproduction* plagues institutionalists, who often assume behavior shifts automatically as rules change—yet knowledge and practices may persist.

40 E.g. Evans, *Embedded Autonomy*; Michael Piore and Charles Sabel, *The Second Industrial Divide* (New York: Basic Books, 1984).

41 Cf. Mark Granovetter, "Economic Action and Social Structure: The Problem of Embeddedness," *American Journal of Sociology* 91 (1985), 481–510; Walter Powell and Laurel Smith-Doerr, "Networks and Economic Life," in Neil Smelser and Richard Swedberg (eds), *The Handbook of Economic Sociology* (Princeton, NJ: Princeton University Press, 1994), 368–402; Viviana Zelizer, "Enter Culture," in Mauro Guillén, Randall Collins, Paula England, and Marshall Meyer (eds), *The New Economic Sociology: Developments in an Emerging Field* (New York: Russell Sage Foundation, 2002), 101–25.

42 David Stark and László Bruszt, *Postsocialist Pathways* (New York: Cambridge University Press, 1998).

43 Michael Burawoy and Katherine Verdery (eds), *Uncertain Transition: Ethnographies of Change in the Postsocialist World* (New York: Rowan & Littlefield, 1999).

44 Elizabeth Dunn, *Privatizing Poland: Baby Food, Big Business, and the Remaking of Labor* (Ithaca, NY: Cornell University Press, 2004).

45 John W. Meyer and Brian Rowan, "Institutionalized Organizations: Formal Structure as Myth and Ceremony," *American Journal of Sociology* 83 (1977), 340–63; Paul DiMaggio and Walter Powell, "The Iron Cage Revisited: Institutional Isomorphism and Collective Rationality in Organizational Fields," *American Sociological Review* 48 (1983), 147–60.

46 The four forms of isomorphism are: coercive (practices imposed from the outside), mimetic (copying legitimate practices), normative (common socialization), and competitive. William Roy (*Socializing Capital*) used isomorphism to explain the rise of the American corporation: from state–business partnerships to limit risk later reified by Wall Street financiers speculating on shares.

47 William Ouchi, *Theory Z* (Reading, MA: Addison-Wesley, 1981); Geert Hofstede, *Cultures and Organizations: Software of the Mind* (New York: McGraw-Hill, 1991).

48 Fligstein, *The Transformation of Corporate Control* (Cambridge, MA: Harvard University Press, 1990); "Social Skill and the Theory of Fields," *Sociological Theory* 19/2 (2001), 105–25; *The Architecture of Markets* (Princeton, NJ: Princeton University Press, 2001).

49 Frank Dobbin, *Forging Industrial Policy* (New York: Cambridge University Press, 1994); Walter Powell, "Expanding the Scope of Institutional Analysis," in Powell and DiMaggio (eds), *The New Institutionalism in Organizational Analysis*, 183–203.

50 Richard Colignon, *Power Plays* (Stony Brook, NY: SUNY Press, 1997).

51 Paul DiMaggio, "Interest and Agency in Institutional Theory," in Lynne Zucker (ed.), *Institutional Patterns and Organization* (Cambridge, MA: Ballinger, 1988), 3–21.

52 Vladimir Mau and Irina Staroduborskaya, *The Challenge of Revolution: Contemporary Russia in Historical Perspective* (New York: Oxford University Press, 2001). One way to approach social reality is to follow perturbations that disturb taken-for-granted meanings and practices and then watch reconstruction. To know energy levels of electron orbitals, scientists "perturb" an electron from its orbit with an energy blast. As it returns to its ground state, the electron emits quanta of energy that reveal energy levels.

53 Mustafa Emirbayer and Victoria Johnson, "Bourdieu and Organizational Analysis," *Theory and Society* 37 (2008), 1–44.

54 On fractals, see Goldstone, *Revolution and Rebellion in the Early Modern World*, 46–7.

55 Tim Hallett, "Symbolic Power and Organizational Culture," *Sociological Theory* 21 (2003), 128–49; also Gary Alan Fine, "Negotiated Orders and Organizational Cultures," *Annual Review of Sociology* 10 (1984), 239–62.

1 Power-culture, practice, and economic change

1 Thomas Kuhn, *The Structure of Scientific Revolutions* (Chicago: University of Chicago Press, 1970).
2 William Sewell, *Work and Revolution in France* (New York: Cambridge University Press, 1980); Lynn Hunt, *Politics, Culture, and Class in the French Revolution* (Berkeley, CA: University of California Press, 1984). Chikako Usui and Richard Colignon, "Corporate Restructuring: Converging World Pattern or Societally Specific Embeddedness?" *Sociological Quarterly* 37 (1996), 551–78. Consider economic imperialism: economists realized the theoretical inconsistency of assigning different theories to different spheres and so imposed their paradigm on families, discrimination, and the like.
3 Among others, see: Weber, *General Economic History*, and *Economy and Society*; North, *Institutions, Institutional Change, and Economic Performance*; Richard Nelson and Sidney Winter, *An Evolutionary Theory of Economic Change* (Cambridge, MA: Harvard University Press, 1982); Fligstein, *The Transformation of Corporate Control*.
4 Bourdieu, *The Logic of Practice* (Stanford, CA: Stanford University Press, 1990), and *The State Nobility* (Stanford, CA: Stanford University Press, 1996).
5 Charles Tilly, *Popular Contention in Great Britain* (Cambridge, MA: Harvard University Press, 1995); David A. Snow and Robert D. Benford, "Master Frames and Cycles of Protest," in Aldon D. Morris and Carol McClurg Mueller (eds), *Frontiers in Social Movement Theory* (New Haven, CT: Yale University Press, 1992), 133–55.
6 Williamson, *Economic Institutions of Capitalism*; John Waterbury, *Exposed to Innumerable Delusions* (New York: Cambridge University Press, 1993); Piore and Sabel, *The Second Industrial Divide*; DiMaggio and Powell, "The Iron Cage Revisited."
7 Jeffrey Pfeffer, *Power in Organization* (Marshfield, MA: Pitman, 1981) and *Managing with Power: Politics and Influence in Organizations* (Boston, MA: Harvard Business School Press, 1992).
8 We can apply these insights in a fractal manner. At one level, the field is economic polity, and owners and managers are polity members. One level lower, the firm is polity, managers and employees polity members cooperating or fighting over authority and meanings.
9 Bourdieu, *The Rules of Art* (Stanford, CA: Stanford University Press, 1996), 178.
10 Burawoy, "The Extended Case Method," in Michael Burawoy *et al* (eds), *Ethnography Unbound* (Berkeley, CA: University of California Press, 1991), 271–87.
11 Charles Tilly, *Big Structures, Large Processes, Huge Comparisons* (New York: Russell Sage, 1984).
12 I focus primarily on firms in St. Petersburg. Networks facilitated interviews and observation, and helped me check the veracity of claims. St. Petersburg is home to several sectors (electronics, shipbuilding, machine-tool, engineering and energy equipment). For comparison I did a few interviews in Tula, a military-industrial city, but found no fundamental deviation from processes in Petersburg.
13 My thinking on "practice" comes from Bourdieu, *The Logic of Practice*, and Anthony Giddens, *The Constitution of Society*.
14 My ideas about "logics" come from Roger Friedland and Robert Alford, "Bringing Society Back In: Symbols, Practices, and Institutional Contradictions," in Walter Powell and Paul DiMaggio (eds), *The New Institutionalism in Organizational Analysis*, 232–63; Roger Friedland, "Money, Sex, and God: The Erotic Logic of Religious Nationalism," *Sociological Theory* 20 (2002), 381–425.
15 In East Europe, semblances of market practices existed in varying forms. This shortened distances between socialism and capitalism. Michael D. Kennedy, *Cultural Formations of Post-Communism: Emancipation, Transition, Nation, and War* (Minneapolis, MN: University of Minnesota Press, 2002), ch. 3.
16 Bourdieu, *The Logic of Practice*, 52–66; Berger and Luckmann, *The Social Construction of Reality*; Robert Wuthnow, *Meaning and Moral Order* (Berkeley, CA: University of

California Press, 1987); Paul DiMaggio, "Culture and Cognition," *Annual Review of Sociology* 23 (1997), 263–87.

17 Economists conceptualize culture in simplistic or bizarre ways: e.g. Robert J. Shiller, Maxim Boycko, and Vladimir Korobov, "Hunting for *Homo Sovieticus*: Situational versus Attitudinal Factors in Economic Behavior," *Brookings Papers on Economic Activity* 1992/1 (1992), 127–81.

18 Ann Swidler, "Culture in Action: Symbols and Strategies," *American Sociological Review* 51 (1986), 273–86.

19 Charalambos A. Vlachoutsicos, "How Managerial Learning Can Assist Economic Transformation in Russia," *Organizational Studies* (Spring 1996), at www.findarticles. com; Vlachoutsicos and Paul Lawrence, "What we don't Know about Soviet Management," *Harvard Business Review* 68/6 (1990), 50–64. Other problems included "need for radical restructuring of the large state enterprises" that "stubbornly stuck to their traditional ways of operating."

20 This compresses four levels Paul DiMaggio proposes, but it also follows Polanyi's levels of knowledge and Anthony Giddens's discursive versus practical consciousness. Paul DiMaggio, "Cultural Aspects of Economic Action and Organization," in Roger Friedland and A. F. Robertson (eds), *Beyond the Marketplace: Rethinking Economy and Society* (New York: Aldine de Gruyter, 1990), 113–36; Michael Polanyi, *The Tacit Dimension* (Garden City, NY: Doubleday Anchor, 1967); Nelson and Winter, *An Evolutionary Theory of Economic Change*; Giddens, *The Constitution of Society*, ch. 3 and pp. 334–43.

21 Hammad Akbar, "Knowledge Levels and the Transformation: Towards the Integration of Knowledge Creation and Individual Learning," *Journal of Management Studies* 40 (2003), 2000. Akbar characterizes levels of learning as superficial "know-what/how" and "know-why." See also Chris Argyris, *On Organizational Learning* (Cambridge: Blackwell, 1993).

22 Pamela Hinds and Jeffrey Pfeffer, "Why Organizations Don't 'Know What They Know': Cognitive and Motivational Factors Affecting the Transfer of Expertise," Research Paper 1697 (July 2001), Graduate School of Business, Stanford University. "Because tacit knowledge does not reside at the conscious level, it is difficult to articulate and, therefore, difficult to share with others…[Experts] may have trouble articulating the specific information novices need to learn and perform effectively" (p. 9).

23 Cf. Tversky and Kahneman, "Judgment under Uncertainty: Heuristics and Biases," and "The Framing of Decisions and the Psychology of Choice."

24 Legitimation and normality have levels. Superficially, legitimation masks interests or makes them palatable. Fundamentally, legitimation involves defending and promoting logics one takes for granted.

25 David A. Snow, E. Burke Rochford Jr., Steven K. Worden, and Robert D. Benford, "Frame Alignment Process, Micromobilization, and Movement Participation," *American Sociological Review* 51 (1986), 464–81. One can talk of the logic of a frame (principles of systematizing meaning) and a tacit level.

26 Margaret Somers and Fred Block, "From Poverty to Perversity: Ideas, Markets, and Institutions over 200 Years of Welfare Debate," *American Sociological Review* 70 (2005), 260–87.

27 Snow and Benford, "Master Frames and Cycles of Protest."

28 Cf. Nelson and Winter, *An Evolutionary Theory of Economic Change*; Connie J. G. Gersick, "Revolutionary Change Theories: A Multilevel Exploration of the Punctuated Equilibrium Paradigm," *Academy of Management Review* 16 (1991), 10–36.

29 Nelson and Winter, *An Evolutionary Theory of Economic Change*, part 2.

30 Consider learning another language. One level is memorizing vocabulary and formal grammar rules. A deeper level is fluency: reflexively using correct words and syntax in the right context.

31 Hinds and Pfeffer, "Why Organizations Don't 'Know What They Know'." Discussing obstacles to transferring expertise, Hinds and Pfeffer note differences between abstract, conceptual "structures" and concrete but superficial representations. Post-Soviet managers might learn of "marketing" from books, but such knowledge is concrete, not systemic or conceptual.

32 Kennedy, *Cultural Formations of Post-Communism*, chs. 1–3.

33 E.g. Woodruff, *Money Unmade*, on barter and troubled monetization of the economy.

34 E.g. Kathryn Stoner-Weiss, *Local Heroes: The Political Economy of Russian Regional Governance* (Princeton, NJ: Princeton University Press, 1997).

35 Steven Lukes, *Power: A Radical View* (London: Macmillan, 1974); John Gaventa, *Power and Powerlessness* (Urbana, IL: University of Illinois Press, 1980).

36 Ákos Róna-Tas argues socialist state power derived from controlling the labor market (wage dependency), which vanished with liberalization. This restricts power to the first dimension. *The Great Surprise of the Small Transformation* (Ann Arbor, MI: University of Michigan Press, 1997).

37 The American Right used 1970s economic failure, social disorder, and racism to create a narrative delegitimating welfare and state regulation as abnormalities. Over-the-top propaganda and stagnation weakened the Soviet narrative; but Yeltsin could not create a strong alternative.

38 James C. Scott, *Domination and the Arts of Resistance* (New Haven, CT: Yale University Press, 1990), 73–82.

39 This has affinity with vertical and horizontal social capital. Robert Putnam, *Making Democracy Work* (Princeton, NJ: Princeton University Press, 1993).

40 In escrow or third-party practices, both sides invoke power voluntarily. This is not vertical domination; it is a measure to enforce a particular action (e.g. a contract) that does not affect inherent autonomy.

41 Charles Tilly, *Coercion, Capital, and European States A.D. 990–1992* (Cambridge: Blackwell, 1990).

42 Fligstein, *The Transformation of Corporate Control*, ch. 1.

43 Challengers to the Party took control of the state through negotiated transfer, rather than by dismantling state authority. In the USSR, reforms invited challenges and began decomposition of state power, when liberalization facilitated local elites' grabbing. Mark Beissinger, *Nationalist Mobilization and the Collapse of the Soviet State* (New York: Cambridge University Press, 2002).

44 James Millar (ed.), *Politics, Work, and Daily Life in the USSR* (New York: Cambridge University Press, 1987); Alexei Yurchak, *Everything Was Forever, Until It Was No More: The Last Soviet Generation* (Princeton, NJ: Princeton University Press, 2006).

45 On "living the lie," see Slavenka Drakulic, *How We Survived Communism and Even Laughed* (London: Hutchinson, 1992). Yurchak (*Everything Was Forever*) notes how people maneuvered "the Lie," acting according to belief while holding that belief in abeyance. Yet this distracts him from how "the Lie" could be a game of power, resistance, and empowerment.

46 Jeffrey K. Hass, "The Great Transition: The Dynamics of Market Transitions and the Case of Russia, 1991–1995," *Theory and Society* 28 (1999), 383–424.

47 A crucial question is *why* each path occurs when it does. Here contingency contributes. Structure is an artifact of power-culture, and as enforcement weakens and contexts become fluid, contingency overtakes path dependency.

48 Note that marketplace coevolution to common logics and practices involves one set of actors imposing criteria: e.g. Wall Street brokers and financial analysts (experts), or state technocrats in France or Japan.

49 One explanation is that by law managers had to retain large staffs and welfare functions; but managers could get around this by not paying wages and claiming financial hardship.

50 Lotman, *Kul'tura i vzryv*, in *Semiosfera* (St. Petersburg: Iskusstvo-SPb, 2000).

51 One analysis of blaming and collective action is Debra Javelin, "The Role of Blame in Collective Action: Evidence from Russia," *American Political Science Review* 97 (2003), 107–21.

52 In 2004, Putin demanded the elite "fully recognize their social duties" to contribute to "a system of new social guarantees for the population." Maria Levitov, "Corporations Flaunt their Social Conscience," *Moscow Times*, April 1, 2004.

53 East European technocrats mimicked market clichés for aid donors. Janine Wedel, *Collision and Collusion: The Strange Case of Western Aid to Eastern Europe, 1989–1998* (New York: St Martin's Press).

54 Brian Humphreys, "Russia Urged to Improve its Accounting Standards," *St. Petersburg Times*, October 5, 2000. Various managers I interviewed in 1995 expressed confusion about managerial accounting.

55 To argue that competitive markets automatically wash out those lacking knowledge assumes *deus ex machina*. Fields of power may be in flux; older knowledge may not kill off a firm.

56 "With exogenous dependency and learning costs remaining high…a rational response, *ceteris paribus* is to erect information entry barriers" hindering learning. Akbar, "Knowledge Levels and Transformation," 2008.

57 Gordon Smith, *Reforming the Russian Legal System* (Cambridge: Cambridge University Press, 1996).

58 Solnick's *Stealing the State* is a useful account that is trapped in one-dimensional instrumentalism.

59 Blasi *et al*, *Kremlin Capitalism*, 157–65.

60 On exchange, see Kathryn Hendley, Peter Murrell, and Randi Ryterman, "A Regional Analysis of Transactional Strategies of Russian Enterprises," *McGill Law Journal* 44 (1999), 433–72; Kathryn Hendley, "How Russian Enterprises Cope with Payment Problems," *Post-Soviet Affairs* 15/3 (1999), 201–34; Vadim Volkov, *Violent Entrepreneurs* (Ithaca, NY: Cornell University Press, 2002).

61 Tim McDaniel, *Autocracy, Capitalism, and Revolution in Russia* (Berkeley, CA: University of California Press, 1988); Daniel Brower, *The Russian City between Tradition and Modernity, 1850–1900* (Berkeley, CA: University of California Press, 1990); Richard Pipes, *Russia under the Old Regime* (New York: Charles Scribners' Sons, 1974).

62 Thomas Owen, *Capitalism and Politics in Russia: A Social History of the Moscow Merchants, 1855–1905* (New York: Cambridge University Press, 1981); Alfred Rieber, *Merchants and Entrepreneurs in Imperial Russia* (Chapel Hill, NC: University of North Carolina Press, 1982); Roberta Manning, *The Crisis of the Old Order in Russia* (Princeton, NJ: Princeton University Press, 1982).

63 V. Ia. Kantorovich, *Sovietskie sindikaty* (Moscow and Leningrad: Tsentral'noe Upravlenie Pechati VSNKh SSSR, 1925); G. Dyperovich, *Sindikaty i tresty v dorevoliutsionnoi Rossii i v SSSR* (Leningrad: Tekhnika i Proizvodstvo, 1927); G. V. Lakin, *Reforma upravleniia promyshlennosti v 1929/30 g* (Moscow: Gosudarstvennoe tekhnicheskoe izdatel'stvo, 1930).

64 Kantorovich, *Sovietskie sindikaty*, 74; Dyperovich, *Sindikaty i tresty*, 442–5.

65 Mark Beissinger, *Scientific Management, Socialist Discipline, and Soviet Power* (Cambridge, MA: Harvard University Press, 1988), chs. 7–9; William J. Conyngham, *The Modernization of Soviet Industrial Management* (Cambridge: Cambridge University Press, 1982), 136; Abraham Katz, *The Politics of Economic Reform in the Soviet Union* (New York: Praeger, 1972), 137–40.

66 Katz, *Politics of Economic Reform*, 155, 157–60; Ed Hewett, *Reforming the Soviet Economy: Equality versus Efficiency* (Washington, DC: Brookings, 1988), 240–4.

67 James Millar, "The Little Deal: Brezhnev's Contribution to Acquisitive Socialism," *Slavic Review* 44/4 (1985), 694–706.

68 Valerie Bunce, "The Political Economy of the Brezhnev Era: The Rise and Fall of Corporatism," *British Journal of Political Science* 13 (1983), 129–58.

69 Caroline Humphrey, "Russian Protection Rackets and the Appropriation of Law and Order," in Josiah Heymann (ed.), *States and Illegal Practices* (Oxford: Berg, 1999), 199–232.

70 Marshall Goldman, *USSR in Crisis: The Failure of an Economic System* (New York: Norton, 1983).

71 Stephen Kotkin, *Armageddon Averted* (New York: Oxford University Press, 2001), 61.

72 Donna Bahry, "Politics, Generations, and Change in the USSR," and Brian D. Silver, "Political Beliefs of the Soviet Citizen: Sources of Support for Regime Norms," in James R. Millar (ed.), *Politics, Work, and Daily Life in the USSR* (New York: Cambridge University Press, 1987), 61–99 and 100–41.

73 Russian reformers perceived a short window of opportunity and felt shock therapy was the only option. William Tompson, "Putin's Challenge: The Politics of Structural Reform in Russia," *Europe–Asia Studies* 54/6 (2002), 933–57.

74 On path dependency, see *American Journal of Sociology* 104 (1998), 722–845.

75 Some crucial texts are: René Fülöp-Miller, *The Mind and Face of Bolshevism* (New York: G. P. Putnam's Sons, 1927), tr. F. S. Flint and D. F. Tait; McDaniel, *Autocracy, Capitalism, and Revolution in Russia*; Joseph Berliner, *Factory and Manager in the USSR* (Cambridge, MA: Harvard University Press, 1957); Kornai, *The Socialist System*; David Granick, *Management of the Industrial Firm in the USSR* (New York: Columbia University Press, 1954).

76 This is akin to Neil Fligstein's "manufacturing conception of control." Pre-1930s American firms were a collection of *production* units. Profit was important, but strategy focused on producing and selling a line of goods identified with the firm. Top managers rose through production.

77 Katherine Verdery, "What Was Socialism, and Why Did It Fall?" in Daniel Orlovsky (ed.), *Beyond Soviet Studies* (Washington, DC: Woodrow Wilson Center Press, 1995), 27–46.

78 Reinhard Bendix, *Work and Authority in Industry* (Berkeley, CA: University of California Press, 1974).

79 McDaniel, *Autocracy, Capitalism, and Revolution in Russia*; Stephen Kotkin, *Magnetic Mountain: Stalinism as Civilization* (Berkeley, CA: University of California Press, 1995), chs. 5–7.

80 Given constant falsification of economic reports and people's manipulation of "front stage" behavior, the regime relied on police reports on economic performance and public opinion.

81 Reinhard Bendix, "The Cultural and Political Setting of Economic Rationality in Western and Eastern Europe," in Gregory Grossman (ed.), *Value and Plan: Economic Calculation and Organization in Eastern Europe* (Berkeley, CA: University of California Press, 1960), 245–61; Eugenia Belova, "Economic Crime and Punishment," in Paul Gregory (ed.), *Behind the Façade of Stalin's Command Economy* (Stanford, CA: Hoover Institution Press, 2001), 131–58. Ed Hewett noted about the 1965 Kosygin reforms, "The entire 'culture' of the economic system under Stalin involved direct supervision of enterprises, the philosophy being that things only get done if enterprises are told what to do." Hewett, *Reforming the Soviet Economy*, 241.

82 James C. Scott, *Weapons of the Weak* (New Haven, CT: Yale University Press, 1985) and *Domination and the Arts of Resistance*.

83 Berliner, *Factory and Manager in the USSR*, chs. 10–12; Alena Ledeneva, *Russia's Economy of Favors* (New York: Cambridge University Press, 1998). Reliance on networks and informality stemmed from historical collectivist traditions such as peasant *zemliachestvo* and a totalitarian system that denied *formal* private spaces and in which the unknown (*chuzhoi*) person might be an informer.

84 Stephen Hoch, *Serfdom and Social Control in Russia: Petrovskoe, a Village in Tambov* (Chicago: University of Chicago Press, 1986); Daniel Field, *Rebels in the Name of the Tsar* (Boston, MA: Houghton Mifflin, 1976).

85 Donald Filtzer, *Soviet Workers and Stalinist Industrialization* (Armonk, NY: M. E. Sharpe, 1986); David Lane, *Soviet Labour and the Ethic of Communism* (Boulder, CO: Westview, 1987).

86 Caroline Humphrey, *The Unmaking of Soviet Life*, chs. 5 and 6. *Prikhvatizatsiia*, meaning "grabbing," is a play on "privatization" and implies state capture or insider privatization of the state.

87 A popular Russian joke in 2002 illustrates the culture of resistance. A psychologist bets a sociologist that he can get an American, Frenchman, and Russian standing on a bridge to jump to their deaths. The psychologist tells the American his business failed; the American jumps out of panic. He tells the Frenchman he slept with both his wife and lover; the Frenchman jumps out of despair. The psychologist then tells the Russian that it is illegal to jump off the bridge.

88 Berliner, *Factory and Manager in the USSR*; Eugenia Belova, "Economic Crime and Punishment," in Gregory (ed.), *Behind the Façade of Stalin's Command Economy*, 131–58.

89 Gregory Grossman, "The 'Second Economy' of the USSR," *Problems of Communism* 26/5 (1977), 25–40, and "The Second Economy: Boon or Bane for the Reform of the First Economy?" *Berkeley–Duke Occasional Papers on the Second Economy in the USSR* 11 (1987); K. M. Simis, *USSR: The Corrupt Society: The Secret World of Soviet Capitalism* (New York: Simon & Schuster, 1982); Arkadii Vaksberg, *The Soviet Mafia* (New York: St Martin's Press, 1991).

90 Alena Ledeneva, *How Russia Really Works* (Ithaca, NY: Cornell University Press, 2006), notes how opportunism became a core logic to informality after 1991, although *prikhvatizatsiia* has a logic of resistance.

91 William Tompson, "Old Habits Die Hard: Fiscal Imperatives, State Regulation and the Role of Russia's Banks," *Europe–Asia Studies* 49 (1997), 1159–85. "During the Brezhnev era…Soviet administrative bureaucracies were far more concerned than their Western counterparts with *directing* economic and social activities rather than *regulating* them…Russian officials since 1991 have often approached the business of marketisation in a 'task-fulfilling' frame of mind" (p. 1169).

92 Michael Burawoy, "From Sovietology to Comparative Political Economy," in Daniel Orlovsky (ed.), *Beyond Soviet Studies*, 72–102.

93 Alexei Yurchak (*Everything Was Forever*) claims younger Soviets, in the last years of the USSR, decoupled meaning from performance. Komsomol members could take their usual performances seriously (attending meetings, participating in rituals) while not giving them significance. Laws, too, were performed without meaning. The rule of law requires law be sacred; going through the motions is not enough. The USSR collapsed when performances were questioned and sanctity could not provide support.

94 William L. Blackwell, *The Beginnings of Russian Industrialization. 1800–1860* (Princeton, NJ: Princeton University Press, 1968), 58.

95 Bendix, *Work and Authority in Industry*, ch. 3.

96 Stephen Kotkin, *Steeltown USSR* (Berkeley, CA: University of California Press, 1990).

97 Humphrey, *The Unmaking of Soviet Life*, ch. 7.

98 While categorization does injustice to reality, I use some terms as ideal types for analytic purposes and as rhetorical devices (e.g. to talk of "managers" having interests or "the firm" taking some action), at the same time understanding that "state officials" or "managers" include individuals with other identities and interests. By "Red Directors" I mean managers socialized in the managerial hierarchy before 1985. "Entrepreneur" is a heuristic for people engaged in independent business and oriented to creation rather than fulfilling bureaucratic tasks. When I asked subjects what "entrepreneur" means, most noted one who owns and runs a firm (leadership and ownership).

99 For an overview of the interest–identity link, see Denise Anthony, "Cooperation in Microcredit Borrowing Groups: Identity, Sanctions, and Reciprocity in the Production of Collective Goods," *American Sociological Review* 70 (2005), 496–515; James D.

Montgomery, "Toward a Role-Theoretic Conception of Embeddedness," *American Journal of Sociology* 104 (1998), 92–125.

100 *Kompromat*, "compromising legal materials," is formal, documented violations. At heart is how such data are interpreted and used—not automatically, as in the rule of law, but selectively against political opponents. "Blackmail" (*shantazh*) is general dirt anyone can wield (e.g. revealing another's extramarital affairs). *Kompromat* is specific to the state and has a *political* connotation.

101 On Soviet-era managerial conservatism, see David Granick, *Management of the Industrial Firm in the USSR* and *The Red Executive* (Garden City, NY: Doubleday, 1960).

102 On this legacy of the Komsomol, see Yurchak, *Everything was Forever.*

103 Putin's innovation was linking local officials' interests—personal gain (corruption) or implementing law—to increasing economic control to expand state power and national glory.

104 One can see this as remaking principal–agent relations. In the Soviet system, the state was principal, managers were agents. With reforms and shifts in power, principals and agents became muddled.

105 Charles Sabel, "Studied Trust: Building New Forms of Cooperation in a Volatile Economy," in Richard Swedberg (ed.), *Explorations in Economic Sociology* (New York: Russell Sage Foundation, 1993), 105–44. Sabel claims ritualized practices and myths create identities and pressures for commonality and cooperation. "Studied distrust," as ritualized opposition and opportunism, follows logically.

2 Remaking strategy and structure in post-Soviet entrepreneurship

1 V. Listovskaia (ed.), *Biznesmeny Rossii. 40 istorii uspekha* (Moscow: OKO, 1994), 228.

2 Capitalist structures and practices vary (e.g. Japan, the USA, Germany). Yet Marx's and Weber's insight was that capitalism is a form of control, based on private property, commodification, rationalized structure and practice, structured hierarchy, and exploitation through discipline.

3 Speculation could aid production. Commodities exchanges (*birzhi*) for oil or timber began as speculation of state resources, but these helped buyers and sellers find each other (but made parasitical rather than productive entrepreneurship attractive).

4 Richard Edwards, *Contested Terrain* (New York: Basic Books, 1979).

5 Small firms in East Europe had historical legacies that provided some capital, knowledge, and practices on which post-socialist reform could build. Ivan Szelenyi, *Socialist Entrepreneurs. Embourgeoisement in Rural Hungary* (Madison, WI: University of Wisconsin Press, 1988).

6 Simon Clarke and Vadim Borisov, "New Forms of Labour Contract and Labour Flexibility in Russia," *Economics of Transition* 7/3 (1999), 593–614; Vladimir Gimpelson and Douglas Lippoldt, "Private Sector Employment in Russia. Scale, Composition, and Performance," *Economics of Transition* 7/2 (1999), 503–33; Simon Clarke and Inna Donova, "Internal Mobility and Labour Market Flexibility in Russia," *Europe–Asia Studies* 51/2 (1999), 213–43; OECD, *OECD Economic Surveys 2001–2002: Russian Federation* 2002/5 (Paris: OECD Publications, 2002).

7 Murrell, "Can Neoclassical Economics Underpin the Reform of Centrally Planned Economies?"; "Evolutionary and Radical Approaches to Economies Reform," *Economies of Planning* 25 (1992), 79–95; "What is Shock Therapy? What Did it Do in Poland and Russia?" *Post-Soviet Affairs* 9/2 (1993), 111–40. Chinese development was the gradualists' foil to shock therapy's Latin America.

8 Cf. T. Alimova, V. Buev, B. Golikova, and T. Dolgopiatova, "Problemy malogo biznesa glazami predprinimatelei," *Voprosy ekonomiki* 11 (1994), 108–23.

9 Ksenia Yudaeva, Konstantin Kozlov, Natalia Melentieva, and Natalia Ponomareva, "Does Foreign Ownership Matter? The Russian Experience," *Economics of Transition* 11 (2003), 383–409; Simon Johnson, John McMillan, and Christopher Woodruff, "Entrepreneurs and the Ordering of Institutional Reform: Poland, Slovakia, Romania, Russia and Ukraine Compared," *Economics of Transition* 8 (2000), 1–36; Elaine Buckberg, "Legal and Institutional Obstacles to Growth and Business in Russia," *Paper on Policy Analysis and Assessment of the International Monetary Fund* (1997).

10 See Gaddy and Ickes, *Russia's Virtual Economy*, on resistance to bankruptcy. Denise complained of vagaries and contradictions in tax law. If Atlas bought theater tickets for a client, when did value-added tax apply—when Atlas purchased tickets from the theater or when they sold them to the client without a mark-up? Tax inspectors gave no consistent answers. For safety Atlas sometimes charged a *double* VAT.

11 David Woodruff, "Property Rights in Context: Privatization's Legacy for Corporate Legality in Poland and Russia," *Studies in Comparative International Development* 38/4 (2004), 82–108.

12 Pfeffer, *Power in Organization* and *Managing with Power*; Fligstein, "Social Skill and the Theory of Fields."

13 James Q. Wilson, *Bureaucracy: What Government Organizations Do and Why They Do It* (Cambridge, MA: Harvard University Press, 1989).

14 On transcripts, power, and resistance, see Scott, *Domination and the Arts of Resistance.*

15 Kennedy, *Cultural Formations of Post-Communism*, 95–7.

16 The meaning of "entrepreneur" is not precise. Thane Gustafson suggests a shift in meaning: from one daring to step outside the state-run system (pre-1991), to one with strategies and vision for developing a dynamic organization. Gustafson, *Capitalism Russian-Style* (New York: Cambridge University Press, 1999), 123–7. The meaning I sensed was one who ran private business for profit or its own sake.

17 While profit might be at work, it is a vague guide to practice and change. *How much* profit should one attain, and *how* does one make it, with what role for sales versus speculation? See Chi-Nien Chung, "Institutional Transition and Cultural Inheritance: Network Ownership and Corporate Control of Business Groups in Taiwan, 1970s–1990s," *International Sociology* 19/1 (2004), 25–50.

18 Cătălin Augustin Stoica shows that socialist cadres were *structurally* well situated to turn to entrepreneurship (better networks for resources), but inevitably they became a rentier class. Non-cadres with better education were more likely to be the classical Weberian/Schumpeterian value-creating entrepreneurs. Stoica, "From Good Communists to Even Better Capitalists? Entrepreneurial Pathways in Post-Socialist Romania," *East European Politics and Societies* 4 (2000), 236–77.

19 I. M. Bunin, "Novye rossiiskie predprinimateli," in Listovskaia (ed.), *Biznesmeny Rossii*, 377. As one commentator noted, *nomenklatura* privatization could not be mass entrepreneurship, "because of the absence in the *nomenklatura* context of a wide stratum of people able to act in the market." T. Boiko, "Rossiiskie predprinimateli," *EKO* 5 (1993), 97.

20 Yurchak, *Everything Was Forever*, 296–8.

21 Peter Drucker, *Innovation and Entrepreneurship* (New York: Harper & Row, 1985).

22 Informal private work accounted for up to 17.8 billion rubles in 1985. Half of physical repair (cars, shoes, apartments, etc.) was done informally. Anders Åslund, *Gorbachev's Struggle for Economic Reform* (Ithaca, NY: Cornell University Press, 1989), 150–2.

23 T. Alimova, V. Buev, B. Golikova, and T. Dolgopiatova, "Problemy malogo biznesa glazami predprinimatelei," *Voprosy ekonomiki* 11 (1994), 114; OECD, *OECD Economic Surveys 2001–2002*, 76; A. Vilenskii, "Etapy razvitiia malogo predprinimatel'stva v Rossii," *Voprosy ekonomiki* 7 (1996), 30–8. Simon Ostrovsky claims, "There were 843,000 small businesses, 262,000 farms and a staggering 4.5 million individual entrepreneurs at the beginning of 2001…or 37 small businesses per 1,000 people. There are 40 to 60

small businesses per 1,000 people in the European Union" ("New Data: More Small Businesses," *St. Petersburg Times* July 2, 2002).

24 I. M. Bunin, "Novye rossiiskie predprinimateli," in Listovskaia (ed.), *Biznesmeny Rossii*, 392–9; Martha de Melo, *Private Service Firms in a Transitional Economy: Findings of a Survey in St. Petersburg* (New York: World Bank, 1994); Martha de Melo, Gur Ofer, and Olga Sandler, "Pioneers for Profit: St. Petersburg Entrepreneurs in Services," *World Bank Economic Review* 9/3 (1995), 425–50; Darrell Slider, "Embattled Entrepreneurs: Soviet Cooperatives in an Unreformed Economy," *Soviet Studies* 43/5 (1991), 797–821. Even in the 1990s profit and personal meaning were the two most important aspects of independent business. A. A. Voz'mitel', *Sposoby biznese i sposoby zhizni rossiiskikh predprinimatelei* (Moscow: Institut sotsiologiia RAN, 1997), 64. One small firm owner who sold car components and rudimentary electronic goods opened one of Petersburg's earliest co-operatives to realize his own autonomy. Interview Carpart-1, Dec. 1995.

25 O. V. Tokarenko claims 93% of early entrepreneurs were in "commerce," 3% in finance, and 4% in production. Tokarenko, "Russkie kak predprinimateli (istoricheskie korni ustanovok i povedeniia)," *Mir Rossii* 5/1 (1996), 195–207, esp. p. 196. I. M. Bunin claimed most small private firms were in industry and construction—most likely because state enterprises spun off construction subdivisions and brigades as "small firms." Bunin, "Novye rossiiskie predprinimateli," in Listovskaia (ed.), *Biznesmeny Rossii*, 379. By 2000 trade and catering dominated small business: *OECD Economic Surveys*, 78.

26 A. Blinov, "Maloe predprinimatel'stvo i bol'shaia politika," *Voprosy ekonomiki* 7 (1996), 39–45; A. Chepurenko, "Problema finansirovaniia v rossiiskom malom biznese (po materialam vyborochnykh sotsiologicheskikh obsledovanii)," *Voprosy ekonomiki* 7 (1996), 59–71; T. Dolgopiatova, I. Evseeva, and V. Shironin, "Rol' zakonodatel'stva i regulirovaniia v stanovlenii malogo biznesa v Rossii," *Voprosy ekonomiki* 11 (1994), 92–107.

27 Small firm owners preferred to close their firms rather than go bankrupt or restructure, given required procedures, time, and costs (around $1000 in 1999). Vadim Radaev, "Informalization of Rules in Russian Economy," Annual Conference of the International Society for New Institutional Economics, Session XV (Tubingen, Sept. 22–4, 2000), 8. Many new firms were *de facto* expansions of existing firms—this was easier under tax law. *OECD Economic Surveys*, 78.

28 A. Vilenskii, "Etapy razvitiia malogo predprinimatel'stva v Rossii," *Voprosy ekonomiki* 7 (1996), 30–8.

29 Listovskaia (ed.), *Biznesmeny Rossii*, 225–7, 248, 296–7, 337. Entrepreneur Dmitrii Elkin criticized banks and businessmen for going for quick money, rather than long-term development strategies. Listovskaia (ed.), *Biznesmeny Rossii*, 307–15; also Bunin, "Novye rossiiskie predprinimateli," in *Biznesmeny Rossii*, 379–82. When I asked one young computer expert who opened a software firm in Tula about hiring and sales strategies, he answered by asking: "I don't know, I've never thought about it. Do you have any ideas?" Interview Rom-2, Nov. 1995.

30 In 1993 entrepreneur Vladimir Dovgan' opened a franchise for his "Doka-Pizza" but admitted, "the franchises made junk" and "money we spent on advertising was thrown to the winds." Practices, not economic instability, killed his idea. Gustafson, *Capitalism Russian-Style*, 117.

31 Listovskaia (ed.), *Biznesmeny Rossii*, 247.

32 Ibid., pp. 332, 345. Economics was stagnant by the 1980s, and the sciences best prepared people for business. D. L'vov, *Razvitie ekonomiki Rossii i zadachi ekonomicheskoi nauki* (Moscow: Ekonomika, 1999), 19–22.

33 Rude clerks were the bane of Soviet stores. The founder of the Antanta store chain (1992) hired young girls with no Soviet work experience, uncontaminated by Soviet rudeness. Simon Clarke and Veronika Kabalina claim: "Many [private firm] employers

also said that they preferred to take on people who were young enough not to have been socialised into the old work ethic, so that they could turn them into employees suitable for work in new conditions." Clarke and Kabalina, "The New Private Sector in the Russian Labour Market," *Europe–Asia Studies* 52 (2000), 12.

34 To entrepreneur Igor Sagirian, shadow business is a response to state interference. He says nothing about why *he* does not work in the shadows. Listovskaia (ed.), *Biznesmeny Rossii*, 227. See also Ledeneva, *Russia's Economy of Favors*.

35 This could appear as shadow behavior inside firms. Entrepreneur Sergei Orlov discovered several employees working *nalevo* (on the side) inside his private firm, using the firm's resources and neglecting formal duties. He fired them. Listovskaia (ed.), *Biznesmeny Rossii*, 361.

36 Small private firms tended to have better discipline and productivity than former state-owned firms, reflected in fewer breaks and partly due to flexible wage schemes and less job security. Clarke and Borisov, "New Forms of Labour Contract and Labour Flexibility in Russia," esp. pp. 601–10.

37 I observed Atlas informally in July 1991 and Feb.–July 1993, and formally in Aug. 1994–Feb. 1995, randomly in 1995, and briefly in summer 1999 and 2001. I observed Economics Inc. formally Aug. 1994–Dec. 1995, and brief observations and interviews in summer 1997, 1999, and 2001. I chose these firms because I had access to their inner workings.

38 My field notes mention little activity. This paragraph is a composite of many days, an "ideal type."

39 In chemistry, this is a means to discover energy levels of components of atoms or molecules: blast the object with energy and perturb its energy levels.

40 This led to a brief confrontation between Aleksei and Denise. Aleksei sometimes used Ivan for tasks, e.g. organizing currency exchange. Denise claimed this interfered with work and was Aleksei's attempt to be the boss. If Aleksei wanted these services he should do them himself or come to the office every day rather than work through Ivan.

41 In April 1993, two Dutch students showed up and asked for rooms they claimed a tour firm (not Atlas) had arranged. The *dezhurnaia* (entrance guard) replied that rooms were only for guests of the Mayor. Aleksei said his networks to the hotel director avoided this restriction.

42 Elizabeth Moss Kanter claims this is a crucial approach to change. *When Giants Learn to Dance* (New York: Free Press, 1990).

43 Contrast this to the experience of another entrepreneur who hired a professionally qualified accountant. The accountant knew the entrepreneur was cheating on taxes—not unusual, given Russia's unclear and onerous tax law—and demanded a bribe or he would take the books to tax authorities. The entrepreneur phoned his bandits, who took the books from the accountant. The entrepreneur decided to hire only trusted acquaintances. Interview MechGood-1, Nov. 1995.

44 On local knowledge versus broader constructions of legitimate knowledge, see Kennedy, *Cultural Formations of Postcommunism*, ch. 3.

45 Note the language and the overall meaning in this evaluation of Ivan's life, repeated by Ivan's acquaintances outside Atlas. To say Ivan "lost his way" assumes a normal "way" to lose—demonstrating how anti-Soviet logics were normal and Soviet values abnormal. (Often people assumed senior citizens with similar values were old, conservative, and had sacrificed their lives for a defunct system and were to be pitied as nostalgic.) Those commenting on Ivan were in their thirties and lived in St. Petersburg. I suspect elsewhere, e.g. Tula (where I also observed daily life), more people would sympathize with Ivan.

46 Misha asked British and American colleagues to help with grant proposals. This provided legitimacy for foreign agencies eager to fund projects for helping the market transition.

47 At any time four secretaries did work that required only two. Yet Misha retained all four—most were near pension age. Only by 2000 were more secretaries in their twenties.

48 Interview D-Com (former commercial director of Economics Inc.), Nov. 1995. This person added that his cousin worked in a Moscow import–export firm that was squeezed by formidable competitors. They had competent managers who enforced discipline and effectively implemented business plans; personal relations were outside the firm's ethos. He sensed this firm's practices were the exception in Russia.

49 Misha blamed "negative" behavior on Soviet influences. When one woman complained of not being paid on time, Misha claimed they were acting as in Soviet days—thinking of nothing but money (!).

50 Interview D-Com.

51 Misha and his assistant managers tried to contact individual bookstores abroad directly. Only a few specialty stores replied. In 2002 Economics Inc. updated the dictionary and used the same tactic of calling small stores, with the same lack of success.

52 Unlike in the West, where authors send manuscripts to publishers who also organize sales, Economics Inc. organized and wrote up literature, ordered it printed, collected the printed material, and distributed it themselves. They made the outlay for printing but also recouped full profits rather than just a royalty.

53 Ironically, as a professor of economics, Misha should have been aware of misreading unit prices *and* of studying demand. Yet unit costs, not marketing, dominated decision-making.

54 Two male employees who did grunt work for courses in autumn 1994—e.g. accompanying clients (managers, accountants) to courses, meals, and tours—used this chance to network. An assistant manager hired them for his finance department, with better pay and experience than Economics Inc. could provide.

55 Scott, *Weapons of the Weak*; Hoch, *Serfdom and Social Control in Russia*.

56 Compare this with American capitalism, where social norms demand work. One need not work but could starve; the choice is the individual's. Jay MacLeod, *Ain't No Makin It* (Boulder, CO: Westview, 1995), and Bendix, *Work and Authority in Industry*.

57 One incident shows Misha's weakness with precise organization. A well-organized American woman working as a guide approached Economics Inc. in early 1995 for help organizing activities for her American clients. Complaining that Mariinskii Theater did not publish its schedule for the next season—hindering planning efforts—she suggested she and Misha check their planning diaries to arrange future meetings. She looked months ahead in her calendar; he sat stunned and went through the motions of looking for a future date. She proposed middle June, many months ahead. Potential joint work did not materialize because Misha did not take her or such planning seriously. Given the emerging crisis at Economics Inc. in early 1995, and his assignment to Inna to find potential business or academic clients, it seems irrational that he did not jump at this opportunity—but this betrayed his own logics.

58 In 1993 and 1994 Economics Inc. sold goods without charging VAT; Misha claimed labor exchange officials said a non-profit institute selling educational literature did not need to do so. In 1995 one female worker—hired because her father ran the school where Economics Inc. was located—left unpleasantly. When she demanded her wages (almost no one was being paid), Misha accused her of sloppy work. She threatened to tell the tax police of the VAT issue, and a tax inspector arrived to levy a hefty fine.

59 This was the typical response to crises I address in Chapter 4: rather than reorient production and sales to real demand, instead to waste time and resources, flooding the market with goods to find solvent consumers.

60 By itself this is no sin. When a project involves considerable time and resources, feasibility should be ascertained as accurately as possible. Yet Economics Inc. managers with whom I talked did not think of studying potential demand—what

buyers might want. As economists who interacted with Western experts, they had basic skills applicable to marketing—or at least they should have been *alert* to marketing.

61 Matvei relayed this account in summer 2007. I was not able to contact Misha to verify the story, but Matvei's earlier accounts held up to scrutiny, and he had no bias for or against Misha or Economics Inc.

62 It might seem Misha was outright incompetent. He lacked knowledge of how to create and enforce habits, structure, and identities of an organized, flexible, productive organization that could survive Russia's economy. He was also kind-hearted, better suited to being a professor than a manager. His failure was due less to inherent faults than the mismatch between his logics and those defined as normal market norms.

63 This is an interesting corrective to Gaddy and Ickes's interpretation, in which firms that cannot produce for the market must go into the virtual economy or die. This assumes quality goods find a market. Yet market adaptation meant learning new sales strategies and practices. Quality producers could be value-destroyers *not* because of inherent production weaknesses (e.g. bad equipment).

3 Contradictions and conflict unleashed

1 *Leningradskii stankostroitel'* Oct. 20, 1993, p. 1.

2 Olga Kuznetsova and Andrei Kuznetsov, "The State as a Shareholder: Responsibilities and Objectives," *Europe–Asia Studies* 51 (1999), 433–45.

3 Cf. Beissinger, *Nationalist Mobilization and the Collapse of the Soviet State.*

4 Melville Dalton, *Men Who Manage* (New York: John Wiley & Sons, 1959).

5 This resembles "garbage can theory": claims are thrown into the "garbage can," from which new policies emerge (i.e. "garbage in, garbage out"). Michael Cohen, James March, and Johan P. Olsen, "A Garbage Can Model of Organizational Choice," *Administrative Science Quarterly* 17 (1972), 1–25.

6 For a quick overview see William P. Barnett and Glenn R. Carroll, "Modeling Internal Organizational Change," *Annual Review of Sociology* 21 (1995), 217–36; J. T. Hage, "Organizational Innovation and Organizational Change," *Annual Review of Sociology* 25 (1999), 597–622; Myeong-Gu Seo and W. E. Douglas Creed, "Institutional Contradictions, Praxis, and Institutional Change: A Dialectical Perspective," *Academy of Management Review* 27 (2002), 222–47.

7 Simeon Djankov defined "restructuring" vaguely and broadly as "changes in operations, interactions and motivation towards success in a changing market environment." Djankov, "The Restructuring of Insider-Dominated Firms," *Economics of Transition* 7 (1999), 467–79. Blasi *et al* (*Kremlin Capitalism*, 125) conceptualize it as changing routines, capital sources, control, and provision.

8 E.g. Harry Braverman, *Labor and Monopoly Capital: The Degradation of Work in the Twentieth Century* (New York: Monthly Review Press, 1974); Michael Burawoy, *Manufacturing Consent* (Chicago: University of Chicago Press, 1979) and *The Politics of Production: Factory Regimes under Capitalism and Socialism* (London: Verso, 1985).

9 See my *Economic Sociology* (New York: Routledge, 2007), ch. 5.

10 Neil Fligstein and Kenneth Dauber, "Structural Change in Corporate Organization," *Annual Review of Sociology* 15 (1989), 73–96; Lynne G. Zucker, "Institutional Theories of Organization," *Annual Review of Sociology* 13 (1987), 443–64.

11 E.g. John R. Sutton and Frank Dobbin, "The Two Faces of Governance: Responses to Legal Uncertainty in U.S. Firms, 1955 to 1985," *American Sociological Review* 61 (1996), 794–811; Frank Dobbin, *Inventing Equal Opportunity* (Princeton, NJ: Princeton University Press, 2009).

12 David Stark, "Rethinking Internal Labor Markets: New Insights from a Comparative Perspective," *American Sociological Review* 51 (1986), 492–504.

13 Michael Burawoy and Pavel Krotov, "The Soviet Transition from Socialism to Capitalism: Worker Control and Economic Bargaining in the Wood Industry," *American Sociological Review* 57 (1992), 16–38; Michael Burawoy and Kathryn Hendley, "Between Perestroika and Privatisation: Divided Strategies and Political Crisis in a Soviet Enterprise," *Soviet Studies* 44 (1992), 371–402; Kotkin, *Armageddon Averted*, ch. 5.

14 Stephen Crowley, *Hot Coal, Cold Steel: Russian and Ukrainian Workers from the End of the Soviet Union to the Post-Communist Transformations* (Ann Arbor, MI: University of Michigan Press, 1997). Crowley's use of cultural frames is less well integrated into his structural account, and his explanation relies on a money nexus to explain coal workers' militancy, despite the underdevelopment of market and money. Debra Javeline's study of blame relies on narrow attitudinal survey data: *Protest and the Politics of Blame: The Russian Response to Unpaid Wages* (Ann Arbor, MI: University of Michigan Press, 2003).

15 Simon Clarke (ed.), *Management and Industry in Russia; Conflict and Change in the Russian Industrial Enterprise* (Cheltenham: Edward Elgar, 1996); *The Russian Enterprise in Transition: Case Studies* (Cheltenham: Edward Elgar, 1996).

16 McDermott (*Embedded Politics*) fits cases into an instrumental logic, rather than analyzing change on its own terms.

17 Clarke *et al* note the *kollektiv* as social identity and boundary. Sarah Ashwin produced important work on *kollektiv* meanings and mobilization, e.g. "Redefining the Collective: Russian Mineworkers in Transitions," in Burawoy and Verdery (eds), *Uncertain Transition*, 245–71.

18 Sabel, "Studied Trust," suggests interests and identities are contingent. On interests and cultural processes, see Paul DiMaggio, "Interest and Agency in Institutional Theory," in Lynne Zucker (ed.), *Institutional Patterns and Organization* (Cambridge, MA: Ballinger, 1988), 3–21. The *search* for new roles and interests in changing contexts is elided in these studies.

19 Hallett, "Symbolic Power and Organizational Culture."

20 Katz, *The Politics of Economic Reform*, 120, 144–7; Hewett, *Reforming the Soviet Economy*, 245–50. See also case histories of electronics firms Pozitron and Svetlana: A. A. V'iunik, *Vsegda v poiske: istoriia Leningradskogo nauchno-proizvodstvennogo obedineniia "Pozitron"* (Leningrad: Lenizdat, 1987); *"Svetlana": Istoriia Leningradskogo obedineniia elektronnogo priborostroeniia "Svetlana"* (Leningrad: Lenizdat, 1986). Informal networks cut across structure, but informality reflected off formal *obedinenie* structures. Berliner, *Factory and Manager in the USSR*, chs. 6, 7, 11, and 12.

21 Alec Nove, *The Soviet Economic System* (Boston, MA: George Allen & Unwin, 1977), 79–84. Terms include *obedinenie*, *predpriiatie*, and *zavod*; and *tsekh* (shopfloor) and *podrazdelenie* (subdivision).

22 Ed Hewett, *Reforming the Soviet Economy*, 249–55.

23 Simon Clarke, Peter Fairbrother, Vadim Borisov, and Pëtr Bizyukov, "The Privatisation of Industrial Enterprises in Russia: Four Case-studies," *Europe–Asia Studies* 46 (1994), 179–214; T. P. Cheremisina, "Arendnye predpriiatiia: analiz opyta privatizatsii," *EKO* 1 (1994), 75–88.

24 Pozitron set up an SP with Daewoo to import and assemble VCRs, but Daewoo dropped Pozitron. *Maiak* Feb. 27, 1992, pp. 1, 3; Dec. 17, 1992, p. 1. Kirov set up a useful SP venture with Caterpillar: *Kirovets* Nov. 3, 1994, pp. 2–4.

25 Interview Stnk/Prod-1, March 1995.

26 *Krasnyi treugol'nik* April 18, 1991, p. 2. Pilot AP "Rezina" was opened to improve waste collection and transport. *Krasnyi treugol'nik* Jan. 11, 1991, p. 1.

27 Claudio Morrison and Gregory Schwartz, "Managing the Labour Collective: Wage Systems in the Russian Industrial Enterprise," *Europe–Asia Studies* 55 (2003), 553–74; Gregory Schwartz, "Employment Restructuring in Russian Industrial Enterprises: Confronting a 'Paradox,'" *Work, Employment and Society* 17 (2003), 49–72.

28 *Leningradskii stankostroitel'* Feb. 7, 1994, p. 2. Iurii Shafranskii, manager of MP Universal, claimed independence helped keep skilled cadres. *Leningradskii stankostroitel'* May 17,

1994, p. 3. By 1997 Universal suffered "financial overstretch." Interview Psk-1, July 1997.

29 T. Boiko, "Rossiiskie predprinimateli," *EKO* 5 (1993), 93–105; Kotkin, *Armageddon Averted*, ch. 5. Sometimes the shell game had a market logic: "new [shell] structures exploited entrepreneurial qualities...AO 'Neftekhim,' created in Nov. 1991 by enterprises of the former Ministry of Chemical and Oil Refining Industry, was headed not by a ministerial bureaucrat or 'Red Director,' but by the head of a consulting firm who began his career as a cooperative boss" (Boiko, p. 98).

30 Boris Sokolin, *Krizisnaia ekonomika Rossii: Rubezh tysiacheletii* (St. Petersburg: Liki Rossii, 1997), 158–9. A good example of the shell game was at St. Petersburg's military-industrial firm Arsenal. In 1990 and 1991 managers created co-operatives, joint ventures, and MPs, that used Arsenal equipment and space at cheap rates. Daughter Arton produced civilian output, and was privatized in autumn 1991 with financial help from independent firm Khoks—which some believed was indirectly owned by Arsenal managers. New firm TOO Arton-Khoks continued to sell goods produced by Arsenal. In 1992 Arton became a private AO (*aktsionernoe obshchestvo*), with 51% of capital and shares owned by Arsenal and 49% by Khoks and Arton-Khoks. The venture made a profit of 8 million rubles, a good sum considering Arton's official worth was 16,000 rubles. *Sankt-Peterburgskoe Ekho* Jan. 27, 1993, p. 22.

31 "Sverkhchernye superdyry," *Ogonëk* 43 (Oct. 1995), 22–3; David E. Hoffman, *The Oligarchs: Wealth and Power in the New Russia* (New York: PublicAffairs, 2002). Using daughters to evade taxes and debts or to launder money was legion, as were problems tracking assets or controlling daughters. "Gazprom vybral bankrotstvo," *Vedemosti* Jan. 24, 2002; "'Dochki' RAO EES deliat imushchestvo," *Vedemosti* Jan. 30, 2002.

32 *Turbostroitel'* Dec. 28, 1992, p. 5.

33 Sokolin, *Krizisnaia ekonomika Rossii*, 158.

34 *Svetlana* Jan. 22, 1992, p. 2.

35 Trade unions (*profsoiuzy*) negotiated labor contracts and articulated employees' claims, but often were no better than workers' clubs. In the 1989 miners' strikes, trade unions played a minor role. Walter Connor, *Tattered Banners: Labor, Conflict, and Corporatism in Postcommunist Russia* (Boulder, CO: Westview, 1996); Peter Rutland, "Labor Unrest and Movements in 1989 and 1990," *Soviet Economy* 6 (1990), 345–84. A workers' club at Krasnaia Zaria expressed these goals: "to render moral and material help and support to laborers...in difficult circumstances" and "the struggle for democratization of trade unions", "the struggle for social justice", "the interaction with trade union organizations, with the goal of the defense of rights and interests of laborers," and "assistance for the moral and cultural development of laborers." "Ustav obshchestvenno-politicheskogo kluba 'Rabochaia Initsiativa' pri LNPO 'Krasnaia Zaria'" (g. Leningrad)," in *Rossiia segodnia: politicheskii portret v dokumentakh* (Moscow: Mezhdunarodnye otnosheniia, 1991), 326, 328.

36 Mst. Afanas'ev, P. Kuznetsov, and A. Fominykh, "Korporativnoe upravlenie glazami direktorata (po materialam obsledovanii 1994-1996 gg)," *Voprosy ekonomiki* 5 (1997), 84–101.

37 See interviews with KB bosses and engineers, *Svetlana* June 19, 1991, p. 5, and Jan. 22, 1992, p. 2.

38 *Elektrosila* Feb. 15, 1990, p. 5; also *Leningradskii stankostroitel'* April 16, 1991, p. 3.

39 Robert Eccles, *The Transfer Pricing Problem* (Lexington, MA: Lexington Books, 1985).

40 *Krasnyi treugol'nik* Feb. 20, 1991, p. 3; also March 6, 1991, p. 2, and April 18, 1991, p. 2.

41 Andrew Walder, *Communist Neotraditionalism* (Berkeley, CA: University of California Press, 1986); Kotkin, *Steeltown, USSR*; Simon Clarke (ed.), *Conflict and Change in the Russian Industrial Enterprise* (Cheltenham: Edward Elgar, 1996), and (ed.) *The Russian Enterprise in Transition: Case Studies* (Cheltenham: Edward Elgar, 1996). Paternalism was not unique to Soviet socialism, but its historical specifics and penetration institutions and meanings more deeply. One might cite political incentives, e.g. provision as bribe

for stability, but this misses how much the safety net unraveled. Political fear did not prevent directors from not paying employees for months. Yet some money *was* spent on construction, renovating churches, and daycare.

42 E. V. Gudkova and A. A. Get'man, "Predpriiatiia mashinostroeniia Dal'nego Vostoka v usloviiakh ekonomicheskoi reformy," *EKO* 4 (1998), 90–1; Simon Clarke, "The Enterprise in the Era of Transition," in Clarke (ed.), *The Russian Enterprise in Transition*, esp. pp. 49–57.

43 Interview Stnk/Sa-2, March 1995. Managers would fire *individual* employees for egregious labor code violations. *Leningradskii stankostroitel'* March 6, 1989, pp. 2–3, and Jan. 29, 1992, p. 1; *Kirovets* Feb. 12, 1993, pp. 1–6, and Feb. 17, 1993, pp. 3–6.

44 P. Ia. Dobrynin, "Privatizatsiia v VPK," *EKO* 4 (1993), 3–16, esp. p. 6. Managers could not pay wages for up to six months; withholding severance pay was not difficult. Yet paternalist duty and labor shortages mitigated against using unemployment to buttress authority. Some firms skirted wage ceilings by hiring employees to two organizations, paying two salaries. *Elektrosila* Nov. 24, 1993, p. 2.

45 *Kirovets* Aug. 9, 1993, p. 4; also Feb. 5, 1993, p. 2; March 3, 1993, p. 1; Aug. 9, 1993, p. 4. Kirov lost one-third of employees in the 1990s to retirement or exit. In 1994 Sergei Beliaev, head of the Federal Administration for Insolvency Affairs (Bankruptcy), criticized Kirov for "hidden unemployment" and "quiet liquidation"—maintaining fictitious employment to dismiss suspicions of insolvency. "Bankrotstvo: Plany, perspektivy, protsedury," *EKO* 8 (1994), 47–53.

46 Shershneva was under suspicion. Otdykh-Servis was founded by Ol'shaniki *pansionat* employees, but an investigation revealed fraudulent protocols and documents. *Baltiets* Aug. 21, 1992, p. 1.

47 *Baltiets* Aug. 28, 1992, p. 3; Sept. 9, 1992, p. 1; Sept. 15, 1992, pp. 3–4. This *pansionat* is still there, on the road along the Gulf of Finland to Zelenogorsk.

48 Beissinger, *Nationalist Mobilization and the Collapse of the Soviet State*.

49 Ship-maker Baltiiskii Zavod split its production divisions (metallurgy, ship-building, machine-building) and reunited them as a shareholder-run *kholding* with legally independent daughters. Baltiiskii's general director cloaked the *kholding* in language of the *kollektiv*. *Baltiets* Dec. 14, 1993, pp. 2–3.

50 Interview Stnk/Sa-1, March 1995, and Stnk/Prod-1, March 1995; *Leningradskii stankostroitel'* Oct. 20, 1993, p. 1.

51 Interview Stank/Gendir-2, Feb. 1995; interview Stnk/Sa-2, March 1995.

52 Ministry of Finance of the Russian Federation, *Predpriiatii na puti reform (polozhitel'nyi opyt raboty)*. *Materialy soveshchaniia rukovoditelei promyshlennykh predpriiatii* (Moscow: Ministry of Finance, 1993), p. 19.

53 Shopfloor bosses and workers blamed financial trouble on the broader crisis, not bad products or work. *Leningradskii stankostroitel'* Feb. 5, 1992, p. 3, and March 5, 1992, p. 2; *Kirovets* Dec. 14, 1992, p. 1; *Elektrosila* Dec. 3, 1992, p. 2, and Dec. 8, 1992, p. 1; Mst. Afanas'ev, P. Kuznetsov, and A. Fominykh, "Korporativnoe upravlenie glazami direktorata (po materialam obsledovanii 1994–1996 gg)," *Voprosy ekonomiki* 5 (1997), 84–101.

54 Interview SevFurn, July 1997.

55 Irina Starodubrovskaia, "Ekonomicheskaia reforma: mnenie direktorskogo korpusa," *EKO* 10 (1993), 123.

56 Tatiana Dolgopiatova, "Povedenie predpriiatii v usloviiakh zhestkikh finansovykh ogranichenii," *Rossiiskii ekonomicheskii zhurnal* 12 (1994), 68.

57 *Oktiabr'skaia magistral'* Jan. 22, 1994, p. 1. October Railroad continued "socialist competitions."

58 *Oktiabr'skaia magistral'* June 7, 1994, p. 2.

59 Interview Beer-2, July 1999.

60 There is a *symbolic* as well as *technical* aspect to organizational structure. It may have been easier to use the shell game at electronics firms. Managers could use "projects" to

obtain research money and use it otherwise, i.e. buying cheap goods to resell at higher prices. The abstract nature of research allowed "grant holders" to keep "investors" at bay. Alas, I found no formal evidence of this in published sources.

61 It is possible, but difficult to prove definitively, that managers playing the shell game were more likely to embrace decentralization to legitimate reforms and deflect attention.

62 Gaventa, *Power and Powerlessness*, ch. 8.

63 In Fligstein's "social skills" framework, this is the danger of "blustering" (confrontation or dictation). Fligstein, "Social Skill and the Theory of Fields," 114.

64 *Turbostroitel'* Jan. 5, 1990, p. 10, June 29, 1990, p. 8, and July 20, 1990, p. 2.

65 *Turbostroitel'* April 28, 1989, p. 5, and Feb. 16, 1990, p. 10. A similar story occurred at SSK, an agricultural machine-maker that turned to apartment construction. The director quickly abandoned AP/MP forms and rebuilt hierarchy. Shopfloor chiefs did not resist; they produced for a single product and client. The assistant director for sales/marketing and a shopfloor chief related these data in July 1999.

66 *Turbostroitel'* Jan. 25, 1991, p. 5.

67 *Turbostroitel'* Feb. 21, 1992, p. 5, and April 3, 1992, p. 3; Feb. 28, 1992, p. 2.

68 At the 1999 labor conference, with LMZ insolvent and under temporary outside administration, managers bragged that despite 375 million rubles ($15 million) of debt LMZ provided goods and services—1,100 employees at summer camps, 1,500 children at a children's camps—unlike LOMO or Western firms. This echoed the Soviet moral economy. *Turbostroitel'* March 25, 1999, p. 2, and June 10, 1999, p. 1.

69 *Turbostroitel'* Jan. 13, 1994, p. 1; Feb. 3, 1994, p. 1; and March 16, 1995, p. 1.

70 One axis of potential variation I bracket is cross-regional. Brief interviews in Tula did not suggest significantly different claims and experiences. See reviews of Stoner-Weiss' *Local Heroes* by Lynn D. Nelson, *Slavic Review* 57 (1998), 933–5; and William M. Reisinger, *American Political Science Review* 93 (1999), 739.

71 Absence of conflict in newspaper accounts might indicate ambivalence as well as managerial control of discourse. The general effect is the same: the second dimension of power is more circumscribed.

72 I examined more cases than Kirov, Sverdlov, and Pozitron. These three capture general variation.

73 Interview Elec-1, July 1997. Sverdlov management may have used less easily discoverable formal and informal tactics (e.g. *kompromat*) to maintain organizational coherence.

74 Svetlana assistant directors whom I interviewed in 1997 studied Pozitron's politics to avoid its fate.

75 We can also view think of these dimensions as *managerial authority* (the *x*-axis, discourse and normality) and *relations between units* (the *y*-axis, structure), with managerial authority as strong or relaxed and opportunity as low or high (strong/weak interdependence).

76 Svetlana electronics fits quadrant III, but for reasons of space I leave it out. Its dynamics initially resembled those of Pozitron, but contingencies altered its outcome. See Conclusion, n.41.

77 *Kirovets* Jan. 12, 1989, p. 2, and Aug. 1, 1989, pp. 1–3.

78 *Kirovets* Feb. 9, 1989, pp. 3–4.

79 *Kirovets* March 28, 1989, p. 2, and June 19, 1989, p. 2.

80 *Kirovets* June 28, 1991, p. 3.

81 *Kirovets* Feb. 1, 1989, p. 3.

82 *Kirovets* Aug. 21, 1989, p. 3.

83 *Kirovets* Jan. 17, 1989, p. 2.

84 *Kirovets* Aug. 1, 1989, pp. 1–3.

85 *Kirovets* Aug. 22, 1989, p. 1.

86 *Kirovets* Aug. 25, 1989, p. 1.

87 One shopfloor boss said, "To make the transition to *khozraschët*...we need to bring in outside specialists, we need long preparation. The most important [aspect] is cadres." *Kirovets* Aug. 25, 1989, p. 1.

88 *Kirovets* Aug. 31, 1989, p. 1.

89 *Kirovets* June 28, 1991, p. 2; and June 18, 1993, p. 2. Kirov also entered six enterprise associations.

90 *Kirovets* May 5, 1991, p. 2.

91 *Kirovets* May 20, 1991, p. 2.

92 *Kirovets* June 3, 1991, p. 2.

93 *Kirovets* June 28, 1991, p. 2.

94 *Kirovets* July 11, 1991, p. 3.

95 *Kirovets* June 28, 1991, pp. 2–3.

96 *Kirovets* Jan. 4, 1992, p. 1.

97 *Kirovets* Sept. 3, 1992, pp. 1, 2; and Sept. 7, 1992, p. 1.

98 *Kirovets* Jan. 4, 1992, p. 2.

99 *Kirovets* Jan. 10, 1992, p. 1.

100 *Kirovets* June 3, 1992, pp. 2–3.

101 *Kirovets* Aug. 27, 1992, p. 1.

102 *Kirovets* Sept. 25, 1992, pp. 1–2; Oct. 12, 1992, p. 1.

103 *Kirovets* May 21, 1992, p. 2. "Pocket banks" were private banks created with enterprise funds and run by enterprises. They would attract funds to provide cheap loans to their founding industrial enterprises.

104 *Kirovets* Oct. 12, 1992, p. 1.

105 *Kirovets* Sept. 16, 1992, p. 2.

106 *Kirovets* April 30, 1993, p. 1, and Aug. 9, 1993, p. 3.

107 The new schema was published in *Kirovets* July 7, 1993, and refined in later issues.

108 *Kirovets* Jan. 29, 1993, p. 1. This boss complained that shopfloor chiefs should not be responsible for finding buyers: "I consider transferring the search for orders to shoulders of shopfloor bosses is at present bringing certain negative results, but it would be significantly more advantageous for the enterprise if this work were taken up on a professional basis by corresponding factory [i.e. central] services."

109 *Kirovets* Feb. 10, 1993, p. 2.

110 *Kirovets* Feb. 19, 1993, p. 2.

111 *Kirovets* March 17, 1993, p. 1.

112 *Kirovets* June 28, 1993, pp. 2–3.

113 *Kirovets* Sept. 25, 1992, p. 1.

114 *Kirovets* Sept. 2, 1992, p. 1.

115 On using moral frames to support a contradictory policy, see Viviana Zelizer, *Morals and Markets: The Development of Life Insurance in the United States* (New Brunswick, NJ: Transaction Books, 1983).

116 *Kirovets* Aug. 9, 1993, p. 3.

117 *Kirovets* March 17, 1993, p. 1.

118 *Kirovets* Feb. 19, 1993, pp. 2–3, and April 30, 1993, p. 2.

119 *Kirovets* Jan. 19, 1995, pp. 2–4.

120 *Kirovets* July 3, 1992, p. 2.

121 *Kirovets* Jan. 29, 1993, p. 3.

122 *Kirovets* Feb. 11, 1994, p. 5.

123 *Kirovets* July 7, 1994, p. 2.

124 *Kirovets* Nov. 20, 1992, p. 1.

125 *Kirovets* Jan. 29, 1993, pp. 2–3.

126 *Kirovets* Aug. 9, 1993, pp. 3–5.

127 *Kirovets* Dec. 10, 1993, p. 2.

128 Another account put the number of daughter firms at 33. *Kirovets* July 24, 1997, p. 3.

129 *Kirovets* Oct. 12, 1995, pp. 2–4.

130 *Kirovets* Nov. 13, 1997, p. 3.
131 On one study of the efficient use of space, see ibid.
132 Ibid., p. 4, and Oct. 30, 1997, pp. 2–3.
133 Andrey Musatov and Thomas Rymer, "200 Years of Industrial Revolution," *Moscow Times* March 19, 2001; John Varoli, "Kirovsky, John Deere Battle for $1 Bln," *St. Petersburg Times* April 20, 1999.
134 *Kirovets* June 12, 1997, p. 2; July 17, 1997, p. 5; April 9, 1998, p. 3.
135 *Kirovets* Dec. 10, 1998, p. 4. In ZAO form, shares could be sold to outside people or organizations only with permission of existing insider shareholders, providing secure control.
136 *Kirovets* Jan. 22, 1998, pp. 6–7. In 1997 this daughter it was "hopelessly" behind in output plans. *Kirovets* June 12, 1997, p. 2.
137 *Kirovets* April 9, 1998, pp. 3, 6.
138 Cited in Musatov and Rymer, "200 Years of Industrial Revolution."
139 *Kirovets* July 17, 1997, pp. 2–3.
140 *Kirovets* Aug. 27, 1998, p. 2; Oct. 8, 1998, pp. 1–2, 4–5. In the late 1990s Petrostal's sales to car makers brought in half of Kirov's income: Varoli, "Kirovsky, John Deere Battle for $1 Bln."
141 *Kirovets* April 22, 1999, p. 3.
142 *Kirovets* March 4, 1999, pp. 4–5. After 1999 *Kirovets* was mostly photographs and articles on Kirov's anniversary, Sergei Kirov, congratulations from shareholders' meetings (akin to earlier annual congratulations from the Party), veteran employees and World War II—Soviet-style identity politics once again. In Aug. 2005 Semenenko fell to his death from a fifteenth floor window in the middle of the night at a Sochi sanatorium—although he was only visiting friends at the hotel. His estimated worth was $95 million. There were rumors the city administration gave a private company the rights to build a port on Kirov territory, but Semenenko wanted to build a port for Kirov itself. A "Petersburg oligarch," he owned 15% of Kirov shares but may have held more indirectly. His son Georgii became general director and in 2007 replaced the board of directors with EES and OMZ specialists (Obedinennye Mashinostroitel'nye Zavody, United Heavy Machinery), reduced the number of daughters, and changed the administrative structure. In an interview with *Vedomosti*, he avoided questions about his father's death, how he became director, and how many shares his family owned. Gleb Krampets and Andrei Musatov, "Kirovskii zavod obezglavlen," *Vedomosti* Aug. 11, 2005; Irina Malkova and Anatolii Temkin, "Direktora OMZ prishli na Kirovskii zavod," *Vedomosti* Jan. 10, 20097; Anatolii Temkin, "Interv'iu: Georgii Semenenko, general'nyi director Kirovskogo zavoda," *Vedomosti* Jan. 18, 2007.
143 *Leningradskii stankostroitel'* Jan. 11, 1989, p. 1.
144 *Leningradskii stankostroitel'* Jan. 25, 1989, p. 2; May 6, 1989, p. 3.
145 *Leningradskii stankostroitel'* June 29, 1989, p. 1; Dec. 28, 1989, p. 2; Jan. 9, 1990, p. 2; and Jan. 22, 1990, p. 3.
146 *Leningradskii stankostroitel'* May 31, 1989, p. 2; March 22, 1990, p. 2; Aug. 1, 1990, p. 2; Aug. 31, 1990, p. 3 (for MPs).
147 *Leningradskii stankostroitel'* April 24, 1990, p. 2.
148 *Leningradskii stankostroitel'* May 16, 1990, p. 3.
149 *Leningradskii stankostroitel'* Sept. 21, 1990, p. 3; Aug. 31, 1990, p. 3.
150 *Leningradskii stankostroitel'* Nov. 2, 1990, p. 1; July 11, 1990, p. 1.
151 *Leningradskii stankostroitel'* Sept. 26, 1990, p. 2. A journalist noted the economist and assistant manager were so pro-market they "consider profane those doubting market transition goals and methods."
152 *Leningradskii stankostroitel'* Oct. 12, 1990, p. 3.
153 *Leningradskii stankostroitel'* April 16, 1991, p. 3. Pokasiuk might have used APs/MPs to skirt price controls—buying inputs from the mother at low prices and reselling them

for profit. Another option was APs and MPs not paying debts to the mother firm, which would go bankrupt and take all debts with it.

154 *Leningradskii stankostroitel'* Oct. 12, 1990, p. 3.
155 Struggles with MPs persisted in 1997. Interview, Sverdlov mother manager, St. Petersburg, July 1997.
156 *Leningradskii stankostroitel'* Nov. 2, 1990, p. 3.
157 *Leningradskii stankostroitel'* March 11, 1991, pp. 1–2.
158 *Leningradskii stankostroitel'* April 16, 1991, p. 3.
159 *Leningradskii stankostroitel'* July 17, 1991, p. 2.
160 *Leningradskii stankostroitel'* Oct. 3, 1991, p. 3.
161 *Leningradskii stankostroitel'* Oct. 18, 1991, p. 3.
162 *Leningradskii stankostroitel'* Nov. 26, 1991, p. 2.
163 *Leningradskii stankostroitel'* Feb. 5, 1992, p. 3, and Feb. 12, 1992, p. 3.
164 *Leningradskii stankostroitel'* March 5, 1992, p. 2.
165 *Leningradskii stankostroitel'* Feb. 19, 1992, p. 2.
166 *Leningradskii stankostroitel'* July 13, 1992, p. 1. Lathe output was down from 127 to 93 (Jan.–June 1991 to Jan.–June 1992); profitability was down from 50% to 10%. Loans kept Sverdlov alive.
167 *Leningradskii stankostroitel'* Oct. 7, 1992, p. 1. In path #1 employees received less than 50% of shares at reduced cost; in path #2 employees paid face value for more than 50% of shares. The dilemma was money versus control.
168 *Leningradskii stankostroitel'* Dec. 30, 1992, p. 2; emphasis in the original.
169 *Leningradskii stankostroitel'* May 21, 1993, p. 3.
170 *Leningradskii stankostroitel'* April 1, 1993, pp. 2–3.
171 Managerial intrigues at the Arsenal enterprise were reported at Sverdlov. *Leningradskii stankostroitel'* Sept. 17, 1993, p. 3; *Sankt-Peterburgskoe EKhO* Jan. 27, 1993, p. 22.
172 *Komitet po Upravleniiu Gosudarstvennym Imushchestvom*, Committee Administering State Property.
173 *Leningradskii stankostroitel'* June 22, 1993, p. 2.
174 *Leningradskii stankostroitel'* Sept. 30, 1993, p. 2.
175 *Leningradskii stankostroitel'* Oct. 20, 1993, p. 1.
176 *Leningradskii stankostroitel'* Feb. 7, 1994, p. 2.
177 Grishpun became assistant director in March 1993, age 31. Trained as an engineer, he worked at Sverdlov from 1983 in various shopfloors; now he handled economic issues. *Leningradskii stankostroitel'* April 1, 1993, p. 1. He claimed he no longer dealt with engineering and technical issues: these were for shopfloors, not the mother, signaling a status shift from technical to economic knowledge.
178 *Leningradskii stankostroitel'* Feb. 16, 1994, p. 1 (italics mine).
179 *Leningradskii stankostroitel'* Feb. 27, 1994, pp. 2–3.
180 Originally the *kholding* was to be called "LSPO-Phoenix" (pre-Revolutionary name), but employees missed the historical significance. After a two-year competition in which no one participated, the *kholding* was named "Stankostroitel'noe obedinenie Sverdlov"—SOS, as one employee noted!
181 *Leningradskii stankostroitel'* April 14, 1994, p. 3.
182 *Leningradskii stankostroitel'* May 17, 1994, pp. 2–3.
183 *Leningradskii stankostroitel'* Sept. 8, 1994, pp. 1–7.
184 *Leningradskii stankostroitel'* June 29, 1994, p. 1. On June 21 Sverdlov was allowed to privatize as a *kholding*. Some were annoyed with the new foreign words used: "Now [Sverdlov] leadership is working on reunification…through a '*kholding*.' What a word. For us it is not enough that we have 'shops' (*shopy*), 'weekends' (*uik-endy*), 'summits' (*sammity*). We have entirely Europeanized." *Leningradskii stankostroitel'* Feb. 7, 1994, p. 2. "Americanized" is more accurate.
185 *Leningradskii stankostroitel'* Nov. 29, 1994, p. 2. Enterprises in which the state held more than 25% of shares could not sell physical property without KUGI permission.

186 *Leningradskii stankostroitel'* Dec. 23, 1994, p. 1.

187 Interviewees Stnk/Gendir and Stnk/T were particularly critical. Stnk/Gendir criticized state control of their firm, although he had no specific gripes. Stnk/T criticized the state for economic chaos and collapse of Russian industry.

188 Stankolit, Sverdlov's first AP, was in crisis in 1993. In 1994, plans were made for MP Universal to absorb Stankolit and form NEVA-MED. Universal would pick up Stankolit's debts, employees, and equipment. The plan was carried out in May 1995. Stankolit managers were depressed. Inflation was killing them, younger employees were leaving, and pay was low. The director was not sure of his fate after the merger, and nobody was happy to lose autonomy. *Leningradskii stankostroitel'* Nov. 4, 1994; interviews with participants, 1995.

189 Interviews Stnk/Prod-1 and Stnk/Sa-1, March 1995.

190 Interview with the author, July 1997, St. Petersburg; interview with assistant managers, Petersburg electronics enterprise, July 1997.

191 From "Karta sobstvennosti Sankt-Peterburga," (www.stockmap.spb.ru), assembled business news and data, some originally published in *Delavoi Peterburg* and *Agenstvo Biznes Novostei.*

192 Other *obedineniia* began to disintegrate by 1991 under radical reforms, although some reintegrated. T. G. Dolgopiatova, "Gosudarstvennye predpriiatiia v perekhodnyi period: izmenenie organizatsionno-khoziaistvennykh struktur," *EKO* 3 (1994), 49–60.

193 Cf. V'iunik, *Vsegda v poiske.*

194 *Maiak* Oct. 11, 1990, p. 4.

195 *Maiak* Aug. 23, 1990, p. 4.

196 *Maiak* Sept. 13, 1990, pp. 4–5.

197 *Maiak* Sept. 6, 1990, p. 4.

198 *Maiak* Oct. 4, 1990, p. 3.

199 *Maiak* Feb. 14, 1991, pp. 1, 3.

200 *Maiak* April 11, 1991, pp. 1, 3.

201 *Maiak* March 14, 1991, p. 3. He was also general director of new industrial concern Farada. *Maiak* May 8, 1991, p. 3.

202 *Maiak* Sept. 26, 1991, p. 3.

203 *Maiak* Oct. 31, 1991, p. 3.

204 *Maiak* Feb. 6, 1992, p. 3; Feb. 20, 1992, p. 3. Kichigin's initial opponent, Vladimir Trenin, withdrew; according to Blokhin, the union "supported" Kichigin (i.e. rigged the vote).

205 Soviet VCRs were not high-quality. A subdivision assembling Daewoo VCRs was a cash cow (*Maiak* Feb. 27, 1992, pp. 1, 3). When it left Pozitron, Viton was excluded from the Daewoo deal and could not use the "Pozitron" trademark; it later went bankrupt. *Kommersant Daily* Jan. 25, 1996, p. 9.

206 *Maiak* Dec. 5, 1991, p. 3. I found no data on "Slava," but one detail is suspicious: "Slava" is Russian for "glory." A Russian-named French firm: coincidence or shell game?

207 *Maiak* Oct. 22, 1992, p. 3. That some shopfloors would do better than others bred accusations that better-off MPs and shopfloors were speculating, not producing value—an echo of moral economy. See the report on Pozitron MP KONEL, *Maiak* Dec. 17, 1992, p. 1.

208 *Maiak* Dec. 17, 1992, p. 1. In a Feb. 1995 interview, Blokhin hinted of problems solved by the exit of a troublesome individual.

209 *Maiak* Nov. 19, 1992, pp. 1–3. The city council's and mayor's reactions from November 4, 1992, were posted on shopfloor bulletin boards; they called separate privatization of shopfloors "pointless" and "inadmissible." Employees claimed *three-quarters* of the original declarations were left out and suspected managers were not disclosing full information on privatization and Pozitron's condition.

210 *Maiak* Oct. 8, 1992, p. 2. Information was vague. I noticed business plans had prices for VCRs but little on *production* figures and strategies.

211 Ibid., p. 3.

212 *Maiak* Feb. 20, 1992, pp. 1–2; March 12, 1992, pp. 1-3; March 19, 1992, pp. 1, 3, 5. One STK representative claimed employees feared privatization as unfamiliar.

213 *Maiak* April 23, 1992, p. 3.

214 *Maiak* Oct. 8, 1992, p. 3, and June 4, 1992, p. 3.

215 *Maiak* April 16, 1992, p. 3.

216 *Maiak* Oct. 8, 1992, p. 3.

217 *Maiak* Oct. 29, 1992, p. 1.

218 Interview Elec-1, July 1997.

219 *Maiak* Nov. 19, 1992, p. 3.

220 *Predprinimatel' Peterburga* 20, June 4–17, 2001, p. 17; "Dzerzhinskii 'Sintez' razdelili na chasti," *Ekspert-Volga* Feb. 5, 2007.

221 "Karta sobstvennosti Sankt-Peterburga" (www.stockmap.spb.ru).

222 Interview Rail-1, March 1995.

223 *Oktiabr'skaia magistral'* Aug. 18, 1994, p. 3, and March 22, 1994, p. 1.

224 In 2005 AvtoVAZ announced 4,000 job cuts. Director Kadannikov encouraged retirement or shifting workers around the firm. "AvtoVAZ Cutting Jobs as Production Drops," *Moscow Times* May 31, 2005.

4 Innovation and confusion

1 Interview Ku-1/1, Jan. 1994. The firm survived on subsistence production and renting space.

2 It is axiomatic in mainstream economics and much political economy that managers optimize a set of variables (costs to self, costs to the firm, etc.). Yet if instrumental rationality dominates, why remove managers, as incentives should change behavior. See Susan Linz, "Restructuring with What Success? A Case Study of Russian Firms," *Comparative Economic Studies* 43/1 (2001), 75–99.

3 Åslund dubs Red Directors "rent-seekers" without exploring logics this entailed or why they predominated. Yet he claims "the most profound problem was that they did not know how to manage their enterprises in a market economy"—which Russia then was not—but decries "irresponsible and parasitical mismanagement" (pp. 138–9). *Russia's Capitalist Revolution* (Washington, DC: Peterson Institution for International Economics, 2007), ch. 4. Stoica ("From Good Communists to Even Better Capitalists?") claimed that former socialist cadres were rentier, not value-adding, entrepreneurs.

4 Marketing can help managers broaden business; train managers might see themselves in the *transport*, not *train*, business and be attentive to non-obvious pitfalls and opportunities.

5 Alfred Chandler, *The Visible Hand* (Cambridge, MA: Harvard University Press, 1977); Michael Porter, *Competitive Strategy* (New York: Free Press, 1980) and *Competitive Advantage* (New York: Free Press, 1985); David E. Gumpert (ed.), *The Marketing Renaissance* (New York: John Wiley & Sons, 1985).

6 T. Alimova, V. Buev, B. Golikova, and T. Dolgopiatova, "Problemy malogo biznesa glazami predprinimatelei," *Voprosy ekonomiki* 11 (1994), 116, 117.

7 Blasi *et al, Kremlin Capitalism*; Annette N. Brown and J. David Brown, *Does Market Structure Matter? New Evidence from Russia*, Working Paper, 130 (Stockholm Institute of Transition Economics, 1998).

8 Alan Blinder *et al, Asking about Prices: A New Approach to Understanding Price Stickiness* (New York: Russell Sage, 1998).

9 Blasi *et al, Kremlin Capitalism*, ch. 5; Paul R. Lawrence, Charalambos A. Vlachoutsicos, *et al, Behind the Factory Walls: Decision-Making in Soviet and US Enterprises* (Boston, MA:

Harvard Business School Press, 1990); Sheila Puffer, *The Russian Management Revolution* (Armonk, NY: M. E. Sharpe, 1992).

10   William Tompson, "The Price of Everything and the Value of Nothing? Unravelling the Workings of Russia's 'Virtual Economy,'" *Economy and Society* 28 (1999), 256–80; Andrei Yakovlev, "Ekonomika 'chernogo nala' v Rossii: mekhanizmy, prichiny, posledstviia," in Teodor Shanin (ed.), *Neformal'naia ekonomika. Rossiia i mir* (Moscow: Logos, 1999), 270–91; Ledeneva, *How Russia Really Works*, ch. 5.

11   Reddy, *The Rise of Market Culture*. Susan Linz and Gary Krueger claim taxes were not the prime force behind barter, which was specific to particular sectors and driven by lack of hard cash: "Enterprise Restructuring in Russia's Transition Economy: Formal and Informal Mechanisms," *Comparative Economic Studies* 40 (1998), 5–52.

12   Herrera notes that shocks are necessary to weaken orthodoxy (*Imagined Economies*, 90), but the generation and emergence of alternatives, and multidimensional culture and learning, need more analysis.

13   Contrast this with McDermott's analysis (*Embedded Politics*, 111–14 and 140–4). Facing falling sales, Czechs, like Russians, used "probing" ("flooding the market"), designing new goods to find a cash stream. In Russia's story, not only was "probing" a search for income amidst capital hunger; it was a panicked, confused search for normality embedded in broader discourses and practices.

14   Burawoy and Verdery (eds), *Uncertain Transition*; Gernot Grabher and David Stark (eds), *Restructuring Networks in Post-Socialism* (New York: Oxford University Press, 1997).

15   Szelenyi, *Socialist Entrepreneurs*; Victor Nee and David Stark (eds), *Remaking the Institutions of Socialism* (Stanford, CA: Stanford University Press, 1989); Hill Gates, *China's Motor: A Thousand Years of Petty Capitalism* (Ithaca, NY: Cornell University Press, 1996).

16   Berliner, *Factory and Manager in the USSR*; David Granick, *Management of the Industrial Firm in the USSR* and *The Red Executive*.

17   Verdery, "What Was Socialism, and Why Did it Fall?" 28–30 and 33–41.

18   Harrison White claims managers orient to their fields to signal legitimacy; but consumers are not unimportant. "Where Do Markets Come From?" *American Journal of Sociology* 87 (1981), 517–47.

19   Stewart Macaulay, "Non-Contractual Relations in Business: A Preliminary Study," *American Sociological Review* 28 (1963), 55–67.

20   Humphrey, *The Unmaking of Soviet Life*, ch. 2; Smith, *Reforming the Russian Legal System*, ch. 7. Up to 100 unclear taxes on wages, income, sales, etc. required meticulous documentation.

21   Recall Denise's complaints about VAT (Ch. 2, n. 10). Entrepreneurs in cottage manufacture routinely rolled out the vodka when the fire inspector stopped by. Interview HomeDir/2, Nov. 1995.

22   Rozalina Ryvkina, "Ot tenevoi ekonomiki k tenevomu obshchestvu," and Leonid Kosals, "Mezhdu khaosom i sotsial'nym poriadkom," *Pro et Contra* 4/1 (1999), 24–54.

23   Berliner, *Factory and Manager in the USSR*, chs. 6 and 10.

24   *Kirovets* July 17, 1991, p. 2. A Sverdlov manager justified a ten-day trip to America in 1994 to learn American finance. "Today we have many contacts with the West, but we do not understand each other because we live by different laws." *Leningradskii stankostroitel'* May 17, 1994, p. 1.

25   Georgine Fogel and Alina Zapalska, "A Comparison of Small and Medium-Size Enterprise Development in Central and Eastern Europe," *Comparative Economic Studies* 43/3 (2001), 60–1.

26   E. Belianova, "Motivatsiia i povedenie rossiiskikh predpriiatii," *Voprosy ekonomiki* 6 (1995), 20.

27   Data from a study at Surgut suggested that employees of state-owned and private commercial firms were generally unprepared and "conservative." L. V. Korel', M. A. Shabanova, Iu. B. Chistiakova, and O. V. Sharnina, "Chto pomogaet i chto meshaet adaptirovat'sia k rynku," *EKO* 3 (1994), 71–85.

28 Yevgeny Kuznetsov, "Learning to Learn. Emerging Patterns of Enterprise Behavior in the Russian Defense Sector, 1992–95," in Bartlomiej Kaminskii (ed.), *Economic Transition in Russia and the New States of Eurasia* (Armonk, NY: M. E. Sharpe, 1996), 315–43. If the main motive was maintaining labor collective integrity, survival strategies dominated: I. Alimova, V. Buev, V. Golikova, and T. Dolgopiatova, "Problemy malogo biznesa glazami predprinimatelei," *Voprosy ekonomiki* 11 (1994), 119–20.

29 An early Petersburg co-operative owner said state-run auto suppliers were useless, and he set up service "as it should be." Interview Carpart-1, Dec. 1995.

30 A. P. Prokhorov, *Russkaia model' upravleniia* (Moscow: ZAO 'Zhurnal Ekspert,' 2002). Prokhorov uses *upravlenie* (administration) and not *menedzhment* (management).

31 E. E. Kogan, "Zakonodatel'stvo o bankrodstve," *EKO* 10 (1994), 130–44; E. E. Smirnova, "Bankrodstvo nesostoiatel'nosti rozn'?" *EKO* 9 (1993), 141–9; "Bankrotstvo: plany, perspektivy, protsedury," *EKO* 8 (1994), 47–53. In 1994 and 1995 an estimated 70% of all large firms were bankrupt, yet in 1994 only thirty real bankruptcies occurred.

32 Kogan, "Zakonodatel'stvo o bankrodstve," 143. On piercing the corporate veil, see Vadim Volkov, *Violent Entrepreneurs*, 46–9. In 2005 legislation made banks work with credit bureaus for credit histories. Resistance is highlighted by a story of American lawyers sent to Nizhny Novgorod to help enforce bankruptcy. Finding a firm in debt, they tried to find managers with proper authority. Each time they found their man, he had "sold" the firm. World Bank Conference, Columbia University, Feb. 4, 1994.

33 Sergei Skaterschikov, founder and former owner of the Skate analysis group, noted that through 2002 only twenty or so stocks showed real trading turnover; 80% of capitalization was in gas, oil, and telecommunications. Catherine Belton and Andrei Zolotov Jr., "Shadow of Wild '90s at Forum in London," *Moscow Times* April 4, 2003.

34 Andrei Kuznetsov, "Economic Reforms in Russia: Enterprise Behavior as an Impediment to Change," *Europe–Asia Studies* 46 (1994), 955–70.

35 Andrei Kuznetsov and Olga Kuznetsova, "Privatisation, Shareholding and the Efficiency Argument: Russian Experience," *Europe–Asia Studies* 48 (1996), 1173–85. Simeon Djankov and Peter Murrell claim privatization is associated with restructuring, yet their survey suggests its effects are less straightforward. Managerial abilities and tactical preferences remain exogenous; gains come when owners hire new managers. "Enterprise Restructuring in Transition: A Quantitative Survey," *Journal of Economic Literature* 40 (2002), 739–92.

36 Tatiana Dolgopiatova suggested that causation between privatization and performance might run in the opposite direction: firms with better survival chances did not fear privatization., *Rossiiskie predpriiatiia v perekhodnoi ekonomike: ekonomicheskie problemy i povedenie* (Moscow: Delo, 1995), 122–6.

37 Susan J. Linz, "Russian Firms in Transition: Champions, Challengers and Chaff," *Comparative Economic Studies* 39/2 (1997), 1–36.

38 One study claims private owners were *less* effective at investment than the state. A. G. Shelomentsev, "Struktura aktsionernogo kapitala promyshlennykh korporatsii i investitsii," *EKO* 2 (1998), 29–42.

39 At Baltika beer, Russian managers answered to foreign owners but enjoyed autonomy and took credit for success. Interviews Beer-1 and Beers-2, July 1999.

40 Cf. Fligstein on "efficiency": *Transformation of Corporate Control*, introduction.

41 I. Boeva, T. Dolgopiatova, and V. Shironin, *Strategii vyzhivaniia gosudarstvennykh i privatizirovannykh predpriiatii promyshlennosti v perekhodnoi period* (Moscow: Vysshaia shkola ekonomiki, 1994).

42 Salesmen at Petersburg's Gostiny Dvor complex sent a letter to the Skorokhod shoe firm, noting poor shoe selection or quality and complaining shoppers would "as a rule leave with nothing. At least nothing from our shoe section." *Skorokhodovskii rabochii* April 20, 1989, p. 3, and May 15, 1990, pp. 1, 3.

43 *Krasnyi treugol'nik* Feb. 20, 1991, p. 3; also April 11, 1991, p. 3, and April 18, 1991, p. 2.

44 *Turbostroitel'* Jan. 6, 1989, p. 5, and Oct. 5, 1990, p. 8.

45 *Molot* April 4, 1991, p. 1; also Feb. 14, 1991, p. 3. Nevskii zavod saw Energomash as a cash stream, but output for Nevskii zavod, ZTL, Elektroapparat, and Proletarii dropped in 1989. *Turbostroitel'* March 24, 1989, pp. 6–7, and Feb. 9, 1990, pp. 1, 6–9.

46 *Krasnaia zaria* Jan. 22, 1991, p. 2.

47 *Maiak* April 25, 1991, p. 2.

48 Burawoy and Krotov ("Soviet Transition from Socialism to Capitalism") claim liberalization wrecked authority and promoted speculation. By not taking *practice* into account, they cannot explain change *away* from speculation except by invoking market institutions—just like neoclassical economics.

49 On Gaidar's reforms, see David Lipton, Jeffrey D. Sachs, Vladimir Mau, and Edmund S. Phelps, "Prospects for Russia's Economic Reforms," *Brookings Papers on Economic Activity* 1992/2 (1992), 213–83.

50 One commentator noted how reforming exchange "required overcoming the routine, centralized system of Gossnab, Gosplan and other 'goses.'" *Molot* Feb. 14, 1991, p. 3.

51 From interviews at a Petersburg lathe-making and castings firm: interview Stnk/T-2 (head engineer), April 1995; Stnk/Prod-1 and Stnk/Prod-2 (assistant director for purchases and production), March 1995; Stnk/Sa-1 and Stnk/Sa-2 (assistant director for sales), March 1995.

52 *Turbostroitel'* Dec. 27, 1991, p. 2. An assistant director at Elektrosila claimed the real economic problem was supplies; "sales" were guaranteed. *Elektrosila,* Jan. 9, 1992, pp. 1–2.

53 Boeva *et al, Strategii vyzhivaniia,* 30–5. Anticipating upcoming (1992) reforms, Krasnyi Treugol'nik's AP director planned to make the supply division independent. There was little on sales strategies. *Krasnyi treugol'nik* Oct. 31, 1991, p. 2. On continuing fixation over supplies, see *Turbostroitel'* Jan. 24, 1992, p. 3.

54 Mark Granovetter argued strong ties and networks make up for absent institutions or access to them: "The Strength of Weak Ties: A Network Theory Revisited," *Sociological Theory* 1 (1983), 201–33. Gary Krueger showed networks were a defensive tactic: "Transition Strategies of Former State-Owned Enterprises," *Comparative Economic Studies* 37 (1995), 89–109.

55 Interview Pz-CDir, March 1995.

56 Up to 82% of firms in one survey suffered this. Dolgopiatova, "Promyshlennye predpriiatiia v usloviiakh," 3.

57 Gregory Schwartz, "Employment Restructuring in Russian Industrial Enterprises: Confronting a 'Paradox,'" *Work, Employment and Society* 17/1 (2003), 49–72. Interview Pz-CDir, March 1995; *Leningradskii stankostroitel'* Jan. 20, 1993, p. 1.

58 *Turbostroitel'* July 10, 1992, p. 5.

59 *Rossiiskii ekonomicheskii barometr* 4 (1992) and 2 (1993); interview Stnk/Ec-1, March 1995; also *Krasnyi tkach* Jan. 23, 1992, p. 4, and April 6, 1992, p. 2.

60 E.g. Berliner, *Factory and Manager in the USSR,* chs. 6, 7, and 10–12.

61 Boeva *et al, Strategii vyzhivaniia,* 44.

62 E. Belianova, "Motivatsiia i povedenie rossiiskikh predpriiatii," *Voprosy ekonomiki* 6 (1995), 15–21; T. Dolgopiatova and I. Evseeva, "Ekonomicheskoe povedenie promysh-lennykh predpriiatii v perekhodnoi ekonomike," *Voprosy ekonomiki* 8 (1994), 40–50; Barry Ickes and Randi Ryterman, "The Interenterprise Arrears Crisis in Russia," *Post-Soviet Affairs* 8 (1992), 331–61. Some firms made changes. Elektrosila stopped producing generators and heavy electrical equipment because Transmash and Zvezda did not pay debts of 70 million and 58 million rubles. *Elektrosila* Dec. 3, 1992, p. 2. Transmash requested 1,400 generators and parts for 1993—more than Elektrosila ever made.

63 Boeva *et al, Strategii vyzhivaniia,* 51–3. Even in 2008 I heard criticism of speculation. Putin reacted to rising food prices in 2007 and 2008 with anti-speculation legislation.

64 Dolgopiatova, "Povedenie predpriiatii v usloviiakh zhestkikh finansovykh ogranichenii, 70–3.

65 I. Boeva *et al, Gosudarstvennye predpriiatiia v 1991–1992 gg: Ekonomicheskie problemy i povedenie* (Moscow: Institut ekonomicheskoi politiki, 1992), 51–4.

66 Interview Stnk/Sa-1, March 1995, St. Petersburg.

67 In one survey of managers, sales were rarely mentioned in January or summer 1992 and were a problem only in March 1992. Boeva *et al, Strategii vyzhivaniia*, 44–6. In 1992 and 1993 tight money versus subsidies pitted Yeltsin against industrialist group Civic Union, Supreme Soviet speaker Ruslan Khasbulatov, and vice president Aleksandr Rutskoi.

68 *Kirovets* July 11, 1991, p. 2, and March 31, 1992, p. 3. The state did not finance first production runs.

69 *Kirovets* Jan. 16, 1992, p. 1.

70 *Kirovets* March 20, 1992, p. 1. Another journalist noted, "the factory is prepared to sell its products to whomever wants them, but alas there are not many purchasers ready to pay insane prices for tractors."

71 *Kirovets* March 17, 1993, p. 1.

72 *Kirovets* Dec. 22, 1993, p. 4.

73 *Kirovets* Nov. 30, 1992, pp. 1–2.

74 Svetlana lost 60% of sales (1.3 billion rubles) in 1992 due to reduced state purchases. *Svetlana* Nov. 3, 1993, pp. 1–2.

75 *Svetlana* Oct. 27, 1993, p. 1. The lesson: "Altruism and the market are not comparable concepts."

76 *Svetlana* Feb. 23, 1994, p. 1, and June 2, 1994, p. 1.

77 *Leningradskii stankostroitel'* April 20, 1992, p. 1, June 10, 1992, p. 1, and July 13, 1992, p. 1. Despite debt and insolvent buyers, managers considered production profitable— "profit" being based on costs and forthcoming receipts.

78 *Leningradskii stankostroitel'* July 16, 1992, p. 1.

79 *Leningradskii stankostroitel'* Jan. 20, 1993, p. 1.

80 Tatiana Dolgopiatova, "Promyshlennye predpriiatiia v usloviiakh ekonomicheskoi transformatsii," *EKO* 4 (1995), 2–23 (esp. p. 20).

81 Interview Ptit-1, July 1997; interview BreadAssoc-1, June 1995.

82 S. P. Aukutsionek, "Oprosy promyshlennykh predpriiatii," *EKO* 2/248 (1995), 15–17.

83 *Turbostroitel'* Feb. 14, 1992, p. 5. One politician and long-time LMZ employee was enraged by price hikes; reforms were "robbing people." *Turbostroitel'* Feb. 7, 1992, p. 2.

84 *Svetlana* Feb. 19, 1992, p. 6.

85 Dolgopiatova, "Promyshlennye predpriiatiia v usloviiakh ekonomicheskoi transformatsii," 6–7.

86 Andrei Kuznetsov and Olga Kuznetsova, "Privatisation, Shareholding and the Efficiency Argument: Russian Experience," *Europe–Asia Studies* 48 (1996), 1179.

87 *Turbostroitel'* March 27, 1992, p. 4; May 29, 1992, p. 7. LMZ turned to barter, but metal received had to be reworked. In 1992 managers experimented with smaller, cheaper low-capacity turbines. *Turbostroitel'* July 10, 1992, p. 5.

88 *Elektrosila* Dec. 8, 1992, p. 2.

89 In Jan. 1992 the Kirov tractor works greeted the post-Soviet market era with the head-lines, "The Plan Lived. The Plan Lives. The Plan Will Live!" *Kirovets* Jan. 6, 1992, p. 1.

90 *Svetlana* Nov. 20, 1991, p. 1.

91 *Svetlana* Jan. 13, 1993, p. 1; April 20, 1993, p. 1. Alas, Svetlana owed more than they were owed.

92 E.g. *Kirovets* Jan. 13, 1992, p. 1, and Aug. 6, 1993, pp. 1–3.

93 *Kommersant Daily* Dec. 5, 1992, p. 5.

94 *Leningradskii stankostroitel'* Feb. 5, 1992, p. 3; March 5, 1992, p. 2; *Kirovets* Dec. 14, 1992, p. 1; *Elektrosila* Dec. 3, 1992, p. 2; Dec. 8, 1992, p. 1.

95 Leningrad Metal Factory and Elektrosila exported electrical generation equipment to China and Sweden (LMZ) and Latin America (Elektrosila). As partial payment from Chinese clients, LMZ accepted sugar, canned meat, and sweaters. *Turbostroitel'* June 5, 1992, p. 6, and April 26, 1993, p. 2. Energomash's Chinese clients paid 30% of the price of turbines or generators in clothes and toys. EMK enterprises sold the goods for money (for wages) or gave them to employees. Interview ArtEnerg, July 1997.

96 T. Dolgopiatova and I. Evseeva, "Ekonomicheskoe povedenie promyshlennykh predpriiatii v perekhodnoi ekonomike," *Voprosy ekonomiki* 8 (1994), 42.

97 In Fligstein's "financial conception of control," corporate identity is profit, not a family of products. *The Transformation of Corporate Control*, ch. 7.

98 *Leningradskii stankostroitel'* April 1, 1992, pp. 2–3; also April 20, 1992, p. 1.

99 *Leningradskii stankostroitel'* June 22, 1992, p. 1; July 13, 1992, p. 2; July 16, 1992, pp. 1, 4; April 29, 1993, p. 1. Pokasiuk was confident solvent buyers had signed contracts and pocket banks would provide funds. *Leningradskii stankostroitel'* Sept. 9, 1992, p. 1.

100 Dolgopiatova, "Promyshlennye predpriiatiia v usloviiakh ekonomicheskoi transformatsii," 8–9.

101 A Girikond manager (Pozitron) claimed to find buyers for new products. *Maiak* March 19, 1992, p. 3.

102 *Leningradskii stankostroitel'* Oct. 7, 1993, p. 1; July 13, 1992, p. 2.

103 *Turbostroitel'* June 22, 1995, p. 1. They celebrated June 24, "Inventors' and Developers' Day."

104 *Elektrosila* March 19, 1992, p. 3. By 1994 few Russian vacuum cleaners were in stores. LOMO did export cameras to Europe. "Local Plants Find Private Successes," *St. Petersburg Times*, Aug. 8, 1995. Elektrosila's generators still had foreign demand. *Elektrosila* Jan. 9, 1992, p. 1, June 30, 1993, p. 3; interview ArtEnerg-1, July 1997.

105 *Elektrosila* Feb. 20, 1992, p. 2.

106 *Svetlana* Jan. 22, 1992, p. 2.

107 For a few (of many) examples: *Svetlana* Aug. 14, 1991, p. 5; May 13, 1992, p. 4.

108 *Svetlana*, June 19, 1991, p. 5; Jan. 22, 1992, p. 2; June 3, 1992, p. 2; Jan. 26, 1994, p. 2. The "super-telephones" were not a success.

109 E.g. *Svetlana* Jan. 27, 1993, p. 2, and Jan. 12, 1994, p. 1.

110 *Vestnik sviazi* 8 (1999) (www.vestnik-sviazy.ru/archive/08_1999/svias.html).

111 *Krasnyi tkach* Sept. 16, 1992, p. 1, and Feb. 24, 1993, p. 2. Uncertain why there was low demand for overcoat fabric, the sales chief reasoned that "it is better to sew something expensive that lasts many years than something cheap which cannot last a year."

112 I. V. Kniazeva, "'Sibirskaia iarmarka—Evroasiia': Problemy i perspektivy rossiiskogo rynka. Real'nyi marketing nachinaetsia s vystavki," *EKO* 4 (1996), 58–66.

113 *Leningradskii stankostroitel'* Nov. 26, 1991, p. 1.

114 *Leningradskii stankostroitel'* May 17, 1994, p. 1.

115 *Kirovets* April 5, 1989, p. 1; July 16, 1993, pp. 1, 3; Oct. 27, 1994, pp. 3–5.

116 *Leningradskii stankostroitel'* July 11, 1991, p. 2.

117 *Svetlana* June 24, 1992, p. 2.

118 *Elektrosila* March 19, 1992, p. 3.

119 *Leningradskii stankostroitel'* April 20, 1992, p. 1.

120 *Kirovets* Sept. 28, 1992, p. 1.

121 *Svetlana* Jan. 12, 1994, p. 1.

122 T. Alimova, V. Buev, V. Golikova, and T. Dolgopiatova, "Problemy malogo biznesa glazami predprinimatelei," *Voprosy ekonomiki* 11 (1994), 118.

123 Interview Chem-3, Sept. 1995. This individual aimed for a steady profit rate of 15%.

124 Interviews: Pz-1 (electronics), Feb. 1995; Stnk/Ec-1 (lathes/castings), March 1995.

125 *Turbostroitel'* Feb. 24, 1989, p. 8.

126 *Svetlana* Jan. 13, 1993, p. 1.

127 *Svetlana* Nov. 3, 1993, p. 2. Some daughter firm chiefs felt competitors forced them to adjust: *Svetlana* Oct. 6, 1993, pp. 1–2.

128 *Svetlana* Feb. 3, 1993, p. 4.
129 *Svetlana* April 21, 1994, p. 1.
130 Tatiana Dolgopiatova, "Perekhodnaia model' povedeniia rossiiskikh promyshlennykh predpriiatii (po dannym empiricheskikh issledovanii 1991-1995 gg.)," *Voprosy ekonomiki* 11 (1996), 124.
131 *Oktiabr'skaia magistral'* May 24, 1994, p. 1.
132 *Turbostroitel'* Jan. 24, 1992, p. 3.
133 *Svetlana* Jan. 26, 1994, p. 2; Interview Elec-1, July 1997.
134 *Kirovets* Feb. 22, 1993, p. 2; March 24, 1993, p. 2; Nov. 3, 1994, pp. 2–3; cite from March 18, 1994, pp. 6–7.
135 *Kirovets* May 19, 1994, p. 3.
136 *Kirovets* March 24, 1993, pp. 1–2; Oct. 15, 1993, pp. 3–4; Sept. 12, 1996, pp. 2, 3; Oct. 17, 1996, pp. 4–5; April 3, 1997, p. 2; April 2, 1998, p. 3; *Delovoi Peterburg* Sept. 28, 1994, p. 5. Locking in to clients could hurt. Universalmash produced a narrow range of road-working equipment for the military and Ministry of Transportation, who did not always pay. Two years later the Ministry of Defense had paid "living money" once. Lipetsk Tractor Factory owed money but went bankrupt.
137 *Kirovets* Jan. 29, 1993, pp. 1–3; *Elektrosila* March 17, 1993, p. 2.
138 *Svetlana* July 1, 1992, p. 3.
139 *Novator* Feb. 3, 1992, p. 3.
140 The following material and quotations are from *Krasnaia zaria* Dec. 8, 1992, p. 2.
141 *Leningradskii stankostroitel'* Feb. 9, 1993, p. 1.
142 Miscommunications exist in capitalist firms, but the Russian economy was in such crisis that mistakes could spell disaster. Promising to sell goods is not producing and selling them.
143 *Turbostroitel'* Nov. 22, 1993, p. 4. LMZ's goods sold better outside the former USSR than those of Sverdlov, Pozitron, and others.
144 To the chagrin of one expert in 1996, even advertising was driven by ad designers, not marketing data. Igor Vikent'ev, "Bez publicity nyet prosperity," *Ekspert* Jan. 22, 1996.
145 *Elektrosila* Dec. 8, 1992, p. 2.
146 Clients claimed MMM must be legitimate: MMM "shares" guaranteed returns!
147 One Russian told of work at a prestigious American consulting firm. The Americans advised a Russian firm to ship goods on consignment. This Russian warned about payment problems and suggested using prepayments; he was overruled. The Russian firm used consignment and never was paid.
148 Interview BreadAssoc-1, June 1995.
149 Interviews PtSb, Nov. 1995, and Rozh-2, Nov. 1995. Andrei also advised an importer of German household goods, who remade his firm *à la* Atlas.
150 *Baltiets* Jan. 12, 1993, p. 2; Dec. 14, 1993, pp. 2–3.
151 R. M. Fomina, "Marketing—novoe poniatie," *EKO* 5 (1995), 90–1.
152 *Elektrosila* March 17, 1993, p. 2.
153 *Leningradskii stankostroitel'* July 13, 1993, p. 1, and May 17, 1994, p. 1.
154 *Oktiabr'skaia magistral'* Jan. 22, 1994, p. 1.
155 *Oktiabr'skaia magistral'* Feb. 2, 1994, p. 1.
156 *Oktiabr'skaia magistral'* Aug. 18, 1994, p. 3. Railroad services still employ byzantine procedures for ticket sales, but there are newer wagons and more expensive services for Moscow–Petersburg trains.
157 *Oktiabr'skaia magistral'* March 26, 1994, p. 1; also April 19, 1995, p. 1.
158 *Oktiabr'skaia magistral'* April 6, 1995, p. 2.
159 *Oktiabr'skaia magistral'* April 19, 1995, pp. 1, 3.
160 E. V. Gudkova and A. A. Get'man, "Predpriiatiia mashinostroeniia Dal'nego Vostoka v usloviiakh ekonomicheskoi reformy," *EKO* 4 (1998), 81–94.
161 S. Tsukhlo, "Formirovanie obemov i struktury vypuska rossiiskikh promyshlennykh predpriiatii," *Voprosy ekonomiki* 6 (1995), 36.

162 Niklas Pettersson and Stefan Nordström, *Western Perspectives on the Russian Shipbuilding Company Almaz* (Linköping: Linköping Institute of Technology, 1994), 67, 104.

163 Institute of Economics, Russian Academy of Sciences (RAN), "Strategiia i neotlozhnye zadachi preobrazovaniia mashinostroeniia Rossiiskoi Federatsii," *Voprosy ekonomiki* 11 (1996), 54–6.

164 I. Gurkov and E. Avraamova, "Strategii vyzhivaniia promyshlennykh predpriiatii v novykh usloviiakh," *Voprosy ekonomiki* 6 (1995), 25.

165 *Svetlana* June 2, 1994, p. 1.

166 "Biznes-plany: opyt i problemy realizatsii," *EKO* 12 (1994), 64–8.

167 *Krasnaia zaria* Dec. 8, 1992, p. 2.

168 Interview Nik-1, Dec. 1995.

169 V. D. Rechin, "Predpriiatie v usloviiakh neplatezhei. Mneniia direktorov predpriiatii," *EKO* 3/285 (1998), 82–90. Numbers of proposals and authorships suggest more than one hundred participants.

170 Rechin, "Predpriiatie v usloviiakh neplatezhei," 86.

171 Ibid., pp. 87–90.

172 *Kirovets* Oct. 12, 1995, pp. 2–4.

173 *Kirovets* July 17, 1997, p. 3; Oct. 24, 1996, pp. 2–4. In 1993 Kirov turned to Germany—they had contacts there and used Bosch parts—and the British Royal Exhibition. *Kirovets* Sept. 3, 1998, p. 3.

174 *Kirovets* March 7, 1996, pp. 6–7. Semenenko hinted accidental diversification and multiple production lines spread risk and revealed dynamics of different niches. *Kirovets* Oct. 30, 1997, pp. 2–3.

175 Interview Kr/Mrkt.

176 *Kirovets* April 18, 1996, pp. 1–2.

177 *Kirovets* March 13, 1997, p. 2; Nov. 13, 1997, p. 7; April 9, 1998, p. 3; Aug. 27, 1998, p. 2; Oct. 8, 1998, pp. 1–2, 4–5.

178 Torrey Clark, "Firms Urged to Study Marketing," *Moscow Times* Oct. 21, 2002.

179 Krom, "Druzheskaia ataka"; Natalia Kalmykova, "Zdes' i seichas," *Ekspert-Ural* Aug. 16, 2004.

180 Sergei Ageev, "V kruge pervom," and Andrei Maksimov, "Pishcha dlia stratega," *Ekspert* Sept. 29, 2003.

181 E.g. Kotkin, *Armageddon Averted*, 117.

182 In a study of integrated holding companies, Simon Clarke notes that top managers focus first on sales, profit, and finance, with production costs addressed in planning. Marketing departments prepare sales targets based on increasing current sales targets. Yet enterprise paternalism also has grown, and typical corporate culture retains Soviet traits. Firms strive for self-sufficiency, piece-rate payment persists, socialist competitions returned with a new name, "the culture of the enterprises…remains a very traditional production-oriented culture with a strong factory patriotism," and "for most people the prime objective of the enterprise is to increase production, provide stable employment, and pay good wages, and making a profit is simply the means of achieving these objectives" (cf. pp. 417–19). The primacy of finance and marketing is far from embedded in practices. Clarke, "A Very Soviet Form of Capitalism? The Management of Holding Companies in Russia," *Post-Communist Economies* 16 (2004), 405–22.

183 Institute of Economics, RAN, "Strategiia and neotlozhnye zadachi preobrazovaniia mashinostroeniia Rossiiskoi Federatsii (doklad IE RAN)," *Voprosy ekonomiki* 11 (1996), 55, 54.

184 Interview Chem-1, June 1995. That these meat factories were state-owned does not mean income was unimportant. Kenneth I. Spenner, Olga O. Suhomlinova, Sten A. Thore, Kenneth C. Land, and Derek Jones, "Strong Legacies and Weak Markets: Bulgarian State-Owned Enterprises during Early Transition," *American Sociological Review* 63 (1998), 599–618; Gerhard Schüsselbauer, "Privatisation and Restructuring

in Economies in Transition: Theory and Evidence Revisited," *Europe–Asia Studies* 51 (1999), 65–83.

185 William Tompson cites comments by Pëtr Karpov, head of the bankruptcy commission. Karpov, "Promyshlennost' ne vyderzhit vysokikh tsen," *Ekspert* 27 (July 20, 1998), and "Tsenovoi absurd," *Ekspert* 39 (Oct. 19, 1998).

186 The formula was refined in paragraph 2, point 2.5, instruction 37 of the State Tax Service (Aug. 10, 1995), "O poriadke ischisleniia i uplaty v biudzhet naloga na pribyl' predpriiatii i organizatsii." In the new formula, the tax assessor compared a firm's price for a good/service to that of a similar good/service, and used the higher value to assess profit tax. This maximized profit but discouraged price competition.

187 Clauses in the 1991 tax code forbidding sales below production cost were repealed in July 1998. In the 2002 code, the definition of profit was unchanged, but if the difference between income and expenses is zero, there is nothing to tax. The new code allows discounts except in exchange between acquaintances.

188 Interview Chem-3. Denise and Aleksei said nothing of taxes and shaping prices.

189 Interview Brkda-2, Dec. 1994.

190 Cf. Marina Grikhiuk, "Fevrial'skii perelom," *Rossiiskaia gazeta* Jan. 29, 2009: Russian Minister of Health and Social Development Tatiana Golikova noted the rise in the number of firms contemplating or actually laying off employees—when American firms had accepted this as necessary. See also "Salary Arrears Sour 16%," *Moscow Times* March 17, 2009; Gleb Stoliarov, "Deripaska uvol'niaet," *Vedomosti* March 10, 2009; Evrenii Rakul', "Prodadut liubomu za \$1," *Vedomosti—Rostov-na-Danu* March 20, 2009. On legal aspects to labor reduction see Maria Landau and Alexandra Bludvan, "Key Points in the Staff Reduction Process," *Moscow Times* Feb. 17, 2009; yet Grigorii Milov shows Russian managers were slower than Western counterparts to lay off employees, although once the shock set in they laid off employees more quickly and with less of a tactical sense: "Shok i smiatenie," *Vedomosti* Jan. 28, 2009.

191 Cf. Daria Nikolaeva, "Ianvarskoi zarplaty na vsekh ne khvatilo," *Kommersant Daily* Feb. 18, 2009; Anton Utekhin *et al*, "Net deneg na zarplatu," *Vedomosti* Feb. 20, 2009; Gleb Zhorga, "Bez dela I bez deneg," *Ekspert Ural* Feb. 23, 2009. Wages under the table and in the shadow economy also reemerged: Mikhail Malykhin, "Pochti dve treti rossiian soglasny na 'chernuiu' zarplatu," *Vedomosti* Feb. 9, 2009. Lukoil owner and oligarch Vagit Alekperov penned an editorial in *Rossiiskaia gazeta* supporting corporate paternalism as a "strategic investment": "Ne liudi dlia nefti, a neft' dlia liudei," *Rossiiskaia gazeta* Dec. 18, 2008.

192 Steven Rosefielde, *Russia in the Twenty-First Century* (New York: Cambridge University Press, 2005).

193 Anna Smolchenko, "National Champions Declared a Dead End," *Moscow Times* Oct. 5, 2006. For a defense of the policy, see Khisamova, "Kol'tsevoe dvizhenie."

5 Fields of battle

1 *Radio Free Europe/Radio Liberty Business Watch* 3/26 (July 15, 2003), "The Yukos File."

2 William Roy, *Socializing Capital*, 15–16: power relations and strategies shape property rules and field logics, which shape resource access and legitimate strategies.

3 KGB-trained officials staffed much of the state bureaucracy and remained dormant. Stephen Kotkin, "Heir, Apparently: Why Russia Wants Putin," *Financial Times Magazine* 45 (March 6, 2004), 16–22; Lilia Shevtsova, *Russia: Lost in Transition* (Washington, DC: Carnegie Endowment for International Peace, 2007). Shevtsova notes *siloviki* logics and practices of secrecy, using power "without moral constraint" (p. 100), and concern with power for its own sake. For a defense of the FSB, see former "chekist" Viktor Cherkesov's letter to *Komsomol'skaia pravda* Dec. 28, 2004.

4 Evgenii Gontmakher, "Stsenarii: Novocherkassk-2009," *Vedomosti* Nov. 6, 2008, and "Kadrovoi perepolokh," *Rossiiskaia gazeta* Nov. 17, 2008.

5 Literature on post-socialist privatization, and privatization generally, is too vast for a detailed review. Standard accounts include Maxim Boycko, Andrei Schleifer, and Robert Vishny, *Privatizing Russia* (Cambridge, MA: MIT Press, 1995); Roman Frydman, Andrzej Rapaczynski, and John S. Earle, *The Privatization Process in Russia, Ukraine, and the Baltic States* (Budapest: Central European University Press, 1993); Roman Frydman and Andrzej Rapaczynski, *Privatization in Eastern Europe: Is the State Withering Away?* (Budapest: Central European University Press, 1994); Lynn D. Nelson and Irina Y. Kuzes, *Property to the People: The Struggle for Radical Economic Reform in Russia* (Armonk, NY: M. E. Sharpe, 1994); and Barnes, *Owning Russia*.

6 Cf. Woodruff, "Property Rights in Context."

7 Pavel Listev was a television journalist killed in 1995. In 1994 I witnessed an entrepreneur negotiating with *mafiia* over a third person's debts and life. This convinced me crucial data are not always worth obtaining. Even Shevtsova's overview uses secondary sources: *Putin's Russia* (Washington, DC: Carnegie Endowment for International Peace, 2005).

8 Sergei Guriev and Andrei Rachinsky, "The Role of Oligarchs in Russian Capitalism," *Journal of Economic Perspectives* 19 (2005), 131–50; "Ownership Concentration in Russian Industry," Country Economic Memorandum for Russia, World Bank (www.cefir.ru/). Guriev and Rachinsky use a broad definition of "oligarchs" as the top 627 owners in 2003. Their conclusions about *habitus* (a term they do not use), human capital, and political practices support my claims.

9 Charles Lindblom, *Politics and Markets* (New York: Basic Books, 1977). Note the centrality of private property's illegitimacy in the narrative of Soviet normality. Kotkin, *Magnetic Mountain*, introduction.

10 Kennedy, *Cultural Formations of Post-Communism*, ch. 2.

11 On privatization scholarship, see William Megginson and Jeffry Netter, "From State to Market: A Survey of Empirical Studies on Privatization," *Journal of Economic Literature* 39 (2001), 321–89.

12 Gary Hamilton and Nicole Woosley Biggart, "Market, Culture, and Authority: A Comparative Analysis of Management and Organization in the Far East," *American Journal of Sociology* 94/supplement (1988), S52–S94.

13 Stark and Bruszt, *Postsocialist Pathways*, chs. 1, 3, and 5.

14 This may be due to empirical cases. McDermott (*Embedded Politics*) also pays less attention to conflict, as he too uses an East European case (the Czech Republic).

15 Bourdieu, *The State Nobility*, part 4.

16 Manager-owners span "managers" and "owners"— positions of power via property *and* bureaucracy. Small firm owner-managers I treat as owners; insider-owners (managers) called themselves "managers."

17 Kennedy, *Cultural Formations of Post-Communism*, chs. 1 and 3.

18 A majority of Russians in a 2005 poll thought the state should prevent foreign ownership of defense and natural resources firms. "Russians Guard Strategic Sectors," *Moscow Times* Oct. 14, 2005.

19 Recall that *kompromat* is legally compromising materials and political capital state officials might have or seek (e.g. by raiding a company) to use in courts—as Khodorkovskii learned to his misfortune.

20 Stefan Hedlund, "Property without Rights: Dimensions of Russian Privatisation," *Europe–Asia Studies* 53/2 (2001), 213–37; McDaniel, *Autocracy, Capitalism, and Revolution in Russia*.

21 Even in 2001 conservative parties and media resisted land privatization, e.g. "Zemlia— nash Stalingrad" (Land—our Stalingrad), *Sovietskaia Rossiia* June 16, 2001, p. 1.

22 Irina Starodubrovskaia, "Financial-industrial Groups: Illusions and Reality," *Communist Economies and Economic Transformation* 7/1 (1995), 5–19; S. Batchikov and

Iu. Petrov, "Formirovanie finansovo-promyshlennykh grupp i gosudarstvo," *Rossiiskii ekonomicheskii zhurnal* 2 (1995), 3–10; Kh. Mingazov, "Stanovlenie novykh organizatsionno-khoziaistvennykh struktur v rossiiskoi industrii," *Rossiiskii ekonomicheskii zhurnal* 9 (1993), 25–34, and 10 (1993), 50–60; Juliet Johnson, "Russia's Emerging Financial-Industrial Groups," *Post-Soviet Affairs* 13/4 (1997), 333–65.

23 Irina Starodubrovskaia conceptualized firms having "survival goals" (attract capital for support) or "development goals" (profit). "Finansovo-promyshlennaia gruppy: illiuzii i real'nost'," *Voprosy ekonomiki* 5 (1995), 143.

24 Taehwan Kim, "Resisting the Market: The Politics of Hierarchies and Networks in Russian Fuel and Metallurgy Industries," PhD dissertation, Columbia University, 2000.

25 Granick, *The Red Executive*, ch. 4; John P. Hardt and Theodore Frankel, "The Industrial Managers," in Gordon Skilling and Franklyn Griffiths (eds), *Interest Groups in Soviet Politics* (Princeton, NJ: Princeton University Press, 1971), 171–208.

26 Hoffman, *The Oligarchs*, 107.

27 Mst. Afanas'ev, P. Kuznetsov, and A. Fominykh, "Korporativnoe upravlenie glazami direktorata," *Voprosy ekonomiki* 5 (1997), 84–101; E. Belianova, "Motivatsiia i povedenie rossiiskikh predpriiatii," *Voprosy ekonomiki* 6 (1995), 15–21.

28 *Maiak* May 8, 1991, p. 3. Pozitron's general director Iurii Blokhin was vice-president.

29 *Smena* May 9, 1992, p. 2.

30 Interview, president, Association of Industrial Enterprises, St. Petersburg, July 1997.

31 Interview, director, Union of Industrialists and Entrepreneurs of St. Petersburg, July 1997.

32 "Energomash," company pamphlet (Leningrad: SMART, n.d.). I suspect this was printed in 1990.

33 O. Ivanov, "Korporativnye formy upravleniia v promyshlennosti," *Rossiiskii ekonomicheskii zhurnal* 3 (1994), 53.

34 *Turbostroitel'* March 24, 1989, p. 6.

35 Ibid., pp. 6-7. One LMZ journalist compared Energomash to liberation of serfs: formally free but financially bound to the state. Member firms Nevskii Zavod and Elektroapparat were in debt to Gosbank and kept borrowing to pay wages.

36 *Turbostroitel'* Aug. 18, 1989, pp. 6–7; *Elektrosila* Feb. 15, 1990, p. 9. Energomashbank was a "pocket bank," created by enterprise managers to attract deposits and gain low-interest loans.

37 *Elektrosila* Feb. 15, 1990, pp. 7–8; *Molot* April 18, 1991, pp. 2–3.

38 Interview BreadAssoc-1 and BreadAssoc-2, June and July 1995.

39 A *tolkach* was an employee with networks to important suppliers.

40 Hoffman, *The Oligarchs*, chs. 2, 5, 6, and 12.

41 In Dec. 1996, FPG Granit was registered as twenty-seven military-industrial firms and banks "to create and perfect a unified system of antiaircraft defense of [CIS] countries, and to concentrate scientific-technological and industrial potential of defense sector enterprises." "Korotko: Sozdana FPG," *Segodnia* Dec. 11, 1996.

42 *Kommersant* Sept. 26, 1995, p. 14.

43 "Evrika: FPG zameniat ministerstva na 'srednem urovne upravleniia,'" *Segodnia* Jan. 26, 1996; "Ukaz: Glava gosudarstva podderzhal FPG," *Segodnia* April 2, 1996.

44 Khanif Mingazov, "Stanovlenie novykh organizatsionno-khoziaistvennykh struktur v rossiiskoi industrii," *Rossiiskii ekonomicheskii zhurnal* 9 (1993), 26.

45 V. Kulikov, L. Latysheva, and A. Nikolaev, "Obrazovanie finansovo-promyshlennykh grupp (neobkhodimost', tseli i mekhanizmy)," *Rossiiskii ekonomicheskii zhurnal* 1 (1994), 17.

46 *Kommersant* Dec. 19, 1995, pp. 11–12.

47 Hoffman, *The Oligarchs*, ch. 12.

48 Starodubrovskaia, "Financial-Industrial Groups," 8–11.

49 Presidential *ukaz* #2096, Dec. 5, 1993, "On the Creation of Financial-Industrial Groups in the Russian Federation."
50 Kulikov *et al*, "Obrazovanie finansovo-promyshlennykh grupp," 18–19; Starodubrovskaia, "Finansovo-promyshlennaia gruppy," 144–5.
51 Cf. Burawoy and Krotov, "The Soviet Transition from Socialism to Capitalism."
52 Interviews Stnk/Gendir-1, Nov. 1994; Stnk/Sa-1, March 1995; Stnk/Prod-1, March 1995; Stnk/T-1, April 1995.
53 O. Botkin and M. Kozlov, "Finansovo-promyshlennaia gruppa 'Ural'skie zavody': pervyi god raboty," *Voprosy ekonomiki* 5 (1995), 147–9. Kozlov was vice-president of FPG Ural'skie zavody.
54 "FPG 'Interros' predpochitaet podkhod k priobreteniiu predpriiatii," *Segodnia* Oct. 22, 1996.
55 Interview KhF-2, Aug. 1995, St. Petersburg.
56 Interview Fur-1, July 1997. Defensive FPGs needed investment, but investors wanted control.
57 Larisa Gorbatova, "Formation of Connections between Finance and Industry in Russia: Basic Stages and Forms," *Communist Economies and Economic Transformation* 7/1 (1995), 21–34; Jane E. Prokop, "Industrial Conglomerates, Risk Spreading and the Transition in Russia," *Communist Economies and Economic Transformation* 7/1 (1995), 35–50.
58 Ia. Sh. Pappe, V. E. Dement'iev, B. I. Makarenko, P. Venediktov, and A. Iu. Zudin, *Finansovo-promyshlennye gruppy i konglomeraty v ekonomike i politike sovremennoi Rossii* (Moscow: Tsentr Politicheskikh Tekhnologii, 1997), 69–72.
59 Kira Andreeva, "Nu ochen' prizrachnyi investor," *NovayaGazeta.Ru* July 17, 2000.
60 "Pervaia Peterburgskaia FPG sozdaetsia ne v interesakh promyshlennosti," *Sankt-Peterburgskoe EKhO* Oct. 9, 1996; "'Morskaia tekhnika' obedinila finansistov i promyshlennikov," *Delovoi Peterburg* March 12, 1996.
61 Interview Fur-1, July 1997.
62 Interview Chem-2 (representative and manager of local chemical FPG), July 1997.
63 Botkin and Kozlov, "Finansovo-promyshlennaia gruppa 'Ural'skie zavody,'" 150.
64 Interview Chem-2, July 1997.
65 *Kommersant* Sept. 26, 1995, pp. 14–16.
66 This is the explanation favored by analysts at *Kommersant* Sept. 26, 1995.
67 Pappe *et al*, *Finansovo-promyshlennye gruppy*, 52.
68 Starodubrovskaia, "Financial-industrial Groups," 18, n. 3; *Ekonomika i zhizn'* 33 (1994), 37.
69 *Kommersant* Dec. 19, 1995, pp. 12–13.
70 Pappe *et al*, *Finansovo-promyshlennye gruppy*, 138–48 and 118–29.
71 Sergei Batchikov and Iurii Petrov, "Formirovanie finansovo-promyshlennykh grupp i gosudarstvo," *Rossiiskii ekonomikcheskii zhurnal* 2 (1995), 3 (Batchikov was an Interros manager). These first five FPGs were Ural'skie zavody, Sokol, Dragotsennosti Urala, Ruskhim, and Sibir'. According to Goskomprom (State Committee for Industry), Interros was to be registered in Oct. 1994 (Presidential decree #2023, Oct. 28, 1994) and on the state registry in Jan. 1995.
72 Lev Makarevich, "Finansovo-promyshlennye gruppy operuiut gigantskimi kapitalami," *Finansovye izvestiia* Nov. 12, 1996, and "Finansovo-promyshlennye gruppy uvelichivaiut proizvodstvo," *Finansovye izvestiia* Jan. 21, 1997; "'Morskaia tekhnika' obedinila finansistov i promyshlennikov," *Delovoi Peterburg* March 12, 1996. Data exclude *de facto* FPGs. In 1995 the St. Petersburg Mayor's office refused my request for data on FPG registration.
73 Thomas Graham, "Novyi russkii rezhim," *Nezavisimaia gazeta* Nov. 23, 1995, p. 5; Andrei Fadin, "The Oligarchs in Charge of 'Russia Inc.'," *Transition* April 4, 1997, pp. 27–9; *Kommersant* June 17, 1997, pp. 14–16.
74 See *Kommersant Daily* throughout July 1996.

75 See the interview with Mikhail Khodorkovskii in *Kommersant* April 16, 1996, pp. 18–19. He later rejected the *chaebol* model: Hoffman, *The Oligarchs*, 298.

76 Hoffman, *The Oligarchs*, 312.

77 *Kommersant* Nov. 28, 1995, pp. 47–50; *Ekspert* Oct. 10, 1995, pp. 20–1, and Nov. 28, 1995, pp. 20–6. See *Ekspert* Sept. 12, 1995, pp. 43–8, for the presidential decree.

78 Hoffman, *The Oligarchs*, 312.

79 *Ekspert* Nov. 28, 1995, pp. 20–6.

80 Rossiiskii Kredit and Kont complained of unfair exclusion and contested auction results. *Kommersant* Sept. 10, 1995, pp. 42–3; *Ekspert* Nov. 28, 1995, pp. 20–6.

81 Johnson, "Russia's Emerging Financial-Industrial Groups," 335–6.

82 McKinsey Global Institute, *Unlocking Economic Growth in Russia* (Moscow: McKinsey & Co., 1999), ch. 3.

83 Johnson, "Russia's Emerging Financial-Industrial Groups," 340–1.

84 *Turbostroitel'* March 3, 1994, p. 2.

85 *Turbostroitel'* April 7, 1994, p. 1.

86 *Turbostroitel'* June 2, 1994, p. 2, and March 30, 1995, p. 1.

87 *Turbostroitel'* Dec. 29, 1994, p. 1, and April 6, 1995, p. 1.

88 *Turbostroitel'* March 30, 1995, p. 1.

89 *Turbostroitel'* June 22, 1995, p. 1. Managers sold Siemens a large amount of shares for investment.

90 Natal'ia Kuraptseva, "AO 'LMZ' vstupilo v svoi prava investora v AO 'ZTL,'" *Sankt-Peterburgskoe EkhO* May 10, 1995.

91 *Nevskoe vremia* April 5, 1995, p. 1; *Turbostroitel'* March 30, 1995, p. 1.

92 "Dual power" was unstable power-sharing between the Provisional Government and Petrograd Soviet in 1917. The second financial-industrial group was unnamed. LMZ owned 45.8% of ZTL shares, while the ZTL board held 35.3%; the only EMK representative on the board was Shevchenko.

93 *Nevskoe vremia* April 14, 1995, p. 1. A leaflet circulated at ZTL, supposedly in the name of ZTL employees, claimed LMZ owed ZTL 10 million rubles.

94 LMZ journalists accused the ZTL board of "acting first and foremost in Stumhammer's interests...not disdaining any means, even unworthy." Shevchenko's language in *Nevskoe vremia* was diplomatic.

95 *Nevskoe vremia* April 14, 1995, p. 3.

96 I gained some of this information from one employee who organized exchange at EMK.

97 However, *Sovietskaia Rossiia* and *Pravda* were more critical, and some of Yeltsin's allies favored natural resource sectors or Red Directors.

98 *Kommersant* Dec. 19, 1995, pp. 12–14.

99 From Hans-Henning Schröder, "El'tsin and the Oligarchs: The Role of financial Groups in Russian Politics between 1993 and July 1998," *Europe–Asia Studies* 51 (1999), 957–88; Hoffman, *The Oligarchs*; Johnson, "Russia's Emerging Financial-Industrial Groups," 346–7; Radio Free Europe/Radio Liberty, *Russian Media Empires IV*. I leave out others, e.g. Lukoil, Sistema, etc. Berezovskii created his empire with few clear, consistent goals; he was content to rent-seek. Al'fa Group focused systematically on the consumer market, Interros on industrial output and natural resources.

100 Albert Speransky, "'Master and Man' in Today's Russia," *Jamestown Foundation Prism* 2/4 (Oct. 1996).

101 *Kommersant* Feb. 13, 1996, pp. 22–5.

102 *Kommersant* March 5, 1996, p. 71.

103 "Yeltsin Enters Wages Dispute in Norilsk," *Moscow News* March 7, 1996.

104 *Kommersant* April 23, 1996, pp. 28–9; "Norilsk Nickel vs Uneximbank: Is This the Outcome of the Conflict?" *Moscow News* April 25, 1996.

105 *Kommersant* Sept. 17, 1996, p. 52, and *Kommersant Daily* May 29, 1996.

106 *Kommersant* April 30, 1996, p. 16.

107 *Kommersant* July 23, 1996, p. 34.
108 "Menedzherov kombinata vyzovut na kover," *Kommersant Daily* Dec. 10, 1996.
109 "Noril'skii kombinat ne priznali bankrotom," *Kommersant Daily* Nov. 14, 1997.
110 "'Norilsk kombinat' trebuiut, chtoby im upravliali po-staromu," *Finansovye izvestiia* Jan. 2, 1997.
111 In 2007 Potanin, partner Mikhail Prokhorov, and Oleg Deripaska fought over control of Norilsk.
112 Some of this discussion on Iukos is based on Yuko Iji, "Corporate Control and Governance Practices in Russia," mimeo, University College London, School of Slavonic and East European Studies, May 2003.
113 Hoffman, *The Oligarchs*, 448–50.
114 Iji, "Corporate Control and Governance Practices in Russia," 24–7.
115 General directors of textile and furniture factories whom I interviewed in St. Petersburg in July 1997 shared this suspicion of financial elites and Financial FPGs.
116 *Kommersant* July 25, 1995, pp. 30–5. Inkombank bought shares in the Babaevskii candy firm without publicly announcing takeover intentions, although by law they had to go public once enrolled on the shareholder register. Courts supported Inkombank, who then turned to a Novosibirsk candy factory, at which a woman of long standing and engineering expertise was appointed director at an emergency shareholders' meeting. She refused Inkombank's advances; her subsequent murder was never solved. *Kommersant Daily* Sept. 30, 1995, p. 9, March 11, 1997, p. 7, and April 17, 1997, p. 10.
117 *Ekspert* Aug. 22, 1995, pp. 28–33, and Dec. 4, 1995, pp. 29–31.
118 For a summary see *Kommersant* Aug. 29, 1995, pp. 20–5.
119 *Federal'noe upravlenie po delam nesostoiatel'nosti (bankrodstvo)*, Federal Administration on Matters of Insolvency (Bankruptcy).
120 *Ekspert* Sept. 26, 1995, p. 8.
121 *Kommersant* Nov. 21, 1995, p. 44, and Dec. 19, 1995, p. 56.
122 *Kommersant* March 5, 1996, pp. 67–8; "Vysshii arbitrazhnyi sud RF otkloniaet isk AO 'Rybinskie motory' k pravitel'stvu," *Segodnia* Jan. 19, 1996; *Kommersant* March 5, 1996, p. 68; "Fond federal'nogo imushchestva perenes konkurs po prodazhe aktsii 'Rybinskikh,'" *Kommersant* March 5, 1996; "Vosvrat: 'Rybinskim motoram' ne udalos' vykupit' 5% svoikh aktsii," *Kommersant* March 23, 1996; "Podopleka: 'Rybinskie motory' ostalis' na shee u gosudarstva," Oct. 25, 1996, *Segodnia* online.
123 Taehwan Kim, "Resisting the Market," 142–79.
124 Cf. Pappe *et al*, *Finansovo-promyshlennye gruppy*, 83–102.
125 Radio Free Europe/Radio Liberty, *How Russia is Ruled—1998*, "Informal Politics," Aug. 28, 1998.
126 Pappe *et al*, *Finansovo-promyshlennye gruppy*, 69–72.
127 Interviews Fur-1, July 1997, and Ptit-1, July 1997.
128 Igor Korol'kov, "Chelovek iz Dikarska," *Moskovskie novosti*, July 3, 2001.
129 Sergei Smirnov, "Poluoligarkh i ego muzy," *Trud*, July 20, 2000.
130 Andreeva, "Nu ochen' prizrachnyi investor"; Smirnov, "Poluoligarkh i ego muzy."
131 "Peterburg dolzhen ostat'sia tsentrom rossiiskogo energomashinostroeniia," *Energetika Peterburga* May 24, 2000.
132 "Konflikt mezhdu 'Elektrosiloi' i korporatsiei EMK vstupil v novuiu fazu," *Nevskoe vremia* Dec. 16, 1998. (Materials from local and national newspapers after 1997, e.g. *Nevskoe vremia*, *Sankt-Peterburgskie vedomosti*, *Vedomosti*, etc.–were usually obtained from internet archives, and so I cite authors and headlines rather than the usual page numbers.)
133 Aleksei Klepikov, "Zatianuvsheesia protivostoianie," *Nevskoe vremia* Jan. 19, 1999; "Konflikt mezhdu 'Elektrosiloi' i korporatsiei EMK vsupilo v novuiu fazu," *Nevskoe vremia* Dec. 16, 1998.
134 Vladimir Novikov, "Nyet, eto ne 'semeinaia' ssora," *Sankt-Peterburgskie vedomosti* Dec. 16, 1998; "Konflikt mezhdu 'Elektrosiloi' i korporatsiei EMK vsupilo v novuiu fazu."

Stepanov tried and failed to replace Energomashbank leadership, making an enemy of director Andrei Bykov. Vladimir Novikov, "Razvaliv, 'prozreli' ne slishkom li pozdno?" *Sankt-Peterburgskie vedomosti* Dec. 24, 1998.

135 "Peterburg dolzhen ostat'sia tsentrom rossiiskogo energomashinostroeniia," *Energetika Peterburga* May 24, 2000.

136 Andreeva, "Nu ochen' prizrachnyi investor"; Novikov, "Nyet, eto ne 'semeinaia' ssora." Korol'kov, "Chelovek iz Dikarska," dubbed the two EMK-1 and EMK-2.

137 Vladimir Novikov, "Pole boia—zavod," *Sankt-Peterburgskie vedomosti* Jan. 15, 1999.

138 John Varoli, "Fight to Control Leading Turbine Maker Heats up," *Moscow Times* Oct. 15, 1999.

139 "Leningradskogo metallicheskogo zavoda bol'she ne budet?" *Nevskoe vremia* Dec. 5, 1998.

140 *Turbostroitel'* Jan. 14, 1999, p. 1.

141 Andrei Tsyganov, "'Dvortsovyi perevorot' na LMZ: dozhivem do 29 dekabria," *Nevskoe vremia* Dec. 23, 1998. A January 15 court decision ruled Shevchenko could not be manager; a January 20 court decision ruled he could. *Turbostroitel'* Jan. 21, 1999, p. 1.

142 Novikov, "Razvaliv, 'prozreli' ne slishkom li pozdno?"

143 Anton Mukhin, "Militsiia gotovitsia k boiu," *Nevskoe vremia* Jan. 21, 1999.

144 "Konflikt na LMZ prodolzhaet razvivat'sia," *Nevskoe vremia* Jan. 14, 1999.

145 "Obrashchenie general'nogo direktora OAO 'Energomashkorporatsiia' Stepanova A. Iu. K trudovomu kollektivu i profsoiuznoi organizatsii AO 'Leningradskii Metallicheskii zavod,'" *Sankt-Peterburgskie vedomosti* Jan. 21, 1999.

146 Andrei Davlitsarov, "Obvineniia vmesto kompromissa," *Nevskoe vremia* Jan. 23, 1999.

147 Dmitrii Starosel'skii, "Pomozhet li miting v bor'be s rynkom?" *Nevskoe vremia* Feb. 25, 1999.

148 Aleksandr Andreev, "Skol'ko stoit effektivnoe energomashinostroenie?" *Nevskoe vremia* Feb. 17, 1999.

149 Aleksei Klepikov, "Padenie poslednego bastiona," *Nevskoe vremia* Feb. 9, 1999.

150 *Turbostroitel'* March 18, 1999, p. 1.

151 "Na LMZ vvedeno vneshnee upravlenie," *Nevskoe vremia* Feb. 20, 1999.

152 *Turbostroitel'* Sept. 9, 1999, p. 1.

153 Viktoriia Mikhailova, "Ssora iz-za lopatok," *Vedomosti* March 14, 2000; Mikhailova, "'Interrosu' vernuli lopatki," *Vedomosti* April 24, 2000.

154 Nikolai Ivanov and Elena Konnova, "'Energomashkorporatsiia' ostalas' bez turbin," *Kommersant Daily* June 30, 2000; Anatolii Temkin and Viktoriia Uzdina, "'Interros' teriaet LMZ," *Vedomosti* July 21, 2000.

155 Dmitrii Butrin, "Engineering Industry: Trends," *Kommersant Vlast'* March 2, 2004 (English version).

156 Simon Pirani, "Oligarch? No, I'm Just an Oil Magnate…" *Guardian* June 4, 2000.

157 Cf. Shevtsova, *Russia: Lost in Transition*, chs. 3 and 4.

158 For an overview of Putin's rise to power, see Shevtsova, *Putin's Russia*.

159 Robert W. Thurston, *Life and Terror in Stalin's Russia, 1934–1941* (New Haven, CT: Yale University Press, 1996).

160 "Chekists in the Corridors of Power," *Novaia gazeta* July 2003; from *Johnson's Russia List* 7255, July 18, 2003. This article lists deputy ministers and regional governors with KGB-FSB experience and/or links to Putin from the KGB or Anatolii Sobchak's St. Petersburg administration. See also Olga Kryshtanovskaya, *Anatomiia rossiiskoi elity* (Moscow: Zakharov, 2005), 256–79; Victor Yasman, "Russia: Siloviki Take the Reins in Post-Oligarchy Era," *Radio Free Europe/Radio Liberty* Sept. 17, 2007, and "Russia: From Siloviki Power to a Corporate State," *Radio Free Europe/Radio Liberty* Sept. 25, 2007; "Twelve Who Have Putin's Ear," *RFERL* Oct. 15, 2007.

161 E.g. the FSB's arrest of Deputy Finance Minister Sergei Storchak in 2007. Viktor Cherkesov, head of the Federal Drug Control Service, openly warned of *siloviki* turf wars before the 2007 Duma election. "'Nel'zia dopustit', chtoby voivy prevratilis' v

torgovtsev,'" *Kommersant Daily* Oct. 9, 2007. Shevtsova (*Russia: Lost in Transition*) suggests *siloviki* splits between those oriented to economic power and those dedicated to social order.

162 On *siloviki* symbolic trappings, expressions of power, and consensus, see Olga Kryshtanovskaya and Stephen White, "Inside the Putin Court: A Research Note," *Europe–Asia Studies* 57 (2005), 1065–75; and "The Making of a Neo-KGB State," *The Economist* Aug. 23, 2007. One former FSB general noted, "A Chekist is a breed."

163 Shevtsova, *Russia: Lost in Transition*, esp. chs. 9–11.

164 Yulia Latynina, "Krasnoyarsk: One Region with Two Tsars," *Moscow Times* Jan. 26, 1999; Kirill Koriukin, "Interior Ministry Troops Raid Tanako Offices in Krasnoyarsk," *Moscow Times* April 2, 1999.

165 Boris Nemtsov and Vladimir Milov, "Putin i 'Gazprom,'" *Novaia gazeta* Aug. 28, 2008.

166 Iulia Bushueva and Elzaveta Osetinskaia, "Mina pod Viakhireva," *Vedomosti* May 31, 2000; Iulia Bushueva, "Osen' oligarkhov," *Vedomosti* June 19, 2000.

167 Iulia Bushueva, "Perevorot v 'Gazprome,'" *Vedomosti* July 3, 2000.

168 Boris Grozovskii and Aleksei Nikol'skii, "Ne otkupites'!" *Vedomosti* Nov. 5, 2003.

169 Yevgenia Albats, "Gusinsky's Arrest Shakes the Rule of Law," *Moscow Times* June 15, 2000; Martin Nesirky, "Putin Says Gusinsky Arrest 'Excessive,'" *Moscow Times* June 16, 2000.

170 Andrei Zolotov Jr., "Charges Dropped Against Gusinsky," *Moscow Times* July 28, 2000; Zoia Kaika and Anton Charkin, "Bez isterik," *Vedomosti* Sept. 22, 2000; Andrei Zolotov Jr., "Lesin Says He Was Wrong to Sign Gusinsky Pact," *Moscow Times* Sept. 21, 2000.

171 Natal'ia Arkhangel'skaia and Iskander Khisamov, "Vam paket ot Borisa Abramovicha," *Ekspert* Sept. 11, 2000.

172 Gregory Feifer, "Oligarch Meeting Judged a Success," *St. Petersburg Times* Aug. 1, 2000.

173 Vladimir Pribylovsky, "What's the Scandal All About?" *Moscow Times* June 11, 2003; Lilia Shevtsova, "Implications of the Yukos Scandal for Russian Domestic Politics," Sept. 16, 2003 (Carnegie Endowment for International Peace).

174 Elena Evstigneeva, "Oligarkhi ustali ot korruptsii," *Vedomosti* Feb. 19, 2003.

175 Catherine Belton, "Khodorkovsky Arrested on Seven Charges," *Moscow Times* Oct. 27, 2003.

176 Analyst Sergei Markov claimed Russians accepted rigged privatization because of a tacit promise that oligarchs would run firms better than the state. Violating this promise left them open to attack. "The Yukos Conflict and Putin's Second Term," *St. Petersburg Times* Aug. 1, 2003.

177 Catherine Belton, "Khodorovsky Makes Veiled Threat about Energy," *St. Petersburg Times* July 11, 2003. Commentators claimed Ivanov, Sechin, and Patrushev (a "Petersburg *mafiia*") were behind attacks.

178 Valeria Korchagina, "Kasyanov: Lebedev Arrest 'Excessive,'" *Moscow Times* July 9, 2003.

179 Sabrina Tavernise, "As Tycoons Slip Overseas, Putin Appears to Lay Siege," *New York Time* Nov. 5, 2003. One Kremlin official feared a larger issue: "It's about all that we have worked for, all that we were trying to do…The law was not supposed to be this way or that way. It was supposed to be straight."

180 Editorial, *Moscow Times* Nov. 17, 2003. RSPP called an emergency meeting but abandoned Khodorkovskii. "Biznesmeny prosiat Vladimira Putina vmeshat'sia," *Vedomosti* Oct. 27, 2003.

181 Chrystia Freeland, "A Falling Tsar," *Financial Times* Nov. 1, 2003.

182 Alex Fak, "Gryzlov: Natural Resources Never Privatized," *Moscow Times* Oct. 30, 2003.

183 Valeria Korchagina and Maria Danilova, "Putin Defends Attacks on Yukos," *Moscow Times* Oct. 28, 2003.

184 Catherine Belton, "Putin Tip Powers Yukos Recovery," *Moscow Times* June 18, 2004; Erin Arvedlund, "Signs of Damage Control in Russia's Oil Scandal," *New York Times* Nov. 3, 2003.

185 Shevtsova hints that *siloviki* factions who gained economic power had to decide what to do with gains. From this their economic logic emerged. This recalls Lachmann's claim that capitalism emerged as elites gained property control in struggles with states and then had to develop strategies for their use. Lachmann, "Origins of Capitalism in Western Europe: Economic and Political Aspects."

186 The interview was published in *Kommersant Daily* on Nov. 30, 2007. Georgy Boyt argues Shvartsman might have exaggerated his role to save his skin. In an interview with Ekho Moskvy, Shvartsman claimed *Kommersant* distorted reality, but eyewitnesses said he looked nervous. Boyt, "Using Pull of FSB Patrons to Make Deals," *Moscow Times* Dec. 13, 2007.

187 Aleksei Whapovalov *et al*, "Oleg Shvartsman rasplatilsia za interv'iu 'Kommersantu,'" *Kommersant Daily* Feb. 19, 2008; "Shvartsman Fund Deals Canceled," *Moscow Times* Feb. 20, 2008.

188 Ekaterina Derbilova, Tat'iana Egorova, and Nikolai Borisov, "Chubais pomog Potaninu," *Vedomosti* Sept. 21, 2005; Tat'iana Egorova *et al*, "OMZ otdadut 'Gazpromu,'" *Vedomosti* Aug. 22, 2005. In November Bendukidze and partners sold OMZ to a Russian group linked to Gazprom. Lyuva Pronina, "Bendukidze Ditches 42% Stake in OMZ," *Moscow Times* Nov. 7, 2005.

189 Greg Walters, "Study: Siloviki's Struggle for Assets Not Over," *Moscow Times* June 27, 2005.

190 Pavel Arabov, "VASO vol'etsia v kholding," *Vedomosti* Feb. 21, 2003; Ivan Lamykin, "An-148 dostroiat obshchim usiliiami," *Vedomosti* September 25, 2003; Pronina, "Aviation Rescue Plan Unveiled," *Moscow Times* June 22, 2005.

191 AvtoVAZ was owned by daughters AVVA, Tsentral'noe otdelenie Avtomobil'noi finansovoi korporatsiiu, and IFK. In turn, AvtoVAZ owned the daughters. In October 2005 Kadannikov resigned under Kremlin pressure. (In the 1990s he ordered AvtoVAZ not to pay taxes, to free up production funds—a debt weapon the Kremlin later used.) Rosoboroneksport gained AvtoVAZ daughters, took over boards of directors, and purged managers. Elena Naumova, "Bez strategii, no s perspektivami," *Ekspert Volga* Jan. 16, 2006; Aleksei Khazbiev, "Spurt voennogo kapitala," *Ekspert-Volga* Jan. 16, 2006; Aleksandr Bekker *et al*, "'Rosoboroneksport khochet stat' goskorporatsiei," *Vedomosti* May 17, 2006.

192 Lenta news, Sept. 4, 2007 www.lenta.ru/news/2007/09/04/rostechnologies/.

193 For the decree and data on the state corporation, see *Rossiiskaia gazeta* July 16, 2008; Vladislav Tiumenev, "Na koreiskie grabli," *Ekspert* July 21, 2008.

194 Cf. Iurii Sakharov, "Oglasite proekt!" *Ekspert Volga* Dec. 24, 2007.

195 Dmitry Butrin, "Engineering Industry 1991–2000: Present," *Kommersant Vlast* (English version) March 2, 2004.

196 This logic has taken root beyond the field of power. Second-tier oligarchs follow the financial logic, subordinate to state logic supremacy. Guriev and Rachinsky, "The Role of Oligarchs in Russian Capitalism" and "Ownership Concentration in Russian Industry."

197 "Determined Deripaska Casts a Long Shadow," *Moscow Times* April 27, 2008.

198 *Kommersant Daily* March 5, 1997, p. 10, and March 7, 1997, p. 9; Mikhail Petrov, "Nedodelannyi KrAZ," *Ekspert* June 16, 1997; Yulia Latynina, "Bykov Arrest And History of Feudalism," *Moscow Times* Oct. 11, 2000; Andrei Zolotov Jr., "Workers Troubled by KrAZ's Fate," *Moscow Times* April 28, 2000.

199 Kirill Koriukin, "Graft Case Opened on Aluminum Boss," *Moscow Times* April 9, 1999.

200 Nikolai Alekseev, "Bykov proshchaetsia s KrAZom," *Kommersant Daily* Feb. 17, 2000.

201 Kirill Vishnepol'skii, "Aluminum Titan," *Kommersant Daily* July 23, 1996.

202 Andrew McChesney, "Winners Take All," *Moscow Times* Feb. 22, 2000.
203 Andrew McChesney, "Aluminum Showdown Ending in Merger," *St. Petersburg Times* April 18, 2000; Igor Semenenko, "Aluminum Holding's Men to Run Smelters," *Moscow Times* July 4, 2000; Yulia Latynina, "Russian Aluminum's Growing Pains," *Moscow Times* June 7, 2000.
204 Yulia Latynina, "Shchit Happens," *Moscow Times* Oct. 1, 2003; Valeria Korchagina, "Abramovich Sells 25% of RusAl to Deripaska," *Moscow Times* Oct. 6, 2003.
205 Ekaterina Safarova and Dmitry Butrin, "Ferrous Metallurgy 2000–2004," *Kommersant* May 31, 2004.
206 Maria Rozhkova, "SibAl Looks to Change its Image," *Moscow Times* Nov. 30, 2001.
207 Igor Semenenko, "Siberian Aluminum Buys up Tank Firm," *Moscow Times* Feb. 27, 2001; Andrei Lemeshenko *et al*, "Deripaska poboretsia s Siemens," *Vedomosti* Nov. 11, 2004; Simon Ostrovsky, "RusAl Ends Dispute, Buys 100% of KrAZ," *Moscow Times* May 19, 2004.
208 Alex Nicholson, "Pulp Non-Fiction Fuels Hostile Takeovers," *Moscow Times* July 1, 2003; Dmitry Butrin, "Timber Industry 2000–2004," *Kommersant* July 5, 2004 (English version).
209 "Determined Deripaska Casts a Long Shadow," *Moscow Times* April 27, 2008; Catherine Belton, "'I Don't Need to Defend Myself," *Financial Times* July 13, 2007.
210 Alex Fak, "Survey: Business Confidence Plummets," *Moscow Times* Dec. 1, 2003. In 2007 the state already owned 35% of Russian stock market capitalization. David Woodruff, "The Expansion of State Ownership in Russia: Cause for Concern?" *Development and Transition* 7 (July 2007), 11–13.
211 Humphrey, *The Unmaking of Soviet Life*, ch. 5.
212 Yulia Latyinina, "Letting the Genies out of the Bottle," *Moscow Times* Aug. 13, 2003.
213 Sergei Dorenko, "Putin Presiding over Centralized Feudal State," *Moscow Times* Feb. 25, 2004; Yulia Latynina, "Goodbye Oligarchs, Hello Feudal Capitalism," *Moscow Times* Dec. 8, 2004; Barnes, *Owning Russia*, ch. 8.
214 In November 2006, Putin replaced Gazprom's second in command with FSB and Petersburg comrade Valerii Golub'ev, former head of Gazprom equipment and services purchasing, consolidating state control. Gaddy and Ickes, "Resource Rents and the Russian Economy"; Miriam Elder, "Gazprom Deputy Ryazanov is Fired," *Moscow Times* Nov. 16, 2006. In 2007 and 2008 attacks on British Petroleum's investments, especially TNK-BP, picked up.
215 Cf. Barnes, *Owning Russia*, ch. 7.
216 In nineteenth-century America, two visions of state–business relations contended for dominance: an activist state participating in corporate governance to guard society against predatory elites; and a neutral state outside the economy so as to avoid corruption. Roy, *Socializing Capital*, ch. 3.

6 Conclusion

1 "The Reluctant Briber," *The Economist: Country Briefings—Russia*, Nov. 2006 (online).
2 Rosefielde, *Russia in the Twenty-First Century*, ch. 7.
3 Alexis de Tocqueville, *Democracy in America*, tr. George Lawrence (New York: Harper & Row, 1966), 340–63.
4 Prokhorov, *Russkaia model' upravleniia*, 317–46.
5 Merely importing Western managing techniques has not led to real change: R. Peter Dickenson, David Campbell, and Vladimir Azarov, "Will Western Managerial Methods Work in Transitional Societies?" *Problems of Post-Communism* 47/3 (2000), 48–56.
6 Kennedy's *Cultural Formations of Post-Communism* (ch. 3) hints at generational cohorts.
7 Cf. Linz, "Russian Firms in Transition."

8 National economic security grew in discourse. One study of machine-tool production claimed the state needed to integrate smaller enterprises to improve capacity, and survive global competition, and maintain "national economic sovereignty." Konstantin Kostrikin, "Marketolog ot stanka," *Kommersant Daily* supplement, Oct. 30, 2007.

9 Beyond the commanding heights, second-tier oligarchs retain the financial logic, combining profit and rent-seeking with political networks. Cf. Guriev and Rachinsky, "The Role of Oligarchs in Russian Capitalism" and "Ownership Concentration in Russian Industry."

10 Clifford Gaddy and Barry W. Ickes, *Russia's Addiction: The Political Economy of Resource Dependence* (Washington, DC: Brookings, forthcoming).

11 Alas, by 2000 access to managers and other data were more limited, although I gained a few interviews that I use here. My schema fits well with others' data: Blasi *et al*, *Kremlin Capitalism*; Gaddy and Ickes, *Russia's Virtual Economy*; Linz, "Restructuring with What Success?"; Linz and Krueger, "Enterprise Restructuring in Russia's Transition Economy."

12 In March 2008 the Duma approved a list of 42 sectors in which foreign investment was forbidden or restricted (media, aerospace, mining, oil, gas). One commentator noted, "The provisions of the bill will likely formalize the current situation, where Kremlin approval is widely seen as essential for any major business deal inside the country." Tai Adelaja and Natalia Krainova, "Strategic Sector Bill Clears Second Reading," *Moscow Times* March 24, 2008; Andrei Evplanov, "Ostorozhno, dveri zakryvaiutsia," *Rossiiskaia gazeta* March 25, 2008; Anatolo Medetsky, "Test Run for Strategic Sector Law," *Moscow Times* August 20, 2008.

13 Aleksei Miller tried to "upgrade" Gazprom managerial skills. "Forsyth Tech and Gazprom Sign International Management Training Agreement," *Business Wire* Oct. 18, 2005.

14 Cf. Gaddy and Ickes on redistribution of hydrocarbon rents ("Resource Rents and the Russian Economy"): Gazprom, Rosneft, and EES did not always use economic rationales to choose suppliers.

15 Interviews Beer-1 and Beer-2, July 1999; "Baltika Takes Beer Market to Heady Heights," *Moscow Times* May 18, 2004; "Interv'iu: Taimuraz Bolloev, president OAO 'Pivovarennaia kompaniia Baltika,'" *Vedomosti* Nov. 2, 2004.

16 Interview Cloth-1, July 1997.

17 Natal'ia Ul'ianova, "Novoe litso FOSP," *Sekret firmy* 5 (Feb. 7, 2005).

18 Guriev and Rachinsky, "The Role of Oligarchs in Russian Capitalism" and "Ownership Concentration in Russian Industry."

19 Younger managers used IPOs to obtain capital. In the 1990s this risked losing control. Henry Ford compromised with his union over wages but never risked control of Ford by selling shares.

20 Cf. Dmitrii Butrin, "Engineering Industry: Trends," *Kommersant Vlast'* March 2, 2004 (in English via the *Kommersant* internet site). Silovye Mashiny also adopted this logic.

21 The autumn 2008 crisis and corporate debt forced Deripaska to sell assets, however. Dmitrii Belikov and Mariia Cherkasova, "Oleg Deripaska lishilsia zapchastei," *Kommersant Daily* Oct. 6, 2008.

22 Catherine Belton, "'I don't Need to Defend Myself,'" *Moscow Times* July 13, 2007.

23 E.g. Anatolii Temkin, "Spad po raspisaniiu," *Vedomosti* March 17, 2005; Sarah Karush, "Severstal's U.S. Bid Backed," *Moscow Times* Nov. 26, 2003; Andrew Hurst, "Cherepovets a Steel Girder in the New Economy," *Moscow Times* April 14, 2003.

24 As for AvtoVAZ, we see a case of the daughter owning the mother—not unique in 1990s privatization.

25 Lina Kalianina, "Inovatsionnyi ukhod ot konkurentsii," *Ekspert* June 6, 2005.

26 "Strategiia golykh raschëtov," *Ekspert* 31 (January 31, 2000).

27 According to one study, firms with a commanding position in their sector are more likely to focus on integration or control, not using marketing to innovate or create

value through production or exchange relations. K. V. Krotov, S. P. Kushch, and M. M. Smirnova, "Marketingovyi aspekt upravleniia vzaimootnosheniiami v tsepiakh postavok: rezul'taty issledovaniia rossiiskikh kompanii," *Rossiiskii zhurnal menedzhmenta* 6/2 (2008), 3–26.

28 "Retseptura vyzovov," *Ekspert* 35 (Sept. 22, 2003).

29 Nikolai Demidov, "Marketing na gliukakh," *Ekspert severo-zapad* (Sept. 29, 2008). This sales logic created problems of data collection and interpretation: were auto sales slowing (as aggregate data on auto shipment suggested), or was it stable (suggested by declining waiting lists)?

30 Iuliia Fedorinova, "Rekord 'Mechela,'" *Vedomosti* May 31, 2005.

31 One tactic was leveraging and corporate debt, creating a debt bomb that the 2008 global crisis set off. Al'fa Bank and others expected Russian companies would have to pay $88 billion in interest and principal; in April 1, 2008 Russian corporate debt was at least $477 billion. Woodruff, "The Expansion of State Ownership in Russia," 10; Dmitrii Butrin *et al*, "VEB prigovoren k krainei mere," *Kommersant Daily* Sept. 30, 2008; Filipp Sterkin, "Dolgovye rezervy," *Vedomosti* Oct. 13, 2008; Aleksandr Ivanter, "Zontik—nepromokaemym," *Ekspert* Oct. 13, 2008. Deripaska's empire started to come undone in early 2009 because of corporate debt. See Iuliia Fedorinova's analyses in *Vedomosti* March 3, 10, 13, and 16, 2009. See also Elena Mazneva, "Kto zamenit Deripasku," *Vedomosti* March 4, 2009, and Tatiana Zykova, "'RUSAL' zalozhil svoi zavody gosudarstvu," *Rossiiskaia gazeta* March 17, 2009.

32 Mariia Rozhkova, "'AvtoVAZ vosvroshchaet potrebitelei," *Vedomosti* July 6, 2005; Zarina Khisamova, "Kol'tsevoe dvizhenie," *Ekspert* Nov. 28, 2005.

33 Iuliia Fedorinova *et al*, "Daite deneg 'AvtoVAZu,'" *Vedomosti* Sept. 27, 2005; Anna Smolchenko, "State Tightens its Grip on AvtoVAZ," *Moscow Times* Nov. 21, 2005; Elena Naumova, "Bez strategii, no s perspektivami," *Ekspert Volga* Jan. 16, 2006.

34 Konstantin Sonin, "The Future that AvtoVAZ Needs," *Moscow Times* Nov. 29, 2005; Iuliia Fedorinova, "'AvtoVAZ ne tonet," *Vedomosti* Dec. 19, 2005.

35 Evgeniia Pis'mennaia and Iuliia Fedorinova, "'Nas interesuet mashinostroeniie'— Sergei Chemezov, general'nyi direktor goskorporatsii 'Rostekhnologii,'" *Vedomosti* July 14, 2008.

36 On *siloviki* rent-seeking and redistributive logic, see Gaddy and Ickes, *Russia's Addiction*.

37 S. Elekoev, H. Zondhof, and H. Kroll, "Restrukturizatsiia promyshlennykh predpriiatii (opyt Rossiiskogo tsentra provatizatsii)," *Voprosy ekonomiki* 9 (1997), 13–22.

38 Interview, President Association of Industrial Entrepreneurs (private voluntary association), July 1997, St. Petersburg, Russia; interviews Ptit-1, July 1997, and Elec-1, July 1997.

39 *Elektrosila* June 14, 1995, p. 2.

40 Interviews Psk-1 (machine-tool), July 1997, and SevFurn (furniture), July 1997.

41 Reform was radical structurally and discursively. Interdependence between subdivisions was weaker, and there was less a material incentive to hold the Svetlana *obedinenie* together. This encouraged internal conflicts over contracts and payments, due to superficial devolution without rethinking authority and accountability. Svetlana's general directors, 1988–92, were fairly open with employees, moderating employee–manager relations. In 1993 employees suspected newly elected general director Vladimir Bashkatov of using shell games and restructuring for immoral personal gain. This strengthened employee identity versus a common threat, bringing the firm together again. Yet Bashkatov's shell games strengthened mother firm control over subdivisions and daughters and helped Svetlana avoid Pozitron's fate.

42 These data come from an interview with assistant directors for sales and economics, July 1997.

43 *Maiak* Feb. 27, 1992, pp. 1, 3.

44 Basic data are from www.positron.spb.ru and www.pplast.spb.ru (summer 2008).

45 *Kommersant Daily* Jan. 25, 1996, p. 9.

46 Pavel Kober, "Raketami po stereotipam," *Ekspert-Ural* Dec. 11, 2006.
47 Especially Gaddy and Ickes, *Russia's Virtual Economy*, and Woodruff, *Money Unmade*.
48 Cf. Gaddy and Ickes, *Russia's Virtual Economy*, and Jeffrey Hass, "Trials and Tribulations of Learning the Market: Culture and Economic Practice in Russia's Market Transition," *The Carl Beck Papers in Russian and East European Studies* (Pittsburgh: University of Pittsburgh Center for Russian and East European Studies, 2005).
49 *Why* firms landed in the virtual economy is less clear. Gaddy and Ickes assume if a firm cannot sell output, it must be unable to produce for the market—a tautology.
50 Gaddy and Ickes, *Russia's Virtual Economy*, ch. 5.
51 Earlier, Neutron and brothers in its *obedinenie* followed flood-the-market strategies.
52 Newtonian physics works for sending rockets to the moon. Quantum mechanics, strong and weak forces, and strings suggest that what lies under Newton's mechanics— ostensibly the model for economic theory—is far more complicated.
53 William Doyle, *Origins of the French Revolution* (New York: Oxford University Press, 1988) and *The Oxford History of the French Revolution* (New York: Oxford University Press, 1989); Alan Knight, *The Mexican Revolution*, 2 vols. (Lincoln, NE: University of Nebraska Press, 1986).
54 E.g. Sheila Fitzpatrick, "The Bolsheviks' Dilemma: Class, Culture, and Politics in the Early Soviet Years," *Slavic Review* 47 (1988), 599–613.
55 Cf. Paul R. Gregory (ed.), *Behind the Façade of Stalin's Command Economy* (Stanford, CA: Hoover Institution Press, 2001).
56 Peter A. Hall and David W. Soskice (eds.), *Varieties of Capitalism: The Institutional Foundations of Comparative Advantage* (New York: Oxford University Press, 2001).
57 "Critique of Modern Civilization," in Rudrangshu Mukherjee (ed.), *The Penguin Gandhi Reader* (New York: Penguin, 1996), 1–66.
58 John Markoff and Verónica Montecinos, "The Ubiquitous Rise of Economists," *Journal of Public Policy* 13 (1993), 37–68.
59 *Condé Nast Traveler* Sept. 2008, p. 176.
60 Roy, *Socializing Capital*; Alfred Chandler, *Scale and Scope* (Cambridge, MA: Harvard University Press, 1990); Paul Kennedy, *The Rise and Fall of the Great Powers* (New Haven, CT: Yale University Press, 1988).
61 Haggard, *Pathways from the Periphery*; Chalmers Johnson, *MITI and the Japanese Miracle* (Stanford, CA: Stanford University Press, 1982); Gereffi and Wyman (eds), *Manufacturing Miracles*.
62 Peter Evans, *Embedded Autonomy* (Princeton, NJ: Princeton University Press, 1995).
63 Joseph Schumpeter, *Capitalism, Socialism and Democracy* (New York: Harper, 1975).
64 Stark and Bruszt, *Postsocialist Pathways*, chs. 4 and 7.
65 McDermott, *Embedded Politics*, conclusion.
66 Susan Shirk, *The Political Logic of Economic Reform in China* (Berkeley, CA: University of California, Press, 1993); Bartlomiej Kaminski, *The Collapse of State Socialism: The Case of Poland* (Princeton, NJ: Princeton University Press, 1991); John Edgar Jackson, Jacek Kilch, and Krystyna Poznańska, *The Political Economy of Poland's New Firms and Reform Governments* (New York: Cambridge University Press, 2005); Connor O'Dwyer, *Runaway State-Building: Patronage Politics and Democratic Development* (Baltimore, MD: Johns Hopkins University Press, 2006).
67 Samuel Huntington, *Political Order in Changing Societies* (New Haven, CT: Yale University Press, 1968).
68 Albert O. Hirschman, *The Passions and the Interests* (Princeton, NJ: Princeton University Press, 1977).

Bibliography

Afanas'ev, Mst., P. Kuznetsov, and A. Fominykh. 1997. "Korporativnoe upravlenie glazami direktorata (po materialam obsledovanii 1994–1996 gg)." *Voprosy ekonomiki* #5: 84-101.

Afanas'ev, Mst., P. Kuznetsov, and P. Isaeva. 1995. "Krizis platezhei v Rossii: chto proiskhodit na samom dele?" *Voprosy ekonomiki* #8: 52-67.

Akbar, Hammad. 2003. "Knowledge Levels and the Transformation: Towards the Integration of Knowledge Creation and Individual Learning." *Journal of Management Studies* 40: 1997–2021.

Akhmeduev, A. 1994. "Gosudarstvennye predpriiatiia: tipy i mekhanizm funktsonirovaniia." *Voprosy ekonomiki* #8: 59-68.

Alimova, T. 1994. "Malyi biznes v zerkale ofitsial'noi statistiki." *Voprosy ekonomiki* #11: 133-141.

Alimova, T., V. Buev, V. Golikova, and T. Dolgopiatova. 1994. "Problemy malogo biznesa glazami predprinimatelei." *Voprosy ekonomiki* #11: pp. 108–23.

Alimova, T., V. Buev, V. Golikova, and I. Yevseeva. 1994. "Formirovanie informatsionnoi sredy malogo biznesa." *Voprosy ekonomiki* #11: 124-132.

Amsden, Alice. 1989. *Asia's Next Giant*. New York: Oxford University Press.

Amsden, Alice, Jacek Kochanowicz, and Lance Taylor. 1994. *The Market Meets its Match: Restructuring the Economies of Eastern Europe*. Cambridge, CA: Harvard University Press.

Anthony, Denise. 2005. "Cooperation in Microcredit Borrowing Groups: Identity, Sanctions, and Reciprocity in the Production of Collective Goods." *American Sociological Review* 70: 496-515.

Argyris, Chris. *On Organizational Learning*. Cambridge: Blackwell.

Arnot, Bob. 1988. *Controlling Soviet Labor: Experimental Change from Brezhnev to Gorbachev*. Armonk, NY: M. E. Sharpe.

Åslund, Anders (ed.). 1992. *Market Socialism or the Restoration of Capitalism?* New York: Cambridge University Press.

—(ed.) 1994. *Economic Transformation in Russia*. London: Pinter Publishers.

—1995. *How Russia Became a Market Economy*. Washington, DC, WA: Brookings Institution.

—2007. *Russia's Capitalist Revolution*. Washington, DC, WA: Peterson Institution for International Economics

Auktsionek, S. P. 1994. "Oprosy promyshlennykh predpriiatii." *EKO* #11: 18-21.

Bahry, Donna. 1987. "Politics, Generations, and Change in the USSR." Pp. 61–99 in *Politics, Work, and Daily Life in the USSR*, edited by James R. Millar. New York: Cambridge University Press.

Ball, Alan. 1987. *Russia's Last Capitalists*. Ithaca, NY: Cornell University Press.

Barnes, Andrew. 2006. *Owning Russia: The Struggle Over Factories, Farms, and Power*. Ithaca, NY: Cornell University Press.

Barnett, William P. and Glenn R. Carroll. 1995. "Modeling Internal Organizational Change." *Annual Review of Sociology* 21: 217-236.

Batchikov, S. and Iu. Petrov. 1995. "Formirovanie finansovo-promyshlennykh grupp i gosudarstvo." *Rossiiskii ekonomicheskii zhurnal* #2: 3-10.

Bates, Robert. 1983. *Essays on the Political Economy of Rural Africa*. New York: Cambridge University Press.

Batizi, E. 1994. Upolnomochennye banki i finansovo-promyshlennaia integratsiia." *Rossiiskii ekonomicheskii zhurnal* #10: 42-46.

Beissinger, Mark. 1988. *Scientific Management, Socialist Discipline, and Soviet Power*. Cambridge, MA: Harvard University Press.

—2002. *Nationalist Mobilization and the Collapse of the Soviet State*. New York: Cambridge University Press.

Belianova, E. 1995. "Motivatsiia i povedenie rossiiskikh predpriiatii." *Voprosy ekonomiki* #6: 15-21.

Belova, Eugenia. 2001. "Economic Crime and Punishment." Pp. 131–58 in *Behind the Façade of Stalin's Command Economy*, edited by Paul Gregory. Stanford, CA: Hoover Institution Press.

Bendix, Reinhard. 1960. "The Cultural and Political Setting of Economic Rationality in Western and Eastern Europe." Pp. 245–61 in *Value and Plan: Economic Calculation and Organization in Eastern Europe*, edited by Gregory Grossman. Berkeley, CA: University of California Press.

—1974. *Work and Authority in Industry*. Berkeley, CA: University of California Press.

Berger, Peter and Thomas Luckmann. 1967. *The Social Construction of Reality*. Garden City: Anchor Books.

Berliner, Joseph. 1957. *Factory and Manager in the USSR*. Cambridge, MA: Harvard University Press.

—1976. *The Innovation Decision in Soviet Industry*. Cambridge: MIT Press.

Blackwell, William L. 1968. *The Beginnings of Russian Industrialization. 1800-1860*. Princeton, MA: Princeton University Press.

Blanchard, Olivier Jean, Kenneth A. Froot, and Jeffrey D. Sachs (eds). 1994. *The Transition in Eastern Europe, vol. 1. Country Studies*. Chicago, IL: University of Chicago Press.

Blasi, Joseph, Maya Kroumova, and Douglas Kruse. 1997. *Kremlin Capitalism. Privatizing the Russian Economy*. Ithaca, NY: Cornell University Press.

Blinder, Alan, Elie R. D. Canetti, David E. Lebow, and Jeremy B. Rudd. 1998. *Asking About Prices. A New Approach to Understanding Price Stickiness*. New York: Russell Sage.

Blinov, A. 1996. "Maloe predprinimatel'stvo i bol'shaia politika." *Voprosy ekonomiki* #7: 39-45.

Boeva, I. N., Tatiana G. Dolgopiatova, and Viacheslav Shironin. 1992. *Gosudarstvennye predpriiatiia v 1991-1992 gg: ekonomicheskie problemy i povedenie*. Moscow: Moscow Institute of Economic Policy.

Boiko, T. 1993. "Rossiiskie predprinimateli." *EKO* #5: 93-105.

Botkin, O. and M. Kozlov. 1995. "Finansovo-promyshlennaia gruppa 'Ural'skie zavody': pervyi god raboty." *Voprosy ekonomiki* #5: 147-155.

Bourdieu, Pierre. 1990. *The Logic of Practice*. Stanford, CA: Stanford University Press.

—1996. *The State Nobility*. Stanford, CA: Stanford University Press.

—1996. *The Rules of Art*. Stanford, CA: Stanford University Press.

Boycko, Maxim, Andrei Schleifer, and Robert Vishny. 1995. *Privatizing Russia*. Cambridge: MIT Press.

Braverman, Harry. 1974. *Labor and Monopoly Capital: The Degradation of Work in the Twentieth Century*. New York: Monthly Review Press.

Brower, Daniel. 1990. *The Russian City Between Tradition and Modernity, 1850-1900*. Berkeley, CA: University of California Press.

Bunce, Valerie. 1983. "The Political Economy of the Brezhnev Era: The Rise and Fall of Corporatism." *British Journal of Political Science* 13: 129-158.

—1998. *Subversive Institutions: The Design and the Destruction of Socialism and the State*. New York: Cambridge University Press.

Burawoy, Michael. 1979. *Manufacturing Consent*. Chicago, IL: University of Chicago Press.

—1985. *The Politics of Production: Factory Regimes under Capitalism and Socialism*. London: Verso.

—1995. "From Sovietology to Comparative Political Economy." Pp. 72–102 in *Beyond Soviet Studies*, edited by Daniel Orlovsky. Washington, DC, WA: Woodrow Wilson Center Press.

Burawoy, Michael, Alice Burton, Ann Arnett Ferguson, Akthryn J. Fox, Joshua Gamson, Nadine Gartrell, Leslie Hurst, Charles Kurzman, Leslie Salzinger, Josepha Schiffman, and Shiori Ui. 1991. *Ethnography Unbound*. Berkeley, CA: University of California Press.

Burawoy, Michael, and Kathryn Hendley. 1992. "Between Perestroika and Privatisation: Divided Strategies and Political Crisis in a Soviet Enterprise." *Soviet Studies* 44 (3): 371-402.

Burawoy, Michael and Pavel Krotov. 1992. "The Soviet Transition from Socialism to Capitalism: Worker Control and Economic Bargaining in the Wood Industry." *American Sociological Review* 57: 16-38.

Burawoy, Michael and Katherine Verdery (eds). 1999. *Uncertain Transition: Ethnographies of Change in the Postsocialist World*. New York: Rowan and Littlefield.

Burkov, S. and S. Skliarov. 1995. "Zakonodatel'stvo ob aktsionernykh obshchestvakh: kakim emu byt'?" *Voprosy ekonomiki* #7: 103-111.

Centeno, Miguel A. 1994. "Between Rocky Democracies and Hard Markets: Dilemmas of the Great Transformation." *Annual Review of Sociology* 20: 125-147.

—1994. *Democracy Within Reason*. University Park, PA: Penn State Press.

Chandler, Alfred D. 1962. *Strategy and Structure*. Cambridge: M.I.T. Press.

—1977. *The Visible Hand*. Cambridge, MA: Harvard University Press.

—1994. *Scale and Scope. The Dynamics of Industrial Capitalism*. Cambridge, MA: Harvard University Press.

Chase, William. 1987. *Workers, Society, and the Soviet State. Labor and Life in Moscow. 1918–1929*. Urbana, IL: University of Illinois Press.

Chepurenko, A. 1996. "Problema finansirovaniia v rossiiskom malom biznese (po materialam vyborochnykh sotsiologicheskikh obsledovanii)." *Voprosy ekonomik* #7: 59-71.

Chibrikov, G. 1994. "O finansovo-promyshlennykh gruppakh." *Rossiiskii ekonomicheskii zhurnal* #2: 82-85.

Clarke, Simon (ed.). 1995. *Management and Industry in Russia. Formal and Informal Relations in the Period of Transition*. Cheltenham, UK: Edward Elgar.

—(ed.). 1996. *Conflict and Change in the Russian Industrial Enterprise*. Cheltenham, UK: Edward Elgar.

—(ed.). 1996. *The Russian Enterprise in Transition. Case Studies*. Cheltenham, UK: Edward Elgar.

—(ed.). 1996. *Labour Relations in Transition. Wages, Employment and Industrial Conflict in Russia*. Cheltenham, UK: Edward Elgar.

—(ed.). 1997. *Structural Adjustment Without Mass Unemployment? Lessons from Russia.* Cheltenham, UK: Edward Elgar.

—1999. *The Formation of a Labour Market in Russia.* Cheltenham, UK: Edward Elgar.

—1999. *New Forms of Employment and Household Survival Strategies in Russia.* Cheltenham, UK: Edward Elgar.

Clarke, Simon and Vadim Borisov. 1999. "New Forms of Labour Contract and Labour Flexibility in Russia." *Economics of Transition* 7: 593-614.

Clarke, Simon and Inna Donova. 1999. "Internal Mobility and Labour Market Flexibility in Russia." *Europe-Asia Studies* 51 (2): 213-243.

Clarke, Simon, Peter Fairbrother, Vadim Borisov, and Pëtr Bizyukov. 1994. "The Privatisation of Industrial Enterprises in Russia: Four Case Studies." *Europe-Asia Studies* 46 (2): 179-214.

Clarke, Simon and Veronika Kabalina. 2000. "The New Private Sector in the Russian Labour Market." *Europe-Asia Studies* 52 (1): 7-32.

Clarke, Simon and Tanya Metalina. 2000. "Training in the New Private Sector in Russia." *International Journal of Human Resource Management* 11 (1): 19-36.

Cohen, Michael, James March and Johan P. Olsen. 1972. "A Garbage Can Model of Organizational Choice." *Administrative Science Quarterly* 17: 1-25.

Colignon, Richard. 1997. *Power Plays.* Stony Brook, NY: SUNY Press.

Connor, Walter. 1988. *Socialism's Dilemmas.* New York: Columbia University Press.

—1991. *The Accidental Proletariat: Workers, Politics, and Crisis in Gorbachev's Russia.* Princeton, MA: Princeton University Press.

—1996. *Tattered Banners: Labor, Conflict, and Corporatism in Postcommunist Russia.* Boulder: Westview.

Conyngham, William J. 1982. *The Modernization of Soviet Industrial Management.* Cambridge: Cambridge University Press.

Cooper, Julian. 2006. "Can Russia Compete in the Global Economy?" *Eurasian Geography and Economics* 47: 407-425.

Crowley, Stephen. 1997. *Hot Coal, Cold Steel: Russian and Ukrainian Workers from the End of the Soviet Union to the Post-Communist Transformations.* Ann Arbor, MI: University of Michigan Press.

Dalton, Melville. 1959. *Men Who Manage.* New York: John Wiley and Sons.

Dickenson, R. Peter, David Campbell, and Vladimir Azarov. 2000. "Will Western Managerial Methods World in Transitional Societies?" *Problems of Post-Communism* 47 (3): 48-56.

DiMaggio, Paul. 1988. "Interest and Agency in Institutional Theory." Pp. 3–21 in *Institutional Patterns and Organization*, edited by Lynne Zucker. Cambridge: Ballinger.

—1990. "Cultural Aspects of Economic Action and Organization." Pp. 113–36 in *Beyond the Marketplace. Rethinking Economy and Society*, edited by Roger Friedland and A. F. Robertson. New York: Aldine de Gruyter.

—1997. "Culture and Cognition." *Annual Review of Sociology* 23: 263-287.

DiMaggio, Paul and Walter Powell. 1983. "The Iron Cage Revisited: Institutional Isomorphism and Collective Rationality in Organizational Fields." *American Sociological Review* 48:147-60.

—1991. "Introduction." Pp. 1–38 in *The New Institutionalism in Organizational Analysis*, edited by Walter Powell and Paul J. DiMaggio. Chicago, IL: Chicago University Press.

Dobbin, Frank. 1994. *Forging Industrial Policies.* New York: Cambridge University Press.

—2009. *Inventing Equal Opportunity.* Princeton, MA: Princeton University Press.

Dobrynin, P. Ia. 1993. "Privatizatsiia v VPK." *EKO* #4: 3-16.

Dolgopiatova, T., 1994. "Povedenie predpriiatii v usloviiakh zhestkikh finansovykh ogranichenii." *Rossiiskii ekonomicheskii zhurnal* 12: 66-73.
—1995. *Rossiiskie predpriiatiia v perekhodnoi ekonomike: ekonomicheskie problemy i povedenie.* Moscow: Delo Ltd.
—1996. "Perekhodnaia model' povedeniia rossiiskikh promyshlennykh predpriiatii (po dannym empiricheskikh issledovanii 1991-1995 gg.)." *Voprosy ekonomiki* #11: 119-130.
Dolgopiatova, T. and I. Evseeva, 1994. "Ekonomicheskoe povedenie promyshlennykh predpriiatii v perekhodnoi ekonomike." *Voprosy ekonomiki* 8: 40-50.
Dolgopiatova, T., I. Evseeva, and V. Shironin. 1994. "Rol' zakonodatel'stva i regulirovaniia v stanovlenii malogo biznesa v Rossii." *Voprosy ekonomiki* 11: 92-107.
Doyle, William. 1988. *Origins of the French Revolution.* New York: Oxford University Press.
—1989. *The Oxford History of the French Revolution.* New York: Oxford University Press.
Djankov, Simeon. 1999. "The Restructuring of Insider-Dominated Firms." *Economics of Transition* 7 (2): 467-479.
Drakulic, Slavenka. 1992. *How We Survived Communism and Even Laughed.* London: Hutchinson.
Drobak, John N. and John V. C. Nye (eds). 1997. *The Frontiers of New Institutional Economics.* New York: Academic Press.
Dunn, Elizabeth. 1999. "Slick Salesmen and Simple People: Negotiated Capitalism in a Privatized Polish Firm." Pp. 125–50 in *Uncertain Transitions,* edited by Michael Burawoy and Katherine Verdery. Lanham, MD: Rowman and Littlefield.
—2004. *Privatizing Poland: Baby Food, Big Business, and the Remaking of Labor.* Ithaca, NY: Cornell University Press.
Dyperovich, G. 1927. *Sindikaty i tresty v dorevoliutsionnoi Rossii i v SSSR.* Leningrad: Tekhnika i Proizvodstvo.
Earle, John S., Roman Frydman, and Andrzej Rapaczynski (eds). 1993. *Privatization in the Transition to a Market Economy.* London: Pinter.
Eccles, Robert. 1985. *The Transfer Pricing Problem.* Lexington: Lexington Books.
Eccles, Robert and Harrison White. 1988. "Price and Authority in Inter-Profit Center Transactions." *American Journal of Sociology* 94 (supplement): 517-552.
Edwards, Richard. 1979. *Contested Terrain.* New York: Basic Books.
Emirbayer, Mustafa and Victoria Johnson. 2008. "Bourdieu and Organizational Analysis." *Theory and Society* 37: 1-44.
Evans, Peter. 1979. *Dependent Development.* Princeton, MA: Princeton University Press.
—1995. *Embedded Autonomy.* Princeton, MA: Princeton University Press.
Ewick, Patricia and Susan Silbey. 1998. *The Common Place of Law: Stories from Everyday Life.* Chicago, IL: University of Chicago Press.
Eyal, Gil, Evan Szelenyi, Eleanor Townsley, and Ivan Szelenyi. 2001. *Making Capitalism Without Capitalists: The New Ruling Elites in Eastern Europe.* London: Verso.
Field, Daniel. 1976. *Rebels in the Name of the Tsar.* Boston, MA: Houghton Mifflin.
Filtzer, Donald. 1986. *Soviet Workers and Stalinist Industrialization.* Armonk, NY: M. E. Sharpe.
—1991. "The Contradictions of the Marketless Market: Self-financing in the Soviet Industrial Enterprise." *Soviet Studies* 43: 989-1009.
Fine, Gary Alan. 1984. "Negotiated Orders and Organizational Cultures." *Annual Review of Sociology* 10: 239-262.
Fitzpatrick, Sheila. 1988. "The Bolsheviks' Dilemma: Class, Culture, and Politics in the Early Soviet Years." *Slavic Review* 47: 599-613.
Fligstein, Neil. 1990. *The Transformation of Corporate Control.* Cambridge, MA: Harvard University Press.

—1996. "Markets as Politics: A Political-Cultural Approach to Market Institutions." *American Sociological Review* 61: 656-673.

—1996. "The Economic Sociology of the Transitions from Socialism." *American Journal of Sociology* 101: 1074-81.

—2001. *The Architecture of Markets*. Princeton, MA: Princeton University Press.

—2001. "Social Skill and the Theory of Fields." *Sociological Theory* 19: 105-125.

Fligstein, Neil and Kenneth Dauber. 1989. "Structural Change in Corporate Organization." *Annual Review of Sociology* 15: 73-96.

Fogel, Georgine and Alina Zapalska. 2001. "A Comparison of Small and Medium-Size Enterprise Development in Central and Eastern Europe." *Comparative Economic Studies* 43 (3): 35-68.

Foucault, Michel. 1977. *Discipline and Punish: The Birth of the Prison*, translated by Alan Sheridan. New York: Pantheon Books

—1980. *Power/Knowledge: Selected Interviews and Other Writings, 1972-1977*, edited by Colin Gordon. New York: Pantheon Books.

Frankel, Lev. 1995. "Financial-industrial Groups in Russia: Emergence of Large Diversified Private Companies." *Communist Economies and Economic Transformation* 7 (1): 51-66.

Franzosi, Roberto. 1987. "The Press as a Source of Socio-Historical Data: Issues in the Methodology of Data Collection from Newspapers." *Historical Methods* 20 (1): 5-16.

—1995. *The Puzzle of Strikes*. New York: Cambridge University Press.

—2004. *From Words to Numbers A Journey in Science*. New York: Cambridge University Press.

Friedland, Roger and Robert R. Alford. 1991. "Bringing Society Back In: Symbols, Practices, and Institutional Contradictions." Pp. 232–63 in *The New Institutionalism in Organizational Analysis*, edited by Walter Powell and Paul DiMaggio. Chicago, IL: University of Chicago Press.

Frank, Robert H. 1990. "Rethinking Rational Choice." Pp. 53–88 in *Beyond the Marketplace: Rethinking Economy and Society*, edited by Roger Friedland and A. F. Robertson. New York: Aldine de Gruyter.

Frieden, Jeffrey. 1992. *Dept, Development, and Democracy*. Princeton, MA: Princeton University Press.

Friedland, Roger. 2002. "Money, Sex, and God: The Erotic Logic of Religious Nationalism." *Sociological Theory* 20: 381-425.

Friedland, Roger and Robert Alford. 1991. "Bringing Society Back In: Symbols, Practices, and Institutional Contradictions." Pp. 232–263 in *The New Institutionalism in Organizational Analysis*, edited by Walter Powell and Paul DiMaggio. Chicago, IL: University of Chicago Press.

Frydman, Roman and Andrzej Rapaczynski. 1994. *Privatization in Eastern Europe: Is the State Withering Away?* London: Central European University Press.

Frydman, Roman, Andrzej Rapaczynski, John S. Earle. 1993. *The Process of Privatization in Russia, Ukraine, and the Baltic States*. London: Central European University Press.

Fülöp-Miller, René. 1927. *The Mind and Face of Bolshevism*, trans. F. S. Flint and D. F. Tait. New York: G. P. Putnam's Sons.

Gaddy, Clifford W. and Barry W. Ickes. 1998. "Russia's Virtual Economy." *Foreign Affairs* 77(5): 53-67.

—2002. *Russia's Virtual Economy*. Washington, DC, WA: Brookings.

—2005. "Resource Rents and the Russian Economy." *Eurasian Geography and Economics* 46: 559-583.

—Forthcoming. Clifford Gaddy and Barry W. Ickes, *Russia's Addiction. The Political Economy of Resource Dependence*. Washington, DC, WA: Brookings.

Gates, Hill. 1996. *China's Motor: A Thousand Years of Petty Capitalism*. Ithaca, NY: Cornell University Press.

Gaventa, John. 1980. *Power and Powerlessness*. Urbana, IL: University of Illinois Press.

Gerber, Theodore and Michael Hout. 1998. "More Shock than Therapy: Market Transition, Employment, and Income in Russia, 1991–1995." *American Journal of Sociology* 104: 1-50.

Gereffi, Gary and Donald Wyman (eds). 1990. *Manufacturing Miracles: Paths of Industrialization in Latin America and East Asia*. Princeton, MA: Princeton University Press.

Gersick, Connie J. G. 1991. "Revolutionary Change Theories: a Multilevel Exploration of the Punctuated Equilibrium Paradigm." *Academy of Management Review* 16: 10-36.

Giddens, Anthony. 1984. *The Constitution of Society*. Berkeley, CA: University of California Press.

Goldman, Marshall. 1983. *USSR in Crisis: The Failure of an Economic System*. New York: Norton.

Goldstone, Jack A. 1991. *Revolution and Rebellion in the Early Modern World*. Berkeley, CA: University of California Press.

Gorbatova, Larisa. 1995. "Formation of Connections between Finance and Industry in Russia: Basic Stages and Forms." *Communist Economies and Economic Transformation* 7(1): 21-34.

Granick, David. 1954. *Management of the Industrial Firm in the USSR*. New York: Columbia University Press.

—1960 *The Red Executive*. Garden City, NY: Doubleday.

Granovetter, Mark. 1973. "The Strength of Weak Ties." *American Journal of Sociology* 78: 1360-1380.

—1974. *Getting a Job*. Cambridge, MA: Harvard University Press.

—1983. "The Strength of Weak Ties: A Network Theory Revisited." *Sociological Theory* 1: 201-233.

—1985. "Economic Action and Social Structure: The Problem of Embeddedness." *American Journal of Sociology* 91: 481-510.

—1993. "The Nature of Economic Relationships." Pp. 3–41 in *Explorations in Economic Sociology*, edited by Richard Swedberg. New York: Russell Sage Foundation.

Gregory, Paul R. (ed.). 2001. *Behind the Façade of Stalin's Command Economy*. Stanford, CA: Hoover Institution Press.

Grossman, Gregory. 1977. "The 'Second Economy' of the USSR." *Problems of Communism* 26 (5): 25-40.

—1987. "The Second Economy: Boon or Bane for the Reform of the First Economy?" *Berkeley-Duke Occasional Papers on the Second Economy in the USSR* No. 11.

Gudkova, E. V. and A. A. Get'man. 1998. "Predpriiatiia mashinostroeniia Dal'nego Vostoka v usloviiakh ekonomicheskoi reform." *EKO* #4: 81-94.

Gumpert, David E. (ed.). 1985. *The Marketing Renaissance*. New York: John Wiley and Sons.

Guriev, Sergei and Andrei Rachinsky. 2005. "The Role of Oligarchs in Russian Capitalism." *Journal of Economic Perspectives* 19: 131-150.

Gurkov, I. and E. Avraamova. 1995. "Strategii vyzhivaniia promyshlennykh predpriiatii v novykh usloviiakh." *Voprosy ekonomiki* 6: 22-30.

Gustafson, Thane. 1989. *Crisis Amid Plenty: The Politics of Soviet Energy under Brezhnev and Gorbachev*. Princeton, MA: Princeton University Press.

—1999. *Capitalism Russian-Style*. New York: Cambridge University Press.

Hage, J. T. 1999. "Organizational Innovation and Organizational Change." *Annual Review of Sociology* 25: 597-622

Haggard, Stephan. 1990. *Pathways from the Periphery*. Ithaca, NY: Cornell University Press.

Hall, Peter. 1986. *Governing the Economy*. New York: Oxford University Press.

Hall, Peter and David W. Soskice (eds). 2001. *Varieties of Capitalism: The Institutional Foundations of Comparative Advantage*. New York: Oxford University Press.

Hallett, Tim. 2003. "Symbolic Power and Organizational Culture." *Sociological Theory* 21: 128-149.

Hamilton, Gary and Nicole Woosley Biggart. 1988. "Market, Culture, and Authority: A Comparative Analysis of Management and Organization in the Far East." *American Journal of Sociology* 94 (Supplement):S52-S94.

Handelman, Stephen. 1995. *Comrade Criminal: Russia's New Maffiya*. New Haven, CT: Yale University Press.

Hardt, John P. and Theodore Frankel. 1971. "The Industrial Managers." Pp. 171–208 in *Interest Groups in Soviet Politics*, edited by Gordon Skilling and Franklyn Griffiths. Princeton, MA: Princeton University Press.

Hass, Jeffrey K. 1997. "Making Markets: Rationality, Institutions, Culture, and Economic Change in Russia." *Problems of Post-Communism* 44 (4): 44-51.

—1999. "The Great Transition: The Dynamics of Market Transitions and the Case of Russia, 1991-1995." *Theory and Society* 28: 383-424.

—2005. *Trials and Tribulations of Learning the Market. Culture and Economic Practice in Russia's Market Transition*. (*The Carl Beck Papers in Russian and East European Studies*.) Pittsburgh: Center for Russian and East European Studies, University of Pittsburgh.

—2007. *Economic Sociology*. New York: Routledge.

Hedlund, Stefan. 2001. "Property Without Rights: Dimensions of Russian Privatisation." *Europe-Asia Studies* 53 (2): 213-237.

Hellman, Joel and Mark Schankerman. 2000. "Intervention, Corruption and Capture. The Nexus between Enterprises and the State." *The Economics of Transition* 8 (3): 545-576.

Hendley, Kathryn. 1992. "Legal Development and Privatization in Russia: A Case Study." *Soviet Economy* 8 (2): 130-157.

—1999. "How Russian Enterprises Cope With Payment Problems." *Post-Soviet Affairs* 15 (3): 201-234.

Hendley, Kathryn, Peter Murrell, and Randi Ryterman. 1999. "A Regional Analysis of Transactional Strategies of Russian Enterprises." *McGill Law Journal* 44: 433-472.

Hendley, Kathryn. 1999. "How Russian Enterprises Cope With Payment Problems." *Post-Soviet Affairs* 15 (3): 201-234.

Herrera, Yoshiko. 2004. *Imagined Economies: The Sources of Russian Regionalism*. New York: Cambridge University Press.

Hewett, Ed. 1988. *Reforming the Soviet Economy. Equality Versus Efficiency*. Washington, DC, WA: Brookings.

Hinds, Pamela and Jeffrey Pfeffer. 2001. "Why Organizations Don't 'Know What They Know': Cognitive and Motivational Factors Affecting the Transfer of Expertise." Research Paper #1697, Graduate School of Business, Stanford University.

Hirsch, Paul. 1986. "From Ambushes to Golden Parachutes: Corporate Takeovers as an Instance of Cultural Framing and Institutional Integration." *American Journal of Sociology* 91: 800-837.

Hirschman, Albert O. 1977. *The Passions and the Interests*. Princeton, MA: Princeton University Press.

Hoch, Stephen. 1986. *Serfdom and Social Control in Russia: Petrovskoe, a Village in Tambov*. Chicago, IL: University of Chicago Press.

Hoffman, David. 2002. *The Oligarchs. Wealth and Power in the New Russia*. New York: PublicAffairs.

Hofstede, Geert. 1991. *Cultures and Organizations: Software of the Mind.* New York: McGraw-Hill.

Hopf, Ted. 2002. *Social Construction of International Politics. Identities and Foreign Policies, Moscow, 1995 and 1999.* Ithaca, NY: Cornell University Press.

Hough, Jerry. 2001. *The Logic of Economic Reform in Russia.* Washington, DC, WA: Brookings.

Humphrey, Caroline. 1999. "Russian Protection Rackets and the Appropriation of Law and Order." Pp. 199–232 in *States and Illegal Practices,* edited by Josiah Heymann. Oxford: Berg.

—2002. *The Unmaking of Soviet Life. Everyday Economies After Socialism.* Ithaca, NY: Cornell University Press.

Hunt, Lynn. 1984. *Politics, Culture, and Class in the French Revolution.* Berkeley, CA: University of California Press, 1984.

Huntington, Samuel. 1968. *Political Order in Changing Societies.* New Haven, CT: Yale University Press.

Ickes, Barry W. and Randi Ryterman. 1992. "The Interenterprise Arrears Crisis in Russia." *Post-Soviet Affairs* 8 (4): 331-361.

Ingram, Paul and Karen Clay. 2000. "The Choice-Within-Constraints New Institutionalism and Implications for Sociology." *Annual Review of Sociology* 26: 525-546.

Isupov, K. and I. Savkin (eds). 1993. *Russkaia filosofiia sobstvennosti.* St. Petersburg: Ganza.

Ivanov, O. 1994. "Korporativnye formy upravleniia v promyshlennosti." *Rossiiskii ekonomicheskii zhurnal* #3: 50-55.

Jackson, John Edgar, Jacek Kilch, and Krystyna Pozna ska. 2005. *The Political Economy of Poland's New Firms and Reform Governments.* New York: Cambridge University Press.

Javeline, Debra. 2003. "The Role of Blame in Collective Action: Evidence from Russia." *American Political Science Review* 97: 107-121.

—2003. *Protest and the Politics of Blame: The Russian Response to Unpaid Wages.* Ann Arbor, MI, University of Michigan Press.

Johnson, Juliet. 1997. "Russia's Emerging Financial-Industrial Groups." *Post-Soviet Affairs* 13 (4): 333-365.

—2000. *Fistful of Rubles: the Rise and Fall of the Russian Banking System.* Ithaca, NY: Cornell University Press.

Johnson, Simon and Heidi Kroll. 1991. "Managerial Strategies for Spontaneous Privatization." *Soviet Economy* 7 (4): 281-316.

Kaminski, Bartlomiej. 1991. *The Collapse of State Socialism: The Case of Poland.* Princeton, MA: Princeton University Press.

Kanter, Rosabeth Moss. 1983. *The Change Masters.* New York: Simon and Schuster.

—1989. *When Giants Learn to Dance.* New York: Simon and Schuster.

Kantorovich, V. Ia. 1925. *Sovietskie sindikaty.* Moscow-Leningrad: Tsentral'noe Upravlenie Pechati VSNKh SSSR.

Katz, Abraham. 1972 *The Politics of Economic Reform in the Soviet Union.* New York: Praeger.

Kennedy, Michael D. 2002. *Cultural Formations of Post-Communism. Emancipation, Transition, Nation, and War.* Minneapolis: University of Minnesota Press.

Kennedy, Paul. 1987. *The Rise and Fall of the Great Powers.* New York: Random House.

King, Lawrence. 2003. "Shock Privatization: The Effects of Rapid Large-Scale Privatization on Enterprise Restructuring." *Politics and Society* 31: 3-30.

Kniazeva, I. V. 1996. "'Sibirskaia iarmarka—Evroasiia': problemy i perspektivy rossiiskogo rynka. Real'nyi marketing nachinaetsia s vystavki." *EKO* #4: 58-66.

Kogan, E. E. 1994. "Zakonodatel'stvo o bankrodstve." *EKO* #10: 130-144.

Korel', L. V., M. A. Shabanova, Iu. B. Chistiakova, and O. V. Sharnina. 1994. "Chto pomogaet i chto meshaet adaptirovat'sia k rynku." *EKO* #3: 71-85.

Kornai, Janos. 1992. *The Socialist System*. Princeton, MA: Princeton University Press.

Kosals, Leonid. 1999. "Mezhdu khaosom i sotsial'nym poriadkom." *Pro et Contra* 4 (1): 40-54.

Kotkin, Stephen. 1990. *Steeltown USSR*. Berkeley, CA: University of California Press.

—1995. *Magnetic Mountain: Stalinism as Civilization*. Berkeley, CA: University of California Press.

—2001. *Armageddon Averted*. New York: Oxford University Press.

—2004. "Heir, Apparently. Why Russia Wants Putin." *Financial Times Magazine*, #45 (March 6): 16-22.

Koval', B. I. (ed.). 1991. *Rossiia segodnia: politicheskii portret v dokumentakh 1985–1991*. Moscow: Mezhdunarodnye otnosheniia.

Knight, Alan. 1986. *The Mexican Revolution*, 2 volumes. Lincoln: University of Nebraska Press.

Krotov, K. V. , S. P. Kushch, and M. M. Smirnova. 2008. "Marketingovyi aspekt upravleniia vzaimootnosheniiami v tsepiakh postavok: rezul'taty issledovaniia rossiiskikh kompanii." *Rossiiskii zhurnal menedzhmenta* 6 (2): 3-26.

Kryshtanovskaia, Olga. 2005. *Anatomiia rossiiskoi elity*. Moscow: Zakharov.

Kryshtanovskaya, Olga and Stephen White. 2005. "Inside the Putin Court: A Research Note." *Europe-Asia Studies* 57: 1065-1075.

Kuhn, Thomas. 1970. *The Structure of Scientific Revolutions*. Chicago, IL: University of Chicago Press, 1970.

Kulikov, V., L. Latysheva, and A. Nikolaev. 1994. "Obrazovanie finansovo-promyshlennykh grupp (neobkhodimost', tseli i mekhanizmy)." *Rossiiskii ekonomicheskii zhurnal* #1: 16-22.

Kuromiya, Hiroaki. 1988. *Stalin's Industrial Revolution. Politics and Workers, 1928–1932*. New York: Cambridge University Press.

Kutyrkin, A. N. 1993. *Usloviia truda na predpriiatii sviazi: ekonomicheskoe upravleniie pri perekhode k rynochnym otnosheniiam*. Moscow: Radio i slova.

Kuznetsov, Andrei. 1994. "Economic Reforms in Russia: Enterprise Behaviour as an Impediment to Change." *Europe-Asia Studies* 46: 955-970.

Kuznetsov, Andrei and Olga Kuznetsova. 1996. "Privatisation, Shareholding and the Efficiency Argument: Russian Experience." *Europe-Asia Studies* 48: 1173-1185.

Kuznetsova, Olga and Andrei Kuznetsov. 1999. "The State as a Shareholder: Responsibilities and Objectives." *Europe-Asia Studies* 51: 433-445.

Kuznetsov, Yevgeny. 1996. "Learning to Learn: Emerging Patterns of Enterprise Behavior in the Russian Defense Sector. 1992–1995." Pp. 315–43 in *Economic Transition in Russia and the New States of Eurasia*, edited by Bartlomiej Kaminski. Armonk, NY: M. E. Sharpe.

Lachmann, Richard. 1989. "Elite Conflict and State Formation in 16th and 17th Century England and France." *American Sociological Review* 54: 141-162.

—1990. "Class Formation Without Class Struggle: An Elite Conflict Theory of the Transition to Capitalism." *American Sociological Review* 55: 398-414.

Lakin, G. V. 1930. *Reforma upravleniia promyshlennosti v 1929/30 g*. Moscow: Gosudarstvennoe tekhnicheskoe izdatel'stvo.

Lane, David. 1987. *Soviet Labour and the Ethic of Communism*. Boulder: Westview.

Lapina, S., and N. Leliukhina. 1994. "Gosudarstvennoe predprinimatel'stvo v Rossii (nachalo XX veka)." *Voprosy ekonomiki* #8: 69-79.

Lawrence, Paul R., Charalambos A. Vlachoutsicos, *et al*, 1990. *Behind the Factory Walls: Decision-Making in Soviet and US Enterprises*. Boston, MA: Harvard Business School Press.

Ledeneva, Alena. 1998. *Russia's Economy of Favors*. New York: Cambridge University Press.

—2006. *How Russia Really Works*. Ithaca, NY: Cornell University Press.

Lie, John. 1997. "Sociology of Markets." *Annual Review of Sociology* 23: 341-360.

Lindblom, Charles. 1977. *Politics and Markets*. New York: Basic Books

Linz, Susan J. 1997. "Russian Firms in Transition: Champions, Challengers and Chaff." *Comparative Economic Studies* 39 (2): 1-36.

—2001. "Restructuring With What Success? A Case Study of Russian Firms." *Comparative Economic Studies* 43 (1): 75-99.

Linz, Susan J. and Gary Krueger. 1998. "Enterprise Restructuring in Russia's Transition Economy: Formal and Informal Mechanisms." *Comparative Economic Studies* 40 (2): 5-52.

Lipton, David, Jeffrey Sachs, Stanley Fisher, and Janos Kornai. 1990. "Creating a Market Economy in Eastern Europe: the Case of Poland." *Brookings Papers on Economic Activity* 1990 (1): 75-133.

Lipton, David, Jeffrey D. Sachs, Vladimir Mau, and Edmund S. Phelps. 1992. "Prospects for Russia's Economic Reforms." *Brookings Papers on Economic Activity* 1992 (2): 213-283.

Lipton, David, Jeffrey Sachs, and Lawrence H. Summers. 1990. "Privatization in Eastern Europe: The Case of Poland." *Brookings Papers on Economic Activity* 1990 (2): 293-341.

Listovskaia, V. *et al* (eds). 1994. *Biznesmeny Rossii. 40 istorii uspekha*. Moscow: OKO.

Litwack, John M. 1991. "Legality and Market Reform in Soviet-type Economies." *Journal of Economic Perspectives* 5 (4): 77-89.

Loginov, V. and I. Kurnysheva. 1996. "Restrukturizatsiia promyshlennosti v usloviiakh krizisa." *Voprosy ekonomik* #11: 33-47.

Lotman, Iuri. 2000. *Semiosfera*. St. Petersburg: Iskusstvo-SPb.

Lukes, Steven. 1974. *Power: A Radical View*. London: Macmillan.

L'vov, D. 1999. *Razvitie ekonomiki Rossii i zadachi ekonomicheskoi nauki*. Moscow: Ekonomika.

Macaulay, Stewart. 1963. "Non-contractual Relations in Business: A Preliminary Study." *American Sociological Review* 28: 55-67.

MacLeod, Jay. 1995. *Ain't No Makin It*. Boulder: Westview.

Manning, Roberta. 1982. *The Crisis of the Old Order in Russia*. Princeton, MA: Princeton University Press.

Marangos, John. 2002. *Preventative Therapy: The Neoclassical Gradualist Model of Transition from Central Administration to Market Relations. (The Carl Beck Papers in Russian and East European Studies)*. Pittsburgh: Center for Russian and East European Studies, University of Pittsburgh.

March, James and Herbert Simon. 1958. *Organizations*. New York: Wiley.

Markoff, John. 1997. *The Abolition of Feudalism*. University Park, PA: The Pennsylvania State University Press.

Markoff, John and Verónica Montecinos. 1993. "The Ubiquitous Rise of Economists." *Journal of Public Policy* 13: 37-68.

Martin, John Levi. 2003. "What is Field Theory?" *American Journal of Sociology* 109: 1-19.

Mau, Vladimir and Irina Staroduborskaya. 2001. *The Challenge of Revolution. Contemporary Russia in Historical Perspective*. New York: Oxford University Press.

McCloskey, Deirdre [Donald]. 2003. "The Rhetoric of Economics." *Journal of Economic Literature* 21: 481-517.

McDaniel, Tim. 1988. *Autocracy, Capitalism, and Revolution in Russia*. Berkeley, CA: University of California Press.

—1998. *Agony of the Russian Idea*. Princeton, MA: Princeton University Press.

McDermott, Gerald A. 2002. *Embedded Politics. Industrial Networks and Institutional Change in Postcommunism*. Ann Arbor, MI: University of Michigan Press.

McFaul, Michael. 2001. *Russia's Unfinished Revolution*. Ithaca, NY: Cornell University Press.

McKinsey Global Institute. 1999. *Unlocking Economic Growth in Russia*. Moscow: McKinsey and Company.

Megginson, William and Jeffry Netter. 2001. "From State to Market: A Survey of Empirical Studies on Privatization." *Journal of Economic Literature* 39: 321-389.

de Melo, Martha, Gur Ofer, and Olga Sandler. 1995. "Pioneers for Profit: St. Petersburg Entrepreneurs in Services." *World Bank Economic Review* 9 (3): 425-450.

Meyer, John W. and Brian Rowan. 1977. "Institutionalized Organizations: Formal Structure as Myth and Ceremony." *American Journal of Sociology* 83: 340-63.

Millar, James. 1985. "The Little Deal: Brezhnev's Contribution to Acquisitive Socialism." *Slavic Review* 44: 694-706.

—1995. "From Utopian Socialism to Utopian Capitalism. The Failure of Revolution and Reform in Post-Soviet Russia." *Problems of Post-Communism* 42 (3): 7-14.

Millar, James (ed.). 1987. *Politics, Work, and Daily Life in the USSR*. New York: Cambridge University Press.

Mingazov, Khanif. 1993. "Stanovlenie novykh organizatsionno-khoziaistvennykh struktur v rossiiskoi industrii." *Rossiiskii ekonomicheskii zhurnal* #9: 25-34 and #10: 50-60.

Ministry of Finance of the Russian Federation. 1993. *Predpriiatii na puti reform (polozhitel'nyi opyt raboty). Materialy soveshchaniia rukovoditelei promyshlennykh predpriiatii*. Moscow: Ministry of Finance.

Mitchell, Timothy. 2002. *Rule of Experts. Egypt, Techno-Politics, Modernity*. Berkeley, CA: University of California Press.

Montgomery, James D. 1998. "Toward a Role-Theoretic Conception of Embeddedness." *American Journal of Sociology* 104: 92-125.

Morozov, L., A. Krutik, and V. Golovach. 1994. "Kholding kak budushchee organizatsii rossiiskogo voennogo proizvodstva." *Rossiiskii ekonomicheskii zhurnal* #10: 25-29.

Morrison, Claudio and Gregory Schwartz. 2003. "Managing the Labour Collective: Wage Systems in the Russian Industrial Enterprise." *Europe-Asia Studies* 55: 553-574.

Mukherjee, Rudrangshu (ed.). 1996. *The Penguin Gandhi Reader*. New York: Penguin.

Murrell, Peter. 1991. "Can Neoclassical Economics Underpin the Reform of Centrally Planned Economies?" *Journal of Economic Perspectives* 5 (4): 59-76.

—1992. "Evolution in Economics and in the Economic Reform of the Centrally Planned Economies." Pp. 35–54 in *The Emergence of Market Economies in Eastern Europe*, edited by Christopher Clague and Gordon C. Rausser. Cambridge: Basil Blackwell.

—1993. "What Is Shock Therapy? What Did it Do in Poland and Russia?" *Post-Soviet Affairs* 9(2): 111-140.

—1996. "How Far Has the Transition Progressed?" *Journal of Economic Perspectives* 10 (2): 25-44.

Nelson, Lynn D. and Irina Y. Kuzes. 1994. *Property to the People: The Struggle for Radical Economic Reform in Russia*. Armonk, NY: M. E. Sharpe.

Nelson, Richard and Sidney Winter. 1982. *An Evolutionary Theory of Economic Change*. Cambridge, MA: Harvard University Press.

North, Douglass. 1981. *Structure and Change in Economic History*. New York: W. W. Norton.

—1990. *Institutions, Institutional Change, and Economic Performance*. New York: Cambridge University Press.

—2005. *Understanding the Process of Economic Change*. Princeton, MA: Princeton University Press.

Nove, Alec. 1972. *An Economic History of the USSR*. New York: Penguin.

—1977. *The Soviet Economic System*. Boston, MA: George Allen and Unwin.

O'Dwyer, Connor. 2006. *Runaway State-Building: Patronage Politics and Democratic Development.* Baltimore: Johns Hopkins University Press.

Organization for Economic Cooperation and Development [OECD]. 2002. *OECD Economic Surveys 2001–2002. Russian Federation.* Volume 2002/5. Paris: OECD Publications.

Owen, David and David O. Robinson. 2003. *Russia Rebounds.* Washington, DC, WA: International Monetary Fund.

Owen, Thomas. 1981. *Capitalism and Politics in Russia. A Social History of the Moscow Merchants, 1855–1905.* New York: Cambridge University Press.

Ouchi, William. 1981. *Theory Z.* Reading, MA: Addison-Wesley.

Panarin, A. 1995. "Paradoksy predprinimatel'stva, paradoksy istorii." *Voprosy ekonomiki* #7: 62-73.

Pappe, Ia. Sh., V. E. Dement'iev, B. I. Makarenko, P. Venediktov, and A. Iu. Zudin. 1997. *Finansovo-promyshlennye gruppy i konglomeraty v ekonomike i politike sovremennoi Rossii.* Moscow: Tsentr Politicheskikh Tekhnologii.

Peck, Merton J. and Thomas J. Richardson (eds). 1991. *What Is To Be Done? Proposals for the Soviet Transition to the Market.* New Haven, CT: Yale University Press.

Perlamutrv, V. 1993. "K rynochnoi ekonomike ili k ekonomicheskoi katastrofe?" *Rossiiskii ekonomicheskii zhurnal* #8: 11-21.

Perrow, Charles. 1986. *Complex Organizations: A Critical Essay.* New York: Random House.

Pettersson, Niklas and Stefan Nordström. 1994. *Western Perspectives on the Russian Shipbuilding Company Almaz.* Linköping: Linköping Institute of Technology.

Pfeffer, Jeffrey. 1981. *Power in Organization.* Marshfield, MA: Pitman. 1992. *Managing with Power: Politics and Influence in Organizations.* Boston, MA: Harvard Business School Press

Piore, Michael and Charles Sabel, 1984. *The Second Industrial Divide.* New York: Basic Books.

Pipes, Richard. 1974. *Russia under the Old Regime.* New York: Charles Scribners' Sons.

Polanyi, Karl. 1944. *The Great Transformation.* Boston, MA: Beacon.

Polanyi, Michael. 1962. *Personal Knowledge: Towards a Post-Critical Philosophy.* New York: Harper.

—1967. *The Tacit Dimension.* Garden City, NJ: Doubleday Anchor.

Porter, Michael. 1980. *Competitive Strategy.* New York: Free Press.

—1985. *Competitive Advantage.* New York: Free Press.

Powell, Walter. 1991. "Expanding the Scope of Institutional Analysis." Pp. 183–203 in *The New Institutionalism in Organizational Analysis*, edited by Walter W. Powell and Paul DiMaggio. Chicago, IL: University of Chicago Press.

Powell, Walter and Laurel Smith-Doerr. 1994. "Networks and Economic Life." Pp. 368–402 in *The Handbook of Economic Sociology*, edited by Neil Smelser and Richard Swedberg. Princeton, MA: Princeton University Press.

Prokop, Jane. 1995. "Industrial Conglomerates, Risk Spreading and the Transition in Russia." *Communist Economies and Economic Transformation.* 7 (1): 35-50.

Prokhorov, A. P. 2002. *Russkaia model' upravleniia.* Moscow: ZAO 'Zhurnal Ekspert'.

Puffer, Sheila. 1992. *The Russian Management Revolution.* Armonk, NY: M.E. Sharpe.

Putnam, Robert. 1993. *Making Democracy Work.* Princeton, MA: Princeton University Press.

Radaev, Vadim V. 1993. *Novoe predprinimatel'stvo v rossii. (Perviie resul'taty issledovaniia).* Moscow: Institute of Economics, Russian Academy of Sciences.

—(ed.). 1993. *Fenomen predprinimatlia: interpretatsiia poniatii.* Moscow: INTERTsENTR.

—1993. "Vneekonomicheskie motivy predprinimatel'skoi deiatel'nosti." *Voprosy ekonomiki* #7: 85-97.

—1996. "Malyi biznes i problemy delovoi etiki: nadezhdy i real'nost'." *Voprosy ekonomiki* #7: 72-82.

Radygin, A., V. Gutnik, and G. Mal'ginov. 1995. "Postprivatizatsionnaia struktura aktsionernogo kapitala i korporativnyi kontrol': 'kontrrevoliutsiia upravliaiushchikh?'" *Voprosy ekonomiki* #10: 47-69.

Rapaczynski, Andrzej. 1996. "The Roles of the State and the Market in Establishing Property Rights." *Journal of Comparative Perspectives* 10 (2): 87-103.

Rebel'skii, N. 1995. "Antimonopol'noe regulirovanie bankovskoi sfery." *Voprosy ekonomiki* #11: 68-79.

Rechin, V. D. 1998. "Predpriiatie v usloviiakh neplatezhei. Mneniia direktorov predpriiatii." *EKO* #3: 82-90.

Reddy, William. 1984. *The Rise of Market Culture: The Textile Trade and French Society. 1750–1900*. Cambridge: Cambridge University Press.

Rieber, Alfred. 1982. *Merchants and Entrepreneurs in Imperial Russia*. Chapel Hill: University of North Carolina Press.

Rivera, Sharon Werning. 2004. "Elites and the Diffusion of Foreign Models in Russia." *Political Studies* 52 (1): 43-62.

Rizinskii, I. 1996. "Rossiiskie predpriiatiia: 'Dilemma vnutrennikh aktsionerov.'" *Rossiiskii ekonomicheskii zhurnal* #2: 30-40.

Róna-Tas, Ákos. 1997. *The Great Surprise of the Small Transformation*. Ann Arbor, MI: University of Michigan Press.

Rosefielde, Steven. 2005. *Russia in the 21st Century*. New York: Cambridge University Press.

Roshchina, Ia. 1995. "Stil' zhizni predprinimatelia: typi potrebitel'skikh orientatsii." *Voprosy ekonomiki* #7: 91-102.

Roy, William. 1997. *Socializing Capital*. Princeton, MA: Princeton University Press.

Rozhkov, K. 1993. "Mezhotraslevye sviazi v reformiruiemoi ekonomika." *Rossiiskii ekonomicheskii zhurnal* #3: 12-21.

Rueschemeyer, Dietrich, John Stephens, and Evelyne Stephens. 1992. *Capitalist Development and Democracy*. Chicago, IL: University of Chicago Press.

Rumiantseva, Z. 1993. "K obosnovaniiu novoi upravlencheskoi paradigmy." *Rossiiskii ekonomicheskii zhurnal* #8: 61-70.

Rutland, Peter. 1990. "Labor Unrest and Movements in 1989 and 1990." *Soviet Economy* 6: 345-384.

Ryvkina, Rozalina V. 1998. *Ekonomicheskaia sotsiologiia perekhodnoi Rossii. Liudi i reformy* Moscow: Delo.

—1999. "Ot tenevoi ekonomiki k tenevomu obshchestvu." *Pro et Contra* 4 (1): 25-39.

Sabel, Charles. 1982. *Work and Politics: The Division of Labor in Industry*. New York: Cambridge University Press.

—1993. "Studied Trust: Building New Forms of Cooperation in a Volatile Economy." Pp. 105–44 in *Explorations in Economic Sociology*, edited by Richard Swedberg. New York: Russell Sage Foundation.

Sakwa, Richard. 1990. *Gorbachev and His Reforms. 1985-1990*. New York: Prentice-Hall.

Schoors, Koen. 2003. "The Fate of Russia's Former State Banks: Chronicle of a Restructuring Postponed and a Crisis Foretold." *Europe-Asia Studies* 55: 75-100.

Schröder, Hans-Henning. 1999. "El'tsin and the Oligarchs: The Role of financial Groups in Russian Politics Between 1993 and July 1998." *Europe-Asia Studies* 51: 957-988.

Schüsselbauer, Gerhard. 1999. "Privatisation and Restructuring in Economies in Transition: Theory and Evidence Revisited." *Europe-Asia Studies* 51 (1): 65-83.

Schwartz, Gregory. 2003. "Employment Restructuring in Russian Industrial Enterprises: Confronting a 'Paradox.'" *Work, Employment and Society* 17 (1): 49-72.

Scott, James C. 1976. *The Moral Economy of the Peasant*. New Haven, CT: Yale University Press.

——1985. *Weapons of the Weak*. New Haven, CT: Yale University Press.

——1990. *Domination and the Arts of Resistance*. New Haven, CT: Yale University Press.

Seo, Myeong-Gu and W. E. Douglas Creed. 2002. "Institutional Contradictions, Praxis, and Institutional Change: A Dialectical Perspective." *Academy of Management Review* 27: 222-247.

Sewell, William. 1980. *Work and Revolution in France*. New York: Cambridge University Press.

Shevtsova, Lilia. 2005. *Putin's Russia*. Washington, DC, WA: Carnegie Endowment for International Peace.

——2007. *Russia—Lost in Transition*. Washington, DC, WA: Carnegie Endowment for International Peace.

Shiller, Robert J., Maxim Boycko, and Vladimir Korobov. 1992. "Hunting for *Homo Sovieticus*: Situational versus Attitudinal Factors in Economic Behavior." *Brookings Papers on Economic Activity* 1992 (1): 127-181.

Shimko, V. 1995. "Korporativnye formy organizatsii v radioelektronnoi promyshlennosti v usloviiakh rynka." *Voprosy ekonomiki* #10: 113-123.

Shirk, Susan. 1993. *The Political Logic of Economic Reform in China*. Berkeley, CA: University of California Press.

Siegelbaum, Lewis. 1988. *Stakhanovism and the Politics of Productivity in the USSR. 1935–1941*. New York: Cambridge University Press.

Silver, Brian D. 1987. "Political Beliefs of the Soviet Citizen: Sources of Support for Regime Norms." Pp. 100–141 in *Politics, Work, and Daily Life in the USSR*, edited by James R. Millar. New York: Cambridge University Press.

Simis, K. M. 1982. *USSR: The Corrupt Society. The Secret World of Soviet Capitalism*. New York: Simon and Schuster.

Simon, Herbert. 1945. *Administrative Behavior*. New York: Wiley.

Skocpol, Theda. 1979. *States and Social Revolutions*. New York: Cambridge University Press.

——1992. *Protecting Soldiers and Mothers*. Cambridge, MA: Harvard University Press.

Slider, Darrell. 1991. "Embattled Entrepreneurs: Soviet Cooperatives in an Unreformed Economy." *Soviet Studies* 43: 797-821.

Smirnova, E. E. 1993. "Bankrodstvo nesostoiatel'nosti rozn'?" *EKO* #9: 141-149.

Smith, Gordon. 1996. *Reforming the Russian Legal System*. Cambridge: Cambridge University Press.

Smith, Kathleen. 2002. *Mythmaking in the New Russia*. Ithaca, NY: Cornell University Press.

Snow, David A. and Robert D. Benford. 1992. "Master Frames and Cycles of Protest." Pp. 133–44 in *Frontiers in Social Movement Theory*, edited by Aldon D. Morris and Carol McClurg Mueller. New Haven, CT: Yale University Press.

Snow, David A., E. Burke Rochford Jr., Steven K. Worden, and Robert D. Benford. 1986. "Frame Alignment Process, Micromobilization, and Movement Participation." *American Sociological Review* 51: 464-81

Solnick, Steven. 1998. *Stealing the State*. Cambridge, MA: Harvard University Press.

Sokolin, Boris M. 1997. *Krizisnaia ekonomika Rossii: rubezh tysiacheletii*. St. Petersburg (Russia): Liki Rossii.

Somers, Margaret and Fred Block. 2005. "From Poverty to Perversity: Ideas, Markets, and Institutions over 200 Years of Welfare Debate." *American Sociological Review* 70: 260-287.

de Soto, Hernando. 1989. *The Other Path*. New York: Harper and Row.

Spenner, Kenneth I., Olga O. Suhomlinova, Sten A. Thore, Kenneth C. Land, and Derek Jones. 1998. "Strong Legacies and Weak Markets: Bulgarian State-Owned Enterprises During Early Transition" *American Sociological Review* 63: 599-618.

Stark, David. 1986. "Rethinking Internal Labor Markets: New Insights from a Comparative Perspective." *American Sociological Review* 51: 492-504.

Stark, David, and László Bruszt. 1998. *Postsocialist Pathways.* New York: Cambridge University Press.

Starodubrovskaia, Irina V. 1993. "Ekonomicheskaia reforma: mnenie direktorskogo korpusa." *EKO* 10: 111-123.

—1995. "Financial-industrial Groups: Illusions and Reality." *Communist Economies and Economic Transformation* 7 (1): 5-19.

Starr, Paul. 1982. *The Social Transformation of American Medicine.* New York: Harper.

Stoner-Weiss, Kathryn. 1997. *Local Heroes: The Political Economy of Russian Regional Governance.* Princeton, MA: Princeton University Press.

Straus, Kenneth. 1997. *Factory and Community in Stalin's Russia.* Pittsburgh: University of Pittsburgh Press.

Sutton, John R. and Frank Dobbin. 1996. "The Two Faces of Governance: Responses to Legal Uncertainty in U.S. Firms, 1955 to 1985." *American Sociological Review* 61: 794-811.

"Svetlana": Istoriia Leningradskogo obedineniia elektronnogo priborostroeniia "Svetlana." Leningrad: Lenizdat. 1986.

Swartz, David. 1997. *Culture and Power. The Sociology of Pierre Bourdieu.* Chicago, IL: University of Chicago Press.

Swidler, Ann. 1986. "Culture in Action: Symbols and Strategies." *American Sociological Review* 51: 273-286.

Szelenyi, Ivan. 1988. *Socialist Entrepreneurs. Embourgeoisement in Rural Hungary.* Madison, WI: University of Wisconsin Press.

Szelenyi, Ivan and Szonja Szelenyi. 1995. "Circulation or Reproduction of Elites During the Postcommunist Transformation of Eastern Europe." *Theory and Society* 24: 615-638.

Tarrow, Sidney. 1998. *Power in Movement. Social Movements and Contentious Politics,* second edition. New York: Cambridge University Press.

Thurston, Robert W. 1996. *Life and Terror in Stalin's Russia, 1934-1941.* New Haven, CT: Yale University Press.

Tikhomirov, I. Iu. *et al* 1994. *Biznes v rossii. Universal'nyi iuridicheskii spravochnik predprinimatelia.* Moscow: IuRINFORMTsENTR.

Tilly, Charles. 1978. *From Mobilization to Revolution.* New York: Random House.

—1984. *Big Structures, Large Processes, Huge Comparisons.* New York: Russell Sage.

—1990. *Coercion, Capital, and European States A.D. 990–1992.* Cambridge: Blackwell.

—1995. *Popular Contention in Great Britain.* Cambridge, MA: Harvard University Press.

de Tocqueville, Alexis. 1955. *The Old Regime and the French Revolution,* translated by Stuart Gilbert. New York: Doubleday.

—1966. *Democracy in America.* Translated by George Lawrence. New York: Harper and Row.

Tourevski, Mark and Eileen Morgan. 1993. *Cutting the Red Tape. How Western Companies Can Profit in the New Russia.* New York: Free Press.

Tokarenko, O. V. 1996. "Russkie kak predprinimateli (istoricheskie korni ustanovok i povedeniia)." *Mir Rossii* 5 (1): 195-207.

Tompson, William. 1997. "Old Habits Die Hard: Fiscal Imperatives, State Regulation and the Role of Russia's Banks." *Europe-Asia Studies* 49: 1159-1185.

—1998. "The Politics of Central Bank Independence in Russia." *Europe-Asia Studies* 50: 1157-1182.

—2000. "Financial Backwardness in Contemporary Perspective: Prospects for the Development of Financial Intermediation in Russia." *Europe-Asia Studies* 52: 605-625.

—2002. "Putin's Challenge: The Politics of Structural Reform in Russia." *Europe-Asia Studies* 54: 933-957.

—2006. "A Frozen Venezuela? The Resource Curse and Russian Politics." Pp. 189-212 in *Russia's Oil and National Gas: Bonanza or Curse?*, edited by Michael Ellman. New York: Anthem.

Tourevski, Mark and Eileen Morgan. 1993. *Cutting the Red Tape. How Western Companies Can Profit in the New Russia*. New York: Free Press.

Tsukhlo, S. 1995. "Formirovanie obemov i struktury vypuska rossiiskikh promyshlennykh predpriiatii." *Voprosy ekonomiki* #6: 31-41.

Tversky, Amos and Daniel Kahneman. 1974. "Judgment Under Uncertainty: Heuristics and Biases." *Science* 185: 1124-1131.

—1981. "The Framing of Decisions and the Psychology of Choice." *Science* 21: 453-458.

Usui, Chikako and Richard Colignon. 1996. "Corporate Restructuring: Converging World Pattern or Societally Specific Embeddedness?" *Sociological Quarterly* 37: 551-578.

Vaksberg, Arkadii. 1991. *The Soviet Mafia*. New York: St. Martin's Press.

Varese, Federico. 1994. "Is Sicily the Future of Russia? Private Protection and the Rise of the Russian Mafia." *European Journal of Sociology* 35: 224-258.

—2001. *The Russian Mafia: Private Protection in a New Market Economy*. New York: Oxford University Press.

Verdery, Katherine. 1993. "What Was Socialism and Why Did It Fall?" *Contention* 3 (1): 1-23. Reprinted in *Beyond Soviet Studies*, edited by Daniel Orlovsky. Washington, DC, WA: The Woodrow Wilson Center Press, 1995), pp. 27–47.

Vilenskii, A. 1996. "Etapy razvitiia malogo predprinimatel'stva v Rossii." *Voprosy ekonomiki* #7: 30-38.

V'iunik, A. A. 1987. *Vsegda v poiske: istoriia Leningradskogo nauchno-proizvodstvennogo obedineniia 'Positron.'* Leningrad: Lenizdat.

Vlachoutsicos, Charalambos A. 1996. "How Managerial Learning Can Assist Economic Transformation in Russia." *Organizational Studies* (www.findarticles.com).

Vlachoutsicos, Charalambos A. and Paul Lawrence. 1990. "What We Don't Know About Soviet Management." *Harvard Business Review* 68 (6): pp. 50–64.

Voitolobskii, V. N. and B. V. Priankov (eds). 1993. *Tipy predpriiatii i ikh ekonomicheskoe povedenie v usloviiakh rynka*. St. Petersburg: St. Petersburg University of Economics and Finance.

Volkov Vadim. 2002. *Violent Entrepreneurs*. Ithaca, NY: Cornell University Press.

Voz'mitel', A. A. 1997. *Sposoby biznese i sposoby zhizni rossiiskikh predprinimatelei*. Moscow: Institut sotsiologiia RAN.

Wade, Robert. 1990. *Governing the Market*. Princeton, MA: Princeton University Press.

Walder, Andrew. 1986. *Communist Neotraditionalism*. Berkeley, CA: University of California Press.

—1994. "The Decline of Communist Power: Elements of a Theory of Institutional Change." *Theory and Society* 23: 297-323.

—1996. "Markets and Inequality in Transitional Economies: Toward Testable Theories." *American Journal of Sociology* 101: 1060-1073.

Waterbury, John. 1993. *Exposed to Innumerable Delusions*. New York: Cambridge University Press.

Weber, Max. 1978. *Economy and Society*. Berkeley, CA: University of California Press.

—1987. *General Economic History.* New Brunswick: Transaction Books.

Wedel, Janine. 1998. *Collision and Collusion. The Strange Case of Western Aid to Eastern Europe, 1989–1998.* New York: St. Martin's Press.

Weiner, Elaine. 2007. *Market Dreams: Gender, Class, and Capitalism in the Czech Republic.* Ann Arbor, MI: University of Michigan Press.

White, Harrison. 1981. "Where Do Markets Come From?" *American Journal of Sociology* 87: 517-547.

Willerton, John P. 1992. *Patronage and Politics in the USSR.* New York: Cambridge University Press.

Williamson, Oliver. 1975. *Markets and Hierarchies.* New York: Free Press.

—1985. *The Economic Institutions of Capitalism.* New York: Free Press.

Wilson, James Q. 1989. *Bureaucracy. What Government Organizations Do and Why They Do It.* Cambridge, MA: Harvard University Press.

Woodruff, David. 1999. *Money Unmade. Barter and the Fate of Russian Capitalism.* Ithaca, NY: Cornell University Press.

—1999. "It's Value That's Virtual: Bartles, Rubles, and the Place of Gazprom in the Russian Economy." *Post-Soviet Affairs* 15 (2): 130-48.

—2000. "Rules for Followers: Institutional Theory and the New Politics of Economic Backwardness in Russia." *Politics and Society* 28 (4): 437-482.

—2004. "Property Rights in Context: Privatization's Legacy for Corporate Legality in Poland and Russia." *Studies in Comparative International Development* 38 (4): 82-108.

Wuthnow, Robert. 1987. *Meaning and Moral Order.* Berkeley, CA: University of California Press.

Yakovlev, A. A. 1993. "Chastnyi biznes i vlast': v poiskakh vzaimoponimaniia." *EKO* #9: 95-102.

Yakovlev, Andrei. 1999. "Ekonomika 'chernogo nala' v Rossii: mekhanizmy, prichiny, posledstviia." Pp. 270–91 in *Neformal'naia ekonomika. Rossiia i mir,* edited by Teodor Shanin. Moscow: Logos.

Yasin, Ye. G., *et al* 1993. *Predpriiatiia na puti reform (polozhitel'nyi opyt raboty).* Moscow: Poligran.

Yudaeva, Yudaeva, Konstantin Kozlov, Natalia Melentieva, and Natalia Ponomareva. 2003. "Does Foreign Ownership Matter? The Russian Experience." *Economics of Transition* 11 (3): 383-409.

Yurchak, Alexei. 2006. *Everything Was Forever, Until It Was No More. The Last Soviet Generation.* Princeton, MA: Princeton University Press.

Zakharchenko, V. 1993. "Stankostroenie mezhdu proshlym i budushchim." *EKO* #: 87-93.

Zarubina, N. 1995. "Rossiiskoe predprinimatel'stvo: idei i liudi." *Voprosy ekonomiki* #7: 82-90.

Zaslavskaia, Tat'iana I. 1994. "Biznes-sloi rossiiskogo obshchestva: poniatie, struktura, identifikatsiia." *Informatsionnyi biulleten' monitoringa* (Sept.-Oct.): 7-15.

Zelizer, Viviana. 1979. *Morals and Markets: The Development of Life Insurance in the United States.* New York: Columbia University Press.

—1988. "Beyond the Polemics on the Market: Establishing a Theoretical and Empirical Agenda." *Sociological Forum* 3(4): 614-634.

—1997. *The Social Meaning of Money: Pin Money, Paychecks, Poor Relief, and Other Currencies.* Princeton, MA: Princeton University Press.

—2002. "Enter Culture." Pp. 101–25 in *The New Economic Sociology: Developments in an Emerging Field,* edited by Mauro Guillén, Randall Collins, Paula England, and Marshall Meyer. New York: Russell Sage Foundation.

—2005. *The Purchase of Intimacy.* Princeton, MA: Princeton University Press.

Zubakin, V. 1994. "'Vtoraia ekonomika.'" *Voprosy ekonomiki* #11: 156-160.
Zucker, Lynne G. 1986. "Production of Trust: Institutional Sources of Economic Structure. 1840-1920." in *Research in Organizational Behavior* 8: 53-111.
—1987. "Institutional Theories of Organization." *Annual Review of Sociology* 13: 443-464.
—1988. "Where Do Institutional Patterns Come From? Organizations as Actors in Social Systems." Pp. 23–52 in *Institutional Patterns and Organization*, edited by Lynne Zucker. Cambridge: Ballinger.
Zysman, John. 1983. *Governments, Markets, and Growth*. Ithaca, NY: Cornell University Press.

Index

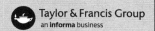

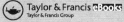

Research Methods: The Basics

Nicholas Walliman, Oxford Brookes University, UK

Research Methods: The Basics is an accessible, user-friendly introduction to the different aspects of research theory, methods and practice. Structured in two parts, the first covering the nature of knowledge and the reasons for research, and the second the specific methods used to carry out effective research, this book covers:

- Structuring and planning a research project
- The ethical issues involved in research
- Different types of data and how they are measured
- Collecting and analysing data in order to draw sound conclusions
- Devising a research proposal and writing up the research

Complete with a glossary of key terms and guides to further reading, this book is an essential text for anyone coming to research for the first time, and is widely relevant across the social sciences and humanities.

Pb: 978-0-415-48994-2
Hb: 978-0-415-48991-1

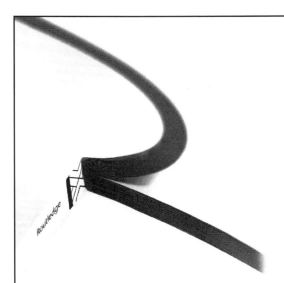